Anonymous

New Letters

Between Napoleon I and Lady Mary

Anonymous

New Letters
Between Napoleon I and Lady Mary

ISBN/EAN: 9783337350055

Printed in Europe, USA, Canada, Australia, Japan

Cover: Foto ©Thomas Meinert / pixelio.de

More available books at **www.hansebooks.com**

BONAPARTE,
AS FIRST CONSUL OF THE FRENCH REPUBLIC.

NEW LETTERS OF
NAPOLEON I

OMITTED FROM THE EDITION

PUBLISHED UNDER THE AUSPICES OF

NAPOLEON III

From the French by

LADY MARY LOYD

LONDON

WILLIAM HEINEMANN

1898

PUBLISHER'S NOTE

IT is well known to all students of Napoleon's history that the collected Letters published in Paris, under the direction of the Commission appointed by Napoleon III. to edit and arrange his uncle's Correspondence, were by no means complete. Interesting and valuable as the twenty-eight volumes are, they are often reticent just where the reader most wishes for illumination. The causes of their *lacunæ* are not far to seek. The work was to be a sort of literary Vendome Column, setting forth the glory and the greatness of the *chef de famille*. The appointment of Prince Napoleon as President of the Committee ensured the suppression not only of evidence that might reflect unpleasantly on Napoleon's personal character, but of anything that might dim the lustre of the Napoleon epic as a whole, by detracting from the dignity of his nearest relatives and most trusted agents. The Commission accordingly set aside many letters of extraordinary interest—letters dealing with Napoleon's relations with his own family, his violent conflict with the Pope, his high-handed methods for the Gallicising of conquered States, or containing trenchant criticisms on the capacity and conduct of famous generals and highly placed officials.

This important store of unpublished letters has, of course, been laid under contribution of late years by many writers of monographs, essayists and reviewers, who have given passages or single letters omitted from the earlier volumes. But a complete edition of all the suppressed documents has only now been published in two volumes supplementing the former issue.

The edition now offered to the English public is a selection from these volumes containing all the hitherto unpublished letters of the greatest interest ; the publishers have in the main chosen such as have never before appeared, though they have included one or two that have only been given (in some cases fragmentarily) in fugitive publications. To those admirers of Napoleon's genius, who believe that his greatness is not to be impaired by the admission that he too was human, the book cannot fail to be welcome as revealing him more intimately, more fully to the world, while to all students of the great drama of the First Empire it must be of importance.

LETTERS

			PAGE
To General Brune :	29 Jan. 1800,	. . . .	1
„ „ Lefebvre :	„ „	. . . .	2
„ „ Chambarlhac :	1 Feb. „	. . . .	3
„ „ Sahuguet :	10 „ „	. . . .	3
„ „ Lefebvre :	14 „ „	. . . .	3
„ „ Hédouville :	21 „ „	. . . .	4
„ „ Augereau :	8 Mar. „	. . . .	6
„ „ Lacuée :	15 May „	. . . .	6
„ Madame * * * :	13 Oct. „	. . . .	7
„ Citizen Lucien Bonaparte :	22 Dec. „	. . . .	7
„ „ „ „	15 Jan. 1801,	. . . .	8
„ General Berthier :	16 Feb. „	. . . .	9
„ Citizen Lucien Bonaparte :	28 „ „	. . . .	9
„ „ „ „	18 Mar. 1801,	. . . .	10
„ „ „ „	15 May „	. . . .	11
„ „ „ „	1 June „	. . . .	12
„ „ „ „	17 „ „	. . . .	13
„ „ „ „	22 „ „	. . . .	16
„ „ Talleyrand :	3 July „	. . . .	17
„ „ Forfait :	11 Aug. „	. . . .	18
„ „ Talleyrand :	7 Mar. 1802,	. . . .	18
Note annexed to a letter to the Pope, dated 4th Prairial, Year x.,			19
To Pope Pius VII. :	18 Oct. 1802,	. . . .	20
„ M. de Barral :	30 April 1803,	. . . .	21
„ Citizen Barbé-Marbois :	15 June „	. . . .	21
„ „ Fabre de l'Aude :	8 Oct. „	. . . .	21
„ General Soult :	13 Feb. 1804,	. . . .	22
„ Citizen Melzi :	20 Feb. „	. . . .	22
„ Madame Mère :	22 April 1805,	. . . .	23
„ M. Fouché :	30 May „	. . . .	23
„ Jerome Bonaparte :	9 June „	. . . .	25
„ M. Fouché :	1 July „	. . . .	25
„ „	15 „ „	. . . .	25
„ Prince Eugene :	27 „ „	. . . .	26

		PAGE
To M. Fouché :	6 Aug. 1805, .	26
„ M. de Champagny :	7 „ „ .	26
„ M. Fouché :	22 „ „ .	27
„ „	29 „ „ .	27
Letter to be sent by Princess Augusta to the States-General of Bavaria :	15 Jan. 1806, .	28
To M. Fouché :	14 Feb. „ .	29
„ Marshal Berthier :	31 Mar. „ .	29
„ M. de Talleyrand :	28 Feb. „ .	29
„ Marshal Berthier :	7 July „ .	30
„ Princess Stephanie de Beauharnais :	8 „ „ . .	30
„ M. Fouché :	8 „ „ . .	30
„ „	19 Aug. „ . .	31
„ M. de Talleyrand :	3 Sept. „ . .	31
„ „ „	12 „ „ . .	31
„ Marshal Berthier :	16 Nov. „ . .	35
„ M. Fouché :	3 Dec. „ . .	35
„ „	31 „ „ . .	35
„ General Lagrange :	13 Jan. 1807, . .	36
„ Prince Cambacérès :	27 „ „ . .	38
„ General Clarke :	21 Feb. „ . .	38
„ M. Fouché :	15 Mar. „ . .	39
„ M. de Talleyrand :	30 „ „ . .	39
„ M. Fouché :	19 April „ . .	40
„ „	21 „ „ . .	41
„ Prince Cambacérès :	16 May „ . .	41
„ the Landamman of Switzerland :	18 „ „ .	42
„ M. Fouché :	18 „ „ .	43
„ M. de Lavallette :	14 Aug. „ .	43
„ M. Fouché :	28 „ „ .	44
„ „	1 Sept. „ .	44
„ M. de Champagny :	7 „ „ .	45
„ „ „	7 „ „ .	47
„ M. Fouché :	7 „ „ .	48
„ „	29 „ „ .	49
„ M. Daru :	12 Oct. „ .	49
„ M. Fouché :	18 „ „ .	50
„ M. de Champagny :	27 „ „ .	52
„ General Clarke :	28 „ „ .	53
„ M. de Lavallette :	9 Nov. „ .	55

			PAGE
To M. Gaudin :	9 Nov. 1807,	.	56
„ Elisa Napoleon :	13 „ „	.	56
„ M. Gaudin :	13 „ „	. .	56
„ M. de Lavallette :	14 „ „	. .	57
„ M. Fouché :	17 Dec. „	. .	57
„ M. de Talleyrand :	19 „ „	. .	59
„ Princess Pauline Borghese :	20 „ „	. .	59
„ Joseph Napoleon :	20 „ „	. .	59
„ Jerome Napoleon :	4 Jan. 1808,	. .	61
„ „ „	4 „ „	. .	62
„ „ „	4 „ „	. .	63
„ General Junot :	7 „ „	. .	64
„ „ „	28 „ „	. ·.	65
„ Jerome Napoleon :	16 Feb. „	. .	67
„ M. Fouché :	16 „ „	. .	68
„ M. de Champagny :	17 „ „	. .	68
„ General Junot :	29 „ „	. .	69
„ Jerome Napoleon	1 Mar. „	. .	69
„ „ „	6 „ „	. .	70
„ General Junot :	7 „ „	. .	71
„ Prince Murat :	10 „ „	. .	71
„ M. Fouché :	10 „ „	. .	72
„ Joseph Napoleon :	11 „ „	. .	73
„ „ „	12 „ „	. .	73
„ „ „	16 „ „	.	74
„ Marshal Berthier :	24 „ „	.	75
„ M. de Lavallette :	29 „ „	.	75
„ M. de Champagny :	1 April „	.	76
„ Prince Murat :	17 „ „	.	76
„ M. Fouché :	21 „ „	.	78
„ „	25 „ „	.	78
„ Prince Murat :	26 „ „	.	79
„ Marshal Bessières :	26 „ „	.	81
„ Prince Murat :	28 „ „	.	81
„ „ „	29 „ „	.	83
„ „ „	30 „ „	.	84
„ General Clarke :	8 May „	.	85
„ M. de Talleyrand :	9 „ „		86
„ M. Fouché :	21 „ „		87
„ Prince Murat :	23 „ „		88
„ M. Fouché :	26 „ „		89
„ „	26 „ „		90
„ Princess Pauline Borghese :	26 „ „		90

PAGE

To M. Fouché :	11 June 1808,	.	.	.	90
., M. de Champagny :	16 ,, ,,	.	.	.	91
,, Marshal Berthier :	22 ,, ,,	.	.	.	91
,, M. de Lavallette :	26 ,, ,,	.	.	.	92
,, M. Fouché :	28 ,, ,,	.	.	.	92
., M. de Champagny :	28 ,, ,,	.	.	.	92
,, M. Fouché :	29 ,, ,,	.	.	.	93
,, Prince Cambacérès :	29 ,, ,,	.	.	.	93
,, ,, ,,	13 July ,,	.	.	.	94
,, General Duroc :	15 ,, ,,	.	.	.	95
,, Jerome Napoleon :	16 ,, ,,	.	.	.	96
,, ,, .,	16 ,, ,,	.	.	.	96
,, ,, ,,	16 ,, .,	.	.	.	97
,, Prince Cambacérès :	17 ,, ,,	.	.	.	97
,, M. de Champagny :	25 ,, ,,	.	.	.	98
,, the Prince de Neufchâtel :	26 ,, ,,	.	.	.	99
,, Joachim Napoleon :	30 ,, ,,	.	.	.	100
,, Joseph Napoleon :	31 ,, ,,	.	.	.	100
,, Marshal Soult :	23 Aug. ,,	.	.	.	101
,, M. de Champagny :	2 Sept. ,,	.	.	.	102
,, Marshal Soult :	4 ,, ,,	.	.	.	103
,, Joseph Napoleon :	8 ,, ,,	.	.	.	103
,, ,, .,	9 ,, ,,	.	.	.	104
,, General Clarke :	9 ,, ,,	.	.	.	105
,, M. Fouché :	9 Oct. ,,	.	.	.	106
,, Joachim Napoleon :	12 Nov. ,,	.	.	.	107
,, ,, ,,	18 ,, ,,	.	.	.	107
,, M. Fouché :	18 ,, ,,	.	.	.	108
,, General Menou :	28 ,, ,,	.	.	.	108
,, ,, ,,	28 ,, ,,	.	.	.	108
,, M. de Lavallette :	6 Dec. ,,	.	.	.	109
,, M. Fouché :	7 ,, ,,	.	.	.	109
,, M. de Champagny :	10 ,, ,,	.	.	.	110
,, the Prince de Neufchâtel :	15 ,, ,,	.	.	.	110
,, M. de Champagny :	16 ,, ,,	.	.	.	111
,, M. Fouché :	31 ,, ,,	.	.	.	111
,, Comte Fouché :	1 Jan. 1809,	.	.	.	112
,, M. Bigot de Préameneu :	1 ,, ,,	.	.	.	112
,, Comte de Champagny :	7 ,, ,,	.	.	.	113
,, ,, ,,	8 ,, ,,	.	.	.	114
., the Prince de Neufchâtel :	9 ,, ,,	.	.	.	114
,, Comte de Champagny :	25 ,, ,,	.	.	.	115
,, ,, Fouché :	27 ,, ,,	.	.	.	116

			PAGE
To Comte de Champagny :	8 Feb. 1809,	. . .	116
„ Jerome Napoleon :	11 „ . „	. . .	117
„ Comte de Champagny :	23 „ „	. . .	118
„ „ „	23 „ „	. . .	118
„ M. Bigot de Préameneu :	3 Mar. „	. . .	119
„ General Clarke :	6 „ „	. . .	119
„ Comte Fouché : ·	14 „ „	. . .	120
„ Jerome Napoleon :	15 „ „	. . .	120
„ Comte Fouché :	23 „ „	. . .	121
„ „ „	24 „ „	. . .	122
„ General Clarke :	27 „ „	. . .	122
„ Comte Fouché :	27 „ „	. .	122
„ „ „	27 „ „	. .	123
„ „ „	3 April „	. . .	123
„ Jerome Napoleon :	29 „ „	. .	124
„ Frederick, King of Wur-			
temberg :	1 May „		124
„ Comte de Champagny :	14 „ „		125
„ General Clarke :	19 „ „		126
„ Prince Cambacérès :	20 „ „		126
„ Comte Fouché :	20 „ „		127
„ „ „	14 June „		127
„ Joachim Napoleon :	20 „ „		128
„ Comte Fouché :	20 „ „		128
„ General Andréossy :	25 „ „		128
„ Comte Fouché :	30 „ „		131
„ the Prince de Neufchâtel :	3 July „		131
„ Comte Fouché :	14 „ „		132
„ „ Gaudin :	15 „ „		132
„ „ Fouché :	16 „ „		132
„ „ „	17 „ „		133
„ Jerome Napoleon :	17 „ „		133
„ Comte Régnier :	18 „ „		134
„ „ Fouché :	20 „ „		134
„ „ „	24 „ „		135
„ Jerome Napoleon :	25 „ „		135
„ Comte Fouché :	26 „ „		139
„ Marshal Lefebvre :	26 „ „		139
„ Comte Fouché :	28 „ „		140
„ „ „	28 „ „		140
„ Marshal Lefebvre :	30 „ „		142
„ M. Bigot de Préameneu :	2 Aug. „		143
„ Comte Fouché :	2 „ „		143

			PAGE
To Comte Fouché :	2 Aug. 1809,	.	144
„ the Prince de Neufchâtel :	5 „ „	.	144
„ Comte Fouché :	6 „ „	.	145
„ General Clarke :	7 „ „	.	145
„ Comte Fouché :	9 „ „	.	146
„ „ „	10 „ „	.	146
„ „ „	11 „ „	.	147
„ Prince Borghese :	13 „ „	.	147
„ General Clarke :	16 „ „	.	148
„ Elisa Napoleon :	17 „ „	.	150
„ Comte Fouché :	17 „ „	.	150
„ General Clarke :	18 „ „	.	151
„ Comte de Champagny :	20 „ „	.	152
„ Comte Fouché :	22 „ „	.	154
„ „ „	2 Sept. „	.	155
„ Comte de Champagny :	4 „ „	.	155
„ Comte Fouché :	6 „ „	.	155
„ M. Bigot de Préameneu :	7 „ „	.	156
„ Comte Fouché :	12 „ „	.	157
„ „ „	15 „ „		158
„ „ „	15 „ „	.	158
„ „ „	18 „ „	.	159
„ Louis Napoleon :	21 „ „	.	159
„ Comte Fouché :	23 „ „	.	162
„ Comte de Champagny :	8 Oct. „	.	162
„ General Clarke :	10 „ „	.	163
„ „ „	21 „ „	.	164
„ M. Fouché :	26 „ „	.	164
„ the Prince Borghese :	26 „ „	.	164
„ Marshal Bessières :	20 Nov. „	.	165
„ General Clarke :	9 Dec. „	.	165
„ M. de Champagny :	17 „ „	.	166
„ Prince Cambacérès :	22 „ „	.	167
„ M. Fouché :	24 „ „	.	167
„ „	27 „ „	.	168
„ M. de Champagny :	30 „ „	.	168
„ „ „	17 Jan. 1810,	.	168
„ M. Fouché :	21 „ „		169
„ M. de Champagny :	24 „ „		170
„ „ „	27 „ „		170
„ M. de Rémusat :	13 Feb. „		171
„ M. de Champagny :	18 „ „		171
„ M. Fouché :	18 „ „		172

			PAGE
To Mme de la Rochefoucauld : 24 Feb. 1810,			173
„ M. de Champagny :	26 „	„	173
„ „ „	2 Mar.	„	174
„ M. Fouché :	12 „	„	175
„ M. de Champagny :	3 April	„	176
„ Prince Eugène Napoleon :	3 „	„	176
„ M. Fouché :	14 „	„	177
„ M. de Champagny :	24 „	„	178
„ M. Fouché :	24 „	„	178
„ General Clarke :	26 „	„	179
„ Prince Eugène Napoleon :	26 „	„	179
„ Louis Napoleon :	20 May	.,	180
„ M. Fouché :	23 „	„	183
„ Louis Napoleon :	23 „	„	184
„ the Prince de Neufchâtel :	23 „	„	185
„ General Savary :	6 June	„	185
„ M. de Champagny :	9 „	„	186
„ General Savary :	24 „	„	186
„ M. de Champagny :	24 „	„	186
„ General Clarke :	6 „	„	187
„ General Savary :	29 „	„	187
„ M. de Champagny :	29 „	„	188
„ M. Fouché :	1 July	„	189
„ M. Savary :	1 „	,	189
„ „	3 „	„	190
„ General Clarke :	3 „	„	190
„ Comte Bigot de Préameneu :	13 „	„	190
„ Comte de Montalivet :	16 „	„	192
„ Prince Lebrun :	17 „	„	194
„ General Savary :	20 „	„	195
„ „ „	4 Aug.	„	196
„ General Clarke :	8 „	„	197
„ M. de Champagny :	18 „	„	197
„ Prince Lebrun :	11 „	„	197
„ General Savary :	21 „	„	198
„ Comte Bigot de Préameneu :	22 „	„	198
„ M. de Champagny :	20 „	„	199
„ General Savary :	31 „	„	199
„ M. de Champagny :	5 Sept.	„	200
„ Marshal Bernadotte :	10 „	„	200
„ the Prince de Neufchâtel :	16 „	„	200
„ „ „	16 „	„	201
„ Prince Lebrun :	19 „	„	202

					PAGE
To Prince Lebrun :	25 Sept. 1810,	.	.		202
„ „ „	26 „ „	.	.		203
„ Comte Laplace :	27 „ „	.	.		204
„ General Savary :	28 „ „	.	.		205
„ General Clarke :	2 Oct. „	.	.		206
„ Jerome Napoleon :	4 :, „	.	.		206
„ Comte Mollien :	5 „ „	.	.		206
„ M. de Champagny :	7 „ „	.	.		207
„ „ · „	12 „ „	.	.		207
„ Comte de Montalivet :	13 „ „	.	.		208
„ General Savary :	14 „ „	.	.		209
„ M. de Champagny :	16 „ „	.	.		210
„ General Savary :	17 „ „	.	.		211
„ „ „	18 „ „	.	.		211
„ Joachim Napoleon :	18 „ „	.	.		212
„ General Savary :	20 „ „	.	.		212
„ M. de Champagny :	21 „ „	.	.		213
„ General Savary :	25 „ „	.	.		213
„ M. de Champagny :	8 Nov. „	.	.		214
„ „ „	9 „ „	.	.		214
„ General Savary :	14 „ „	.	.		215
„ „ „	21 „ „	.	.		216
„ Comte de Lavallette :	28 „ „	.	.		216
„ General Savary :	28 „ „	.	.		216
„ Prince Borghese :	31 Dec. „	.	.	.	217
„ General Savary :	31 „ „	.	.	.	217
„ Comte Bigot de Préameneu :	1 Jan. 1811,	.	.	.	218
„ Prince Borghese :	1 „ „	.	.	.	218
„ Elisa Napoleon :	1 „ „	.	.	.'	219
„ General Savary :	2 „ „	.	.	.	219
„ Prince Borghese :	2 „ „	.	.	.	220
„ „ „	2 „ „	.	.	.	221
„ General Savary :	3 „ „	.	.	.	221
„ the Prince de Neufchâtel :	4 „ „	.	.	.	222
„ Prince Borghese :	6 „ „	.	.	.	222
„ Elisa Napoleon :	8 „ „	.	.	.	224
„ General Savary :	15 „ „	.	.	.	224
„ Prince Borghese :	15 „ „	.	.	.	225
„ General Savary :	20 „ „	.	.	.	225
„ Comte Daru :	22 „ „	.	.	.	226
„ General Savary :	10 Feb. „	.	.	.	227
„ Comte de Montalivet :	21 „ „	.	.	.	227
„ M. de Champagny :	3 Mar. „	.	.	.	227

			PAGE
To General Savary :	14 Mar. 1811,	. .	228
„ „	16 „ „	. .	228
„ „	18 „ „	. . .	229
„ Prince Lebrun :	18 „ „	. . .	229
„ „	18 „ „	. . .	229
„ General Savary :	14 April „	. . .	230
„ „	14 „ „	. . .	230
„ Prince Lebrun :	17 „ „	. . .	231
„ General Savary :	21 „ „	. . . .	232
„ M. Maret :	24 „ „	. . .	232
„ Prince Lebrun :	3 May „	. . .	233
„ General Savary :	3 „ „	. . .	233
„ „	7 „ „	. . .	234
„ Prince Lebrun :	12 „ „	. . .	234
„ Marshal Davout :	17 „ „	. . .	234
„ Prince Lebrun :	20 „ „	. . .	235
„ General Savary :	24 „ „	. . .	235
„ M. Maret :	26 „ „	. . .	236
„ „	1 June „	. . .	236
„ „	13 „ „	. . .	237
„ General Savary :	22 „ „	. . .	237
„ Prince Lebrun :	22 „ „	. . .	237
„ „	29 „ „	. . .	238
„ Marshal Davout :	5 July „	. . .	238
„ Cardinal Fesch :	12 „ „	. . .	239
„ Comte de Montalivet :	19 „ „	. . .	239
„ General Comte Bertrand :	22 „ „	. . .	240
„ „ Hullin :	25 „ „	. . .	240
„ M. Maret :	26 „ „	. . .	241
„ General Savary :	26 „ „	. . .	241
„ „	27 „ „	. . .	241
„ M. Maret :	29 „ „	. . .	242
„ General Savary :	29 „ „	. . .	242
„ „ Clarke :	30 „ „	. . .	243
„ „ Savary :	1 Aug. „	. . .	243
„ „ „	4 „ „	. . .	243
„ „ Clarke :	4 „ „	. . .	244
„ M. Maret :	5 „ „	. . .	244
„ General Clarke :	15 „ „	. . .	245
„ „ Savary :	20 „ „	. . .	245
„ „ „	22 „ „	. . .	246
„ M. Maret :	24 „ „	. . .	246
„ Comte Mollien :	3 Sept. „	. . .	247

				PAGE
To M. Régnier :	3 Sept. 1811,	.	.	247
„ „	6 „ „	.	.	248
„ General Clarke :	7 „ „	.	.	248
„ Marshal Bessières :	11 „ „	.	.	248
„ General Savary :	12 „ „	.	.	249
„ „ „	30 „ „	.	.	249
„ „ „	30 „ „	.	.	250
„ „ „	7 Oct. „	.	.	252
„ „ „	7 „ „	.	.	252
„ Comte de Montalivet :	20 „ „	.	.	252
„ M. Gaudin :	23 „ „	.	.	254
„ Marshal Davout :	27 „ „	.	.	254
„ Comte Mollien :	1 Nov. „	.	.	255
„ General Clarke :	16 „ „	.	.	256
„ M. Maret :	18 „ „	.	.	257
„ General Savary :	21 „ „	.	.	257
„ „ „	24 „ „	.	.	258
„ „ „	30 „ „	.	.	258
„ „ „	30 „ „	.	.	258
„ Queen Julie of Spain :	4 Dec. „	.	.	258
„ Comte de Montalivet :	9 „ „	.	.	259
„ Jerome Napoleon :	10 „ „	.	.	259
„ General Savary :	10 „ „	.	.	260
„ Comte de Lavallette :	25 „ „	.	.	261
„ M. Maret :	26 Jan. 1812,	.	.	261
„ „	9 Feb. „	.	.	262
„ „	29 „ „	.	.	262
„ Jerome Napoleon :	4 July „	.	.	262
„ M. Maret :	5 Oct. „	.	.	263
„ „	18 Nov. „	.	.	264
„ Jerome Napoleon :	23 Dec. „	.	.	265
„ Princess Stephanie :	29 „ „	.	.	265
„ General Savary :	8 Jan. 1813,	.	.	266
„ Comte Defermon :	24 „ „	.	.	266
„ Comte Bigot de Préameneu :	24 „ „	.	.	266
„ General Savary :	24 „ „	.	.	267
„ „ Clarke :	24 „ „	.	.	267
„ Elisa Napoleon :	25 „ „	.	.	268
„ General Savary :	26 „ „	.	.	268
„ Princess Pauline Borghese :	27 „ „	.	.	269
„ General Savary :	28 „ „	.	.	269
„ „ Clarke :	28 „ „	.	.	269

				PAGE
To Prince Eugène Napoleon :	28 Jan. 1813,	. . .	270
„ General Duroc :	3 Feb. „	. . .	270
„ Vice-Admiral Ganteaume :	6 „ „	. . .	271
„ General Clarke :	18 „ „	. . .	271
„ M. Gaudin :	19 Mar. „	. . . .	271
„ General Savary :	19 „ „	. . . .	272
„ „ Clarke :	20 „ „	. . . .	272
„ Prince Lebrun :	22 „ „	. . . .	273
„ General Savary :	23 „ „	. . . .	273
„ M. Maret :	24 „ „	. . . .	273
„ Comte Bigot de Préameneu :	25 „ „	. . . .	274
„ Marshal Kellerman :	27 „ „	. .:. .	274
„ General Savary :	30 „ „	. . . .	274
„ „ Clarke :	31 „ „	. . . .	275
„ „ Savary :	2 April „	. . . .	276
„ „ Clarke :	8 „ „	. . . .	277
„ „ „	8 „ „	. . . .	278
„ „ „	14 „ „	. . . .	278
„ Prince Cambacérès :	19 „ „	. . . .	279
„ Baron de Serra :	20 „ „	. . . .	280
„ „ Reinhard :	20 „ „	. . . .	281
„ General Clarke :	5 May „	. . . .	283
„ Marie Louise :	6 „ „	. . . .	283
„ the Prince de Neufchâtel :	7 „ „	. . . .	284
„ Prince Cambacérès :	11 „ „	. . . .	286
„ M. Maret :	1 June „	. . . .	286
„ „	2 „ „	. . . .	287
„ Marshal Davout :	7 „ „	. . . .	288
„ Jerome Napoleon :	10 „ „	. . . .	288
„ M. Maret :	17 June 1813,	. . . .	289
„ General Savary :	18 „ „	. . . .	289
„ Prince Cambacérès :	18 „ „	. . . .	290
„ the Prince de Neufchâtel :	18 „ „	. . . .	291
„ Vice-Admiral Duc Decrès :	24 „ „	. . . .	291
„ Prince Cambacérès :	30 „ „	. . . .	292
„ General Savary :	30 „ „	. . . .	292
„ Joseph Napoleon :	1 July 1813,	. . . .	293
„ Prince Cambacérès :	1 „ „	. . . .	293
„ „ „	1 „ „	. . . .	294
„ General Clarke :	1 „ „	. . . .	295
„ General Savary :	1 „ „	. . . .	296
„ General Clarke :	3 „ „	. . . .	297

PAGE

To General Savary :	3 July 1813,		297
,, ,, Clarke :	6 ,, ,,		297
,, Marshal Davout :	9 ,, ,,		298
,, Prince Cambacérès :	11 ,, ,,		299
,, General Clarke :	11 ,, ,,		300
,, M. Maret :	12 ,, ,,		301
,, ,,	15 ,, ,,		302
,, Prince Cambacérès :	16 ,, ,,		303
,, Marshal Davout :	16 ,, ,,		304
,, the Prince de Neufchâtel :	19 ,, ,,		305
,, Prince Cambacérès :	20 ,, ,,		306
,, General Savary :	20 ,, ,,		307
,, Frederick, King of Wurtemberg :	22 ,, ,,	.	308
,, Elisa Napoleon :	22 ,, ,,	.	308
,, General Savary :	29 ,, ,,	.	308
,, ,, Clarke :	31 ,, ,,	.	309
,, the Prince de Neufchâtel :	31 ,, ,,	.	309
,, General Clarke :	1 Aug. ,,	.	310
,, ,, Savary :	6 ,, ,,	.	311
,, ,, ,,	7 ,, ,,	.	312
,, ,, ,,	7 ,, ,,	.	312
,, ,, ,,	7 ,, ,,	.	313
,, ,, Clarke :	7 ,, ,,	.	313
,, ,, Savary :	11 ,, ,,	. .	313
,, Comte de Rémusat :	12 ,, ,,	. .	314
,, Prince Cambacérès :	14 ,, ,,	. . .	314
,, General Savary :	14 ,, ,,	. . .	315
,, ,, ,,	14 ,, ,,	. . .	315
,, Comtesse de Montesquiou :	14 ,, ,,	. .	316
,, the Prince de Neufchâtel :	29 ,, ,,	. . .	316
,, Marshal Gouvion St. Cyr :	1 Sept. ,,	. . .	316
,, General Comte Friant :	3 ,, ,,	. . .	317
,, the Prince de Neufchâtel :	4 Oct. ,,	. . .	317
,, Prince Cambacérès :	23 ,, ,,	. . .	318
,, Comtesse de Montesquiou :	3 Nov. ,,	. . .	318
,, Prince Cambacérès :	5 ,, ,,	. . .	318
,, ,, ,,	6 ,, ,,	. . .	319
,, Madame Mère :	6 ,, ,,	. . .	320
,, Prince Cambacérès :	6 ,, ,,	. . .	321
,, M. Maret :	12 ,, ,,	. .	322

PAGE

To Ferdinand, Prince of the
    Asturias :   12 Nov. 1813, ...   323
 „ M. Maret :   19 „   „   323
 „ General Savary :   6 Dec. „   323
 „ Duc Charles de Plaisance : 16 „   „   324
 „ King Louis :   4 or 5 Jan. 1814,   .   .   .   325
 „ King Joseph :   7 Jan. 1814, ...   326
 „ General Savary :   13 „   „   327
 „ M. de Caulaincourt : 19 „   „   327
 „ General Savary :   21 „   „   328
 „ Prince Cambacérès : 6 Feb. „   .   :   .   .   329
 „ King Joseph :   21 „   „   .   :   .   .   329
 „ General Savary :   22 „   „   330
 „ Comtesse de Montesquiou : 4 Mar. „   .   .   .   331
 „ Baron de la Bouillerie : 14 „   „   331
 „ Prince Cambacérès : 16 „   „   331
 „ King Joseph :   2 April „   332

THE HUNDRED DAYS.

To King Joseph :   25 Mar. 1815, ...   333
 „ Marshal Davout :   26 „   „   334
 „ Comte Defermon :   27 „   „   333
 „ Prince Cambacérès : 13 April „   334
 „ Marshal Davout :   13 „   „   334
 „ M. Fouché :   14 „   „   335
 „ M. de Caulaincourt : 27 „   „   336
 „ M. Gaudin :   1 May „   336
 „ Prince Cambacérès : 2 „   „   337
 „ Marshal Davout :   2 „   „   337
 „ M. Fouché :   3 „   „   337
 „ Vice-Admiral Duc Decrès : 5 „   „   338
 „ M. Fouché :   5 „   „   338
 „ Marshal Davout :   5 „   „   338
 „   „   „   11 „   „   338
 „ M. Fouché :   13 „   „   339
 „ Marshal Davout :   13 „   „   339
 „ M. Fouché :   15 „   „   340
 „   „   „   16 „   „   340
 „ Marshal Davout :   18 „   „   341
 „ Comte Réal :   19 „   „   341
 „ Marshal Davout :   20 „   „   341

		PAGE
To Comte Mollien :	23 May 1815, .	· 342
„ M. Fouché :	25 „ „ ·	· 343
„ Marshal Davout :	25 „ „ ·	· 343
„ General Comte Drouot :	25 „ „ ·	· 344
„ „ Comte Lemarois:	25 „ „ ·	· 344
„ M. Fouché :	29 „ „ ·	· 345
„ „ „	1 June „ ·	· 345
„ Vice-Admiral Duc Decrès :	1 „ „ ·	· 346
„ Marshal Soult :	3 „ „ ·	· 347
„ King Joseph :	19 „ „ ·	· 347

NEW LETTERS OF

NAPOLEON I

PARIS, *9th Pluviôse, Year* VIII.
(*29th January* 1800.)

YOUR extraordinary massing of troops on Vannes, and the information transmitted to me by General Hédouville, lead me to suppose you are threatened with an attempted landing. If, by good luck, they should land some 15,000 or 20,000 men, see to it, by God! that not one escapes. I imagine that if you have not been forestalled, your first attention will have been given to Fort Penthièvre. In any case, give all orders necessary to insure its being put into the best possible state of defence. However that may be, I hope the guns supplied to Georges will soon be in our hands. No mercy to that ruffian! Bernier has arrived here. I have treated him well. He seems inclined to join the Government.

The measures you have taken have completely stripped the Sarthe, the Mayenne, and the Orne, of troops. About a week ago I sent General Chambarlhac, with 1600 men, into the last named Department. He has beaten Frotté, and put him to utter rout. I am sending a reserve to Verneuil, consisting of 1500 men, under the Brigadier of the 43rd regiment, and 200 dragoons of the 5th, commanded by my brother, who is Brigadier in that regiment. These two columns, over 3000 men altogether, made up the whole of the Paris garrison. I have only one battalion left here. I should not send you these 3000 men unless a landing had been effected, or was seriously threatened, and that by a force of 15,000 or 20,000 men. Send my aide-de-camp back to me quickly, and send me frequent couriers, so that I may know what happens in your quarter.

A

II

TO GENERAL LEFEBVRE, COMMANDING 15TH AND 17TH MILITARY DIVISIONS.

PARIS, *9th Pluviôse, Year* VIII.
(*29th January* 1800.)

GENERAL BRUNE has sent all the troops in the Departments of the Sarthe, the Mayenne, and the Orne, towards Vannes. He has also, I should imagine, sent for General Gardanne. Thus the 22nd and 14th Military Divisions are almost stripped. My intention is that General Chambarlhac shall remain fixed in the Department of the Orne, whatever orders he may receive from General Brune, keeping you informed, meanwhile, by special courier, of all orders he receives. If, in consequence of General Brune's orders, General Guidal has started for Vannes, General Chambarlhac will take chief command of the Department of the Orne. He will open correspondence with the generals remaining in the Sarthe and the Mayenne.

M. Bourmont, who commands the Chouans in that Department, has agreed to the pacification. This does not make it less necessary for General Chambarlhac to press sharply on any gatherings that may yet take place, either in the Orne, the Sarthe, or the Mayenne. For this purpose he will have strong columns commanded by General Nesle and General Champeaux. To-morrow you will despatch the 2nd battalion of the 43rd, and the 2nd battalion of the 76th, with three pieces of light artillery, and the whole of the 5th Dragoons. This column will be commanded by the Brigadier of the 43rd. It will proceed to Verneuil and remain there in reserve. You will inform General Chambarlhac, who will not call upon it except in imminent emergency. The commandant of this column will warn you, by special couriers, of everything which may come to his knowledge, either in the Evreux direction or in that of Nogent-le-Républicain. If the Chouans collect in force, he will pursue them. You will point out that his chief mission is to keep watch, and to remain at your disposal, according to circumstances, and to whatever later news I receive.

III

TO GENERAL CHAMBARLHAC, WITH THE WESTERN ARMY.

PARIS, 12*th Pluviôse, Year* VIII.
(1*st February* 1800.)

I HOPE that by this time you have succeeded in destroying Frotté's main body. I have just placed the 14th Division under the orders of General Lefebvre, whose headquarters will continue to be in Paris. A reserve of 1500 men, commanded by the Brigadier of the 43rd, will be at Verneuil to-morrow. Pursue Frotté wherever he may seek refuge, and disarm the most disaffected of the districts in your neighbourhood. I desire earnestly that my aide-de-camp, whom I send you, may bring me back news of Frotté's complete destruction.

IV

TO GENERAL SAHUGUET, COMMANDING THE 22ND DIVISION, AT TOURS.

PARIS, 21*st Pluviôse, Year* VIII.
(10*th February* 1800.)

I AM assured that Bourmont has not disarmed his bands, and that there are disturbances in the division under your command. Use sufficient force against the rebels to overwhelm them. Send me, by the aide-de-camp I now send you, the army establishment of your division. Send me also notes on the Generals and superior officers under your orders, and also on the central administration of the Department and on the municipal administration of the principal communes. If any mob assembles, march on it instantly, rout it, and disarm any communes that favour the Chouans.

V

TO GENERAL LEFEBVRE, COMMANDING THE 14TH, 15TH, AND 17TH MILITARY DIVISIONS.

PARIS, 25*th Pluviôse, Year* VIII.
(14*th February* 1800.)

YOU have already given orders at Orleans to send 400 or 500 men to Nogent-le-Rotrou. Order General Béthencourt to add to these 400 or 500 men, all the available troops in the Department, to divide them into as many columns, of 400 men each, as possible, and to sweep the Department of the Sarthe so as to disperse all the armed bodies he may meet. He will inform the General in command at Le Mans of this movement, so that he, on his part, may take similar action with the troops under his command. Make General Béthencourt aware that there is to be no question of parleying, but simply of falling, at the double, on every armed gathering. Tell him I rely on his zeal for the prompt dispersal of all the bands infesting the Department of the Sarthe. Inform him that to fulfil this duty thoroughly, he must, after the bands are dispersed, employ good spies, make night marches, and surprise the rebel chiefs at dawn, in the country houses where they take refuge.

VI

TO GENERAL HÉDOUVILLE, ASSISTING THE COMMANDER-IN-CHIEF OF THE WESTERN ARMY.

(Dictated by the First Consul to General Clarke, head of the dépôt of the War Department.)

PARIS, *2nd Ventôse, Year* VIII.
(*21st February* 1800.)

IT is by order of the First Consul that I reply, as I am about to do, to the letter you did me the honour to address to me on 27th Pluviôse, and which, in accordance with my duty, I communicated to him.

The doubt as to Bourmont was probably caused by a letter written by him to General Brune, Commanding in Chief, which he signed with the title of Count, and which he sealed with a seal bearing the three *fleurs de lis.* Independently of these points, which are in manifest contradiction with the established Government, and the (terms of) pacification, Bourmont has ventured to threaten General Brune. This act was taken by the Government, and necessarily so, as one of rebellion. By virtue of the pacification, Bourmont retired into the condition of a private individual. But his letter to General Brune was not the letter of a private citizen. It was simply the letter of a Chouan leader. The

Government was obliged to take measures to check this audacity. Hence the order sent to you, which you received on 27th Pluviôse. I have the honour to transmit you a copy of Bourmont's letter. I cannot believe your judgment of it will be more indulgent than mine.

Before receiving the First Consul's orders, you had decided to authorise Bourmont to proceed to Paris. He has arrived. I presented him to the First Consul, who spoke to him very frankly, and advised him to conduct himself like a peaceable citizen. Bourmont appeared to me resolved to conform to this advice, and to settle here. But none the less is it indispensable, whatever his private intention may be, to make it impossible for him to re-organise civil war in the district he has commanded ; and the future tranquillity of that country depends on its complete disarmament. Without disarmament, the Chouans' present submission offers no guarantee of any kind for the future. Is not their organisation, indeed, still quite intact? May not a summons from their chiefs call them to arms, just when the absence of our troops, marched against some foreign enemy, would enable them to repeat all their former excesses? I transmit a copy of a letter from the Chouan leader Henry, and you will see that the Government cannot really consider a country where such addresses are circulated, to have thoroughly submitted. The First Consul, then, desires you will specially apply yourself to the disarmament. Bourmont has promised to behave himself well. The death of Frotté and his accomplices cannot have failed to make a great impression on him, and the punishment of that desperate leader will doubtless contribute to the complete pacification of the Western Departments. If any of what those gentlemen denominate 'Chefs de Légion' still exist, who have refused to submit to the laws of the Republic, it is urgently important that all necessary measures should be taken for their immediate arrest. The same thing applies to all vagabonds. The First Consul's intention is, that as soon as a certain number have been collected, they shall be sent, under good and safe escort, to Brest, where orders have been received to enrol them in the St. Dominguan troops. As for the leaders who have surrendered at discretion, he desires you to inform them that as they have trusted themselves to the Government, they shall experience its generosity. The

First Consul directs you to demand, from each in succession, his word of honour to avoid the Departments infested by Chouans, while the war lasts. You will invite them to name the town where each proposes to reside. They will be under surveillance, and provision will be made for the support of such as have no private means. You will do well to inform the First Consul as to the towns they mention to you, and he requests you, meanwhile, to watch them carefully.

When these measures have been taken, you will still have to send in the conscripts to their dépôt at Versailles, and to raise the battalion of irregulars which I have discussed with you in my previous letters. The moment is a favourable one for completely stamping out this war: the First Consul is convinced you will not let it slip.

VII

TO GENERAL AUGEREAU, COMMANDER-IN-CHIEF OF THE FRENCH ARMY IN BATAVIA.

PARIS, 17*th Ventôse, Year* VIII.
(*8th March* 1800.)

GENERAL MARMONT goes to Amsterdam with a letter from me to the municipality and leading citizens, to arrange a loan. We are in want of money. The Vendée is pacified, and everything is working towards a war worthy of us. I greatly regret I cannot call you back to the Rhine; but your presence is too necessary in Batavia.

VIII

TO GENERAL LACUÉE, MINISTER OF WAR
ad interim.

LAUSANNE, 25*th Floréal, Year* VIII.
(*15th May* 1800.)

GENERAL PEYROU, who was with the Army of the Pyrenees under General Dugommier, is a bad officer. I do not therefore approve of the position you propose to allot him in the Reserve Army. It is far simpler to give him his half-pay. He is quite useless.

IX

TO MADAME * * * *

PARIS, 21st *Vendémiaire, Year* IX.
(13*th October* 1800.)

I PERFECTLY recollect, Madame, the touching protesta-
tion sent me by your son, at Douai, almost two years ago.
I resolved, then and there, to let him know, some day, how
much it had struck me. I am very glad you have recalled
it to my memory, and to be able to do something which
may be agreeable to you.

X

TO CITIZEN LUCIEN BONAPARTE, AMBASSADOR
AT MADRID.

PARIS, 1st *Nivôse, Year* IX.
(22*nd December* 1800.)

I HAVE received your letters of 12th, 16th, and 23rd
Frimaire. Citizen Talleyrand will have written to inform
you of the desire of the Government that you should at
once send the vessels to Egypt. Arrange so that the first
should start a week or ten days after the receipt of this
letter. Citizen Clément, a senior officer of the Guard, starts
the day after to-morrow, with despatches. You will cause
him to sail by that ship.

Enclosed you will find a note sent me by Berthier. You
will see by it, that several Spanish merchants offer to send
wine to Egypt. There are always Ragusan, Tunisian,
Algerian, or Moorish vessels in the Spanish · ports, which
would undertake this transport.

The Government has two objects in view, in sending
these ships to Egypt:—1st. To send European news, guns,
bullets, and medical necessaries into the country twice every
month; 2nd. To send over large shiploads of wine, brandy,
iron, steel, sulphur, and liqueurs. Although action is being
taken in Italy as well as in Spain, you must none the less
consider yourself as the only person sending ships to Egypt.
I need not enter into the thousand and one reasons we
have for succouring that brave and interesting Army.

I shall not make any definite appointment to the Ministry
of the Interior, until Citizen Alquier returns to Paris.

I still hope you will have war declared against Portugal, and that you will make peace. Neglect nothing to this end.

The Minister for Foreign Affairs will not have left you in ignorance of the brilliant victories won by the Army of the Rhine, and of the satisfactory condition of the Republic.

Let me know, shortly, that several ships are sailing for Egypt. You can make use of some of the French privateers which habitually put into Spanish ports. You will offer them advantageous terms to carry the news and goods above mentioned to Egypt.

(*Autograph Postscript.*)—Write to the Army of the East in lofty terms, calculated to kindle it with a sense of its own importance. Say that Europe, that Spain, takes deep interest in its greatness and glory.

XI

TO CITIZEN LUCIEN BONAPARTE, AMBASSADOR
AT MADRID.

PARIS, 25*th Nivôse, Year* IX.
(15*th January* 1801.)

CITIZEN CLÉMENT, a former aide-de-camp of General Desaix, who has already been in Egypt, proceeds to Madrid on his return thither. See that he does not spend more than four-and-twenty hours at Madrid, and that he takes ship at once.

I hope you have already sent off three or four despatch-boats to Egypt. The season advances, and you know the importance of this matter. Write by Clément to General Menou. Inform Citizen Leroy, Maritime Prefect in Egypt, that he is appointed Commissary-General at Cadiz, whither he must proceed as quickly as he can.

I am very anxious you should rid us of Mazzaredo ; the Minister for Foreign Affairs must already have warned you of this.

Campi was to have started for Madrid. This would have been a fresh cause of expense to you. I will see to his being provided for in some way.

The peace negotiations are beginning to take shape. I am momentarily expecting news of an armistice in Italy.

The great point is to keep up the Egyptian Army.

Hurry on and increase the number of your consignments. Write by every vessel to Menou, and send each month's newspapers. For this purpose I give orders that you should be sent, every day, fifteen copies of the *Moniteur*, and fifteen of the *Défenseurs*. I am expecting to hear what you have arranged with the Barbary Moors, to insure communication with Egypt during the summer.

(*Autograph Postscript.*)—I desire you will behave with reserve. You must be respected, and that cannot be unless you are reserved. Talleyrand's despatches explain my plan of campaign. Communicate it, in my name, to the Prince of Peace, to whom you will express my satisfaction. Conclude the convention of which I send you the basis, with him, as quickly as possible.

XII

TO GENERAL BERTHIER, MINISTER OF WAR.

PARIS, 27*th Pluviôse, Year* IX.
(16*th February* 1801.)

I BEG you will inform General Brune that I am extremely displeased with the conduct of General Clément at Leghorn ; that by his carelessness, he has compromised the safety of the ship *Régulus*; that he has permitted English officers to enter the Port of Leghorn under a flag of truce, received them at dinner, and allowed them to remain several days in the town, which is against all regulations ; and that I have been pained to see that French Generals could forget the outrages with which the English never cease to overwhelm our prisoners.

XIII

TO CITIZEN LUCIEN BONAPARTE, AMBASSADOR AT MADRID.

PARIS, 9*th Ventôse, Year* IX.
(28*th February* 1801.)

REAR-ADMIRAL GANTEAUME reached Toulon on 30th Pluviôse, having taken two English corvettes and one English frigate. Rear-Admiral Dumanoir must have arrived in Madrid. Whatever it may cost, we must become masters of the Mediterranean, or force the English to efforts which they will not long be able to continue.

General Murat, commanding the Army of Observation in the South, concluded an armistice, on 30th Pluviôse, with the King of the Two Sicilies, by the terms of which that Prince has laid an embargo on all English and Turkish ships.

I have received the treaty you have concluded with regard to the fortified towns. As a result of Article 4, the remainder of the Spanish forces are to join the French force in the Mediterranean. I should like to know how many ships may be reckoned on.

The five vessels to be furnished by Spain for the American expedition can sail from Cadiz just as well as from Ferrol.

The Spaniards owe us six ships of war; and it is important that we should have them as soon as possible. If they gave us three or four of those now at Cadiz, Rear-Admiral Dumanoir might select them, and take command. You might then collect all the Frenchmen to be found in the Spanish ports, and as many sailors as possible should be sent from Toulon to Malaga, whence they would proceed to Cadiz overland.

Let me therefore hear shortly, 1st, that the five Ferrol ships have sailed for Cadiz; 2nd, that seven or eight other ships have been fitted out at Cadiz—all the ships, in fact, which the Spaniards are giving us.

We will buy four dismantled frigates from Spain, on the understanding, of course, that the rigging and equipment are sold to us at the same time, and that Rear-Admiral Dumanoir approves their quality.

XIV

TO CITIZEN LUCIEN BONAPARTE, AMBASSADOR
AT MADRID.

PARIS, 27th Ventôse, Year IX.
(18th March 1801.)

THE Corps of Observation is not yet very strong, but troops are marching to join it. If the news of the peace with the Emperor and the Empire does not induce the Portuguese Court to make its own, the vanguard of 4000 men can march, and enter Spanish territory.

A brigade of 4000 men is about to embark at Rochefort, and can be landed at Ferrol, if that becomes necessary.

The Prince of Parma must not lose an instant about coming to Paris, however the Duke of Parma's business may turn out. Let him first take possession of the Duchy of Tuscany. This is very urgent.

The English have hardly any garrison at Port Mahon. If the Spaniards would stir themselves a little at Cadiz and at other ports, the island might be seized, at some moment when their squadron is engaged in another part of the Mediterranean.

XV

TO CITIZEN LUCIEN BONAPARTE, AMBASSADOR AT MADRID.

PARIS, 26th Floréal, Year IX.
(15th May 1801.)

THE King of Tuscany will be lodged, in Paris, at the Spanish Embassy. This custom was established by Joseph II., the Comte du Nord, the Kings of Denmark and Sweden, and all the Sovereigns who have come to Paris.

M. d'Araujo is arrived at L'Orient. His passport to Paris was refused, and he was informed of the ultimatum of the French Government, the conditions of which are much more severe than those proposed by the Court of Spain.

Azara is seventy years old. He is worthy of respect, and for many reasons I desire that the King of Spain shall keep him in Paris.

Set the Court of Madrid against the Pope, by informing it, as a certainty, that, at the request of Paul I., and without consulting any other Power, he has re-established the Jesuits. The Pope is an honest man, but narrow-minded. He is surrounded by the old Neapolitan priesthood, which follows in Busca's steps, and misbehaves itself.

The four Spanish frigates which were to have repaired to Leghorn have not appeared. Redouble your pressure, so that they may start without delay. Porto-Longone, which has been occupied by our troops, will serve as a haven for them.

Admiral Bruix is on the point of starting with five vessels and five frigates, laden with troops to be landed, and will appear before Cadiz. I desire the five Spanish vessels shall

be put under his orders. As he will be able to supply 500
or 600 sailors, I trust Dumanoir will be able to furnish
two or three of his ships. Take all necessary measures
for enabling the five ships which are at Cadiz to join the
French squadron which will appear before that place, and
act according to circumstances, either making an incursion
into the Mediterranean, or turning back, if necessary, to
proceed to the East or West Indies.

The five vessels furnished by Gravina are to join six ships
commanded by Admiral Villaret-Joyeuse, and seven Batavian
ships, and proceed to sea, to take action either in America
or in the Indies. Let it be understood that these operations
must be directed by one person only, and are not to be
carried out on any irrevocable plan.

Further, you will keep profound secrecy as to this movement of Admiral Bruix. It is quite unnecessary to inform
Dumanoir of it. It will be sufficient if he fits out two or
three ships, ready to set sail on short notice. At a pinch,
even one month's provisions on board each would suffice.

XVI

TO CITIZEN LUCIEN BONAPARTE, AMBASSADOR
AT MADRID.

PARIS, 12*th Prairial, Year* IX.
(1*st June* 1801.)

THE Count and Countess of Leghorn[1] have been in Paris
for several days. They have been well received. I am very
much pleased with them.

M. d'Araujo has received orders to go to Madrid, and to
disembark at Corunna. Apart from the 8000 men already
in Spain, 10,000 Frenchmen are on the march thither. See
that provision is made for their support. I do not think
there is a moment to be lost. I wish the Prince of Peace
to place 10,000 Spaniards, and the French corps, under
General St. Cyr's command, and desire him to occupy Oporto,
and the three provinces which it is indispensable for us to
hold, to serve as our indemnity. If, however, the Prince
of Peace has confidence in General St. Cyr, and wishes

---

[1] Louis, Prince of Parma, in whose favour the kingdom of Etruria had just
been created, and who had married the Infanta Maria-Louisa of Spain.

to keep him near him, to direct the war, this body of men may be confided to General Leclerc. I earnestly desire that General St. Cyr may render essential service to both nations. His great talents, and the confidence I have in him, are worthy of very high consideration on the part of the Spanish Court, and the Staff.

You may take it for granted that I will not ratify any treaty of peace which does not provide—(1) That provisionally, and until a general peace is signed, the three provinces of Minho, Tras-los-Montes, and Beiramar shall be occupied by the French and Spanish troops. (2) The payment of twenty millions to France. (3) The vessels which have blockaded Malta and Alexandria (*sic*). (4) The exclusion of the English from Portugal.

Take the crews, as many of them as possible, from Cadiz. Send off the four Spanish frigates to Leghorn.

15,000 or 18,000 men, asked for by the Court of Spain, must by now have entered Spanish territory, and 5000 more are massing at Bordeaux and Bayonne. If the English were to send troops to Lisbon, we should send an equal number into Spain.

XVII

TO CITIZEN LUCIEN BONAPARTE, AMBASSADOR AT MADRID.

PARIS, 28*th Prairial*, Year IX.
(17*th June* 1801.)

I HAVE just received your packet of 19th Prairial. I have not told you what I thought of your treaty of peace, because I dislike saying disagreeable things. Joseph, who was with me when I received it, will tell you what a really painful impression it made on me. You negotiate a great deal too fast. In such a matter as this, fifteen days' discussion are nothing at all.

Your letters, explaining your treaty, clearly prove you should not have made it ; for if England had permitted Portugal to make peace, on condition of its offering nothing in the way of compensation, our policy should have been the very reverse. As I have often told you in my letters, the only interest of Portugal to us, now-a-days, lies in the fact that she may provide us with a guarantee for the general peace.

However, nothing of what M. Pinto assured you will happen, and once we refuse to garrison Lisbon and the neighbourhood, the Regency will agree to all we ask. The fate of the French Bourbons, of the King of Sardinia, and of the Stadtholder, is a striking example of the danger of emigration. England will not go to war with Portugal, because that would oblige us to take possession of Lisbon. It will think itself very lucky if we only seize certain provinces, which it will be able to recover by returning a few islands in America. For the last century, Portugal has really been nothing but an English province, and the port of Lisbon, being under English influence, is all-important to that power.

One article of your treaty, which appears quite inconceivable, is that which stipulates that we should guarantee the Portuguese possessions in other parts of the world. This is an absolute reversal of the question; we ask for compensation with regard to England, and you give compensation to that power, which might take possession of some Portuguese territory.

You ask that the Spanish Treaty should be guaranteed, and fail to send it. . . .

Portugal at one time consented to pay sixteen millions to the Directory. M. d'Araujo agreed to give twenty millions, and these are reduced to sixteen, as we have already had four millions of expenses. Your stipulation that these should be paid at Madrid causes us a loss of one million on the exchange, and finally, by arranging for fifteen monthly payments, you make the transaction perfectly useless to the Public Treasury. Fifteen millions, paid in one month, partly in specie, partly in diamonds, and partly in saleable goods of two or three descriptions, may be of some use to us for our naval equipment; but spread over fifteen months, the payments will not only be perfectly useless, they will even have a parsimonious character which will be hurtful to our credit.

Further, this treaty lacks diplomatic form and style. It is contrary to custom to say that hostilities will not cease until ratification is exchanged. It is contrary to custom to provide, in a definite treaty, that if anything is stipulated elsewhere, the treaty becomes null and void. The safest course always is to wait for news. You must surely be aware that you are not likely to be three days without knowing the issue of M. d'Araujo's negotiations.

Finally, it is against the order and out of harmony with the importance of diplomatic business, to sign a definite treaty without having submitted the draft to your Government, unless the different articles have been successively debated by protocol, and successively adopted by that Government. Now the treaty with Portugal demanded fully ten or twelve days, at the least, of discussion by protocol.

The wording of the Treaty is frequently faulty: I will only quote one passage which struck me. The terms ' Portuguese monarchy ' and ' French people ' should not be placed in opposition. The customary form is ' between the two Nations,—the two States.'

You know that, according to the Treaty signed with Spain, a fourth part of Portugal is to be under the power of the two nations, as a compensation for the American Islands and Trinity Island.

You can, further, communicate the following information to the Spanish Court :—

Negotiations with England are proceeding with a certain amount of activity. The English do not appear disposed to relinquish Malta, Ceylon, the States of Tippoo-Sultan, nor Trinity Island. I have proposed the *status quo ante bellum* in the Mediterranean and America, with the same condition in Portugal, and certain compensations in India. There we are at present. Your treaty with Portugal would have rendered all this nugatory. As to the war, I am too far away to be able to prescribe its exact plan, but I have great confidence in General St. Cyr. I should much like the first act of the war to be to take possession of the three provinces we are to occupy, and to draw contributions and supplies from them. The enemy will probably not allow their Army to be cut, by endeavouring to defend the country on the right of the Mondego, and will concentrate their forces in the Estramadura. Small divisions would suffice to seize the three provinces, once the Army lay with its left on the Tagus and its right on the Estramadura. Once you were in that position, and the Regency was convinced you did not threaten Lisbon, it would do anything you chose. You must tell the Portuguese plenipotentiary, and repeat it over and over again, that we are not making war on Portugal, but that we treat it as an English province.

It is impudence on M. Pinto's part to assert that three Portuguese ships and two frigates did not blockade Alexandria. We spoke them.

All your letters convince me that you are very far from realising all the strength, and all the obstinacy, even, that must be put into a negotiation. You may be sure that your treaty, when it is sent to England, will betray your want of business habits to that Court, and to M. Pinto. This is pardonable. But in such a case a man should seek much counsel, and be less sure about his conclusions. You will be convinced of the great importance I attach to the proper drawing up of a treaty when I tell you, that even if the three provinces had been granted, there are certain articles—that, for instance, by which we should have guaranteed the Portuguese possessions—which would have prevented me from ratifying this one.

XVIII

TO CITIZEN LUCIEN BONAPARTE, AMBASSADOR AT MADRID.

PARIS, *3rd Messidor*, *Year* IX.
(*22nd June* 1801.)

I HAVE received your letter of 24th Prairial. Affairs of such importance are no child's play.

Your last letters from the Minister for Foreign Affairs, and mine, will have informed you that all the present plan depends on our taking possession of two or three Portuguese provinces.

Can it be possible that with your good sense, and knowledge of the human heart, you can have let yourself be deceived by Court flatteries, and that you should not have been able to make Spain aware of her real interests?

In a word, here lies the whole question. If the three provinces are occupied, we shall have an honourable peace with England before the month of Vendémiaire; and if we should be obliged to abide by the Peace of Badajoz, the war would go on for several years. It is because everything, in the political system, hangs so closely together, that a Minister should always move with great caution, and never make any hurried decision.

How can you possibly have imagined that, after the Treaty of Lunéville, I would send 15,000 men into Portugal, to make peace on the same, or perhaps on less advantageous, terms, than those obtained by the Directory six months before the Treaty of Campo-Formio, and at a time when we were still at war with Austria?

I have already caused the English to be informed that I will never depart, as regards Portugal, from the *ultimatum* addressed to M. d'Araujo, and that the *status quo ante bellum* for Portugal must amount, for Spain, to the restitution of Trinity Island ; for France, to the restitution of Martinique and Tobago ; and for Batavia, to that of Cūraçoa and some other small American isles.

In the conversation which followed the presentation of this Note, the English Minister gave it to be understood that this appeared to him reasonable.

Influence the Court to which you are sent. Do not allow yourself to be influenced by it.

Make your declaration to M. Pinto. Make it likewise to the Court of Spain. Let the armies do the rest. When so small an effort is all that is needed to insure the world's peace, it is worth the while of the Spanish Court, and the French Agents, to make it.

As for you personally, you must remain in Spain.

Felix Desportes spends his time at Madrid gossiping with all the Ambassadors, who write a heap of nonsense, which comes back to me, to their various Courts. He also writes a great deal too much to Bayonne journalists.

XIX

TO CITIZEN TALLEYRAND, MINISTER FOR FOREIGN AFFAIRS.

PARIS, 14*th Messidor, Year* IX.
(3*rd July* 1801.)

I REQUEST you will inform M. Azara that I should wish the Count of Leghorn to be beyond Chambéry by the 14th of July. For it will not be fitting that he should witness the festivities held on that day, in all the great towns of the Republic.

XX

TO CITIZEN FORFAIT, MINISTER FOR NAVAL AFFAIRS.

PARIS, 23rd *Thermidor*, *Year* IX.
(11th *August* 1801.)

I BEG you will inform Rear-Admiral Ganteaume that his not being included in the list of State Councillors is no proof of any dissatisfaction on my part, since Citizen Chaptal, Minister of the Interior, who enjoys the greatest confidence, is also omitted from the list; but that it is the result of my intention to employ him on duty which may necessitate his absence for a long time.

In a separate letter, you will express my regret that he did not succeed in carrying out his mission to bring help to the Colony. You have, no doubt, already complimented him on his capture of the *Swiftshire* (*sic*).

XXI

TO CITIZEN TALLEYRAND, MINISTER FOR FOREIGN AFFAIRS.

PARIS, 16th *Ventôse*, *Year* X.
(7th *March* 1802.)

I DESIRE you will instantly send for the Spanish Ambassador, and communicate the following Note to him :—

' Admiral Bruix has just informed the Government, that he is blockaded in the Port of Brest by twenty-one English ships only; that he has seventeen French ships in the best order, and thoroughly equipped; that M. Gravina has fifteen Spanish ships, ready to weigh anchor; that the First Consul considers it shameful and humiliating to both nations, that their fleets should be blockaded by such an inferior force; that he is sending orders by telegraph to Admiral Bruix, to leave port at once, and give chase to the twenty-one English vessels; that His Catholic Majesty's intention, in sending fifteen ships to Brest, was not to render them useless to the service and glory of the two Powers; that the First Consul requests orders to support the French Fleet in this sortie, may be sent by telegraph to General Gravina.

You will make him understand that in the present position,

political and military, of Europe, the sortie of the two fleets,
even with no object beyond that of chasing the English
Squadron for twenty-four hours, would be extremely advantageous in its results, for both nations.

XXII

NOTE ANNEXED TO A LETTER TO THE POPE, DATED 4TH PRAIRIAL, YEAR X.

IT will be expedient, for the dignity of the Government of
France, and beneficial, for the dignity of the Church, to grant
a warrant of secularisation to Citizen Talleyrand.

This Minister has rendered service both to the Church and
to the State. He has publicly and irrevocably renounced
all his clerical functions and dignities. He desires that this
renunciation should be confirmed by the formal recognition
of the Head of the Church; he deserves this special favour.

On political grounds it is inexpedient, now that France
again becomes a Catholic nation, that a Minister who holds
the chief confidence of the Government should be the subject
of doubt and controversy as to his former status.

As regards his efforts to reunite the Church and the
Government, he must be in a position to reap the free
expression of the gratitude of all who care for it,—the
reward of the zeal he has shown for the re-establishment of
religion.

Such weighty considerations will at once appeal to the
benevolence and the justice of the Holy Father.

There shall be no mention of the form such an instru-
ment should take. His Holiness will select that which
appears most fitting and most complete. As for precedents,
the Holy Father will find many in history.

In the seventeenth century, under Innocent X., Camillo
Panfili, a Cardinal, and the Sovereign Pontiff's nephew, was
secularised, and died a layman.

In the fifteenth century, Cæsar Borgia, Archbishop of
Valencia, became Duc de Valentinois, married a Princess
of the House of Albret, and died a layman.

Ferdinand di Gonzaga, who was first an ecclesiastic and
then Duke of Mantua; Maurice of Savoy, who married in
1642, after having taken orders; the two Cardinals Bourbon,

uncle and nephew, both of them Archbishops of Lyons—all of whom laid down their ecclesiastical dignities with the consent of the Holy See—died laymen.

Two Kings Casimir of Poland—one, who succeeded in the eleventh century, another, who was elected in the seventeenth, —were freed, not only from the bonds of the clerical order, but from monastic vows ; the first was a Benedictine, the second a Jesuit, and this last, besides being declared a lay-man, received permission to marry his sister-in-law.

Henry of Portugal, Archbishop of Lisbon, and successor, in 1588, to the crown of Sebastian, died a King and a layman.

François de Lorraine, who surrendered his right to the Dominions of his brother Charles IV. in 1634, and afterwards became the father of Leopold, passed from the priesthood into the laity, and remained faithful to the Church.

All these instances are taken from the period during which the Holy See was in the fulness of its authority. The use then made of it by the predecessors of Pius VII. was dictated by motives of expediency, for the Church's good. These motives still exist, and it is doubtful whether, at any of the epochs referred to, the same request was based on such weighty reasons.

XXIII

TO POPE PIUS VII.

ST. CLOUD, 26th Vendémiaire, Year XI.
(18th October 1802.)

MOST HOLY FATHER,—Since the Concordat, we have observed, in the person of M. de Belloz, Archbishop of Paris, all the virtues, qualities, and talents necessary to the highest dignities and most important functions in the Church. He could not fail to perform the duties, and support the dignity, of a Cardinal, in the most eminent manner, both as to wisdom and holiness. For this dignity we nominate and present the said Archbishop of Paris to Your Holiness, for the next creations to be made, according to custom, for the Christian States.

We pray God will preserve you many years, Most Holy Father, to rule the Church.

XXIV

TO M. DE BARRAL, BISHOP OF MEAUX.

St. Cloud, 10th *Floréal, Year* XI.
(*30th April* 1803.)

I HAVE given orders to the Treasurer to send you the sum you ask for, and to add 60,000 francs to be distributed in works of charity. I shall always be very glad to give you proof of the esteem I feel for you.

XXV

TO CITIZEN BARBÉ-MARBOIS, MINISTER OF THE PUBLIC EXCHEQUER.

26th *Prairial, Year* XI.
(15th June 1803.)

I BEG you will have a valuation made of the finest pearls in the Treasury, and also of an assortment of coloured stones, which my wife desires to purchase. She would require them before her departure for Belgium.

XXVI

TO CITIZEN FABRE DE L'AUDE, PRESIDENT OF THE FINANCE SECTION OF THE TRIBUNATE.

St. Cloud, 15th *Vendémiaire, Year* XII.
(*8th October* 1803.)

I HAVE received your various letters as to the settlement of your family. You do not doubt the interest I feel in everything which affects you. I have ordered the Treasurer, Estève, to remit you 10,000 francs to help towards the fortune of one of your daughters; I have also given orders that from 1st Vendémiaire, Year XII., the expenses of one of your daughters shall be defrayed, at any educational establishment you may select. I desire you will take these arrangements as a proof of my satisfaction with the services you have rendered.

XXVII

TO GENERAL SOULT, COMMANDING THE CAMP AT ST. OMER.

LA MALMAISON, 23rd *Pluviôse, Year* XII.
(13*th February* 1804.)
(*This letter was published in the Correspondence, No.* 7541. *The lines there described as illegible run as follows.*)

HAVE the crew and gear of the fishing-boat which communicated with the English seized at once. I reproach myself with having neglected to have this done sooner. Make the skipper speak, and I even give you authority to promise him his pardon if he gives information ; and if he should seem to hesitate, you can go so far as to follow the custom as to men suspected of being spies, and squeeze his thumbs in the hammer of a musket.

XXVIII

TO CITIZEN MELZI, VICE-PRESIDENT OF THE ITALIAN REPUBLIC.

PARIS, 30*th Pluviôse, Year* XII.
(20*th February* 1804.)

I HAVE instructed M. Mareschalchi to keep you informed of everything that happens here.[1]

You must have absolute confidence in the report made to me by the Chief Judge. There is nothing more to be known. The business would hardly be worthy of the name, save for the part taken in it by General Moreau, who has been the accomplice of those wretches,—a fact which, for three days, I could not believe ; but the proof became so overwhelming that I was unable to interfere with the course of justice. Paris and France are one family, with but one feeling and one opinion. Communicate this fact to the State Council. Place no faith in any false report which may be circulated. I have run no real risk, for the police had its eye on all these machinations, and I have the consolation of not finding reason to complain of a single man, among all those I have placed in this huge administration. Moreau stands alone ; but he had long since drawn away from the Government.

---

[1] The trial of Moreau, Georges, Pichegru, etc.

XXIX

TO MADAME MÈRE.

CASTLE OF STUPINIGI, *2nd Floréal, Year* XIII.
(*22nd April* 1805.)

MONS. JEROME BUONAPARTE has arrived at Lisbon, with the woman with whom he lives. I have ordered this prodigal son to proceed to Milan, passing through Perpignan, Toulouse, Grenoble, and Turin. I have informed him that if he diverged from that road he would be arrested. Miss Patterson, who lives with him, has taken the precaution of bringing her brother with her. I have given orders that she is to be sent back to America. If she were to evade the orders I have given, and to come to Bordeaux or Paris, she would be brought back to Amsterdam, and put on board the first American vessel. I shall treat this young man severely, if he shows himself unworthy of the name he bears, during the only interview I shall grant him, and if he persists in carrying on his *liaison*. If he shows no inclination to wash away the dishonour with which he has stained my name, by forsaking his country's flag on land and sea, for the sake of a wretched woman, I will cast him off for ever. I may make him an example which will teach young soldiers the sacredness of their duty, and the enormity of the crime they commit when they forsake their flag for a woman.

Write to him, on the supposition that he will go to Milan. Tell him I have been a father to him, that his duty to me is sacred, and that the only chance of salvation remaining to him, is to obey my instructions. Speak to his sisters, so that they may write to him too. For, once I have pronounced sentence upon him, I shall be inflexible, and his life will be blasted for ever.

XXX

TO M. FOUCHÉ, MINISTER OF POLICE.[1]

MILAN, *10th Prairial, Year* XIII.
(*30th May* 1805.)

I HAVE told you what you are to think of the reports the English are endeavouring to spread, so as to give colour to

---

[1] The rough draft of this letter is very ill-written, and almost illegible.

the step taken by the Emperor of Russia. Yet the newspapers must not be permitted to take a line favourable to
Russia, to that corrupt . . . weak, and silly Cabinet. At
this moment, indeed, it is showing some spirit, but more
from a feeling that it can do nothing, than from any other.

A contrast must be drawn with the shameful position of
the English. They must be compared to a besieged fortress.
From the top of the towers on which we see them, they
fancy they will save the country (?). The Englishman, strong
in the position of his army of observation, and in the space
which separates him from his enemy, does not glance behind
him. If he sees dust rise in the distance, he does not inquire
whether it is raised by a convoy of provisions or an enemy.
It is certain that in war, as in love, nothing is done without
. . . [*several illegible words*]. In opposition to this, set the
bravado and the cringing (?) of the Russians. Say they are
a barbarous nation, whose strength is in its cunning, a nation
without funds, which could not send 30,000 men to campaign
outside its own borders, without sacrificing them all.

What became of this bond (?) the moment war was
declared? Russian intervention was refused. And in this
connection their inconsistency and rashness must be demon-
strated. Official documents were actually garbled so as to
persuade the people that Russia did not offer her mediation
to prevent the war from breaking out.

Have caricatures made: An Englishman, purse in hand,
entreating the various Powers to take his money, etc. This
is the real direction to give the whole business; and the
huge care the English are taking to gain time, by spreading
false news, all the symptoms together, prove its extreme
importance.

Have it put about in Holland that news comes from
Madeira (?) that Villeneuve has fallen in with and captured
an English convoy of one hundred sail, on its way to
India.

Do not allow M. Musset to remain in the Bavarian States.
Write and have him arrested, wherever he may be. A
perusal of Drake's documents suffices to show what that
ruffian is. It is by this name that my agents, in whatever
country they may be, will describe him.

XXXI

TO JEROME BUONAPARTE.

MILAN, 20th *Prairial*, *Year* XIII.
(9th *June* 1805.)

I HAVE received your letter of the 10th Prairial. I shall shortly proceed to Genoa. Nothing you can say to me can affect my determination. Lucien prefers a disgraced woman, who bore him a child before he had married her, and who was his mistress while her husband was at St. Domingo, to the honour of his own name and family. I can only mourn over such an amount of mental alienation, in a man on whom Nature has bestowed much talent, and who has been snatched from a brilliant destiny by his unexampled selfishness, which has carried him far from the path of honour and duty.

Miss Patterson has been in London, and caused great excitement amongst the English. This has only increased her guilt.

XXXII

TO M. FOUCHÉ, MINISTER OF POLICE.

GENOA, 12th *Messidor*, *Year* XIII.
(1st *July* 1805.)

I CANNOT help seeing with surprise, that the intrigues and bad advice of that Mdme Hulot tend to prevent her son-in-law from going to America, and will force me to do what I would rather have avoided. I do not intend her to remain in Paris. Send her forty leagues away. She is not to go and see the Empress at Plombières : that would give her an opportunity to commit some impertinence, which would oblige me to punish her severely.

XXXIII

TO M. FOUCHÉ, MINISTER OF POLICE.

FONTAINEBLEAU, 25th *Messidor*, *Year* XIII.
(15th *July* 1805.)

THE *Gazette de France* seems to me to be doing very badly. I do not know why it reports that foolish story of the marriage of the Prince Eugene with the Queen of Etruria. It has many other improper items. Advise the Editor to be more sensible.

XXXIV

TO PRINCE EUGENE.

St. Cloud, *8th Thermidor*, *Year* XIII.
(*27th July* 1805.)

I AM informed that you are in correspondence with a person named D——. I do not know if you are aware that this person is nothing but a woman of the town, an intriguer of whom the police have frequently made use. A woman of this kind ought not to receive any letter from you. She is the filth of Paris. I think it my duty to warn you of this, that you may rule yourself accordingly in future.

XXXV.

TO M. FOUCHÉ, MINISTER OF POLICE.

Boulogne, *18th Thermidor*, *Year* XIII.
(*6th August* 1805.)

THE conscription in the Department of the Eure is a complete failure. All the conscripts have deserted. It is also a blank in the Eastern Pyrenees. My intention as regards the Eure, which is at the very gates of Paris, is that you should come to an understanding with the new Prefect, and take measures to have all the conscripts arrested and marched off. I send you a proclamation with reference to the same object. Of all abuses, that which touches the conscription is the most worth consideration, for it is the one which entails the most serious consequences.

XXXVI

TO M. DE CHAMPAGNY, MINISTER OF THE INTERIOR.

Boulogne, *19th Thermidor*, *Year* XIII.
(*7th August* 1805.)

I DESIRE you will express my displeasure to the Prefects of the Gironde, the Hérault, the Loire, the Upper Loire, the Cantal, the Lot, and the Deux-Nèthes. Inform them that they are the seven Prefects who have given least atten-tion to the conscription, who permit the greatest amount of desertions, and who are altogether most behind-hand. Order them to take efficacious measures to remove this blot from their Departments and government. Tell them that the smallest neglect of so important a matter is an injury to the State.

XXXVII

TO M. FOUCHÉ, MINISTER OF POLICE.

BOULOGNE CAMP, 4*th Fructidor, Year* XIII.
(*22nd August* 1805.)

I HEAR that General Lecourbe has returned to his country house a few leagues from Paris. I had sent him orders to go to the Franche-Comté. If he is still at his country house, have him arrested, and brought back to the Franche-Comté by the police. The general officer in question has conducted himself so ill, that he cannot be allowed in the neighbourhood of Paris. Inform him that the first time he ventures within forty leagues of Paris, I will have him arrested and deported. Advise him to sell his property near Paris, and make him understand that he had better behave himself; that I am aware of his share in the Georges conspiracy, and of his conduct in general. I must take this opportunity of expressing my displeasure at your having allowed him to come so near. He is a cunning fellow, a bad and dangerous man,— hand and glove with all my enemies.

I must also tell you that the conduct of the police lacks consistency. The Lenormant affair proves this. If Lahorie and three or four other individuals belonging to Moreau's party, whom I had banished to different departments, were not seen openly in Paris, the many foolish and ridiculous plans, which will only result in their own destruction, would never come into their heads. Fix all your attention on this point, and clear Paris of everything which should not be there.

XXXVIII

TO M. FOUCHÉ, MINISTER OF POLICE.

BOULOGNE CAMP, 11*th Fructidor, Year* XIII.
(*29th August* 1805.)

ALLOW me to tell you that your conduct is utterly unintelligible to me. Either you are profoundly ignorant of mankind, or you are trying to make me look into matters which should not concern me. Lecourbe is in Paris. He has no business there. A falser and more thorough rogue does not live. Let him be out of Paris in twelve hours, and never permit him to return. Anybody with the most

clementary ideas of government must feel that Lecourbe
must never be allowed within a hundred leagues of Paris.
You should never have advised him to come there.

Another matter is that of Mdme de Staël. She claims
that I gave her leave to come to Paris, and wants to stay
there. She must betake herself to Coppet. You must
feel I am not such a fool as to prefer her presence in Paris
to her being twenty leagues off. At Geneva, which is every
one's country, French affairs are her sole occupation. . . . .[1]
Inform her friends that she will stop at a distance of forty
leagues. All elements of discord must be removed from
Paris. It is impossible for me to leave bad citizens free to
disturb my capital, whilst I myself am two thousand leagues
away, at the far end of Europe.

XXXIX

LETTER TO BE SENT BY PRINCESS AUGUSTA TO THE
STATES-GENERAL OF BAVARIA.

THE PALACE AT MUNICH, 15th January 1806.

GENTLEMEN OF THE STATES-GENERAL OF BAVARIA,—I
have to thank you for the kind things you say of me in the
address you have presented to His Majesty the Emperor, my
august father-in-law. I accept with pleasure the gift the
States-General desire to offer me. But permit me to dispose
of it, with the consent of the Prince, my husband, by giving
dowries to fifty girls of my own age, chosen amongst the
most virtuous in the various towns and cantons in Bavaria,
and to two soldiers, either wounded or distinguished by
bravery during the last war—out of each Bavarian regiment
in the brave army of my much honoured father. I wish
these marriages to take place on the 14th of next February,
but would leave all other executive details entirely to you.
On that 14th of February I shall, wheresoever I may be, take
part in thought in the festivities in my own land, and I shall
feel my happiness increased by the happiness of fifty good
and virtuous couples.

Be assured, gentlemen, of my esteem, and of my desire to
give you proof of it, in every circumstance.

---

[1] Here follow several illegible words.   This rough draft is very badly
written.

XL

TO M. FOUCHÉ, MINISTER OF POLICE.

PARIS, 14th February 1806.

I SEE in your report of 13th January, under the heading of Deux-Sèvres, that Mlles La Rochejaquelin, Gibot, and others, harbour dissident priests. Give orders to send them into exile, to towns in the Dauphiné, such as Vienne, and let no time be lost in arresting those priests.

XLI

TO MARSHAL BERTHIER, MINISTER OF WAR.

PARIS, 31st March 1806.

I HOLD official documents to prove that War-Commissary Grobert has received 44,000 francs from the province of Padua, to buy back the stores of salt and tobacco which he threatened to remove, that Commissary Masséna has received 80,000 francs, and Adjutant-Commandant Delort 20,000 francs, from the same province of Padua. Write to these three officers to pay the sums in question into the Army Chest within twenty-four hours, under pain of a criminal prosecution, if they make the smallest delay.

XLII

TO M. DE TALLEYRAND, MINISTER FOR FOREIGN AFFAIRS.

PARIS, 28th February 1806.

MAKE known my displeasure at the bad behaviour of the Zamorra regiment, when crossing the Genoese Riviera, to the Spanish Court. The regiment killed two gendarmes. Write to my Minister at Florence, to positively demand reparation for the death of my two gendarmes, killed at Rapallo, to desire that six men of the Zamorra regiment may be shot, and that if justice is not done me, I will send two regiments into Tuscany, and will have every man of the regiment they can meet with massacred.

XLIII

TO MARSHAL BERTHIER, MAJOR-GENERAL OF THE GRANDE ARMÉE.

St. Cloud, 7th July 1806.

I SEND you a report, the subject of which strikes me as being very extraordinary. It seems to me that the only course is to advise the young lady's father to marry her to General D——. It is that which prudence renders necessary in such a case. Find out whether General D—— intends to marry the girl, and speak to the King of Bavaria on the subject. The father, after making a great deal of noise, will come to feel that if the matter is not arranged in this fashion, he will end by regretting it. If it cannot be so arranged, and if General D—— refuses to marry the girl, I intend to put him under arrest. But go about the whole business wisely and prudently.

XLIV

TO PRINCESS STEPHANIE DE BEAUHARNAIS, ELECTORAL PRINCESS OF BADEN.

St. Cloud, 8th July 1806.

I SEND you back a letter from the Margravine of Baden; the seal was broken by mistake. I desire news of you. Was not your health affected by the heat on the road? Tell me that you are happy and content.

XLV

TO M. FOUCHÉ, MINISTER OF POLICE.

St. Cloud, 8th July 1806.

I LEARN that Brigadier-General D—— has arrived in Paris, at the Hotel d'Angleterre, and has with him Mlle Catherine Eugénia von E——. Are they married or not? Is the General in Paris without leave? I can scarcely allow him to elope with a girl, in a country where he is receiving hospitality. Send for him and clear up this business, about which great complaint has already been made to me.

XLVI

TO M. FOUCHÉ, MINISTER OF POLICE.

RAMBOUILLET, 19th August 1806.

MY intention is, that, if you know where General D——
is, you should send for him and question him as to a woman
named K——, whom he is said to have married two months
before he eloped with Mlle von E. I cannot possibly tie
the hands of justice, and the law must make an example
of so shameful a crime. Is the General aware that the
criminal court will sentence him to the galleys? How
can he have forgotten the laws of honour to such an extent?
There is something very humiliating to every French soldier
about it all. If you know where he is, take measures to
make a report to me on the subject.

XLVII

TO M. DE TALLEYRAND, PRINCE DE BENEVENTO,
MINISTER FOR FOREIGN AFFAIRS.

ST. CLOUD, 3rd September 1806.

GIVE the most positive instructions to dissolve that
ecclesiastical academy in Tuscany, and to have the present
Nuncio at Florence, a good-for-nothing fellow, and an enemy
to France, sent about his business. Write to the Spanish
Ambassador about it and let him make a complaint on the
subject to the Court of Etruria.

XLVIII

TO M. DE TALLEYRAND, PRINCE DE BENEVENTO,
MINISTER FOR FOREIGN AFFAIRS.

Note on the present position of my Affairs.

ST. CLOUD, 12th September 1806.

I HAVE no interest in disturbing the peace of the Continent.
The House of Austria is not in a condition to undertake
anything. Much hatred and rivalry part Russia from Prussia.
The wounds of Austerlitz are still too fresh. It may be pre-
sumed that no considerable body of Russians will enter

Europe for some time to come. They might make sacrifices to attack the Porte; they might keep reserve forces in Poland; I do not think they will again venture to send 100,000 men into Germany.

The idea that Prussia might attack me single-handed appears to me so absurd as not to be worth discussion.

I cannot have any real alliance with any great European Power; that I now have with Prussia is founded on fear. The (Prussian) Cabinet is so despicable, the King so weak, and the Court so ruled by young officers eager to attempt adventures, that no reliance can be placed on that Power. It will continue to act as it has done; it will arm and disarm; it will arm, will lie by while others fight, and will then make terms with the victor.

All Europe is astonished at Prussia's present armament, and yet the motive power which, for the last twelve years, has constantly and solely impelled that Cabinet, has induced it to arm again. This being so, we must give it full time to recover its courage, and allow it peacefully to disarm. It might, however, be, that Prussia, after having taken up arms in a fright, and being reassured by my condescension, might become alarmed as to her own strength, and might contract alliances with other European Powers. The bond would doubtless be a frail one: yet I must foresee the possibility, and provide against it.

I must do two things: first, I must reassure Prussia, and find the easiest possible means of restoring her to her former tranquil condition; second, I must, by every means in my power, reinforce my armies in Germany, both with men and war material. But these two measures are contradictory. If they are alarmed by the troops I have there already, they will inevitably be alarmed by those I may send. Hence there must be a certain amount of confidence, and also a little fear, in Prussia's disarmament; this is the essence of the language of the country—the only real means of touching it.

M. de Lucchesini's arrival at Berlin will be an event. M. de Talleyrand must refer to my review of my Guard yesterday, and of that I held the day before yesterday, at the camp at Meudon, whence the cavalry have already started. Let him think over a conversation which, if possible, may lead up to his getting M. de Lucchesini to write him a note, giving a positive assurance of the pacific intentions of his Government, and let him undertake to await his arrival at Berlin before sending off the Guard;—which I could not do without informing the Senate and the public. If M. de Talleyrand prefers it, he will have this note written by the new Minister, before M. de Lucchesini's departure. This new Minister will say, that he requests the Emperor will not take any extraordinary action, until the courier bringing the answer to Sunday's interview has returned.

My object in taking this step is to change my tone, and instead of saying 'Disarm, or I go to war!'—which would frighten Prussia rather too much—to say 'Disarm, if you do not desire me to arm still further.' There is something more reassuring about this form. There is a certain touch of friendliness in it. We do not want to do anything against Prussia—the action of France depends upon hers. This proceeding is partly reassuring and partly threatening. The first half calms her fears, the second rouses them a little. This middle course will thoroughly suit the Prussian mind.

The manner in which M. de Talleyrand must attain this result is very simple. He will tell the new Minister, or perhaps the new and the old together (for the matter is so distinctly national that whatever the opposition between the two men, they must be glad to join upon it), that 'The Emperor thought the King's letter satisfactory', and had sent a satisfactory reply, when he heard that the garrison of Berlin had departed,—a week, that is to say, after the arrival of the said letter. Yet the King's letter appeared to show he had recovered from the alarm he had felt. Why then continue his armament? Is it not natural to think, when these preparations are taken in conjunction with the false report that Russia had not ratified, with the new Minister's arrival, and the King's letter, that all this is a means of gaining time, so that the Russians may be able to get their army together? The Emperor, on his own account, is inclined to disbelieve it, but so many other strange things have come to pass that this may be the case. He has therefore reinforced his army in Germany by nearly 100,000 men; he has called up all his conscript reserve, and prepared all this year's conscripts. He would have called out his two reserve conscriptions, but that cannot be done without a Decree of the Senate, and the motive for that would have to be explained to the

nation. It is not customary that the Guard and the Emperor should leave the country without some explanation.
Yet what can I do in face of the military men who are
pressing for a decision, in view of the simultaneous armaments
of Russia and Prussia?   But on the other hand, if the Emperor starts, I have no further hope of peace.   Once the
matter has been brought publicly before the Senate, it will be
very difficult to arrange anything.   What am I to say to the
Emperor to-day?'   They will say to you what they have
said to me.   You will take them at their word.   'Well, write
it down ; I will take it to the Emperor ; it will carry some
weight, for, after all, we are not at war !'   The document
will run thus :—'We, the undersigned, having been notified
by the Minister for Foreign Affairs that His Majesty has
been informed that preparations were still being carried on
in Prussia, after the satisfactory letter brought His Majesty
by M. de Knobelsdorf ; that even the Berlin garrison had
started ; that Prussia had, notwithstanding, already been
reassured as to any fear of an invasion by the French Army ;
that many persons were, in consequence, led to believe in the
existence of a secret alliance with some other Powers, which
made it indispensable for the Emperor to complete his
armies by calling out the reserves of his conscription, and
even by sending forward the troops in his capital,—which
step would give a false idea of the existing relations between
the two States and tend to impair the harmony between the
two Courts, which has not been substantially destroyed,—
reiterate to His Excellency our assurance that the King
of Prussia has no other alliance but that which binds him
to France ; that he is only arming for his own security,
and that he is very far from desiring to commit any hostile
act.   And if these assurances do not suffice, we beg that no
strong and overt step may be taken by the French Government until after the arrival of the Berlin courier.   The
undersigned flatter themselves that when His Majesty the
King of Prussia becomes aware of the peaceful and amicable
intentions of the Emperor of the French, he will hasten to
do everything to re-establish the good understanding so unfor-
fortunately disturbed.' Or let them draw up something of
this nature.   The point is that they should make the request
that no operation should be undertaken, till the courier's
arrival.

The arrival of the second courier at Berlin will suffice to reassure people as to the movements of troops I have already made. All that will be left will be to let M. de Laforest know what he should do, a few days later.

XLIX

TO MARSHAL BERTHIER, MAJOR-GENERAL OF THE GRANDE ARMÉE.

BERLIN, 16*th November* 1806.

YOU must reply to General Bisson, that it is quite useless to remove the Duke of Brunswick's body; such a proceeding would only reawaken feelings of attachment in the minds of his former subjects. The result could not fail to be bad.

L

TO M. FOUCHÉ, MINISTER OF POLICE.

POSEN, 3*rd December* 1806.

I HAVE your letter of 24th November. You must give the greatest attention to the stoppage of all apocryphal proclamations and Orders of the Day published in my name. Several have been circulated already. That at Strasburg, which makes me say I have duchies to give away, and 100 millions of money for the soldiers, appears to me more a work of imagination than of spite.

LI

TO M. FOUCHÉ, MINISTER OF POLICE

PULSTUCK, 31*st December* 1806.

IF M. Chénier ventures on the smallest sign, let him know I will order him to be sent to the Isles of Ste. Marguerite. The time for joking is quite gone by. Let him keep quiet. That is the only right he possesses.

Do not allow that jade, Madame de Staël, to come near Paris. I know she is not very far off.

The last bulletins will show you the great successes we have had over the Russian armies. The supposed treaty of alliance between Russia and the Porte is an invention. The Turks entered Wallachia the very moment the Russians entered Moldavia. Have articles written in this sense, and dated from Bucharest. The thing is true; but still public opinion must be enlightened. Have the same thing done with respect to Persia, from Tiflis. The fact is, that the Russian Empire is attacked on every side.

LII

TO GENERAL LAGRANGE, GOVERNOR OF CASSEL.

WARSAW, 13*th January* 1807.

I SEND you details of the offences committed in the country of Hesse, and which you do not mention in your letters to me. They tell me nothing. And yet you should have known these facts, and you should have given an account of them.

The inhabitants of Hersfeld appear to be guilty. You will send a flying column of 4000 men, and have the town thoroughly sacked, to punish the insult offered to the sixty men of my troops.

You must proclaim an order that all arms are to be given up, and declare that any man found with arms shall be punished with death.

The town of Wacht is guilty. Either it will give up the four principal authors of the revolt, or it must be burnt.

At Eschwege, which was the headquarters of the riotous gatherings, the guilty persons must be given up, otherwise the town will be burnt. And also, no matter how, the captain who was the chief leader must be arrested and shot.

You have sufficient forces. If, with a weakness which I cannot credit, you have sent them to a distance, you must recall them. You must even ask General Loison, at Münster, for the 19th Regiment of the Line.

Thus you have two provisional regiments, the Paris Regiment, the Fusiliers of the Guard, and one Italian regiment. General Thiébault has 1500 men. I calculate, then, that you must have nearly 10,000 men. Increase the number, if necessary, and have the country disarmed once for all. Stop the arms factory at Schmalkalden; take hostages, and burn a town or a few big villages. Have the Elector's arms

removed wherever they may still remain ; let all officers
who have not taken service with me be arrested on the spot,
and sent to France.

All this business has been mismanaged. It is ridiculous
that the officers should have been sent by the captains to
arm the soldiers (*sic*). I have never desired to force them
to engage ; but, after all, this outrage on my arms must be
washed out in blood. If 10,000 men are not enough for you,
I will send you 20,000.

When you have taken all your measures thoroughly, issue
a proclamation. Say I have been shocked by the conduct
of such and such towns. Indicate the men each town is to
give up, on pain of being burnt. Add that the Elector's
House shall never reign in Hesse, for the events which have
taken place are the fruit of the bad impulse it has given to
the public mind. Visible traces must be left, to frighten the
evil-intentioned in Germany. It was thus, by burning the
big village of Bignasco, that I kept Italy quiet, in the Year IV.

You must not hide the truth from me. Make a return
of all the offences committed, with a statement of the men
who have been killed, and report things to me in their true
colours. Certain men, such as the Mayor at Schmalkalden,
have behaved well. Express my satisfaction to them.

Cause the Consistories to write the Ministers that troops
are pouring in, that many more are coming, and that if the
people desire to save themselves from great misfortune, they
must submit, and make known the authors of this revolt.

I see nothing but weakness in your letter of 3rd January.
You say Captain Huscart was forced to take service with the
insurgents. I have never accepted that excuse. No man
ever takes service to command, in spite of himself. He
must pay for his conduct with his head.

The arms may possibly have been taken from Treffurt,
but none the less is it true that the insurgents also seized
the very weapons you sent to arm the soldiers.

I am distressed to observe that you intend to send me
back the troops you have with you. I, on the contrary, am
taking measures to increase their number. No troops of any
sort are to leave Cassel until the affront put upon my arms
is avenged. I can spare 15,000 men at present ; later on,
that might be no longer possible. I expect you to show
activity and firmness. One of my couriers passes through

Cassel every day. Send me a report by every one. Go so far as to send special couriers, if that should appear necessary. I long to hear my eagles are avenged.

LIII

TO PRINCE CAMBACÉRÈS, GRAND CHANCELLOR OF THE EMPIRE.

WARSAW, *27th January* 1807.

I HAVE your letter of 17th. You may possibly hear I am making some movement : do not be the least alarmed by that.

If the Prince of Prussia comes to Paris, he must not be aired about too much, for he is a very conceited young man.

LIV

TO GENERAL CLARKE, MINISTER OF WAR.

LIEBSTADT, *21st February* 1807.

THE measures you are taking are insufficient. Write to Crossen that I have given most positive orders ; that the instant the Prussian partisans are received into the town, I shall send a detachment to subject the place to military punishment. It is their business to ward this off, and to consider what they should do. As soon as you can send a column to Crossen, you will require the names of the four chief persons who have corresponded with the partisans, and you will do the same thing at Güntersberg and Mescritz (?), where a courier, and one of the King of Naples' aide-de-camps, have been stopped. You will have these twelve persons shot ; and failing that, the towns must be given over to military punishment. Yon will have the man Koch arrested. Major Letort did wrong not to shoot him. That is not the way in which to perform such missions as his. You will arrest the Burgomaster, and you will have him shot. You will cause the Commandant of Cüstrin to publish a proclamation—which will not be inserted in the Berlin newspapers—in which he will say that an effort is being made to disturb the peace of the country and turn it

into a desert; that every village which harbours partisans
will be responsible for the harm they may have done to
members of the French Army; and that the Burgomaster
who has not warned the Commandant of his Province, and
betaken himself to Cüstrin, will be arrested and treated as
being in secret correspondence with them; that the Posting
Master will be held responsible for every courier who is
stopped by the partisans, and has not been warned by him.
I have ordered you to send a detachment to the village
where the convoy was looted, and to lay it under a heavy
fine. Keep up a ceaseless pursuit of the partisans. Prince
Jérome has sent out troops to pursue them, from his side.

LV

TO M. FOUCHÉ, MINISTER OF POLICE.

OSTERODE, 15*th March* 1807.

I HAVE your letter of 2nd March. You are to see to my
orders being carried out, and not to allow Mdme de Staël
to come within forty leagues of Paris. That wicked schemer
ought to make up her mind to behave herself, at last.

LVI

TO M. DE TALLEYRAND, PRINCE DE BENEVENTO,
MINISTER FOR FOREIGN AFFAIRS.

OSTERODE, 30*th March* 1807.

M. DUPONT-CHAUMONT'S letter of 18th March has filled
me with the deepest astonishment. I can hardly believe it.
M. Dupont ought to have sent me the document,[1] so that
I might have gathered some idea of this piece of folly.
I might expect anything from that sort of conscientious
vermin, but I did not believe I need look forward to such a
ridiculous measure, so opposed to his own interests, and to
those of the Dutch. Write and inform General Dupont, by
special courier, that he is to see the King, and express all
my displeasure, and assure him that if he does not instantly

---

[1] The King of Holland's Decree, re-establishing the nobility.

withdraw his decree, I will no longer recognise him as
King, as a French citizen, nor as a Prince of my blood, and
that he has perjured himself to the Dutch nation ; that his
kingship has depended entirely on his fulfilling the after-
mentioned conditions.   I am writing in very strong terms
to the King of Holland.   But I am sorry not to have the
Decree by me—for if it verifies M. Dupont's letter, we must
believe the man to be mad.

Write also to M. Dupont to send all the original Dutch
Decrees.   Tell him he should write every day, and let us
know everything, good and bad, and the details of the Army
establishment, so that I may form some idea of its capa-
bilities.

LVII

TO M. FOUCHÉ, MINISTER OF POLICE.

FINKENSTEIN, 19th April 1807.

AMONG the thousand and one things that come into my
hands with regard to Mdme de Staël, this letter will show
you what a good Frenchwoman she is.   If it had been
Prince Louis, our furious enemy, and the author of the
loss of his monarchy, she would have spared no pains to
see him.   I am resolved she shall never leave Geneva.
Let her consort, if she chooses, with the friends of Prince
Louis!   Paying court, one day, to the great—a patriot, a
democrat, the next!   One's indignation boils over at the
sight of all the shapes assumed by this . . .—a fright into
the bargain!   I do not tell you of the plans already made
by this ridiculous set, in case, by some good luck, I had
been killed, for a Police Minister ought to know all that.
Everything I hear of that worthless woman shows I should
leave her in her Coppet, with her Genevans and her house of
Necker.

Let me know where M. Rippaut, my librarian, is.   I gave
him orders to send me the last publications, and information
as to the newest literature.   I have no news of him.   Is he
dead? or has he gone to the country?   That would be a
very convenient way of doing his work.   Send for him, and
find out why he does not carry out my intentions.

LVIII

TO M. FOUCHÉ, MINISTER OF POLICE.

FINKENSTEIN, 21*st April* 1807.

YOU must have a great fuss made—especially in the departmental newspapers in Brittany, the Vendée, Piedmont, and Belgium—over the persecution of the Irish Catholics by the Anglican Church. For this purpose you must collect every incident, so as to paint the persecution in the most vivid colours. I should advise M. Portalis to make secret arrangements with certain Bishops, so that when the articles have produced an impression, prayers may be offered for the cessation of the persecution of the Irish Catholics by the Anglican Church.

But the Government must proceed very delicately in the matter, and must make use of the newspapers without allowing any suspicion of its object to get about. The editors of the *Journal de l'Empire* would serve the purpose well. The cruelty and baseness of England with regard to the Irish Catholics, who have been, for the last century, in a perpetual condition of St. Bartholomew (against the Catholics), must be insisted upon. You must always say 'Anglican Church' instead of 'Protestant'; for we have Protestants in France, and we have no Anglican Church.

LIX

TO PRINCE CAMBACÉRÈS, GRAND CHANCELLOR
OF THE EMPIRE.

FINKENSTEIN, 16*th May* 1807.

I HAVE your letter of 7th May. I am sorry you did not tell me there was a disagreement as to the good to be done by Princess Pauline's journey to Provence. You know I opposed it in the first instance, and was averse to it; but I was written to the effect that the whole Faculty desired it, and I have consented. If I had received your letter sooner, I should certainly not have authorised it.

LX

TO THE LANDAMMANN OF SWITZERLAND.

FINKENSTEIN, 18*th May* 1807.

I HAVE your letter of 24th April. I can only thank you for the care with which you inform me of the zeal shown by the different cantons for the recruiting of the Swiss regiments. I trust the four regiments will shortly be complete, and that the Swiss of our day will, like their fathers, make a glorious appearance on the field of honour. I value the bravery, fidelity, and loyalty of the Swiss; and this feeling has led me to decide that all these regiments should consist of citizens of the country, without any admixture of deserters or other foreigners. For it is not the numerical strength of soldiers, it is their fidelity and good feeling, which makes the strength of armies. The Act of Mediation will always be a sacred law to me; I shall always scrupulously fulfil the duties imposed by it, and I cannot but be daily confirmed in this view, since the work, in which you shared, appears to me to have been sanctioned by time, and to have considerably improved the position of your country.

If I could form a wish—one which I am sorry not to have proposed inserting in the Act of Mediation—it would be that the Swiss should not permit any foreign power, except Spain, Holland, and the States connected with my system, to recruit in their country. I am the more anxious that this prohibition should become law, because all enlightened men must be pained to see brother fighting against brother. Those persons who have thoughtlessly and wrongly blamed the Swiss for taking foreign service have laid stress on this drawback, which is a serious one, and wounds the character of any well-conditioned man. If you submit this idea to the next Diet, a decision on the subject would be agreeable to me, because it will be in conformity with the honour and dignity of the Swiss.

I recollect with great pleasure the sagacity and dignity of which you gave proof on the occasion when I knew you. Never doubt my regard, nor my desire to be agreeable to you, and assure the Cantons of my friendship, and my constant protection.

LXI

TO M. FOUCHÉ, MINISTER OF POLICE.

FINKENSTEIN, 18*th May* 1807.

I HAVE your letters of 8th and 9th. That of the 8th contains such an extraordinary thing touching Gombez that it must be an anonymous letter.

I have been very much afflicted by the misfortune which has befallen me.[1] I had hoped for a more brilliant destiny for that poor child.

I am not astonished at what you tell me of the Prince of Prussia. I have noticed that he is an extremely insignificant and narrow-minded man.

LXII

TO M. DE LAVALLETTE, STATE COUNCILLOR.

ST. CLOUD, 14*th August* 1807.

I GREATLY approve the idea that M. Bertin-Devaux should withdraw from all connection, direct or indirect, with the *Journal de l'Empire*. I am too fully informed as to his former relations with foreign countries not to be pleased at his present decision. The only way, indeed, in which he can make himself safe, and provide against all the vicissitudes of unforeseen circumstances, is to cease all attempts to influence politics. And even if this were not so, I have the strongest feeling that there is no man in France who has greater need to behave prudently, and avoid everything that might tend to mix him up with politics.

For it is time, at last, that those who have taken up the Bourbon cause, directly or indirectly, should remember their Scripture history, and what David[2] did to the house of Ahab. This observation also applies to M. de Chateaubriand and his clique. The slightest doubtful conduct on their part will put them outside the pale of my protection.

As regards the position of stockbroker, I will make inquiries. If M. Bertin's financial reputation is good, as I believe it to be, I will appoint him, and shall be glad that M. Fiévée should acquire the two twelfth-shares of the newspaper from

---

[1] The death of the eldest son of King Louis of Holland.
[2] He means *Jehu*.

him by purchase. I conclude him to be well acquainted, by this time, with the spirit in which I desire the paper to be directed, and to be thoroughly convinced that a man who receives my bounty, and whose writings have a direct influence on public opinion, must steer a straight and open course, without any backsliding,—act and speak, in fact, as one of David's faithful servants would have spoken to the partisans of the preceding dynasty.

LXIII

TO M. FOUCHÉ, MINISTER OF POLICE.

St. Cloud, 28th August 1807.

HAVE articles written, bringing the conduct of the King of Sweden, who has shamefully abandoned one of his towns to the enemy, into strong relief. The articles must be conceived in a serious tone, and must make it evident that to surrender a town, and leave it to the enemy's mercy, is not only an action unworthy of a prince, but a violation of his duty to the people, even in a conquered country; that to give up 400 pieces of artillery and a town, the counterscarp of which has not been crossed, nor even a breach made in the walls, is to disgrace his arms, and be false to his honour. You must have long articles, which develop these two ideas, and faithfully depict the King of Sweden's weakness, inconsistency, and folly. You must have one specially long article which will be a sort of indictment of him.

LXIV

TO M. FOUCHÉ, MINISTER OF POLICE.

St. Cloud, 1st September 1807.

THAT man Partarieux of Bordeaux has been long noted as a worthless fellow. I know the Police Commissary's reports are not very much to be depended on, because of the well-known enmity between the two men. You must write to the President, to the Imperial Commissary, and to the Mayor, and get me their opinion of the man, and about the incident of the blood on the Emperor's bust, and the still more important one of his having refused to take the oath, and having torn up the voting paper. If either of these two facts be true, he must be arrested and taken to Paris, under a police warrant.

My intention is that the income of the Spa play-tables, from 1st January 1807 (seven months) shall be paid over, on the spot, for the relief of the sufferers by the fire. By the Decree which you will receive from the Minister-Secretary of State, I grant the next ten years' revenue of the gaming-tables to repair the damage caused by the said fire.

I cannot conceive how the Archbishop of Lyons came to send to Rimini for priests, nor how you can have permitted and approved his behaviour. Send me a report on this subject. The fact appears in the reports for the 30th and 31st.

You will have the man Dufour, aide-de-camp to Georges, arrested, together with the two brothers Lalande, and Geslin and Beauchamp. These five persons will be arrested at the same time, and sent with post-horses to the Temple, that very day. Whether they are guilty or not of the act they are now accused of, I have been displeased with them for a long time.

You will inform me whether the Prefect's report shows that La Crochaix, (?) Tromelin, and the three others have unmasked their evil intentions on this occasion.

Last winter certain individuals in the Morbihan, the Côtes-du-Nord, and Ille-et-Vilaine, showed themselves ill-disposed. Make out a list of some score of those who seemed most inclined to disturbance.

LXV

TO M. DE CHAMPAGNY, MINISTER FOR FOREIGN AFFAIRS.

'*Memorandum on the present state of Continental Affairs.*'

RAMBOUILLET, *7th September* 1807.

THE step taken by England against Copenhagen would seem to have failed, since on the 28th of August, twelve days after the troops were landed, they had gained no success, had allowed the garrisons of Copenhagen and Cronenburg time to man those fortresses, and had given the Prince-Royal time to make arrangements for arming all the militia. But if England were to succeed, the greatest loss would be the Danish ships she would destroy.

This operation by England seems to have been a false calculation. She expected to take Copenhagen without any resistance, and even without having to declare war, for she unquestionably allowed the Danish ships free navigation up till the 1st of September. More probably yet, England has not dared to take any hostile step against the Russian flag. What harm can she do Russia? All she can do her is to intercept her Mediterranean squadron. But I sent orders long ago to Cadiz and Corfu, that the admiral commanding the Russian squadron was to be warned of the new position of affairs, and to be advised, as from me, to retire into my ports, or those of Spain, until the whole matter was cleared up. I shall have one great anxiety the less when I hear the Russian admiral has taken my advice. I am sorry the Russian Ambassador is not yet arrived, for he could have given positive orders. I have reason, however, to think that when these lines are read the ships of the Russian squadron will be in safety, either at Cadiz or at Toulon.

The garrison of Cattaro has arrived safely at Venice, that of Corfu is on the road. The Emperor Alexander need have no anxiety about his troops, which will be properly treated. As soon as I received news of the English expedition against Copenhagen, I caused Portugal to be informed that all her ports must be closed to England, and I massed an army of 40,000 men at Bayonne, to join the Spaniards in enforcing this action, if necessary. But a letter I have just received from the Prince Regent leads me to presume this last measure will not be necessary, that the Portuguese ports will be closed to the English by the time this memorandum is read, and that Portugal will have declared war against England.

On the other hand, my flotilla will be ready for action on 1st October, and I shall have a large army at Boulogne, ready to attempt a *coup de main* on England.

England can thus do nothing against Russia. If she persists in her present plans, the following course should be adopted against her:—

Drive all English diplomatic establishments out of Europe. The Viennese Court stands alone; it must be forced to join the common cause, and the moment events have led Russia to drive the English Legation out of St. Petersburg, the Russian Ambassador at Vienna, in concert with mine, must present a note requesting that the English Ambassador may be sent out of Vienna, and that the port of Trieste may be closed to the English. This expulsion of all English Ministers from the Continent will make a great impression in London, and will especially and strongly affect their trade.

The Emperor Alexander must endeavour by negotiation to force Sweden into making common cause with us; and that Power can hardly resist Russia, France, and Denmark. Such negotiations may suffice to draw Sweden into the common cause. If she refuses, the prospect of a rupture with Russia would suffice to persuade her. The Swedish nation is too much opposed to the English system for the Prince, foolish as he is, to care to run so heavy a risk.

LXVI

TO M. DE CHAMPAGNY, MINISTER FOR FOREIGN AFFAIRS.

RAMBOUILLET, *7th September* 1807.

HEREWITH you will find a letter from M. Daru. Reply that I have been shocked by the incident to which his letter refers;[1] that I order him to present a Note demanding exemplary justice on the officers who committed the insult; that I shall refuse all evacuation until the two ringleaders have been shot; and that if the King of Prussia proposes to offer me such insults, he need not take the trouble of going to Berlin, for he will not stay there long. You, on your part, will send for the two Prussian envoys who are in Paris; you will make them aware of all the indignation I feel at this outrage on the part of the Prussians, with whose impertinence I am well acquainted; you will say that I demand that the two ringleaders shall be shot; that this affair is no slight matter; that it is of much more importance to me than the getting in of the taxes; that the King's weakness has already caused the war which has just come to an end; and that if a set of blackguards, who are as cowardly on the battle-field as they are arrogant behind the scenes of the theatres, go on behaving themselves after this fashion, the

---

[1] Two actors who had appeared on the Königsberg stage, dressed as French officers, had been hissed by the German officers present.

Prussian Monarchy will have a short lease of life. You will express yourself in the strongest terms; you will let it be known that the country will not be evacuated unless I am given satisfaction, and that if there is any delay about it, I will declare war against Prussia.

LXVII

TO M. FOUCHÉ, MINISTER OF POLICE.

RAMBOUILLET, *7th September* 1807.

I SEE, by your report of the 25th, that a certain Frémont, a priest in the Department of Seine-et-Marne, exercises his functions without having made his submission, in the village of Bois-le-Roi. Have him arrested; have him examined by my Procurator-General at the criminal court, and let me see everything relating to this priest, so that I may go on to decide what should be done about him. A priest who performs his functions without his bishop's cognisance revolts against the State, and must be punished. Let the Imperial Procurator understand that you are employing him, in this case, on a confidential, and not on an official mission. Make him acquainted with my principles on the subject.

I see the names of various *Emigrés* in your list of 25th August. Let me know whether they are borne on the first list, and if it is not to hand, give me the names of some sixty people whose residence near the Comte de Lille is well known to you, with such fully detailed notes that no mistake can be made.

Give orders to have Mr. Kuhn, the American Consul at Genoa, put under arrest, for wearing a Cross of Malta given him by the English, and as being an English agent. His papers will be seized, and an abstract of them made, and he will be kept in secret confinement until you have made your report to me. This man, having received a foreign decoration, ceases to be an American. I am sorry, by the way, you should have communicated with the Ambassador of the United States. My police knows no Ambassadors. I am master in my own house. If I suspect a man I have him arrested. I would even have the Ambassador of Austria arrested, if he was hatching anything against the State.

Draw me up a report on the 'white penitents,' 'blue

penitents,' etc., and on the places in France where they exist, so that I may judge whether measures ought to be taken with respect to them.

I see in your report of the 26th, one from the Police Commissary at Bordeaux, to the effect that the nobility did not attend the ball given by M. Lamartinière, Senator. I wish for details on the subject, and desire to be informed, family by family, as to the persons referred to in this document, and to know whether they were in Bordeaux ; for, at this fine season, they might have been in the country, and, in that case, the Commissary-General does wrong to impute this fact to them as a crime. If, on the contrary, any of these lordlings have ventured to fail in the respect due to the Senator, it will be well for me to know the fugle-men, so that the police may remove them from Bordeaux.

LXVIII

TO M. FOUCHÉ, MINISTER OF POLICE.

FONTAINEBLEAU, 29th September 1807.

YOU must make sure whether M. Lahaye, formerly a Deputy, is settled at Antwerp. If he is, you will have him arrested and taken to the Temple, and you will have his papers seized.

Order the goods of the Abbé Ratel to be sequestered. I am informed he still has something left under other people's names.

Certain members of La Haye-St.-Hilaire's family have come from Rennes to Paris, to sue my mercy for that wretch. Order them not to venture into my presence. They should hide their faces for shame at having produced such a monster.

You will give similar orders to Madame Polignac, and you will make her aware that if she prefers the smallest request for leave to present herself before me, she will be exiled from Paris.

LXIX

TO M. DARU, COMMISSARY-GENERAL OF THE 'GRANDE ARMÉE.'

FONTAINEBLEAU, 12th October 1807.

I HAVE your letter of 3rd October. The reckoning given you by the Prussians is absurd. If they want to count all the possible pilferings by individual officers, very soon I shall be owing them money instead of their owing it to me! As to the property of private individuals, if that had not been contrary to my honour and my principles, I might have taken it all. It would be comical if the victor's conduct had to be justified to the vanquished! All that is a very poor joke. I intend that nothing which has been taken, whether from the Savings bank, Mines' department, that of firewood, etc., shall be deducted.

As for what they say about M. de Knobelsdorp, he is not the Prussian Minister, and nobody listens to him. It is true that he made a proposal to M. de Champagny, seven or eight days ago, to pay nineteen millions for the evacuation of Berlin. We laughed in his face, and he doubtless wrote that if terms were not made with you, the evacuation would be delayed.

LXX

TO M. FOUCHÉ, MINISTER OF POLICE.

FONTAINEBLEAU, 18*th October* 1807.

I HAVE been distressed to observe that you did not pay the expenses of the theatres for 1806. It is my intention that in future, when, for any reason, a diminution occurs in the Police receipts, the reduction, until I may order otherwise, shall be made on every head, at so much in the pound, and not on any special one.

Great inconvenience has been caused by your failure to pay the *Ponts et Chaussées*. This having been reckoned on, and the season having run on too far, the confusion caused in the works of that Department, by the interruption in the payments, will cost us 200,000 francs extra; whereas if you had reduced equally, under every head, nothing would have suffered seriously, and I could have supplied the deficit out of other funds. The Budget is my law. It must be complied with, because the finance of every branch of the Administration is the most important point of my affairs.

I do not know enough about the receipts. I must have a statement of the earnings of the gambling-tables, of what has been collected in the towns where such tables exist, and of what has been brought in by sporting licenses and passports in the Departments for the years 1806 and 1807.

My approbation should have been obtained before the Farmers-general of the tables were changed, and so considerable a reduction should not have been made without any warning to me. This rule must be adhered to in future, it being my firm intention not to permit any confusion or abuse.

When I turned my attention to the details of the accounts they struck me as being insufficient. M. Miot should not have been paid beyond the day on which he left, yet he was given 15,000 francs. M. Demarest appears too frequently in these accounts. The expense of letter-transport should form a separate account. The greatest confusion results from expenses being entered under heads to which they do not belong. The cost of sending letters should not appear under the head of 'Unforeseen Expenses.' Besides the assistance given to colonists, wives of deported persons, etc., which are under separate headings, there is assistance given to a certain M. St. Aubin, to a General Besneval, etc. etc., entered in the expenses of the Inspector-General and his agents. In the Unforeseen Police Expenses, I see assistance given to this same General Besneval, to Neapolitan refugees, etc. All this is not orderly. I have already informed you that I desire the sum for assisting colonists to be fixed every year, and distributed as fairly as possible. The same system must hold good in every ministerial department. The War Minister does not give fifty francs to an officer without my signature. Therefore 300,000 francs at a time must not be given to people who believe they receive them from other persons than myself. This is contrary to the welfare of the Services, and of the internal administration of the State. Let me have the Budget for 1808 this very month. Add explanatory observations as to every account, for I will have a real Budget. Cut down every useless expense. I do not intend to permit any but useful expenditure, either for the town of Paris or for other objects.

Indemnities have been granted to head officials and cashiers. That was well enough when your accounts were kept in a capricious and quite irregular manner. But now that no difference is made between the receipts of the Police Treasury, and those of the other departments in the Empire, I do not see why these officials should enjoy special privileges. The officials employed on these accounts are to receive pay corresponding with that of the officials of the Public Treasury.

It is very important that a large general diminution should be made in the Police expenses. Many of these are abuses, and the Prefects and other agents are not the persons who benefit the most.

The receipts for 1808 will be at least 4,400,000 francs. Send me the rough draft of a Budget, with a saving of at least one-fourth for every heading, the expenditure under which I fixed by the Budget for 1807—apart, however, from all salaries.

Good order demands, also, that the Minister for the Treasury should be informed as to these funds. Every State expenditure must be verified by that Minister.

Get secret information as to what I have granted for the Governor of Paris, the Prefect of Police, and the Chief Inspector-General of the Gendarmerie. Does the sum I gave them for office expenses really reach that destination? Or did I give it in the form of a gratuity?

LXXI

TO M. DE CHAMPAGNY, MINISTER FOR FOREIGN AFFAIRS.

FONTAINEBLEAU, 27*th October* 1807.

I DESIRE you will draw up despatches (which you will bring me to-morrow) to my Minister at Madrid, in which you will inform him that my intention is that my troops shall go to Lisbon; that he must try to arrange that they shall come in a friendly manner, and seize the squadron; that such a thing is only possible so long as the Court of Portugal continues to deceive itself, and that being the case, he must back up that inclination.

It is very probable—in the extreme difficulty in which Portugal will shortly be placed—that the Minister of that Court at Madrid will be sent to speak to him. General Junot's army will hardly have reached the position of Ciudad-Rodrigo before 10th November; there will therefore be no difficulty, when he is addressed, about his replying that he thinks the whole matter may easily be arranged. He must not discourage that Power, and must give a hope that everything may be settled, if the Prince consents to receive

French troops as auxiliaries, on the same footing as in Bavaria and other European countries.

But he must not settle anything, nor ever make any attempt to retard the march of the Army, but only speak in that sense, and do all he can to help the Army to get to Lisbon, and seize the fleet. He should even cause the selection of General Junot to be considered a pleasing one.

LXXII

TO GENERAL CLARKE, MINISTER OF WAR.

FONTAINEBLEAU, 28*th October* 1807.

YOU will send a courier to General Junot with orders, the moment his leading troops have reached Salamanca, to fix his headquarters there, so as to be in a position to correspond with my Ambassador at Madrid, and with the Portuguese Ministers.

I have given Hermann orders to join him. He will employ him as Secretary-General, and will make use of his experience. You will inform him that I desire Hermann shall have knowledge of all communications that pass, so that he may be able to send circumstantial reports to the Minister for Foreign Affairs.

I suppose his Army will have reached Ciudad-Rodrigo some time between 1st and 15th November. He must, therefore, be able to march for Lisbon between the 20th and 30th, and whatever the Prince Regent does, whether he declares war with England or not, my troops must go to Lisbon.

I have given my instructions to my Ambassadors at Madrid, to whom he will report himself. General Junot is to listen to every proposal, but he is to sign nothing, having no authority to do so from the Department of Foreign Affairs. He must refer everything to my Ambassador at Madrid, and must keep you exactly informed of all overtures made to him.

I desire my troops shall arrive at Lisbon as soon as possible, to seize all English merchandise. I desire they shall, if possible, go there as friends, in order to take possession of the Portuguese fleet. I am ordering the Minister for Naval Affairs to send a certain number of naval officers to General Junot. They will be useful to him for keeping order in the port of Lisbon.

The Portuguese Government will take one of these two measures.

Either (1) on seeing the French Army approach, it will march forward its own troops, and stand on the defensive. Then everything falls into the military province. Three thousand Spanish cavalry and 8000 infantry will join General Junot's troops, which will reach an effective strength of 35,000 men, with 30,000 actually under arms. Two Spanish divisions, one of 10,000, and the other of 6000 men, are to march on Oporto and the Algarves. General Junot is to march straight on Lisbon. He will keep up frequent correspondence with the Commandant of the 2nd Corps of the Gironde, which, you may inform him, will be massed at Bayonne, by the end of November, to the number of 25,000.

Or (2) the Portuguese Government will make up its mind to submit, will declare war with England, and will send messengers to meet the Army, and negotiate. In this case, General Junot must speak in the following terms :—

' My sovereign's orders are that I am not to delay one day in marching upon Lisbon. My mission is to close that great port to the English. I ought to use force against you, but as the shedding of blood is repugnant to the noble heart of the Emperor Napoleon, and to the character of the French people, I have orders,—if you agree not to keep your troops massed together, if you place them in positions where they cannot cause any anxiety, and if you will receive us as auxiliaries, until the negotiations begun at Paris are concluded,—to consent to that arrangement.'

By these means, General Junot may contrive to get to Lisbon as an auxiliary. The date of his arrival will be calculated here to a couple of days, and, twenty-four hours later, a courier will be sent to inform him that the Portuguese proposals have not been accepted, and that he is to treat the country as that of an enemy. Eight or ten ships of war, and those dockyards, would be an immense advantage to us. All General Junot's discourse, then, must be directed to the execution of this great plan. There is reason to think he will succeed, because it is not likely that Portugal will dare to resist, and still less likely that the Prince will want to go to Brazil.

The secret convention concluded with Spain, which the first courier will carry to General Junot, will make him aware that it is agreed that the Spanish troops which are to form part of his force shall be under his own command ; that if the King of Spain or the Prince of Peace joined the Army, they would have the command ; but it has been settled that they are not to come. If they were to come for a parade, General Junot should show them all the respect due to Generals-in-Chief. But if they came to stay, he must adhere strictly to his instructions to keep his troops together, not to detach any whatever, and to march straight on Lisbon.

My intention is that General Junot shall in no wise diverge from the direct path ; he will neither go to Madrid nor elsewhere, and the moment his leading body of troops reaches Ciudad-Rodrigo, he will proceed there personally.

General Junot's operation will be a real success, if by dint of prudence, and wise use of his tongue, he makes himself master of the Portuguese Fleet. He must make use of his nomination to convey the impression that he has been sent to smooth down everything.

He may say anything he pleases, so long as he gets hold of the Portuguese Fleet. In no case is he to sign any convention with the Portuguese.

LXXIII

TO M. DE LAVALLETTE, DIRECTOR-GENERAL OF THE POSTAL SERVICE.

FONTAINEBLEAU, *9th November* 1807.

THE British Correspondence goes through Holland. Take measures to have all the Dutch mails stopped in France, and all letters from England seized and burnt, after they have been read, and extracts made from the more important documents.

I cannot but express my dissatisfaction at the small amount of activity you show about stopping this correspondence. You seem quite indifferent about it. Let me hear what has been seized since my Decree. A great deal has reached Paris. Of all the measures taken against England, this is the most distressing to her.

LXXIV

TO M. GAUDIN, MINISTER OF FINANCE.

FONTAINEBLEAU, *9th November* 1807.

YOU will receive a Decree by which I authorise the lending of 1,800,000 francs out of the Sinking Fund to the King of Westphalia. You will notify this Decree to Prince Jerome's comptroller; you will see that the [receipts] are signed by Prince Jerome, and that the repayments are punctually made.

You will also inform him that I have authorised the Public Treasury to advance him his income as a French Prince for November and December: which will about make up the two millions owed by the Prince. But, in consideration of these advances, I will not permit the Prince to have a single debt in Paris.

From the 1st of January, I assign his appanage as a French Prince to Madame.

LXXV

TO ELISA NAPOLEON, PRINCESS OF LUCCA AND PIOMBINO.

FONTAINEBLEAU, *13th November* 1807.

THAT villain Hainguerlot is still in communication with you. I do not intend you to keep up any intercourse, direct or indirect, with that schemer. And if you do not conform to this order, you will, in the first place, be the cause of my having him arrested and confined in a fortress, and in the next, you will do a thing which will cost you my esteem.

LXXVI

TO M. BAUDIN, MINISTER OF FINANCE.

FONTAINEBLEAU, *13th November* 1807.

IT is a matter of public notoriety that all the vessels which are supposed to reach Antwerp and Bordeaux from America really come from England. I intend you shall give M. Collin orders to make a raid on the ships still in port, to make an unexpected seizure of the captains' papers, to arrest some of the crews, to cross-question them, get proof that they come from England, and that their cargoes are English, and make a report to me, on which I shall order their confiscation.

I have signed the Decree for applying that of 6th August to merchandise brought to the mouth of the Weser. I should like to know if the same legislation exists for Antwerp and Bordeaux, and whether vessels coming from England, which have touched at Antwerp and Bordeaux, are confiscated.

LXXVII

TO M. DE LAVALLETTE, DIRECTOR-GENERAL OF THE POSTAL SERVICE.

FONTAINEBLEAU, 14th *November* 1807.

I HAVE your undated letter. The measures you have taken do not suffice. You have only stopped 12,000 letters ; that is a very trifling matter. If you had had them intercepted at Bayonne, Bordeaux, etc., you would have had a great many more. Whenever a ship from England reaches these coasts, take care to have all the letters seized and sent to you. Take further steps, and let me hear you have a great quantity of letters.

LXXVIII

TO M. FOUCHÉ, MINISTER OF POLICE.

FONTAINEBLEAU, 17th *December* 1807.

A CERTAIN Perrier, a dissident priest, in the Department of the Deux-Sèvres, who is mentioned in your report of 9th December, must be sent under surveillance to Fénestrella.

It will be a good thing to collect, and print in pamphlet form, all of St.-Hilaire's papers which tend to show up those small London schemers. You will submit them to me before they are published. I will read them, and will see whether it would be well to have a good number of copies struck off, to be disseminated in England. This would unmask, and cast ridicule on, the inferior class of rogues who dabble in petty intrigues in London.

I also wish you to watch the Perlet business, which I consider important, and the documents in which I propose to have printed. Past experience proves that such questions are ended in this way. The good done by the publication of the Drake, Taylor, and Spencer Smith correspondences is incalculable. That of Perlet will have the same effect. It must not be circulated in France, but it must be distributed over Hamburg and London.

I think I have signed the first List of Emigrés. I conclude you have sent it to the Chief Judge, for communication to the different Courts, so that they may be acquainted with the names of all those persons who are beyond the pale of the civil code. A second list must be drawn up.

Find out what that agent of Sainte-Foix is doing at Rastadt; and if any certain knowledge can be had as to the object of his journey, he must be arrested.

You will make arrangements with M. Portalis to break up every congregation of the *Pères de la Foi*. You will endeavour to find the gentlest, and at the same time the most thorough, means of doing this. You will extend this measure to the whole Empire. You will take care that these people have no meeting-place, and I hold you responsible for every religious society of this order. Can it be that we are in one of those periods of weakness and inertia, during which the will of the Government cannot be carried out? The first diocese on which you will begin is the Archbishopric of Lyons; but in the case of this Prelate, as with all others, you must only mention the proofs in your hands, and you must not enter into any theological discussion. I do not choose to have any *Pères de la Foi*, more especially as they interfere with public education, and poison the youth of the country, with their absurd ultramontane principles. You will be able to procure the information you need as to these Fathers from their Superior, Father Varin, who seems to be an adventurer.

I see by your report of 27th November, that a certain actor, named Fay, is mentioned by the Prefect of Maine-et-Loire as being an intriguer, a disturber of the peace, and a dangerous character. If these qualities are connected with his political opinions, have him arrested and flogged, as such riff-raff deserves to be, when it meddles with matters of importance. I wish for a short report on this subject, which may appear of little moment, but to which the attention of the Police should be given.

LXXIX

TO MONSIEUR DE TALLEYRAND, PRINCE OF BENEVENTO, VICE-GRAND ELECTOR.

MILAN, 19th December 1807.

WHO is a *Chef d'Escadron* Chipault, of whom the *Journal de l'Empire* of the 14th speaks, as being presented to the Empress on the score of his having received fifty-two wounds in one battle? I beg you to let it be understood that this is nonsense, and that nothing of the sort should be inserted without advice.

LXXX

TO THE PRINCESS PAULINE BORGHESE.

MILAN, 20th December 1807.

I HAVE your letter of December 15th from Nice. How can you think of coming to Turin by the bad roads you would have to travel over? Stay all this season at Nice, and get well, so as to be able to come to Paris in the spring.

LXXXI

TO JOSEPH NAPOLEON, KING OF NAPLES.[1]

MILAN, 20th December 1807.

I SAW Lucien at Mantua. I had several hours' conversation with him. He will doubtless have acquainted you with his feelings when he started. His thoughts and speech are both so far removed from mine, that I can hardly understand what he wanted. I have an idea he told me he wished to send his eldest daughter to Paris, to her grandmother. If he is still disposed to do this, I wish to be instantly informed of it, for the young girl must be in Paris in the course of January, whether Lucien accompanies her himself, or sends a governess to take her to Madame. Lucien appeared to me swayed hither and thither by conflicting feelings, and not to have sufficient strength of mind to make any decision.

---

[1] Part of this letter was published in the *Correspondence*, No. 13,402, but the most important portion was suppressed. It is given in full in Baron du Casse's Supplement to the *Correspondence*.

I must tell you, however, that I am prepared to restore his rights as a French prince, and recognise all his daughters as my nieces. Only he must begin by annulling his marriage with Mme Jouberthon ; either by divorcing her, or in any other way.

This being done, all his children will be provided for. If Mme Jouberthon really is in an interesting condition at this present time, and bears a daughter, I see no objection to the adoption of the child. If it is a boy, it may be considered as Lucien's son, but not born in open wedlock. And I am willing to enable this child to inherit the sovereignty I may confer on his father, independently of the rank to which his father may be raised by the general policy of the Empire, but not to allow this son any pretension to succeed his father in his own real rank, nor to be called to the succession of the French Empire.

You will see that I have exhausted every means in my power to recall Lucien, who is still in his first youth, to the employment of his talents, in my service, and that of his country. I do not see what he can now allege against this course.

His children's interest is protected ; thus I have provided for everything.

Once Lucien has divorced Mme Jouberthon, and has been raised to a great position at Naples or elsewhere, if he chooses to recall her and live with her, not as with a Princess who is his wife, but in any intimacy he chooses, I shall make no difficulty, for the political aspect is all I care for. Apart from that, I have no desire to run counter to his tastes and passions.

These are my proposals. If he means to send me his daughter, she must start without delay, and he must reply by sending me a formal declaration that his daughter is starting for Paris, and that he places her entirely at my disposal ; but there is not a moment to be lost, events are hurrying on, and destiny must be accomplished. If he has changed his mind, I must know that too, instantly, for I will provide for such an event in another way, however painful that may be for me. For why should I disown these two young nieces, who have no active share in the intrigue of which they may be made the victims ?

Tell Lucien that his grief, and the nature of the feeling he expressed for me, have touched me, and make me regret all the more that he will not be reasonable and contribute to his peace and mine. I hope you will have this letter on the 22nd.

My last news from Lisbon is dated 17th November. The Prince Regent had taken ship for Brazil; he was still in the port of Lisbon. My troops were only a few leagues from the forts which close the entrance of the roadstead. I have no news from Spain, except the letter you have read.

I impatiently await a clear and frank answer, especially concerning Lolotte.

Postscript.—My troops entered Lisbon on 30th November. The Prince Royal has sailed on board a man-of-war. Everything was going on well at Lisbon on 3rd of December. On 6th December, the English declared war against Russia. Have this news sent to Corfu. The Queen of Tuscany[1] is here. She wants to go to Madrid.

LXXXII

TO JEROME NAPOLEON, KING OF WESTPHALIA.

PARIS, *4th January* 1808.

I HAVE received your letter with regard to the speech you addressed to your Council of State. I think the speech absurd. No Frenchman, excepting those to whom I may give permission to enter your service, will take the oath you ask for. My Councillors of State cannot take this oath, and not even my officers. If Beugnot and Siméon desire to stay with you, they are free to do as they choose. If they have taken the oath you demanded of them, I shall remove them from the list of my Councillors of State. You might very well have dispensed with making that speech.

I have to nominate a Commissary, to put you in possession of half the domains which fall to you ; I have appointed M. Jollivet to this position. As I believe my Councillors of State to be overwhelmed with ill-treatment at your Court, I desire they may return as soon as possible.

I am anxiously expecting you to send me a statement of the Frenchmen whom you keep in your service. I will allow them the following advantages :—

[1] Marie Louise of Spain, Queen of Etruria.

Those who remain in your service can swear any allegiance to you they please : when they leave your service I will give them back the grade they held when they left mine, without taking the services they may have rendered you into consideration : this is how I acted with regard to the King of Naples, and the King of Holland. It is very necessary to make the list in question ; without it there would be a great deal of confusion. In general, if you desire to please me, you will show no indulgence to any Frenchman without my advice. I ask you this, with reference to those who are permanently attached to your service, as a matter of courtesy to me. I demand it imperatively, as to those whom I may authorise to take service with you, and who hold to the intention of returning. As for the Westphalians, I do not concern myself about them. You must be prepared for the fact that there are certain Frenchmen to whom I shall not grant permission to remain in your service.

As to H——, I can only be astounded at your weakness. The man has been prosecuted for forgery, and for criminal acts which have made him a horror to France. Can you possibly have carried your want of confidence in me to such a point? Ask Siméon, Beugnot, and Jollivet what they know of him. He is a very clever man, but a gallows-bird, and his natural home is in the galleys. You do not know men yourself, and you try to teach me to know them. I repeat that this proceeding on your part shows very little mature consideration.

Send me, when my courier returns, the statement of the Frenchmen in your service, carefully distinguishing those who are in command of my army from those who have become your subjects.

LXXXIII

TO JEROME NAPOLEON, KING OF WESTPHALIA.

PARIS, 4th January 1808.

I HAVE your letter of December 15th with regard to General Lagrange. I disapprove of your conduct. General Lagrange is not your subject; he is not accountable to you for what he has done in his administration, and you therefore had no right to disgrace him. He has served me in Egypt; he has fought several campaigns under me in Italy; he might have rendered me services of such a nature that I alone could judge what ought to be done. And, besides, General Lagrange was authorised to take the Elector's horses; he had a right to do it. You committed an injustice when you had them brought back to your stables. You should have contented yourself with taking information as to the money he had received, and reporting to me. What pleasure can the dishonouring of the military uniform be to you? It was that garb which conquered your kingdom, and gave me the throne on which I sit. Your conduct shows very little consideration, and that is what distresses me most.

But you must imbue yourself with the conviction that you have no jurisdiction whatever over the Frenchmen I send to you, and that you are only to inform me as to what they may do. I reserve myself the right of taking whatever step with regard to them conduces to my interest, and agrees with my experience. If this course of conduct does not suit you, send me back the Frenchmen who are with you, and govern with Germans.

LXXXIV

TO JEROME NAPOLEON, KING OF WESTPHALIA.

PARIS, 4th January 1808.

I HAVE your letter of the 28th December, by which I see you propose to give the property of Fürstenstein, and 40,000 francs a year, to M. Lecamus. I know nothing more mad than this proceeding, which is at one and the same time contrary to your interests, harmful to the State, and, above all things, harmful to yourself. What has this Lecamus done? He has done no service to his country; he has rendered some personal service to you. Is this reward in proportion to the service he has given you? I have not planned such an arbitrary proceeding during the whole of my reign. I have more than ten men, each of whom has saved my life, to whom I only give a pension of 600 francs. I have Marshals who have won ten battles, who are covered with wounds, and who have not the reward you give this Lecamus. Services rendered to your individual person are not services done to the King, nor to the Kingdom of Westphalia. It is therefore indispensably necessary that you should revoke this measure; and I presume that you have not closed so important a matter so very precipitately. If you have concluded it, you must revoke it, or Mons. Lecamus must renounce his French Citizenship, and then he will lose all his hereditary rights in France. If Lecamus has 40,000 francs a year, what is to be given to Marshals Berthier, Lannes, Bernadotte, and over a score of persons who have paid for the throne on which you sit, with wounds of every kind? What ought you to have done with that property of Fürstenstein? You should have taken it for the Crown, (you are rather poor, as you do not enjoy the benefit of half your domains), or you should have kept it in reserve for ten years. You might then have had a Minister who had served you well enough to deserve such a reward. I have Ministers who might have made ten millions, who have not a halfpenny, and who never dream of claiming such rewards. I have already told you, with reference to General Lagrange—what distresses me about all this is your lack of consideration.

[¹ I have your letter of 24th December, as to the condition of your finances. What sort of finances can you expect to have, when you behave as you do? You have squandered three millions in Paris in two months; you will squander thirty without rhyme or reason, in a shorter time.]

But you must not imagine, all the same, that the Kingdom of Westphalia is a landed property. I shall have to make war to support you, and I foresee that, instead of your weighing advantageously in the balance, I shall find a deficit in my strength.

LXXXV

TO GENERAL JUNOT, COMMANDING THE ARMY OF OCCUPATION IN PORTUGAL.

PARIS, *7th January* 1808.

I HAVE your letter of 21st December. I am distressed to observe that from 1st December—the day of your entry into Lisbon—until the 18th—when the first symptoms of insurrection began to show themselves,—you did nothing at all. Yet I never ceased writing to you: 'Disarm the inhabitants; send away all the Portuguese troops; make severe examples;

---

¹ The passage in parenthesis was struck out of the draft.

keep up an appearance of severity, which will cause you to
be feared.' But your head, it appears, is full of fancies, and
you have no knowledge of the Portuguese spirit, nor of the
position in which you are placed.   I do not recognise this as
the action of a man who has been brought up in my school.
I do not doubt that in consequence of this insurrection, you
have disarmed the town of Lisbon, caused some sixty people
to be shot, and taken proper steps.   All my letters have
foretold what is now beginning, and what will shortly happen
to you.   You will be shamefully hunted out of Lisbon, as soon
as the English have effected a landing, if you continue to
behave with such weakness.   You have lost precious time,
but you have time yet.   I hope my letters, which you have
received in succession, will have decided you as to the course
you should take, and that you have adopted strong and
vigorous measures, without feeding yourself on fancies and
twaddle.   You are in a conquered country, and you behave
as if you were in Burgundy !   I have no inventory, either of
the Artillery or of the fortified towns.   I know neither their
number nor their situation.   I do not even know if you are
holding them.   You have not yet sent the Minister the list
of your halting-places from Bayonne· to your first fortified
town, nor any report on the condition of the country.

Yet I had strong reasons for desiring this.   Indeed, I am
inclined to believe my troops have not yet entered Almeida.
If anything were to happen you would find yourself blockaded by the Portuguese.   There is an extraordinary want
of foresight about the whole thing.

LXXXVI

TO GENERAL JUNOT, COMMANDING THE ARMY OF OCCUPATION IN PORTUGAL.

PARIS, 28th January 1808.

I HAVE fixed the salary of the Administrator-General of
the Portuguese Finances at 100,000 francs, and I have
granted him 50,000 francs for preliminary expenses.   I
have read his report.   He proposes two things :—

First, Not to divide the kingdom.   That is my full
intention.   I have already informed you, and I now repeat
it, that the administration is to be single and undivided

.E

until circumstances permit of the publication of the Treaty, and the partition of the country. You will therefore take measures for the strict execution of this arrangement.

Second, He calculates the consolidated debt at 160,000,000 francs, and the unconsolidated debt at 80,000,000 francs. My answer to that is, that not a halfpenny must be paid,—without however repudiating anything ; but, until the fate of Portugal is decided, no attention must be given to this matter, any more than was done in the case of Vienna and Berlin. When the fate of the country is settled, we will see what is to be done about the debt. If the interest on the 160,000,000 francs is at 5 per cent., you are making a saving of 8,000,000. You have expenditure for the Portuguese army, on the civil list. Send all those troops to France, and reduce these expenses to a very small figure. Home expenses must always be reduced in time of war. By stopping the expenditure on the Public Debt, on the army, the navy, and internal affairs, the payments must be reduced to something very small, and you will have almost the whole of the revenue to feed and support my army.

I have no news of you since 9th January. Article 9 of my Milan Decree fixes the rate of the gratuities I allot to my army. Nothing has been paid in Poland, for a long time. It never was anything but a momentary payment, and only to certain corps.

I have sent a Commissary-General of Police, according to your wish.

I suppose you have not lost a moment in thoroughly organising your artillery, and putting your transport and your cavalry on the best possible footing.

I have not yet received the Engineer Officers' report on Abrantés, Almeida, Santarem, and the other fortresses.

Make up your mind to be worried and disturbed in your conquest, this spring. You will be absolute ruler for these two months. If you do not take advantage of them, you will repent your negligence ; the mischief will be irremediable. Disarm the country — do it thoroughly ; occupy the fortresses, turn batteries of mortars upon the towns. Arm and provision the fortresses, so that any one may be able to defend them. Get rid of the prominent men ; punish the smallest faults with severity. You will be free to do all that during February and March. If you wait for a landing to be effected, it will cost you bloodshed to quiet things down.

General Dupont is at Valladolid. I have no return of your army. Send it me when the orderly-officer, Turenne, returns. Acquaint me fully, at the same time, with the condition of the country, of the fortified towns, of the artillery, and send me a description of the roads. Have the battalion of army service waggons horsed. Get them into good condition, and send a portion to General Dupont.

If I wanted two divisions of 5000 men, with twelve guns horsed, one to march on Badajos, the other on Alcantara, could you furnish them, during the winter, without interfering with the tranquillity of the country? If you could not furnish two, could you furnish one, of 6000 men? How many days would they take to reach their destination? How many troops are there at Oporto? and in the lower part of Spanish [Galicia]?[1]

If unexpected events arose in Spain, what would you fear from the Spanish troops? or could you easily rid yourself of them? You would, on that supposition, have the natives of the country on your side.

Do not be weak and idiotic enough to allow your departments, and your troops, to be short of money. Have several hundred thousand biscuits, either in your rear, or at your front. Double your artillery teams. There were Swiss, and other foreigners, in the Portuguese service, who might be useful to you in this matter. You might even employ some of the native battalions.

LXXXVII

TO JEROME NAPOLEON, KING OF WESTPHALIA.

PARIS, 16th February 1808.

I WOULD have held my peace as to all your doings: but my Ambassador at Vienna informs me you have sounded the Ministry, as to whether you might not send the Abbé de Meerfeldt, brother of the Austrian Minister at St. Petersburg, as your Minister to the former Court. You really have lost your head. Such a piece of folly is unexampled. France, and I myself, have no more bitter enemy than Meerfeldt,

---

[1] This word is blank in the original.

and you take this step, at Vienna, at the very moment when
I am demanding his recall from St. Petersburg! Your hint
has produced the greatest astonishment at Vienna. If you
should have appointed M. de Meerfeldt, I request you will
recall him on the spot. You might really consult me as to
your choice of diplomatic agents. What the devil do you
want with a Minister at Vienna? To spend money? I
have already written to you about M. de Hardenberg's
brother.

You have things notified at Vienna, too, by the Dutch
Minister. I must have your assurance as to this before I
can believe it. It really is too ridiculous.

LXXXVIII

TO M. FOUCHÉ, MINISTER OF POLICE.

PARIS, 16th *February* 1808.

YOUR police work is not as active and energetic as it
should be. How comes it that Prince Esterhazy, Count
Potocki, and others, not belonging to the Austrian Legation,
that a M. Casimir, a Mdme Dufour, and other supposititious
servants of M. de Starhenberg's, land in France from English
packets? You no longer follow up this matter as you ought.

I have informed my Minister of the Navy of my positive
intention, that every part of the Empire should be watched
by the police. There are to be no favoured spots.

By the same packet a great quantity of letters arrived, all
of which ought either to have been given over to the postal
authorities, or seized by the police.

LXXXIX

TO M. DE CHAMPAGNY, MINISTER FOR FOREIGN AFFAIRS.

PARIS, 17th *February* 1808.

THE *Argus* is a newspaper which public opinion accepts
as official. It is cackling about expeditions to Africa. This
cannot do otherwise than make a bad impression at Constantinople, and will drive all the Regencies to declare war
against us. This newspaper should either be done away
with, or steps should be taken to have it better managed.

In to-day's newspapers I see an article on M. de Caulaincourt's reception, which will do that Ambassador a great deal of harm. The article is written with so little tact, that it is easy to see it emanates from the Foreign Affairs Department. There is one passage in particular—about people who are punctilious as to etiquette—which will offend the Russians intensely. The whole thing is stupidly done.

XC

TO GENERAL JUNOT, COMMANDING THE ARMY OF OCCUPATION IN PORTUGAL. .

PARIS, 29th February 1808.

I HAVE your letter of 14th February. Tascher has not arrived yet. He will doubtless come to-morrow, or the day after. I conclude he will not make any delay. I note with pleasure that you have disarmed the town of Lisbon, and the country, and that you are hurrying on the despatch of the Portuguese troops into France : but I am distressed to observe that you have no other means of burning the town and reducing it, in case of revolt, except that supplied by your sea-going ships. This is but a poor and sorry resource. You want a good citadel, which, however weak it may be, should, when garrisoned by 400 or 500 men, be impregnable to the populace. It should be provisioned and armed with mortars. Nothing but the news that such a citadel has been established, will give me the security and confidence I need.

There is no doubt that you must keep great state at Lisbon. I have authorised the remittance of a sum of 50,000 francs a month, to be placed at your disposal, for the expenses of your position, and for secret expenditure, and another monthly sum of 50,000 francs to be spent on extra pay, secret-service money, etc., for generals, commanding officers, and officers sent on special duty. This will enable you to supply all your needs.

XCI

TO JEROME NAPOLEON, KING OF WESTPHALIA.

PARIS, 1st March 1808.

I HAVE your letter of 23rd. I do not write to you, because I can have nothing to say to you,—you, who in the second

month of your reign, apply to a Dutchman to give hints for
you at Vienna.   Is this spite or ingratitude?   Is it frivolity,
thoughtlessness?   All I know is, that in such circumstances
I have no tongue to speak with!

XCII

TO JEROME NAPOLEON, KING OF WESTPHALIA.

PARIS, 6th March 1808.

I HAVE read the letter you are writing to Beugnot.   I
thought I had told you you might keep Beugnot and Siméon
as long as you needed them ; but the idea of making
them swear allegiance is ridiculous.   None but thoughtless
Frenchmen, who had not concerned themselves about the
result of such a step, can have taken the oath, and I pardon
them, for I believe their heart was not in it.   If the oath is
one of fidelity to your person, that is included in the
allegiance every Frenchman has sworn to me.   If it is
the oath of a Westphalian subject, you ask a thing which the
meanest drummer in my army would not do.   Besides, the
Senators and Councillors of State who are employed at
Naples have taken no oath.   The Frenchmen employed in
the King's household have sworn allegiance to him as a
French Prince.   And even if these reasons did not suffice, it
is not when you are surrounded by foes and strangers, that
you should insist that men, who may be useful to you, shall
renounce their own country, and make themselves criminals.
I have met few men with so little circumspection as you.
You are perfectly ignorant, and you follow nothing but your
own fancy.   Reason decides nothing in your case, everything
is ruled by impetuosity and passion.   I do not desire to
have any correspondence with you, beyond what is indispensable as regards Foreign Courts, because they make you
dance steps, and expose your want of harmony before the
eyes of Europe ; which I am not inclined to permit you to
do.   As for your household and financial affairs, I have already
told you, and now tell you again, that nothing you do
accords with my opinion and experience, and that your
mode of action will bring you little success.   But you would
oblige me by using less pomp and ostentation with respect
to steps, the consequences of which you do not appreciate.

Nothing could be more ridiculous than the audience you gave the Jews. Nothing can be more mischievous than your attempt to ape the French *Moniteur.* I have undertaken to reform the Jews, but I have not endeavoured to draw more of them into my realm. Far from that, I have avoided doing anything which could show any esteem for the most despicable of mankind.

(*Postscript in the Emperor's own hand.*)—I love you, my dear fellow, but you are terribly young! Keep Siméon and Beugnot, without any oath, for another year at least. All in good time!

XCIII

TO GENERAL JUNOT, COMMANDING THE ARMY OF
OCCUPATION IN PORTUGAL.

PARIS, 7th March 1808.

(*The following paragraph was suppressed when this letter was published
in the Correspondence, No.* 13,627.)

ONE of your divisions must hold (Spanish) Galicia in check. You will not fail to hint in the course of conversation (but without divulging anything), that my disagreement with Spain is caused by my not choosing to divide Portugal, one half of which Spain would like to give to the Prince of Peace, and the other to the Queen of Etruria.

If these reports so impress the Portuguese that you think you might make use of them, you could employ half at Elvas, and the other half at Almeida, to keep the Spanish part of Galicia in order. Your communication being cut, you must act according to circumstances, and whatever news you may receive.

XCIV

TO PRINCE MURAT, GRAND-DUC DE BERG, THE
EMPEROR'S LIEUTENANT IN SPAIN.

PARIS, 10th March 1808.

I HAVE your letter of the 7th, with General Duhesme's despatch. General Duhesme has nothing to fear, as he is master of the Citadel of Barcelona. You did wrong to order him to seize Figuera. You desire him to concentrate his troops, and then you tell him to take Figuera. These two orders are contradictory. I intend him to stay in Barcelona, with all his division massed. He must have a Paymaster, War Commissaries, and his eighteen pieces of artillery. Besides, he has his Italian War Commissaries, and one can get on very well without a Paymaster. Thus he is very well provided. As for Inspecting Officers for his reviews, what the devil does he want with them, on active service? He must do that duty for himself.

There is no discontent whatsoever at Barcelona. General Duhesme is a gossip. Some Neapolitans have been stabbed with stilettos; that is the local habit. On the whole, the people are well disposed, and when we have the Citadel we have everything. I have given orders to the Minister, Mollien, to send a Paymaster, with funds, to that Division; he should have arrived by now. If Generals Dupont and Moncey had sent in their returns, they would have been given the officers they are short of, but as they have sent nothing for the last three months, they are supposed, for that reason, to be on a satisfactory footing.

You must have received my orders. This letter will find you just beginning your forward movement, on the 15th.

XCV

TO M. FOUCHÉ, MINISTER OF POLICE.

PARIS, 10th March 1808.

MAKE known my displeasure to the editor of the *Journal des Débats*, who prints nothing but nonsense in his paper. He must indeed be a simpleton to say, in an article from Hamburg, that the King of Sweden could, with the help of England, raise an army of 100,000 men. Let him write an article making game of these 100,000 men, for to-morrow's issue. The King of Sweden could not raise more than 15,000 men; and the English will not send him any, except a few regiments of deserters. It is ridiculous, therefore, to draw attention to such a struggle. Sweden will lose Finland, that is the clearest point about it. Truly our newspapers are all very silly, and their folly has evil consequences, because it gives a certain moral importance to Princes who are nothing at all.

XCVI

TO JOSEPH NAPOLEON, KING OF NAPLES.

St. Cloud, 11*th March* 1808.

LUCIEN is misconducting himself at Rome, even going so far as to insult the Roman officers who take my side, and is more Roman than the Pope himself. I desire you will write to him to leave Rome, and retire to Florence or Pisa. I do not choose him to remain at Rome, and if he refuses to take this course, I only await your answer to have him removed by force. His conduct has been scandalous; he is my open enemy, and that of France. If he persists in these opinions, America will be the only refuge left him. I thought he had some sense, but I see he is only a fool. How could he remain in Rome after the arrival of the French troops? Was it not his duty to retire into the country? And not only this, but he sets himself up in opposition to me. There is no name for his conduct. I will not permit a Frenchman, and one of my own brothers, to be the first to conspire, and act against me, with a rabble of priests.

XCVII

TO JOSEPH NAPOLEON, KING OF NAPLES.

Paris, 12*th March* 1808.

REAR-ADMIRAL COSMAO's conduct is preposterous. All I can do is to deplore my sailors' folly. Admiral Ganteaume's instructions to him were to raise the blockade of Corfu: he has been master of the Mediterranean for a fortnight, and he comes and shuts himself up in Tarento. Admiral Ganteaume, when he gave him orders to go to Tarento, only did so in case he should find his strength inferior to the enemy's; but finding himself superior in strength, as the Rear-Admiral did, the first rules of common-sense should have led him to proceed to Corfu.

I do not approve of your keeping my ships at Baiæ, or at Naples. Once the expedition is over, they must return to my ports.

The advice you gave Cosmao was not sufficiently clear: you should have ordered him to start an hour after his arrival

(all the more so because at Corfu he is safe from all
hostile forces); to take all the Brindisi and Otranto convoys
under his escort, and to raise the blockade of Corfu; and if
the Admiral sent him no other orders, to make a cruise, and
then return to Toulon. The long-windedness and indecision
of your letter distressed me. Only six lines were necessary,
and you would have been obeyed. You talk at random
with a set of poor wretches who are dying of uncertainty
and fear. I am sorry you did not consult Saliceti. He would
not have given you such advice.

It is indeed a misfortune that when all the luck was with
him, the stupidity of a naval officer should prevent his
seizing the chance fate offered him. I verily believe that if
a galleon, laden with 30,000,000 of piastres, was to take up
its position in the centre of all the squadrons, they would not
have the sense to seize it.

I conclude that Ganteaume has been at Corfu, since the
24th February. I cannot understand why he has delayed
so long. Certainly there would have been an extra chance
of their meeting, if you had ordered Cosmao to go straight
to Corfu.

XCVIII

TO JOSEPH NAPOLEON, KING OF NAPLES.

PARIS, 16th March 1808.

I HAVE your letter of the 7th. Rear-Admiral Cosmao's
answer is inconceivable; a man may be a fool,—but, to be
such a fool as that, is too much! Ganteaume's instructions
were that his principal object was to be to raise the blockade
of Corfu; that no one ship was to touch there independently,
and that if the enemy was in superior force, he was to take
shelter at Tarento. How comes it that Cosmao, who was
stronger than the enemy, did not enter Corfu? It is un-
heard of. Your first letter to Cosmao was worth nothing,
your second is no better. My fine store-ships will be taken.
You should have held a council. There was no objection to
Cosmao's going into Corfu; four ships together had nothing
to fear.

I do not know what has become of Ganteaume. This is
an expedition that has failed through the greatest folly in

the world! That Cosmao is a wretched fellow. Does he really not know that the number of ships at Corfu is well known at Otranto? Those men do not understand the French language. Ganteaume's instructions might have been better drawn, but they were sufficient for ordinary common sense, and, of course, it is impossible to foresee every circumstance. I trust Ganteaume will be at Corfu.

XCIX

TO MARSHAL BERTHIER, PRINCE DE NEUFCHÂTEL, MAJOR-GENERAL OF THE GRANDE ARMÉE.

ST. CLOUD, 24th March 1808.

WRITE to Marshal Soult, that he is no longer to say 'King of Sweden,' but is to use the generic expression 'Head of the Swedish Government'; that he is to say everywhere, that since his violation of the Constitution of 1778, we no longer recognise the King of Sweden; that we shall not recognise him until that Constitution is restored; that, besides, he is not to accept any letter which does not describe him as 'Marshal Soult, Commanding the Imperial French Army'; and that, as a general rule, he must avoid parleying of every kind. The supposition is, that no communication, political or commercial, is held with Sweden. Nevertheless, no opportunity should be neglected for scattering pamphlets along the coasts, to disturb the people, and cast discredit on the King.

C

TO M. DE LAVALLETTE, DIRECTOR-GENERAL OF THE POSTAL SERVICE.

ST. CLOUD, 29th March 1808.

IT is necessary that all letters belonging to Foreign Ministers, resident in Madrid, should be stopped in the Post. They must be kept back for a fortnight, after which delay they may be allowed to pass.

It is very essential, under present circumstances, that the despatches of Mons. Henry, the Prussian Chargé d'Affaires at Madrid, should be deciphered.

It is also necessary that all letters coming from Spain,

and addressed to the Spanish Division, commanded by the Prince of Ponte-Corvo,[1] should be kept back. Take steps about this, and let me know what you have done. All these letters must be delayed about twenty days; they must be carefully examined, and all those of an evil tendency suppressed.

CI

TO M. DE CHAMPAGNY, MINISTER FOR FOREIGN AFFAIRS.

St. Cloud, *1st April* 1808.

You will write to my Minister in Denmark that his language is not correct; that there is no change in the Emperor's arrangements; that the Expedition has never been anything more than a plan; and that it is absurd for him to want to direct military matters; that it was his business to let me know, by official despatches, what Mons. de Bernstorf was saying, and by reports, what the public was saying, or what prominent persons had told himself (provided he gave the names); that I do not perceive that either Mons. de Bernstorf or the Court have complained; that the troops, instead of relaxing their march, have pressed forward, and that if we have arrived at a later date, it is because the Court of Denmark made up its mind too late.

I desire you will see Mons. Lacépède, and desire him to send the Grand Cordon of the Legion of Honour to the King of Denmark. You will at the same time send a short letter for my signature, to serve as an answer to the notification he has made me by his letter, which I shall consider as official. You will also see the Grand Master of the Ceremonies, and give him my orders about the Court mourning.

CII

TO PRINCE MURAT, GRAND-DUC DE BERG, THE EMPEROR'S LIEUTENANT IN SPAIN.

Bayonne, *17th April* 1808.

Savary is starting at this moment; he is going to the Prince of the Asturias, and brings him the letter of which I

---

[1] In the Baltic Provinces.

enclose a copy. I have desired him to write you everything that happens, from Vittoria. If the Prince of the Asturias comes to Bayonne, you will have time to receive orders as to what you are to do. If the Prince of the Asturias returns to Burgos, I have given the necessary orders to Bessières. If he returns to Madrid, you will send to meet him, and you will have him arrested, and, if necessary, you will publish the letter I send you, and King Charles's protest, and you will force O'Farill and the rest, and the Infant Don Antonio, to swear allegiance to King Charles. You will cause the Grand Inquisitor to publish a Proclamation,- to the effect that as King Charles made a protest against his abdication, he is King. Take vigorous action.

The Governors, the Commissaries, the Bishops, will have to account for any disorder that may arise in the communes and villages. You must declare that I recognise King Charles IV.; that I guarantee the integrity of the two Spains; that the Prince of Peace is banished; and that I undertake to help King Charles with my advice, and the forces of my Empire, to establish good order in his kingdom; that the fate of Spain is in the hands of the Spaniards. You will have pamphlets and newspaper articles written, to lead the public mind in this direction. If the Prince of the Asturias remains at Vittoria, with Savary, he will inform you of what occurs. If communication is open, and nothing presses, you will await my orders. If the Prince of the Asturias should come to Bayonne, and communication were interrupted by brigandage, and the matter became urgent, you must have my letter, and the protest, printed. You will declare that you recognise Charles IV., and the protest will be sent to all the Ministers, by my Chargé d'Affaires. But I hope that will not happen; I hope the Prince of the Asturias will come to Bayonne, and that I shall be able to direct everything, which I greatly desire, because of the extreme delicacy of the circumstances, which call for so thorough a knowledge of my position.

I learn, by your letter of the 12th, that King Charles IV. left the Escurial on the 14th; he will therefore be at Burgos to-day or to-morrow. I shall be very glad to see him here.

If it should come to a rupture, you would make known, through the newspapers, that the French army had come to Spain for the purposes of an African expedition, which I was to have directed myself, from Madrid ; that the Prince of Peace, thinking I desired to advise his King, and perhaps advise him against himself, had taken flight ; and that this had been the cause of everything that had happened.

CIII

TO M. FOUCHÉ, MINISTER OF POLICE.

BAYONNE, *21st April* 1808.

THE *Publiciste*, and the *Journal des Débats*, take pains to print all the most atrocious and vilest, and even the most silly calumnies, against the Prince of Peace.   The Prince's enemies have all these printed in Spain, as extracts from French newspapers.   Have a quantity of articles written, which, though showing no great consideration for that Minister, will point out the meanness of these accusations.

The facts are, that not a halfpenny has yet been discovered of his immense fortune ; that he had no correspondence whatsoever with the English, that the fleet he was said to have sent them, had really been despatched to Toulon, and that, though he may have governed the two Spains badly, it is fair to say they are still intact, while most of the European States have diminished in size, and suffered losses. I say this less out of political interest, than because I think it a horrible thing to inveigh against people in misfortune. I desire the newspapers shall not be allowed to be used as the instruments of these low calumnies.   The *Journal des Débats* makes itself particularly remarkable by its perpetual insertion of absurdities.

If the man Pillichadi, mentioned in your report of the 14th, comes to Paris, have him arrested, and keep him in prison. The case of the Neufchâtel bookseller should teach you what Swiss spies are.   You must not be taken in by them a second time.

CIV

TO M. FOUCHÉ, MINISTER OF POLICE.

BAYONNE, *25th April* 1808.

THE *Journal de l'Empire* still goes on badly.   What business has it to insert Mr. Canning's speech in the Copenhagen intelligence?   Had the editor that speech before him?

Ought he to have inserted it without knowing that it suited me? That young man is either an ill-disposed person, or a fool; tell him so from me. If he does not change his ways, I shall change the editor. I conclude him to be a fool who allows himself to be swayed by the *Clique*.

The difference between the *Journal de Paris*, and the *Journal de l'Empire*, clearly appears in the manner in which the Copenhagen news is edited in each. The *Journal de Paris* avoids saying anything objectionable. Make that clear, and send me Mr. Canning's speech.

Mons. Etienne is the cause of the present agitation in France, about Roman affairs. Pray have all the old editors, who are so hot against the present Administration, turned away.

I had also forbidden the newspapers to refer to priests, sermons, or religion. Does not the *Journal des Débats* give extracts from sermons, homilies, and other things of that kind? Will the police be good enough to do my will at last? Is it not absurd, and contrary to the nature of sacred subjects, to see them called into question in newspapers full of falsehoods, and idle matters?

Cause the newspaper articles which assert that 400 millions were found in the possession of the Prince of Peace, to be turned into ridicule. Let it be known that not a half-penny was found; that if the Government found all that money, we wish it joy; that, in that case, it will be able to give its troops their pay. The real truth is, that the Prince of Peace has nothing, either in England, in Italy, in France, or at Genoa; and that not a million's worth of diamonds and current cash was found in his house.

CV

TO PRINCE MURAT, GRAND-DUC DE BERG, THE EMPEROR'S LIEUTENANT IN SPAIN.

BAYONNE, *26th April* 1808.

I HAVE just seen the Prince of Peace, with whom I conversed for an hour. It will be necessary for you to send him his children, the other members of his family, and his personal effects, to Bayonne. I have received him kindly, because he is unfortunate, and has been abominably treated.

I wrote to you to-night.

It is time for you to show fitting energy. I imagine you will not spare the Madrid mob, if it stirs, and that you will have it disarmed immediately afterwards. I authorise you, if necessary, to have the Body-Guard arrested and disarmed ; in any case, it will be necessary for you, if a rising should occur, to have ten of the chief culprits arrested and shot.

I have just (at midnight) received your letter of the 23rd. You have commuted the sentence of a soldier condemned to death, to that of five years in chains. You have no right to do this. Do not permit yourself such liberties in future. You may venture on such action amongst the troops of Berg, but not amongst French troops. Keep the soldier in prison until the Privy Council makes known its opinion. I have forwarded his appeal to the Chief Judge.

I have informed you, in my letter of yesterday, that you are to cause King Charles's protest to the Regency, and the decision adopted by the latter, to be printed in the *Gazette de Madrid.* Your reason for not finding printers is absurd. I told you to take the government into your hands. When a man is at the head of 50,000 men, he does not write as you wrote to the Infant Don Antonio, and he does not resort to intrigue. King Charles having made a protest, I do not recognise King Ferdinand. King Charles is the only King of Spain. Take care that nothing is done or printed, to disturb the public peace, and make use of the newspapers to give the proper impulse to public opinion.

Your Order of the Day to the soldiers about the Burgos affair is a wretched thing. Good God! where should we be if I was to write four pages to the soldiers, to tell them not to allow themselves to be disarmed, and to quote the fact that a guard of fifteen men fired on the mob, as a trait of heroism? Frenchmen are too clever not to laugh at such proclamations. You never learnt that in my school! What are you to do in critical moments, if you lavish proclamations in this way? Three words were all that was necessary. 'The Madrid mob has risen ; there is an insurrection ; the first soldier who allows himself to be disarmed, or the first sentry who is forced, will be declared unworthy to belong to the army.' And I doubt whether even this would have been necessary. You have committed an offence against discipline, by not having reduced the officer who

gave over those two soldiers to the mob. I intended to
degrade him before the whole army, when I arrived at
Madrid, and you have done very wrong to forgive him.
Your proclamation has made me blush. If it was drawn up
by Belliard, you will let him know my displeasure. To
bring order into the city of Madrid, 3000 men, and 10
pieces of artillery, are needed. Three orders of the day like
yours would demoralise an army.

CVI

TO MARSHAL BESSIÈRES, COMMANDING THE IMPERIAL GUARD, AT BURGOS.

BAYONNE, 26th April 1808, 10 P.M.

THERE was a disturbance on the 22nd at Santander, which
threatened the French. Send an officer there, and warn the
inhabitants that if the meanest Frenchman is touched, they
will pay for it dearly ; that I know all about it ; and that I
have desired you to warn them of the risk they are running,
if they allow themselves to be swayed by the partisans of
England ; and that it would be distressing if honest folk had
to suffer for the good-for-nothing people whom they had not
restrained. I intend, in fact, if I hear of the slightest disturbance, to send a Brigade with cannon, and burn the town
to the ground.

The Archbishop must send me a priest, and the Captain-
General an officer, that they may learn, from my own lips,
the indignation I feel against their town, and that, on the
smallest insurrection taking place, it would cease to exist.

CVII

TO PRINCE MURAT, GRAND-DUC DE BERG, THE EMPEROR'S LIEUTENANT IN SPAIN.

BAYONNE, 28th April 1808, 5 P.M.

I SEND you a thousand copies of the *Journal de Bayonne* ;
you can circulate them quite naturally, and without attracting attention. It would be well for the Junta to publish a

F

proclamation on the subject, making known the fact that King Charles has protested, and that, before leaving the Escurial, he renewed his protest to the Regency; that King Charles must have reached Bayonne; that the two Sovereigns have left the decision of this great quarrel entirely in the hands of the Emperor; that it is the interest of the two Spains to be at one with France; that His Majesty the Emperor has already authorised the Junta to announce, that the integrity and independence of Spain will be guaranteed, as well as the preservation of all privileges; that if the Spaniards think any changes in their Constitution necessary, these will only be made as they wish, and according to their judgment and opinion. If the Junta refuses to make this proclamation, make it yourself, in French and in Spanish.

I send a hundred copies of the same newspaper to Bessières, and desire him to have a proclamation in the same sense made, by the Captain-General of Old Castile.

Send an officer to Generals Solano and Caraffa,[1] to give them notice of the Junta's proclamation, or your own, and to advise them to have confidence in the Emperor, and to do all they can to help on the settlement of good order and tranquillity in Spain.

I have your letter of the 23rd. I note with pleasure what you say in it.

I expect King Charles to-morrow, or the day after. I have no news of his arrival at Burgos, Bessières not having written to me.

You will not fail to induce the Archbishops of Madrid and Toledo to publish charges, exhorting the people to have confidence in me; and you will give the leaders of the clergy and nobility to understand, that the preservation of their privileges depends on how they behave to me. Write also to the heads of the Religious Orders, which must exist in Madrid; and finally, have newspaper articles written in the same sense, so that the public may be thoroughly aware that King Charles has protested; that this is a quarrel between father and son; that the issue of events must be awaited with confidence; and that I shall arbitrate, and decide everything as to the transfer of the Crown.

---

[1] Who commanded the Spanish Divisions in Galicia and Estramadura.

CVIII

TO PRINCE MURAT, GRAND-DUC DE BERG, THE EMPEROR'S LIEUTENANT IN SPAIN.

BAYONNE, *29th April* 1808, 10 A.M.

YOUR letter of 25th April reached me at midnight. King Charles should have arrived at Burgos on the 27th. I do not know whether he will have spent the 28th there, or have come on to Vittoria.

I do not approve of your scattering your troops. I am informed that you have sent a regiment from the Escurial, to a village ; you may detach a regiment for the purpose of making an example, but it must return instantly. If you send a regiment, or a battalion, to every rising that occurs, I shall have no army left. If you accustom the villages to having garrisons, they will revolt the moment you withdraw them. You are to send flying columns, which will not be absent more than a week, and will return the moment their mission is accomplished.

Write to General Dupont to treat the family of Canon Escoïquiz, at Toledo, with consideration.

You are to inform the Junta that it is to stop sending couriers to Mons. de Cevallos,[1] and that in future it is only to correspond with Charles IV. ; that I have given orders that the couriers from Bayonne shall be sent to the Court of Charles IV., as I no longer recognise the Prince of the Asturias as anything but Prince of the Asturias, conformably with the notification I have this day caused to be made. If the nation were to be induced, by its fear of Charles IV., or of the Queen, to press you forward, you must let it have its way. We are drawing near the dénouement. Take the management of the *Gazette* into your own hands, by fair means or foul, and let it appear every day. Make the grandees, and other influential persons of the country, thoroughly understand that the fate of Spain depends on their behaviour ; that if Spain is disturbed, and the safety of my troops compromised, the country will be dismembered. State positively that I no longer recognise the Prince of the Asturias.

---

[1] Whom Ferdinand had appointed Minister of State.

TO PRINCE MURAT, GRAND-DUC DE BERG, THE
EMPEROR'S LIEUTENANT IN SPAIN.

BAYONNE, 30*th April* 1808, 3 P.M.

KING CHARLES has arrived at Irun; I expect him here
within two hours. Berthier has gone as far as the frontier
to meet him. The Prince of Peace is here, and is beginning
to recover.

You have seen, by the Note sent you by Champagny, that
I no longer recognise Cevallos, nor any agent of Ferdinand.
I have stopped a packet sent them from Madrid, which
gives the same account of the state of public opinion
there, as you do. I have stopped another which they were
sending to Bayonne. It contained a letter from the Prince
of the Asturias to the Infant Don Antonio, which will prove
to you what a fool and a hypocrite the man is,—for the Empress has been enthusiastically received here. You need not
show any consideration. I have written you to take command of the troops. Send to Caraffa and Solano, to let them
know that this must be so ; you can have Champagny's Note
sent to them. Send off the Queen of Etruria, send off the
children ; they cannot stay at Madrid any longer. Let them
start day or night. You will tell Don Antonio that there is
an order from Charles IV. for him to come at once. There
is no urgency about sending for the Spaniards. All those
who are here are worthless. It is necessary that I should
get all this business settled within the next two days.

My Chargé d'Affaires is to stay at Madrid. He will give
an account of himself to Mons. Laforest, who will have the
rank of Minister, without, however, holding any communication with the authorities, except through my Chargé d'Affaires.

I think I have told you this already. Dissolve the Junta,
and let it cease to govern, if it obeys King Ferdinand. Tell
them that to despatch the smallest packet, or report, will be
a crime. Above all, let Don Antonio and the rest of the
family depart.

The moment I have seen the King, I will write to you. I
suppose you to be in possession of the *Gazette de Madrid*,
and that you have articles inserted every day.

I think it would be a good thing to disarm and dismount
the Body-Guard. King Charles treated those who were at

Vittoria very severely. They had taken possession of his palace, and he turned them out of it, in a very vigorous manner.

Send an officer to General Junot to inform him of what is happening, so that he may concur, by every means in his power, in holding back the Galician troops, and those of Solano, if they should attempt a movement on Madrid.

(*Postscript in Napoleon's own hand.*)—7 P.M. I have just seen the King and Queen, who are very glad to be here. The King received his children very coldly. All the Spaniards, even the Infantado, etc., kissed his hand, but the old King seems very much incensed against them.

CX

TO GENERAL CLARKE, MINISTER OF WAR.

BAYONNE, *8th May* 1808.

I AM displeased with the behaviour of the pupils of the School of Artillery at Metz, and with the weakness of the Commandant. These young men make scenes in the theatre, which shock all respectable people. You will have it put in orders, in my name, that they are to remain under arrest for a month, without going beyond barracks, and that they are to be forbidden to go to the theatre for a year. Any seen there, will be punished for disobedience to a published order. Express my displeasure to the Colonel, and to the Commandant; they betray the most extreme weakness. The pupils, as soldiers, are under the orders of the Commandant, when they are out of school.

Let me hear no more of this business. I will not allow a handful of urchins to disturb a whole town. If such excesses were tolerated, the result would be that they would be nursed in insubordination. Have a list of the six most mutinous sent you, and have them put in the prison of the School, for two months.

In future, the Colonel will be responsible for any insubordination occurring in the School. You will write to the police at Metz, so that any pupils who go to the theatre, whether in disguise or not, during the next year, may be arrested.

CXI

TO M. DE TALLEYRAND, PRINCE DE BENEVENTO
VICE-GRAND ELECTOR.

BAYONNE, *9th May* 1808.

THE Prince of the Asturias, his uncle, the Infant Don Antonio, and his brother, the Infant Don Carlos, leave this on Wednesday, spend Friday and Saturday at Bordeaux, and will be at Valençay on Tuesday.

Be there yourself on Monday evening. My Chamberlain, Tournon, is posting there, to make all preparations for their reception. See they have table and bed linen, and cooking utensils; they will have eight or ten persons in waiting, and as many, or twice as many, servants. I am ordering the General acting as Chief Inspector of the Gendarmerie, at Paris, to go there, and organise the Gendarmerie Service. I desire these Princes may be received without external show, but politely, and respectfully, and that you should do all in your power to amuse them. It will not be a bad thing, if you have a theatre at Valençay, to bring a few actors down. You might bring down Madame Talleyrand, and four or five other women. If the Prince of the Asturias were to become attached to some pretty woman, whom we were sure of, it would be no disadvantage, for it would give us another means of watching him. It is most important to me that the Prince of the Asturias should not make any false step. I therefore wish him to be amused, and occupied. In strict policy, he should have been sent to Bitche or to some fortress, but as he has thrown himself into my arms, and has promised me he will do nothing without my orders, and as everything in Spain is going on as I wish, I have decided to send him to a country place, and there surround him with amusements, and keep him under supervision. You will keep this up through May, and a part of June. By that time Spanish affairs will have taken shape, and I shall know what course to pursue.

As far as you are concerned, the mission is fairly creditable. To entertain three illustrious personages, for purposes of amusement, is quite in accordance with the national character, and with your rank. The week or ten days you will spend with them, will make you thoroughly acquainted with what they think, and will help me to decide what I am to do.

The Gendarmerie companies will be reinforced, so that you may have forty gendarmes, who will make certain of his not being carried off, and prevent his flight. You will talk to Fouché, who will send agents into the neighbourhood, and among the servants. For it would be a great misfortune, if, somehow or other, this Prince were to make a false step.

There must be a guard at the castle. I think this might be furnished by the Departmental Company.

I have undertaken, by the treaty I have made with King Charles, to allow these Princes 400,000 francs a year. They have more than that from their Commanderies; they will thus have 3,000,000 between the three of them.

If you think, that to do them honour, and for every other reason, you need a company of Grenadiers or Cavalry of my Guard, you will speak about it to General Walther, and you will send them down with post-horses. Herewith is an order for General Walther.

CXII

TO M. FOUCHÉ, MINISTER OF POLICE.

BAYONNE, 21st May 1808.

A HEAP of nonsense about Spanish affairs is being circulated in Paris. This is caused by a mischievous article about Toledo, which has been hawked about in all the papers. As a matter of fact, no blood was shed at Toledo, nor even at Burgos. The only place where blood flowed was Madrid; there were not twenty-five Frenchmen killed, and not more than fifty wounded. The Spaniards who were killed, were all sedition-mongers, or rioters of the lower class; not one peaceable man perished, and the Spanish loss is not so considerable as it was first thought to be. You must take care that the newspapers do not speak of Roman and Spanish affairs, except on the lines given by the *Moniteur*.

On the 2nd of April, I united the four Legations of Ancona with the Kingdom of Italy. I have sent the Decree of the Senate, as to the union of Tuscany with France, to a Privy Council. This measure is indispensable, on account of the Gulf of Spezzia, where I intend to have a great naval establishment. It is necessary that the newspapers should not mention this, until the *Moniteur* has referred to it.

All this idle talk about the divorce does terrible mischief, and is as indecent as it is harmful ; the police can stop it in a thousand ways.   I do not know why none of these are resorted to, but it is very necessary to put an end to it.   All well-conditioned men in France are grieved by it ; it distresses me exceedingly, and the Russian Court, which cannot understand this gossip, quite as much.

CXIII

TO PRINCE MURAT, GRAND-DUC DE BERG, LIEUTENANT-GENERAL OF THE KINGDOM OF SPAIN.

BAYONNE, 23rd *May* 1808, 10 A.M.

IT would appear, by a letter from Laforest to Champagny, that the Council of Castile has refused to have anything to do with the business, or to ask that the King of Naples may be made King.   This behaviour is neither good nor handsome ; try and discover its motive.

In Spain's present position she needs money.   What are the plate, diamonds, and other Crown valuables worth ?   They should certainly be worth 40,000,000.   There will be no difficulty in pawning them for that sum.

When the Minister of Finance arrives, I have no doubt I shall find resources in the country itself, but we must get on for another month, without that.   Meanwhile, money must be found, both for the necessities of the sea-ports, and to facilitate administration.   Pawn the Crown diamonds ; and —as the sum will be too considerable to be procured in the country—borrow 60,000,000 of reals, and pawn diamonds and jewels to that amount.   This is quite a natural proceeding ; they will be redeemed later.   I am persuaded money can be had in Spain, but, to get it, we must know how things are situated ; I await the arrival of the Minister of Finance for that.

Postscript.—I have no money.   If I had, I should not hesitate to lend it, but the Bank of France, when authorised by me, will make no difficulty about lending 20,000,000 of francs or 80,000,000 of reals, receiving part of the Crown diamonds in pledge for the amount.

The Crown has a great number of sheep, which might be turned into money. In present circumstances it will be quite correct that all stocks, interest in the Sinking Fund, or on charitable funds, should wait, and that everything should be given to the War and Naval Departments.

CXIV

TO M. FOUCHÉ, MINISTER OF POLICE.

BAYONNE, *26th May 1808.*

I HAVE read in your Report, in the paragraph headed Antwerp, the answer given by the smuggler Vieusseux.[1] It could hardly have been more impudent. Talk it over a little with the Chief Judge, and with Treilhard, and see if there is no means of getting those rascals hanged. In any case, an answer to these arguments should be inserted in the newspapers.

Have these smugglers rigorously prosecuted, and have the seals put on their goods, furniture, and effects. Write to my Minister in Holland, and to the Dutch Minister here, to have the man Florent, of Breda, arrested. You suggest my appointing a Commission. I think I have already appointed a Committee of the Council of State for this business.

Give orders that the man Desruisseaux, accused of having been at Bayeux, in 1801, in connection with an English correspondence, shall be arrested, and sent to a fortified castle. I cannot but blame your culpable indulgence of such scamps. What hope can you have of successfully watching wretches of that kind? Have them seized, and shut up in the fort of Joux.

Send me a general report on all the smugglers. Could we not get eight or ten millions out of them? What means can we take of bringing them to justice?

[1] Stephen Vieusseux was one of the partners in an Antwerp house, which had branches at Hamburg and in Paris, and which practised smuggling on a large scale. When he was arrested, he replied, 'I have sold the merchandise I had stored in Holland, without troubling myself as to where it came from, or whither it was to be sent. I afterwards bought this merchandise in France, without inquiring whether it had been brought in illegally. No law has forbidden me these speculations, nor does any law forbid them at this moment.' *National Archives,* AF. iv. 1502, Police Report, 20th May 1808.

CXV

TO M. FOUCHÉ, MINISTER OF POLICE.

BAYONNE, *26th May* 1808.

WE intend, having reason to be displeased with Madame de Chevreuse, *Dame du Palais*, that she shall remain in banishment, in her property of Luynes, near Tours, and that she shall be punished for her disobedience, if she trangresses the said order. You will be good enough to see to the execution of the present order.

CXVI

TO PRINCESS PAULINE BORGHESE.

BAYONNE, *26th May* 1808.

I HAVE your letter of the 18th May. I approve of your going to take the waters in the valley of Aosta. I am sorry to learn your health is bad. I suppose you are wise, and that it is by no fault of yours? I observe with pleasure that you are pleased with your lady-in-waiting, and with your Piedmontese ladies. Make yourself loved; be affable with everybody; try to be even-tempered, and to make the Prince happy.

CXVII

TO M. FOUCHÉ, MINISTER OF POLICE.

BAYONNE, *11th June* 1808.

I SEE, in the *Journal de France*, an article on King Charles, dated from Fontainebleau, which seems to me conceived in a bad spirit. Generally speaking, it is time to cease mentioning this family. Let the journalists know this, and see to it.

I do not know why I no longer have a Police report every day. Take measures that I may receive one daily.

The arrest of Préjean and his four comrades is a matter of great importance. I trust he will not escape, and that you will profit by all the information he may be able to give you. If the English agents, and those of the Comte de Lille, who certainly are in Paris, and in the Morbihan, could be arrested, it would be a great thing. I beg you will give me exact information as to all Préjean's depositions.

CXVIII

TO M. DE CHAMPAGNY, MINISTER FOR FOREIGN AFFAIRS

BAYONNE, 16th June 1808.

YOU must have a statement drawn up of all our grievances against Ali Pasha, and send it to my Chargé d'Affaires at Constantinople, and to the Ambassador of the Porte in Paris, requesting satisfaction against the Pasha, or that he should be declared a rebel.

Write in cipher to my Commissary-General at Corfu, that he must stir up the neighbouring small Pashas, who are dissatisfied with Ali Pasha, against him, and weaken him in every way, by giving assistance in arms and money (secretly, of course) to all his enemies.

CXIX

TO MARSHAL BERTHIER, PRINCE DE NEUFCHÂTEL, MAJOR-GENERAL OF THE GRANDE ARMÉE.

BAYONNE, 22nd June 1808.

THE King of Westphalia's Minister has published a circular, dated 3rd June, which is a most humiliating thing for the French Army. Write to the King, that he is to revoke it on the spot, and that it is my intention that French Commanding Officers shall enjoy all the dignities of their rank in his dominions. It is ridiculous that French Commanding Officers should have to refer to Westphalian Commanding Officers—to men, in other words, who were formerly our enemies and bore arms against us—in matters necessary to the wellbeing of our soldiers. Tell the King, that Colonel Morio, in whom I have not the slightest confidence, could not possibly be Chief of the Staff of the French Army; that that gentleman has no head and no sense. What is the meaning of this subordination of French soldiers to Westphalian soldiers? Twenty years hence, at the nearest, such a thing might be tolerated. I await the King's reply, to know what course I must take, to maintain the dignity due to my troops, and my officers.

CXX

TO M. DE LAVALLETTE, DIRECTOR-GENERAL OF THE POSTAL SERVICE.

BAYONNE, *26th June* 1808.

THE Spanish Princes have received a number of letters addressed to them at Valençay, from Bayonne, Perpignan, and various other points on the Spanish frontier ; yet I have strictly desired you to take measures to prevent their receiving any.

CXXI

TO M. FOUCHÉ, MINISTER OF POLICE.

BAYONNE, *28th June* 1808.

MADAME DE STAËL keeps up a steady correspondence with the man Gentz, and has allowed herself to be drawn into the clique of London intriguers. I wish her to be watched at Coppet, and desire you will give orders to that effect, to the Prefect of Geneva, and the Commandant of the Gendarmerie. Her intercourse with this individual cannot be otherwise than harmful to France. You will let it be known that up till now she has been looked on as a mad woman, but that, from this day forward, she enters a circle detrimental to the public peace. I have also given orders to the Minister for Foreign Affairs, to have this made known to all my agents at foreign Courts, and to have her watched wherever she goes.

CXXII

TO M. DE CHAMPAGNY, MINISTER FOR FOREIGN AFFAIRS.

BAYONNE, *28th June* 1808.

As Madame de Staël is in regular correspondence with Gentz, the author, and as this intercourse cannot be anything but reprehensible, it is my intention that you shall inform my Ministers and agents, in Germany, and especially at Weimar, that if that lady should enter the countries where they reside, they are to abstain from seeing her, and they are to have her watched.

CXXIII

TO M. FOUCHÉ, MINISTER OF POLICE.

BAYONNE, 29th June 1808.

I HAVE your letter of the 26th. The changes made in the Police Council are irregular. You should not have made them without my order.

I have carefully read all the examinations sent me by the Prefect of Police. They seem to me important. But it is a calumny to say he attacks the Senate. In what he has sent me, there is not one word that can compromise a single Senator. Your duty is to support the Prefect of Police, and not to disown him, and give currency to false rumours against that magistrate.

CXXIV

TO PRINCE CAMBACÉRÈS, GRAND CHANCELLOR OF THE EMPIRE.

BAYONNE, 29th June 1808.

I HAVE received your letter of 26th. The report of the Prefect of Police, and the examination and confrontation of General Guillaume and Gariot, seem to me very important.

Nothing can exceed my displeasure with this Minister of Police, who displays his hatred of the Prefect of Police, instead of supporting, encouraging, and directing him. The Minister tries to cast blame on the Prefect of Police, by saying he makes reflections on the Senate. There is not one word against the Senate in everything the Prefect of Police has sent me. Speak to Pélet and Réal in my name. I desire you will support M. Dubois in every particular, and give him public proof of your esteem. Warn his enemies and detractors, that the more they endeavour to depreciate his zeal, the more striking will be the proofs of esteem I myself shall bestow upon him. I am guided by my own reason and judgment, and not by other people's opinion.

It is a certain thing, that since the Year VIII. the anarchist party has never ceased hatching underhand plots in France. I have forgiven this, over and over again. We must now make an example, which will cut all these machinations short.

Why have not you, who are a lawyer, pointed out to the Minister of Police, that he had no right to create a new system? He should have consulted the assembled State Councillors and the Secretary-General, who holds the pen. But he should not have taken a decision as to creating a Police Council. The State Councillors, who know the established rules, should have refused to perform such functions, for this new system could not be called into existence, without my authority.

CXXV

TO PRINCE CAMBACÉRÈS, GRAND CHANCELLOR OF THE EMPIRE.

BAYONNE, 13th July 1808.

SEND for M. Fouché. Ask him what he means by his letter of the 10th, which I send you. Why does he think I should sweep away the Senate? Does he not know the Constitution? Does he not know that I have no reason to complain of any member of that body, which has never failed to prove its attachment to my person? Is the Minister mad? or is he joking? Ask him for his proofs that the Prefect (of Police) used such language. Have this functionary brought face to face with M. Fouché, and clear the business up. Why has the Minister kept this matter from the knowledge of the Police Council? Send me the report, and the Council's proceedings. I found fault with his having taken the pen away from the legally appointed secretary of the Council; but I gave no orders to reverse that action, and you did not tell him to do so. Explain to me, in short, what Fouché is about, with all this. Is he mad? At whom does he aim? Nobody is attacking him. Nobody is attacking the Senate. What does it all mean? I am beginning to be thoroughly puzzled by the Minister's conduct. What do Réal and Pélet de la Lozère say? What do you think of it all? Can his jealousy of the Prefect of Police possibly have carried him to such lengths?

CXXVI

TO GENERAL DUROC, GRAND MARSHAL OF THE PALACE.

BAYONNE, 15*th July* 1808.

HERE are two letters which you will send to Rémusat, that he may present them to the King and Queen (of Spain).[1] The King wishes to go to Nice. He can start as soon as he chooses. He can travel *incognito*, or as I do. He will be free to proceed as he chooses.

If he does not desire to travel *incognito*, all the honours due to his rank must be paid him. He will be given whatever escorts he desires. Of course, he will travel at his own expense, and will establish himself at Nice, at his own cost. One of his officers can go to Nice, with a letter from the Minister of the Interior, to prepare his house. I conclude he will take one of the houses in the suburb. There are some good-sized ones, I think. If he should desire to go to Mentone, I do not know if the Prince of Monaco's house is fit to receive him. At all events, he can drive there, and see if he could settle there. I wish the Queen of Etruria to follow the King; unless she should prefer going to Colorno in the State of Parma. I would, in that case, give her the use of that castle. I do not wish her to go to Paris, —not on her own account, but on her son's. But my will is not to appear in the matter at all. M. Rémusat, to whom you will write about all these arrangements, will proceed entirely by means of hints. On the whole, I think Colorno would be the best. It seems to me, that the best and most convenient method for the King's journey would be for him to take boat on the Seine, and go to Avignon by the Saône. These arrangements will be welcome to me, because I shall thus get Compiègne into my own possession again. So, instead of delaying the departure, Rémusat must rather press it forward.

As for the Prince of Peace, he, being a person of very little importance, may live at Paris, and wherever he pleases. Rémusat will say he is commissioned to give all orders.

[1] Charles IV. and his consort, who were then at Compiègne.

CXXVII

TO JEROME NAPOLEON, KING OF WESTPHALIA.

BAYONNE, 16*th July* 1808.

YOU owe two millions to the Sinking Fund. You have allowed your bills to be dishonoured. That is not like a man of honour. I never allow any one to forget what is due to me. Sell your plate and diamonds. Cease indulging in foolish extravagance, which makes you the laughing-stock of Europe, and will end by rousing the indignation of your subjects. Sell your furniture, your horses, and your jewels, and pay your debts. Honour comes first of all. It ill becomes you not to pay your debts, when people see the presents you give, and the unexampled luxury you live in, which disgusts your subjects. You are young and inconsiderate, and you never pay any attention to money matters, especially at this moment, when your subjects are suffering from the effects of a war.

CXXVIII

TO JEROME NAPOLEON, KING OF WESTPHALIA.

BAYONNE, 16*th July* 1808.

I HAVE your letter, brought by your aide-de-camp Girard. I exhort you to three things : respect, gratitude, and attachment to myself, and the French nation, to whom you owe everything ; the severest economy, so that the wretchedness of the circumstances weighing on your people should not be contrasted with unlimited luxury and expenditure on your part ; an economy, which is always necessary at the beginning of a reign, when public opinion is taking shape, an economy so great that you will not only have no debts, but that, on your civil list of six millions, you will spend three on your household expenses, keep 1,500,000 francs for unforeseen expenses—such as marriages, festivities, and the construction of palaces,—and 1,500,000 francs, which shall in ten years have formed a reserve fund of 15,000,000, and which you will meanwhile lend to accelerate the formation of your army ; and further, employ your time in learning what you do not know—cavalry, artillery, and infantry tactics, the administration of justice, and the management of finance : when you have fulfilled all these conditions, you will deserve my esteem, that of France, and of your own people. To fulfil them all, you will require a great deal of reflection, you must reform many things, and change many of your ways.

CXXIX

TO JEROME NAPOLEON, KING OF WESTPHALIA.

BAYONNE, 16th July 1808.

COURIERS are passing between H——'s country house, and Cassel. I have already informed you that H—— is a wretch, stained with every sort of embezzlement, and guilty of things which I cannot put on paper; I am horrified that after this, you should still continue to correspond with him. I am even told he is in Italy; in that case you may expect to see him shut up in a strong castle. I will have him arrested, even in the very palace he dares to profane ! I give you notice, that the first time you write to H—— you will disobey the head of your family, and you will bring down misfortune on all those people.

CXXX

TO PRINCE CAMBACÉRÈS, GRAND CHANCELLOR
OF THE EMPIRE.

BAYONNE, 17th July 1808.

I SEND you the Police Report.[1] I beg you will read it carefully, and compare it with the documents. I have long thought it was Mons. Fouché's jealousy of the Prefect of Police which caused his behaviour. I am beginning to fear that Fouché, who has lost his head, favours busy-bodies, of whom he hopes to make use, and does not desire to discourage those who count on circumstances connected with death, or on extraordinary incidents,—because he himself thinks so much of the future, as his steps about a certain divorce prove. Under these circumstances, I request you to call the Police Council together, and verify the following assertions—

---

[1] The Police Report for the 13th of July is, in fact, missing from the official collection of Police Reports.

(1st), That there has been only one interview between the accused persons—whereas it is clear, from the cross-examinations, that there were a great many ; (2nd), That it was the result of chance—whereas it is proved that they were arranged beforehand ; (3rd), That no proposal was made by the Senators, or in their name—whereas Servan and Jacquemont declared themselves commissioned to make proposals, without the Senators knowing anything of them,—as is usual with leaders of conspiracies ; (4th), That they had come to no decision of any kind—whereas they never thought of anything else : the day for the rising was already fixed, and the one thing which stopped them short, was the idea of the presence of the Imperial Guard in Paris ; (5th), That they never arranged any meetings—whereas they saw each other every day.

These conclusions are too absurd. I do not see that Malet, Florent-Guyot, nor even Jacquemont, are compromised ; the only person who has plotted, is the Prefect of Police. Mons. Fouché takes me to be too great a fool !

After this item in the Report, comes a still more important note, in the Minister's own hand. I desire you will send for Mons. Regnaud, and ask him if he made the assertion. If he denies it, you will ask the Minister why he invented it. You will likewise send for the Prefect of Police, and clear up all this jumble. Mons. Fouché's cackling has turned a trifling affair, which only reveals the necessity for punishing and putting down a few evil-disposed persons, into a matter of immense importance. The whole business is marked by a spirit and behaviour which I do not understand. Why does Mons. Fouché send me this analysis, instead of sending me the whole of the Police Council Report ? What would happen if evil-doers were never put down till there was an army of them, and if every attempt to alarm or mar the public peace, in a well-ordered State, were not stopped short ?

CXXXI

TO M. DE CHAMPAGNY, MINISTER FOR FOREIGN AFFAIRS.

TOULOUSE, 25*th July* 1808.

I SEND you back your portfolio. I cannot understand all this mess of Mons. Bourgoing's. He does things which compromise the dignity of France and are contrary to my intentions. Long ago I gave two orders : the first, to diminish the number of officers, governors of fortresses, war commissaries, and storekeepers, employed on the military roads in Saxony, by two-thirds ; second, that the remaining third should be paid at my expense, and should not cost the King of Saxony, who, at the very most, is only bound to furnish quarters, anything at all. Instead of this, Bourgoing thanks the King for the orders he has given,—a mean and ridiculous step ; for either the King· is bound, as a member of the Rhenish Confederation, to feed whatever troops of mine pass through his dominions—in which case I owe him no thanks ; or he is not bound to do anything of the sort—and then it is ridiculous for me to thank a small Prince of the Rhenish Confederation for giving me thirty or forty thousand francs. It would have been quite easy not to accept them from him. Write to the Saxon Minister, that I have found fault with Bourgoing's conduct ; that my intention is to have as few employés as possible in Saxony, and that they are not to cost the country anything. You will inform Mons. Bourgoing that he is only to use his good offices in important matters ; that the employés in Saxony receive salaries, and are not to ask for anything.

CXXXII

TO THE PRINCE DE NEUFCHÂTEL, MAJOR-GENERAL OF THE GRANDE ARMÉE.

TOULOUSE, *26th July* 1808.

GIVE orders to have the *Gazette de Bayreuth* suppressed, and let the correspondence of the gazetteer be sealed up— the seals to be affixed by French officers. An examination will be made of all the papers, and all documents relative to correspondence with the English will be sent to Paris. The journalist will be kept in prison, and examined as to his acquaintances, and as to the intrigue he has·been carrying on with the English, these several years past.

CXXXIII

TO JOACHIM NAPOLEON, KING OF NAPLES.

AGEN, *30th July* 1808.

I HAVE your letter. I observe with pleasure that your health is improving.

The news from the Duchy of Berg is not satisfactory. Your agents are packing everything up, and sending it over to the left bank. Your stud is slipping away towards the Tyrol. All this makes a very bad impression in the country, and in Germany. Is it worth while to betray such greediness about trifles? In any case, if you care very much about your horses, are you not sure of having them within fifteen or twenty days? Your behaviour is thoughtless, and has a bad effect on opinion. Write and give orders that nothing is to be taken away, and that no avidity is to be shown.

The heat is so great that I fear, if you start too soon, you will not be able to bear it. Take care of your health, first of all,—that is the chief matter.

CXXXIV

TO JOSEPH NAPOLEON, KING OF SPAIN.

BORDEAUX, *31st July* 1808, 11 P.M.

I HAVE your letters of the 24th, 25th, and 26th. The tenor of your letter of the 24th does not please me at all. There is no question of dying, but of fighting, and being victorious; and that you are, and will be.

I may find the Columns of Hercules in Spain, but not the limits of my power. Ever since I have been in the service, I have met nothing so cowardly as these Spanish mobs and troops. Besides, troops, and help of every kind, are moving towards you. You have a third more strength than you really need, if you use it with the proper precision. Except for Moncey, and his disgraceful retreat from San-Clemente, on Ocaña, and dastardly council of war, I am very much pleased with my troops. Savary is a clever and brave-hearted man, who has failed in his general arrangements, because he has not, as yet, the habit of commanding in chief, but who, nevertheless, is much stronger than those you have around you. Caulaincourt has done very well at Cuenca. The town has been sacked; that is the fate of war: it was carried by main force.

Russia has recognised you. The letter to that effect has been sent to Mons. de Strogonoff. When I reach Paris I shall hear Austria has done the same.

Your position may be a trying one, as a king, but as a general, it is brilliant. There is only one thing to fear: Beware of losing touch with the army, and of sacrificing it to the Spaniards. No mercy must be shown to ruffians who murder my wounded men, and commit every sort of horror. It is very natural that they should be treated as they are; I have told you this already, and now repeat it. Since the splendid victory of Medina de Rio-Seco, which so swiftly settled the Spanish business, Marshal Bessières is absolute master in the north.

I was glad to see you have not sent Morlot's Division to Marshal Bessières, as was suggested. Dupont must be supported. Have no anxiety as to the issue of all this. I know your position thoroughly. Nothing of what has happened has surprised me. Otherwise, should I have sent 150,000 men into Spain, raised two conscriptions, and spent 80,000,000 of money? I would rather have lost a battle than have read Moncey's official report.

CXXXV

TO MARSHAL SOULT, SECOND IN COMMAND OF THE
GRANDE ARMÉE AT STETTIN.

St. Cloud, 23rd August 1808.

DUPONT has utterly disgraced himself, and dishonoured my arms. Folly, cowardice, and infatuation presided over his operations during the end of July, and have quite upset my affairs in Spain. The harm he has done me is a trifling thing, compared with the disgrace. The details of the whole matter, which I am glad to keep as secret as possible, excite the most lively indignation. Yet it will all have to be cleared up some day, and the honour of our arms must be avenged.

I think the evacuation of Prussia will be signed to-morrow or next day, and it will take place towards the end of October. I think it would be well for you to blow up Spandau, but it should be done secretly and promptly, so as not to give rise to any protest. You must have miners with you. The whole thing should be over within five days, without its being suspected at Berlin. You might even have it said, that the damage has been caused by the blowing up of a powder magazine, or of the vaults in which the powder was kept. I hold the fortresses of Glogau, Stettin, and Cüstrin, until the indemnities are paid, and all business matters settled. The first and sixth Corps, and three divisions of dragoons from the Grande Armée, come to Mayence, to finish the Spanish business. Fresh marching regiments, drawn from your dépôts, are proceeding to join the army. Before the month of October, your effective infantry strength will have reached 36,000, and your cavalry 18,000 men. This will give you a body of 60,000 men, which, supported by the Prince of Ponte-Corvo's 10,000 infantry, and by 15,000 men of the Confederation troops, will form a strong army.

Marshal Davout's Corps should be a little stronger yet. The fifth Corps is proceeding to Bayreuth; I have not quite decided to bring it back to France. I am going to take up my winter quarters on the left bank of the Elbe, except for 9000 men, whom I leave to garrison the fortresses, and those who must be left in Pomerania.

CXXXVI

TO M. DE CHAMPAGNY, MINISTER FOR FOREIGN AFFAIRS.

St. Cloud, 2nd September 1808.

I SEND you what, as far as I can understand it, seems a very extraordinary letter.[1] Have it translated, and make a report to me about it. Bring it back to me to-morrow at the *Lever*, so that we may talk it over. Make a report to me, also, on all these papers.

---

[1] An intercepted letter from Herr von Stein to Herr von Wittgenstein, who was Prussian Minister in Cassel during the war of 1806.

CXXXVII

TO MARSHAL SOULT, SECOND IN COMMAND OF THE GRANDE ARMÉE, AT STETTIN.

ST. CLOUD, *4th September* 1808.

HERR VON STEIN'S letter strikes me as being very extraordinary. I think it would be a good plan to have Koppe,
the assessor, conveyed to France, under good and safe escort,
so as to subject him to a detailed examination. Meanwhile,
get all you can out of him, by putting him into secret confinement and cross-questioning him. The Prussians are a
poor wretched set. If you have any suspicion of General
Rüchel, have him arrested, and brought to France, but you
must not let him slip. To-morrow a Decree will appear,
calling out 140,000 men of the conscription. This levy will
raise your Corps to fifty-six battalions, or 48,000 infantry
soldiers. Marshal Davout's will be raised to the same
strength, so that the loss caused the Grande Armée by the
departure of the 1st and 6th Corps is made good, as far as
numbers go. Everything Austria does is done out of fear.
But if thorough measures were not taken, she might grow
bold. As for the present, peace is assured; but there is no
knowing what English intrigues may bring forth, between
this and next May. I desire to have 200,000 men in
Germany, and 100,000 in Italy, by that time.

CXXXVIII

TO JOSEPH NAPOLEON, KING OF SPAIN.

ST. CLOUD, *8th September* 1808.

I CANNOT conceive your wanting to send the Prince of
Masserano to Venice; it is strange policy to choose a man
who will act against both you and me, to be your Ambassador
in Austria. Send one of the Negrete, or the son of your
Minister for Foreign Affairs, or some other man of that kind,
whose fate is closely bound up with yours. Otherwise you
are not to send any one at all.

The five or six persons who have been arrested at Bilbao,
by General Merlin, must be put to death, especially a person
appointed Governor-General by the proclamation of the

Junta. If you do not take some vigorous action, there will be no end to it all. This appears to me very important.

It is very strange that so much should be done to spare Navarre. Biscay, Navarre, and Bilbao, must feed the army, otherwise what am I to do? It is absurd to grant them any indemnities. Bilbao could have paid 4,000,000.

CXXXIX

TO JOSEPH NAPOLEON, KING OF SPAIN.

St. Cloud, 9th September 1808.

I THINK it is necessary you should bring Santander into submission. It would be sufficient merely to move 6000 men on Reinosa, and to send another column from Bilbao. The point is a very important one, entailing the submission of the Montaña, and it is indispensable this should be done before the army makes a general move.

I suppose Marshal Moncey to have remained at Tudela. The troops he has, are more than double what he needs for holding that position, and I imagine he will not allow the enemy to establish itself four marches away from him.

You have also, doubtless, had Burgos occupied in force. You must leave the new troops which are there, in Bilbao; they are quite sufficient. Above all things, you must carry out the disarmament of Biscay and Navarre. I request you will make a severe example of the insurgents at Bilbao, more especially of the officer arrested, in command of the armed force, and send numerous hostages to France.

On Sunday, I shall review the Sebastiani division, which starts on Monday to proceed to Perpignan. It consists of four fine regiments of infantry, a regiment of dragoons, and twelve guns. The roads of France are covered with troops, either from Italy, or from Germany. You must oblige the villages to grind corn, and not get everything from France. The provinces you occupy should, and can, furnish you with provisions. The Spanish population is base and cowardly—very much as I found the Arabs to be. It gives you a good reception at Burgos, and elsewhere, because you have a great number of troops, and are able to crush it; but upon the smallest symptom of retreat, it would fire on you. We must

NEW LETTERS OF NAPOLEON I

have hostages, and a general disarmament. You must not listen to your Ministers, who appear to have no information. Spain has been ruined by a disastrous system of indulgence. The infantry should have been disarmed, the cavalry dismounted, and all made prisoners. Madrid has furnished the enemy's army with 2000 horses; these might have been taken, on leaving Madrid, to horse my artillery. All English colonial merchandise at Bilbao must certainly be confiscated, and that town must pay a tax of at least 2,000,000. If you think these people remain in the path of duty out of sheer good feeling, you are deceived. If they do not rise in rebellion, it is not for lack of inclination, but because they do not dare. Take that for certain.

You must have received the Decree for organising the Spanish army; it must be adhered to as closely as possible, for the present.

CXL

TO GENERAL CLARKE, MINISTER OF WAR.

ST. CLOUD, 9th September 1808.

YOU will have General Marescot arrested, and brought alone to Paris, to a military prison, where he will be kept in solitary confinement. His aides-de-camp will be arrested separately. All their papers will be sealed up, and sent to you. When the General has been separated from his aides-de-camp, and the aides-de-camp from each other, you will have the General subjected to the enclosed cross-examination, which will be returned to you, signed by him, and by the person whom you will depute to examine him. You will subject each of the aides-de-camp to almost the same examination.

Cross-Examination of General Marescot.

QUESTION 1. Where were you on the 13th, 14th, 15th, 16th, 17th, 18th, and 19th of July?

2. How was it that you did not perceive that the enemy was marching and manœuvring in your rear, although General Belair was attacked at Murgibar (?) on the 13th, and was in retreat on the 16th?

3. Why did you separate, instead of marching all together on Baylen, on the 16th?

4. Where were you at three o'clock on the afternoon of the 19th, when General Védel's guns were heard?

5. Why did you not then attack, and force the enemy's line, or die gloriously, like Frenchmen?

6. Who caused General Védel to cease firing?

7. Where were you at six o'clock on the evening of the 19th, and all that night?

8. How did you hear that General Védel was retreating on Madrid? What did the enemy's general say to you? What share did you have in the order sent him to come back to his destruction?

9. How could you, a Great Officer of the Empire, and Chief of the Engineers, light-heartedly add the loss of Védel's and Gobert's Divisions, to that of Dupont's Division?

10. How could you put your hand to the capitulation of Baylen, that eternal disgrace to the French name? Why did you include General Védel and his division in it?

11. How was it that you did not insist on the sanction of an English Commissary, and how came you not to realise, that the French troops would be lost, if they laid down their arms, and would never re-enter France without a guarantee from the English?

12. Why did you sign the dishonour of the French army, by consenting to say that the soldiers had stolen the Sacred Vessels?

13. Why did you go into so much detail about your baggage, and thus increase the disgrace of this infamous capitulation, by your interested conduct?

14. Why did you disguise yourself as a Spanish General, and why did you not follow the troops whom you had surrendered without their weapons? Did you not feel it was a cowardly act to put off your uniform, and to show this panic of fear?

CXLI

TO M. FOUCHÉ, MINISTER OF POLICE.

ERFURT, 9th October 1808.

SINCE, as appears from your report of the 30th, the officer at Valençay does not suit, he must be changed. The dentist

Gallet, who tried to speak to the Prince of the Asturias, must be arrested. I think it is absurd of you not to have taken these measures yourself. If people from Madrid are allowed to prowl round the Palace after this fashion, we must expect something to happen.

CXLII

TO JOACHIM NAPOLEON, KING OF NAPLES.

Burgos, 12th November 1808.

I HAVE seen edicts of yours, which are perfectly senseless. Your sole object is reaction. Why recall exiles, and restore property to men who have taken up arms, and are plotting, against me? I give you notice you must take measures to withdraw these edicts, for I will not permit persons who hatch conspiracies against my troops to be received and protected in your dominions. Your action as to the fishermen is no more prudent: it will only give the English a means of obtaining earlier knowledge of what takes place. You are making concessions to a false popularity. You will lose it by means of such foolish steps. It is absurd to release all the sequestered property, so that the people in Sicily may be supported by it. Really and truly you must have lost your head!

CXLIII

TO JOACHIM NAPOLEON, KING OF NAPLES.

Burgos, 18th November 1808.

I CONCLUDE you have caused the property within your kingdom, owned by the Duke del Infantado, and other Spanish Grandees, to be sequestered. My French and Italian subjects in Spain have been plundered, and I propose to compensate them out of that property. Do not lose a moment about this sequestration, if it has not been already made. I am assured that half the kingdom of Naples belongs to these Spanish Grandees. Have an inventory made of all their possessions, and do not free them from sequestration without my leave. I am losing enough as it is, over this Spanish business.

CXLIV

TO M. FOUCHÉ, MINISTER OF POLICE.

BURGOS, 18*th November* 1808.

I HAVE your letter of the 11th. Have young St. Aignan placed in the Military School at St. Cyr. You will let him know this is my will. You will also let him know that I do not intend him to marry, till he has fought two campaigns. You will have him taken there bodily. This method will have to be followed with several others of the same kidney.

CXLV

TO GENERAL MENOU, GOVERNOR OF THE GRAND DUCHY OF TUSCANY.

ARANDA, 28*th November* 1808.

MARET sends you a Decree which is not to be published till after its execution. Have the valley disarmed. Have thirty or forty persons—those best known as having always taken part in former revolts—arrested, whatever their present behaviour may be. There must be no delay about the execution of this order. Eight-and-forty hours after the receipt of my letter, these thirty or forty persons must be in prison. You will, at the same time, let me know their names, their families, their fortunes, and the part they have played at different periods. If any should escape, you will have their property confiscated. You will have them all taken to the Citadel of Fenestrella. The peace of Italy demands that an example should be made of this town of Arezzo, which needs it badly.

CXLVI

TO GENERAL MENOU, GOVERNOR OF THE GRAND DUCHY OF TUSCANY.

ARANDA, 28*th November* 1808.

I HAVE just received, from Paris, a proclamation dated 3rd November, and bearing your signature, which means nothing at all. What is the use of threats? It is far better to strike.

Who is going to answer for the town of Sienna, which has no organisation? All these proclamations only delight our enemies, and make them think Tuscany is in flames. Would it not have been far simpler to march with two or three columns, of from 300 to 400 riflemen, to appoint a military commission, to shoot the principal mutineers, to take hostages from the towns which have behaved ill, and to disarm the most disaffected cantons? This would have settled everything. Besides, reports should have been sent to the Ministers of War and of Police, and you tell them nothing.

CXLVII

TO M. DE LAVALLETTE, DIRECTOR-GENERAL OF THE
POSTAL SERVICE.

CHAMARTIN, 6th December 1808.

YOUR work is badly done. You send me nothing but fools, and my express from Bayonne has just been captured, because the Postmaster at Bayonne gave the courier two portmanteaux instead of one, and two bottles of wine as well. The courier has saved the portmanteau with the wine, and has allowed that containing Mons. de Champagny's correspondence to be taken. I have just dismissed the Postmaster. Let all the other Postmasters know of his dismissal. Long ago I gave orders that no express was to carry more than twenty-five pounds weight. The Spanish express must not carry any letters but mine, and no one is to make up the packets but Mons. Méneval. This had been regularly done hitherto. Mons. Méneval has the key, and the letters should only be sent when I think fit; instead of which it frequently happens that, contrary to my intention, other people have news from Paris before me.

CXLVIII

TO M. FOUCHÉ, MINISTER OF POLICE.

MADRID, 7th December 1808.

I HAVE received your letters of 28th and 29th. You do wrong to be alarmed about me. The Spaniards are no more wicked than other nations. The weather here is as fine as the loveliest May weather in France. We have taken every advantage of it; for we have beaten all our enemies, and have established ourselves firmly in Madrid.

Send me a good man to be Chief of Police in Madrid, and another for Lisbon. I do not want chatterboxes, but upright and impartial men, who will not take advantage of circumstances, to steal and disgrace themselves.

CXLIX

TO M. DE CHAMPAGNY, MINISTER FOR FOREIGN AFFAIRS.

MADRID, 10th December 1808.

YOU will receive a Decree by which ten Spaniards are declared enemies of France and Spain, and traitors to the two Crowns. You will have this Decree made known in Holland, and at Naples. All these individuals' property belongs to me, to be applied to the war expenses. It must be confiscated, and sequestrated, everywhere. There will be no difficulty about this in the Kingdom of Italy, but it may cause some in Naples. Speak about it to the Duke of Monteleone. Make him understand that nothing must prevent the carrying out of my intention.

CL.

TO THE PRINCE DE NEUFCHÂTEL, MAJOR-GENERAL OF THE ARMY IN SPAIN.

CHAMARTIN, 15th December 1808.

GIVE orders to have the Count de Noblejas' property sequestrated, and let him be warned that if he does not come back within a month, it will all be confiscated. As for the Dowager Duchess of Ossuna, you will not only have all her property sequestered, but you will have her jewels, plate, etc., seized, and taken to the Treasury. Inform the Governor of Madrid, and Mons. Savary, of this decision.

CLI

TO M. DE CHAMPAGNY, MINISTER FOR FOREIGN AFFAIRS.

MADRID, 16th December 1808.

SEND the subjoined order to all my Ministers to the Princes of the Rhenish Confederation, and inform them that Herr von Stein continues to concoct fanciful plots against the Rhenish Confederation, with the English. You will demand that the Prince of Nassau shall sequester his property. You will inform the Prussian Court, that my Minister will not go to Berlin, unless Stein is sent out of that capital, and out of Prussia. You will go still further: you will demand, by letter to the Prussian Minister, that this person shall be given up as a traitor, and as being employed by the English, to stir up enmity between the two Courts. Speak strongly on the subject to the Prussian Minister in Paris. Write to my consul at Königsberg, to mention the subject to the King, and let it be understood that if my troops lay hands on Stein, he will be put to death.

CLII

TO M. FOUCHÉ, MINISTER OF POLICE.

BENAVENTE, 31st December 1808.

I AM informed that the *émigré* families screen their children from the conscription, and keep them in grievous and guilty idleness. Of course those rich old families who do not belong to the system, are opposed to it. I desire you will make a list of ten of these chief families, for each Department, and of fifty for Paris, showing the age, fortune, and rank of each member. I intend to publish an edict which will send all youths of these families, over sixteen, and under eighteen years of age, to the Military School at St. Cyr. If any objection is made, the only answer you will give is, that such is my good pleasure. The future generation must not be allowed to suffer for the hatreds and petty passions of this present one. If you ask the Prefects for information, make this idea evident.

CLIII

TO COMTE FOUCHÉ, MINISTER OF POLICE.

BENAVENTE, 1st January 1809.

I HAVE your letter of the 17th. The English have abandoned the Spaniards in a shameful and cowardly manner. We are pursuing them hotly. The Spaniards who formed their left are crushed. La Romana had a few thousand men left, whom he has lost. The English, it appears, had sent for 10,000 horses, so as to escape more quickly. Have all this shown up in the newspapers. Have caricatures made, and songs and popular ditties written ; have them translated into German aud Italian, and circulated in Italy and Germany.

CLIV

TO M. BIGOT DE PRÉAMENEU, MINISTER OF PUBLIC WORSHIP.

BENAVENTE, 1st January 1809.

LET the Archbishop of Bordeaux know of my extreme displeasure at the sermon preached by the Abbé Langlade, on the 4th December. Tell him I do not recognise in it, either the Bishops' own feelings, nor those I have a right to expect from the Bordeaux clergy. As to this Langlade, I have ordered the Minister of Police to have him arrested, and I will punish him in such a way as will serve to warn others.

You will also inform the Archbishop of my dissatisfaction with the bad spirit evident in his Pastoral, as to the message by which I called my subjects to the defence of their country. This spirit is particularly evident in the expressions : ' You will not fail, when you make this communication to your parishioners, to urge them, with prudent zeal, to submit themselves to the command of Divine Providence, when it calls upon us to purchase that repose which is the object of all Christian hope, by painful but temporary sacrifices.' The Archbishop of Bordeaux is, doubtless, a worthy man, but he is surrounded by ill-conditioned people, whom he either does not distrust, or cannot restrain. Send them to Paris instantly.

CLV

TO THE COMTE DE CHAMPAGNY, MINISTER FOR FOREIGN AFFAIRS.

VALLADOLID, *7th January* 1809.

I HAVE received your letter, and that of Mons. de Caulaincourt. You can reply, that the two Russian vessels at Toulon will be paid for, the crews paid, and all supplies given. There will be no difficulty of any sort about that.

As regards the Grand Duchess, my intention is that Mons. de Caulaincourt should do what is agreeable to the Emperor. My Ambassador must not, and cannot, yield precedence to the Hereditary Prince of Oldenburg ; but he must yield it, without any difficulty, to the husband of the Emperor of Russia's sister, whenever he is recognised as such. Mons. de Caulaincourt may even notify, that if the Prince and Princess came to Paris, they would be treated the same as in St. Petersburg, that is to say, they would be seated in the Court circle, etc. Yet, to make things correct, the Emperor should give his brother-in-law the title of Imperial Highness. The Emperor of Austria did this for Prince Albert of Saxony, and I have done it for the Grand Duke of Berg. The whole thing becomes quite simple, once the Emperor gives notice, by a letter to his Master of the Ceremonies, that he has bestowed this proof of his regard for his sister, and thenceforward his brother-in-law will be treated as an Imperial Highness, in whatever European Court he may visit, without any difficulty being made.

In the matter regarding Sweden, Russia must be left to do as she pleases. Reply, that I care very little what she takes from Sweden ; that I am ready to make peace ; that I am ready to carry on the war ; that I approve anything Russia may do.

As for Austria, Mons. de Caulaincourt must take the correct tone. Be sure he says, ' I am not afraid of Austria, even during the war with Spain.' Mons. de Caulaincourt must press the Emperor to take measures to close matters at Vienna. He must make him understand, that I have 150,000 men in Italy, without counting my army in Naples; 150,000 men in Germany, without counting the forces of the Rhenish Confederation ; 400,000 men, in fact, ready to march into Austria ; that I am raising 80,000 more, and all that without withdrawing a single battalion from my armies in Spain. Mons. de Caulaincourt should tell the Emperor, in confidence, that my Guard is retracing its steps; that it will soon be back in Paris, and ready to move on Austria, if this state of things does not end.

Immediately then, on the receipt of this letter, you will send off a courier to St. Petersburg. Add that the Duke of Dalmatia is at Lugo, that 2000 of the English rearguard have already been made prisoners, and that part of its artillery and waggons are already in our power.

CLVI

TO THE COMTE DE CHAMPAGNY, MINISTER FOR FOREIGN AFFAIRS.

VALLADOLID, *8th January* 1809.

I HAVE your letter of the 23rd, your two letters of the 24th, and those of 26th and 30th of December. There is no harm in having the story of Andreossy's despatch inserted in the minor newspapers. Put it into the mouth of a Viennese lady. It appears you have not yet received letters from my Chargé d'Affaires at Constantinople, and that business is not yet cleared up.

Inform Mons. Otto, and my various Ministers to the Courts of the Rhenish Confederation, that they are to speak with scorn of the Austrian forces, and with confidence of mine. Tell them I have an army of 160,000 men in Italy, and one of 250,000 men (including the Confederate troops) still remaining in Germany, and on the Rhine. Write also to Mons. Otto, and to my Ministers in Saxony and Vienna, that they are to speak as if I were already back in Paris,— Spanish affairs not being worth my attention, once the English had embarked.

CLVII

TO THE PRINCE DE NEUFCHÂTEL, MAJOR-GENERAL OF THE ARMY IN SPAIN.

VALLADOLID, *9th January* 1809.

INFORM General Belliard of my displeasure at the weakness of his government. Frenchmen are murdered every day,

in Madrid, and he has done nothing as yet. Tell him thirty
of the worst characters in the town must be arrested, and
shot ; that this is what I have done at Valladolid ; and that I
shall hold him responsible for the first murder of a Frenchman that occurs, unless it is instantly followed by the
arrest of a Spaniard. The way things are going on at
Madrid is ridiculous.

CLVIII

TO THE COMTE DE CHAMPAGNY, MINISTER FOR FOREIGN AFFAIRS.

PARIS, 25*th January* 1809.

I RETURN your portfolio. Write to my Minister in
Westphalia, to enter into the fullest details as to the administration of the country ; his letters will not be seen. Let
his despatches speak of the King's conduct, of that of his
Ministers, and of all the operations of the Government, both
for the Emperor's information, and to enable him to direct
the action of the said Government, which will not know
whence his information comes. Desire him to add, apart
from the signed formal reports addressed to yourself, an
unsigned sheet, containing the reports, real or false, going
about the town, and a kind of summary of the news of the
country. You will also desire my Ministers at other Courts
to follow this plan. This system is followed by Mons. de
Caulaincourt, who sends, by every courier, a short report of
society news, and of such rumours as tend to show the feeling
of the moment.

Postscript.—I have read Mons. Reinhard's report of the
15th Jan. [No. 9] with pleasure. I do not approve of his
delicacy, in objecting to write in cipher. Desire him, on the
contrary, never to neglect writing in cipher, and sending
letters to inform us of the actions of the Government. If he
uses cipher every day, this will become quite easy. Besides,
I keep an Ambassador at Cassel for the purpose of knowing
what happens in Westphalia.

CLIX

TO COMTE FOUCHÉ, MINISTER OF POLICE.

PARIS, *27th January* 1809.

You do not keep proper order in Paris, and you leave evil-disposed people free to put about all sorts of rumours. Have an eye on the conversations in the establishment of a certain Citerni, an eating-house keeper, on the Place du Palais de Justice, and at the Café de Foy. Look after the police, and not after foreign affairs, in your Ministry.[1] A Police Minister must be responsible for rumours which are circulated to lead the people astray. If you were to pay a little more attention to this branch of the public administration, you would discover the threads of the intrigues of the agents, who are at the bottom of this malevolent system in Paris.[2]

Make me a report, showing in what portions of the town most foolish talk goes on, and take measures to put a stop to it. It is your business to keep me informed of everything that is done and said in Paris, and I only hear it from other people.

Postscript.—The neighbourhood of the Hôtel de Ville is full of people who sow foolish rumours. Why have you not men there to deny them, and point out their absurdity? This method should go hand in hand with the arrest of the disseminators.

CLX

TO THE COMTE DE CHAMPAGNY, MINISTER FOR FOREIGN AFFAIRS.

PARIS, *8th February* 1809.

I DESIRE you will give me the draft of a circular to the various Kings of the Rhenish Confederation, and to the Prince Primate. I desire it may be drawn up in the following sense. The States of the Rhenish Confederation have no peace; they are perpetually disturbed by the richest

---

[1] The last phrase of this sentence is cancelled on the Minute by the Emperor's hand.

[2] All that follows, except the postscript, was struck out on the rough draft.

proprietors, who serve Austria, a country which may be looked upon as being secretly on the offensive against, and hostile to, the Confederation. Independently of the secret anxiety which the influence of these individuals causes the States of the Confederation, their residence at Vienna is a source of prosperity to that country, because the better part of the revenue of the Confederation is spent in the capital; and the interest of these persons being opposed to that of the Confederation, they foment and excite a spirit hostile to us, in Vienna. The Act of Confederation is clearly drawn; the interests of the Confederated States, and of France, are equally clear. I should desire the Princes of the Confederation to publish an order, obliging all persons holding property in their country, who are in the service of any other Power, except those of the Rhenish Confederation, to quit the service of such Power, and to return to their own country, within three months. If, within thirty days of the publication of this order, they have not given notice of their intention to return, their property will be sequestered, and if they do not return within three months, their property will be confiscated to the State. By this means, Austria will be deprived of a great number of officers and officials; the Fürstenbergs, and others of the richest Austrian families, will be forced to remain in the States of the Confederation, and thus to weaken Austria, its natural enemy.

CLXI

TO JEROME NAPOLEON, KING OF WESTPHALIA.

PARIS, 11th February 1809.

I AM astonished at your sending me General Morio, a sort of madman, whom I despise; you will permit me to refuse to receive him.

As for the condition of your Treasury and of your Administration, I have nothing to do with either of them. I am aware that both are in a very bad way. This is a consequence of the measures you have taken, and the luxury in which you live. All your actions bear the stamp of folly. Why should you confer baronies on men who have done nothing? Why display a luxury so out of harmony with the country, and which, were it only for the discredit it casts upon your administration, would be a calamity to West-phalia?

Keep your engagements with me, and recollect that no man ever took such engagements without fulfilling them. And further, never question the great interest I take in you.

CLXII

TO THE COMTE DE CHAMPAGNY, MINISTER FOR FOREIGN AFFAIRS.

PARIS, 23rd *February* 1809.

LET M. Otto know that I will allow him a sum of 10,000 francs a month, for espionage ; that I desire he will organise a spy system at Munich, headed by reliable and intelligent men ; and that, to avoid giving umbrage, he will give the King full knowledge of it. The duty of these spies will be to watch all Austrian movements in Styria and Carinthia, and the roads to Vienna and Prague. It would be well that this spy service should consist, as far at all events as the chiefs are concerned, of men who could be attached to the Military Staff, in case of necessity. You will remit the 10,000 francs a month to M. Otto, according as he spends the money. He must set up this spy system on a large scale, so as to be thoroughly informed as to the Austrian movements. You will place 5000 francs a month at the disposal of M. Bourgoing, for the same purpose, so as to have information of what happens at Warsaw, and on the distant frontiers of Austria and Bohemia. Let MM. Bour-going and Serra understand, that they must arrange this spy system so as to have men who will keep them thoroughly informed of what is done in Bohemia, and Warsaw. Their reports will be sent in direct to you.

CLXIII

TO THE COMTE DE CHAMPAGNY, MINISTER FOR FOREIGN AFFAIRS.

PARIS, 23rd *February* 1809.

BEFORE the Note about obliging the nobility to take service within the Confederation is presented, I desire a requisition may be sent to the Houses of Saxe-Coburg,

Lippe, and other minor Princes, to the effect that all relatives of those reigning houses must leave the Austrian service. Send me the rough draft of this Note by M. Bacher, to-morrow.

CLXIV

TO M. BIGOT DE PRÉAMENEU, MINISTER OF PUBLIC WORSHIP.

PARIS, 3rd *March* 1809.

LET me know why the Archbishop of Aix has ordered a Novena because of the illness of Queen Louise,[1] and why the clergy ask the people's prayers for any person, without leave from the Government.

CLXV

TO GENERAL CLARKE, COMTE D'HUNEBURG, MINISTER OF WAR.

PARIS, 6th *March* 1809.

TWELVE thousand prisoners have arrived from Saragossa. They are dying at the rate of 300 to 400 a day : thus we may calculate that not more than 6000 will reach France. My intention is, that the officers shall be separated, and sent towards the North. As for the rank and file, you will send 4000 of them to Niort, where they will be employed in draining the neighbouring marshes. They will be distributed in the following manner :—1000 men at Niort, 1000 at Saintes, 1000 at La Rochelle, and 1000 at Rochefort. The prisoners will be under the orders of General Dufour, who will have them guarded by the Brigade he is now collecting. The fifth thousand will be sent into Dauphiné, where it will be employed on the drainage works ordered in that country. And the sixth thousand will be sent to the Cotentin, to work at draining the marshes. You will order a system of severity —these people are to be made to work, whether they like it or not. The greater number of them are fanatics, who deserve no consideration whatever. Begin by giving orders, in the course of the day, to the Duc de Valmy and General Dufour, and then go on to make arrangements with the Minister of the Interior.

[1] Ex-Queen of Spain, then in Provence.

CLXVI

TO COMTE FOUCHÉ, MINISTER OF POLICE.

RAMBOUILLET, *14th March* 1809.

PALAFOX, his wife and mother, should have reached, or be just reaching, Bayonne.   Palafox will be taken as a criminal to Vincennes, and kept there in secret confinement, so that no one may know where he is.   His wife and mother will be sent to the Castle of Ham, as hostages for a number of Frenchmen, who are in the hands of the insurgents.

You will have the Prince of Castelfranco removed from Fenestrelle to Naples, where he will be put in the Castle of Gaeta, and placed at the disposal of the King of Naples.

Arrest the Vicar of Noyon, who has ventured to make improper allusions to the conscription, in one of his sermons. You will have him brought to Paris, and examined by one of the Councillors of State.   You will make a report of the inquiry to me.

CLXVII

TO JEROME NAPOLEON, KING OF WESTPHALIA.

RAMBOUILLET, *15th March* 1809.

I HAVE your letter of the 7th.   I could not read it without astonishment.   Nobody is talking about you in France.   I am not aware of what Madame may have caused to be written to you.   You think your extravagant living displeases me, and in that you are not mistaken.   But, as you mention your extravagance, and thus give me an opportunity of telling you what I think of it, I will not conceal from you, that I consider it impolitic, and ruinous to your dominions.

I do not know that you owe me anything, unless it be your debt to the Sinking Fund.   That I thought you had paid, for it was lent for a term only.   You must be scrupulously exact, and you would do better to keep your engagements than to bestow presents.   A certain Morio came here.   I did not see him.   He did you harm by his indiscreet conversation.[1]

---

[1] Here come several illegible lines.   The draft is very badly written.

Do not indulge in foolish expenditure. You tell me you implore [my indulgence]. I can only judge you by your actions. Pray reform your expenses, so as to make a considerable economy on your civil list. The King of Prussia, even at the time of his greatest prosperity, never spent more than 3,000,000. The Household at Vienna, too, is not kept up on half the scale of yours. Mistaken ideas of grandeur, and a very thoughtless generosity, have led you to bestow a Barony on Morio.[1] . . . This being so, I may very well think that you care little to please me, and that, as you take so little notice of my advice, I had better not give you any more of it.

I have begged you to let me have an exact statement of your troops, so that I may calculate accordingly.

I am sorry to hear you are not well ; go to bed early, and live by some rule.

CLXVIII

TO COMTE FOUCHÉ, MINISTER OF POLICE.

PARIS, 23rd March 1809.

ALL couriers belonging to Monsieur Metternich and his Court, whether coming from Austria, or starting from Paris for Vienna, are to be stopped. They are to be seized half-way between this and Strasburg. The despatches will be brought to you, and a report will be drawn up by the agent you send for the purpose. The report will run as follows :—
' In consequence of the violation of the Law of Nations, exercised on a French officer, carrying despatches for the Minister of France—which despatches were taken from him at Braunau, by main force, and in spite of his protests, and of the fact that the arms of France appeared on the packet —all despatches coming from the Austrian Government, or its agents, will be seized and held, until the before-mentioned despatches are restored.' The persons employed on this duty will work quietly, so that the arrests may be kept secret as long as possible, and the greatest possible number of despatches seized.

[1] Here an illegible line.

CLXIX

TO COMTE FOUCHÉ, MINISTER OF POLICE.

PARIS, 24*th March* 1809.

WHY does the *Journal des Débats* publish proclamations by Prince Charles, which do not appear in the *Moniteur*? That Monsieur Etienne must be a great fool! On what does he found the observations he makes, which are utterly ridiculous, and which may cause displeasure in Russia?

CLXX

TO GENERAL CLARKE, COUNT D'HUNEBURG, MINISTER OF WAR.

PARIS, 27*th March* 1809.

THERE is a *Courier d'Espagne*, published in French, by a set of intriguers, which appears at Madrid, and which cannot fail to do great harm. Write to Marshal Jourdan that there is to be no French newspaper in Spain, and that this one is to be suppressed. I do not intend to allow any French newspaper wherever my troops are, except such as are published by my order. Besides, do not the French receive Gazettes from France? and as for the Spaniards, they must be spoken to in their own language. Your letter on this subject must be a positive order.

CLXXI

TO COMTE FOUCHÉ, MINISTER OF POLICE.

PARIS, 27*th March* 1809.

QUEEN MARIE LOUISE[1] is to leave Compiègne on the 4th of April, and go to Italy. It is my intention that she shall be allowed to go as far as Lyons, and that when she has reached that town, she shall take the road to Nice. You had better have one or two boats ready to take her and her carriages on board, and convey her by water to Avignon, whence she will go overland to Nice. She must not make any stay at Lyons, and the baggage-carts which she has sent on beforehand, will be despatched from Lyons to Nice by road. At Lyons the Queen will receive a letter from the Grand

[1] Queen of Etruria.

Marshal of my Palace, informing her that I wish her to go to the South, and that she can inhabit whatever town she prefers on the Genoese Riviera, between Nice and Savona. She may settle at Mentone, or San Remo; she may even spend a few months at Nice, but she must be dissuaded from the idea of settling there permanently. You will give orders that she is to be well treated in all these towns. The Queen must dismiss all the Tuscans she has with her. It would be well to attach some retired officer, about forty years of age, with the rank of *Chef de Bataillon*, or Captain, to her suite. This officer would remain in attendance on her, would look after her business, and draw her income for her.

CLXXII

TO COMTE FOUCHÉ, MINISTER OF POLICE.

PARIS, 27th *March* 1809.

I DESIRE you will write to Mons. d'Arberg, at Valençay, that he is to send away all the Spaniards attached to the Princes' suite, and let them go back into Spain, because the Spanish Government proposes to confiscate their property if they do not return. They must carry out this order forty-eight hours after they receive it. Mons. d'Arberg may except the relations of Canon Escoïquiz, and some ten of the Princes' servants; in fact, he must be left some latitude in this respect. He will send the Spaniards to Auch, where they will receive fresh orders from you.

Postscript.—Canon Escoïquiz might be left with the Prince, and San Carlos might be sent to Liége, or Brussels, under surveillance; but before this is done, the Spaniards must have been got rid of.

CLXXIII

TO COMTE FOUCHÉ, MINISTER OF POLICE.

PARIS, 3rd *April* 1809.

THERE is a work on Suwaroff, many of the notes to which are very objectionable. This book is said to have been written by an Abbé. You must put the seals on that Abbé's papers, you must have all the notes cancelled, and you must even stop the publication of the work, which is anti-national.

CLXXIV

TO JEROME NAPOLEON, KING OF WESTPHALIA.

BURGHAUSEN, *29th April* 1809.

I HAVE your letter of the 22nd ; Mons. Otto sends me one dated the 23rd. I approve of your having kept the Berg regiment. I had sent it orders to come, but you can keep it, if you need it. You can send for the division which is at Hamburg, although it consists of Dutch troops. I am giving Kellermann orders to proceed to Mayence, where he may be in a position to give you such help as circumstances, and his means, will permit.

Your Kingdom has no police, no finances, and no organisation. It is not with foolish display that the foundations of monarchies are laid. What is happening to you now[1] I fully expected. I hope it will teach you a lesson. Give yourself ways and habits suited to those of the country you govern. Thus you will win over the inhabitants, by gaining their esteem, which is always governed by their opinion of your manner of life, and by simplicity of demeanour. However, I feel this is not the moment to preach to you. Make severe examples.

CLXXV

TO FREDERICK, KING OF WURTEMBERG.

BRAUNAU, *1st May* 1809.

I HAVE received your Majesty's letter of 28th April. The Princes of Hohenlöhe, of Stadion, etc., must be judged more by the political, than by the civil code. They are Princes who have ceased to be Princes, and their rights and pretensions give umbrage to the sovereign power. In former times their property would have been confiscated. The Act of Confederation has treated them favourably, but it has imposed certain obligations on them. The first of these is obedience to their Sovereign.

I think, therefore, that your Majesty, without entering into

---

[1] A revolt in the Westphalian Army.

civil formalities, should dispossess the Hohenlöhe, etc., if they have misconducted themselves ; should sequester their persons, and confiscate their property—while allowing them an income which shall save them from poverty. No consideration is due to men who have made use of the facilities their fortune gave them, to stir up disorder. The only way to deprive them of their influence, is to strip them of their property. A decree will shortly be communicated to your Majesty, the object of which is to sequester, for high state reasons, all Princes and Counts, who have not conformed to the Act of Confederation. In France, Frenchmen who bear arms against me are only amenable to the criminal code, but in my opinion it is more in the nature of things that all former or unmediatised Princes should be judged according to the political law.

CLXXVI

TO THE COMTE DE CHAMPAGNY, MINISTER FOR FOREIGN AFFAIRS.

SCHÖNBRUNN, 14th May 1809.

YOU will receive my Decree ordering the sequestration and confiscation of all property in the States of the Rhenish Confederation, belonging to those former Princes and Counts of the Empire, who have not conformed to the conditions of Articles 7 and 31 of the Act of Confederation, and especially of those who have remained in the Austrian service. I include the families of Stadion, Metternich, Lichtenstein, Zinzendorf, Fürstenberg, etc., in this measure, which should, therefore, bring in considerable sums.

All my Ministers must be commissioned to seek out the individuals to whom, and properties to which, this measure is applicable. They must have an understanding with the Commissaries to be appointed by the Princes of the Confederation ; they must look after my interests, and, above all, they must correspond fully with you upon this subject. Give some one in your office orders to give special attention to this business.

CLXXVII

TO GENERAL CLARKE, COMTE D'HUNEBURG, MINISTER OF WAR.

EBERSDORF, 19*th May* 1809.

I SEE by your letter of the 13th, that there is alarm in Paris. People had much better sleep quietly in their beds, go to parties, to the opera, and to the Bois de Boulogne, etc. General Blücher has not stirred. Prussia has very little thought of going to war with me. The Russians are marching against the Austrians. Marshal Davout is at Vienna, and the Prince of Ponte-Corvo is at Lintz. People have not much sense in Paris,—but at the same time the Government must not take measures which cause alarm. You need not mention this comical Prussian war to Fouché, nor to Cambacérès, nor need you let things be seen, which a real artist would hide. You pull the puppet-strings openly, when you send wretched companies of conscripts by the public stage.[1]

If the Minister of Police thinks it necessary to send troops to Beaupréau you can get a battalion of 500 men from the corps under General Dufour's command, drawing them from Rochefort, La Rochelle, or the Isle of Aix. The Commune which has allowed a gendarme to be murdered must receive exemplary punishment.

CLXXVIII

TO PRINCE CAMBACÉRÈS, GRAND CHANCELLOR OF THE EMPIRE.

EBERSDORF, 20*th May* 1809.

I LOOK with contempt on the inconsistency of Paris opinion, with its perpetual terrors, and the results brought about by idle talk and spite. I am sorry both for the people of Paris, and for you, who are living there. Those must be fools indeed who believe in this nonsense, and blindly accept the belief that Prussia is declaring war against us. It is true, indeed, that the Minister of War has done all he can to alarm the public, and has thus given rise to reports which have neither rhyme nor reason.

[1] This had been done on the receipt of news of an invasion of Westphalia, by Schill's men.

CLXXIX

TO COMTE FOUCHÉ, MINISTER OF POLICE.

EBERSDORF, 20*th May* 1809.

YOUR police reports are nothing but reports about England, and foreign affairs; they have no reference to what happens within the borders of France. The Minister of War has informed me of an event which has taken place in the Department of the Loire-Inférieure—the murder of a gendarme at Chaudron, by a band of ruffians, who, after having dragged the soldier about for six hours, put nine bullets through him. I send you the Minister's report. If the fact is a true one, get out a warrant against the Mayor, and the ten chief inhabitants, and have them brought to Paris. Make arrangements with the Minister of War to have a battalion sent to Beaupréau, if that is thought necessary; it can be drawn from the troops at Rochefort.

I request you will leave politics alone, and give me frequent intelligence of everything touching the internal affairs of the Departments. I should have heard the incident I have just quoted from yourself, before I learnt it from any other Minister. It is to such facts as these that I attach importance, and not to blundering nonsense concerning Russia and Prussia, with regard to which you can know nothing at all.

CLXXX

TO COMTE FOUCHÉ, MINISTER OF POLICE.

SCHÖNBRUNN, 14*th June* 1809.

I HAVE received a mischievous rigmarole from that scoundrel Palafox. I am vexed that you should have accepted it, had it translated, and thus made known the fact of his being at Vincennes, which should have been concealed. The villain is stained with the blood of over 4000 Frenchmen, whom he was barbarous enough to have murdered at Saragossa. Let him stay at Vincennes, forgotten, without pens or paper, or any means of attracting the sympathy of the bitter enemies of France.

You have not carried out my intentions; you ought to have ignored the fact of his being at Vincennes. I repeat my intention that he shall live there, cut off from the world, without any means of writing or making himself known. It was on this condition only, that I consented to pass over his crimes, and not to summon him before a military court.

You should not have allowed Mdlle von Stein to come to Paris. Write to Westphalia, that no one is to be sent to France without your authority. This is rather giddy behaviour of hers! In any case, she must be shut up in some establishment for ladies, in Paris, and you must find out what the charges against her are.

CLXXXI

TO JOACHIM NAPOLEON, KING OF NAPLES.

SCHÖNBRUNN, 20th June 1809.

I HAVE this instant received news that the Pope has excommunicated us all. This is an excommunication which will fall upon his own head. No more consideration must be shown. He is a dangerous madman, and must be shut up. Have Cardinal Pacca, and the Pope's other adherents, arrested.

CLXXXII

TO COMTE FOUCHÉ, MINISTER OF POLICE.

SCHÖNBRUNN, 20th June 1809.

THE Grand Duchess did wrong to prevent the execution of the measures I ordered. I do not wish Madame d'Albany to live in Florence; I intend her to remain at Parma.

If you have reason to think the complaints of Escoïquiz well founded, you must begin by removing him from about the Princes, and then you must have him arrested, and sent to Vincennes.

CLXXXIII

TO GENERAL ANDRÉOSSY, GOVERNOR OF VIENNA.

SCHÖNBRUNN, 25th June 1809.

THE town of Vienna is not kept in good order. The popular insolence is the outcome of a neglect of measures of repression, directed against the excesses committed during the last month. These excesses are of such a nature, that not one of them should have received less punishment than the death of several persons. If some examples had been made, the populace would have settled down to its duty more and more every day. The culpable negligence which has reigned, has ended by making the people insolent. This is the first occasion on which I have seen my power set at nought. I have been left in ignorance of these facts, and none of them have been followed up. All the organisation of Vienna yet remains to be done, and everything is still in the hands of the burghers, and of our enemies. The French are annoyed and criticised by the conquered party. This order of things must be promptly changed.

Every day an absurd and frivolous report is submitted, relating obscure incidents, which cannot be of any importance to me. Even in Paris, such matters are never brought to my knowledge. They do not get beyond the local authorities.

But the political report on the popular misconduct as regards the French is not sent to me. It is my intention that you shall submit to me, every day, a report from the Commandants of the various Quarters of the town, of the important incidents of each day, and the measures taken to maintain order, to discover culprits, and avenge affronts put upon Frenchmen.

You must first of all make sure that the Commandants of the different Quarters can talk German ; that is an important point. To each of these Commandants you will attach an officer from the Nassau Regiment, with two non-commissioned officers, and fifteen men, who will form his guard. He will make use of these Germans to procure full information of everything that occurs. Every Police Commissary will recognise the Commandant of his Quarter ; will report everything to him ; and will take every means to carry out his orders.

Each Commandant will also have an officer of the City Guard, and eight intelligent men, drawn from that Guard, whom he will employ to keep order amongst the populace, and to summon the military guard when necessary.

Every Viennese arrested by the City Guard, for any ordinary police matter, will be brought before the Police Commissary.

I

Any Frenchman arrested for quarrelling with the Viennese, and any Viennese arrested by a French patrol, will be brought up before the Commandant of the Quarter, without any interference from the local authorities.

If the Commandants of Quarters are not sufficiently numerous, their numbers must be increased. Everything connected with the order and the surveillance of the city must depend on them.

No German prisoner of war is to set foot in Vienna, on any pretext whatsoever. The prison dépôt will be at Schön-brunn. This order has already been given several times, but it is not enforced, because the commanding officers of military posts, who trangress them, are not punished.

I do not intend the National Guard to exceed 5000 or 6000 men in number. It will not have more than 1500 muskets, and all other muskets, guns, etc., will be taken for the use of my army. You will report to me on the manner in which this disarmament should be carried out, and I will give you the authority to do it to-morrow, 26th. You will forthwith publish an order, enjoining all persons who have cannon balls, or cannon, to give them up. Have this order preceded by the sentence of death pronounced on the person who was found in possession of three cannon.

You will take measures for the paying of domiciliary visits, and for discovering those persons who may still hold arms. You will encourage informers, by desiring the Commandants of Quarters to reward persons who help them to discover arms.

You will order all Englishmen, foreigners, and vagrants of any kind, to be arrested.

Have a list drawn up of the principal rich landowners, or of their men of business, and order them to send for wheat, of which they have a great quantity at their country places ; —such as Prince Albert, who has corn land a few leagues from Vienna, and Prince Esterhazy. You will also oblige the Superiors of convents to bring in corn ; I am certain there are secret stores within the town. Watch all this most carefully, and have any corn you find in Vienna, or its neigh-bourhood, seized. Have it put into store, and make the Communes responsible for it.

The government of Vienna needs firmness and energy. To give you an example of the ignorance in which I am left, I have had no report of the capture of a vehicle, loaded with muskets, which gave rise to an important incident. The French patrols are insulted daily. As yet I have no report on that subject. I send you a report which I asked for, relative to this business of the muskets. It is of importance that this should be followed up, and that you should find out whence the arms come, where they were brought in, and whither they were being sent.

CLXXXIV

TO COMTE FOUCHÉ, MINISTER OF POLICE.

SCHÖNBRUNN, 30th June 1809.

I SEND you a letter from the Duke of Dalmatia, and the inquiry of a Lieutenant of Gendarmerie into a strange and altogether extraordinary event. A certain Argenton, an adjutant-major in the 18th Dragoon regiment in Spain, who has served with us, who fought through the Egyptian campaign, whom I do not know personally, but who had the reputation of being a faithful and reliable man, has, how I know not, been led away by the English. You will see, by several letters taken from him, and which I send you, that his wife's relations live at Tours. You will collect information as to his family. Colonel Lafitte, who is mixed up in this business, is one of the most faithful of soldiers, a man whom every one is ready to answer for. The whole business is a very strange one.[1]

CLXXXV

TO THE PRINCE DE NEUFCHÂTEL, MAJOR-GENERAL OF THE ARMY IN GERMANY.

ÎLE NAPOLÉON, 3rd July 1809.

WRITE General Laroche, that as soon as he can get back to Nuremberg, he must arrest six ringleaders of the insurrection, and have them hanged in the public square. Amongst them, one Reuter, a tinsmith, and Birkner, a vagrant.

[1] In connection with this business, see the *Moniteur* of 14th January 1810.

CLXXXVI

TO COMTE FOUCHÉ, MINISTER OF POLICE.

SCHÖNBRUNN, 14*th July* 1809.

I DESIRE you will see that whenever anything is put on columns, monuments, or elsewhere, relative to the battle of Austerlitz, the word ' Austerlitz ' itself shall never be used. This word causes the Emperor Alexander a great deal of pain and injury.

You will receive a Decree, by which I appoint a Commissary-General of Police at Wesel. Take care he is a Frenchman, and an intelligent and reliable man.

I send you a letter, the subject of which is important. If this Dessort really is that wretch Argenton, whose documents I sent you, let him be brought to Paris, with irons on his feet and hands. This business is worthy of all your anxiety. I conclude all his papers have been seized. It is inconceivable that he should have dared to come to Paris.

CLXXXVII

TO COMTE GAUDIN, MINISTER OF FINANCE.

SCHÖNBRUNN, 15*th July* 1809.

ORDER General Miollis to have Cardinal Pacca, and all the Pope's so-called temporal Ministers arrested, and send them to France. I approve of your dividing the Roman State into two Departments, that of the Tiber, and that of the Trasimenus.

CLXXXVIII

TO COMTE FOUCHÉ, MINISTER OF POLICE.

SCHÖNBRUNN, 16*th July* 1809.

I HAVE your letter of 10th July. Make a severe example of those who show the worst spirit. If you do not see the hand of the foreigner in this, you are quite mistaken. There is no doubt that the English have a regular organisation all over Europe. Nothing happens by chance, and when the same news is bandied about simultaneously in Paris, in the depths of Italy, in Holland, and in Germany, it is evidently the result of some system. The Police in Paris ought to be more firm, and more severe. That is what I should wish to see, and what I do not see.

CLXXXIX

TO COMTE FOUCHÉ, MINISTER OF POLICE.

Schönbrunn, 17th July 1809.

I HAVE your letter of 11th July. Keep that wretch Argenton safely, in secret confinement ; he is a traitor, sold to our enemies, and deserves exemplary punishment. I think you will do well to issue a warrant of arrest, in Spain, against Colonel Lafitte and his brother. They are men whom I know to be upright, but yet Argenton could not have absented himself without their knowledge. Let both of them appear at your office.

CXC

TO JEROME NAPOLEON, KING OF WESTPHALIA.

Schönbrunn, 17th July 1809.

I HAVE seen an Order of the Day of yours, which makes you the laughing-stock of Germany, Austria, and France. Have you not a single friend about you, to tell you a few truths? You are a King, and brother to an Emperor— absurd qualifications in war-time. You should be a soldier, and once more a soldier, and then again a soldier! You should have neither Minister, nor Diplomatic Body, nor display. You should bivouac with your advance-guard, be on horseback day and night, march with your advance-guard, so as to secure information. Otherwise you had better stop at home in your seraglio.

You make war like a satrap. Did you learn that from me? Good God!—from me, who, with my army of 200,000 men, lead my own skirmishers, without allowing even Champagny to follow me, leaving him at Munich or Vienna?

What has happened? That everybody is dissatisfied with you! That Kienmayer, with his 12,000 men, has made game of you and your absurd pretensions, has concealed his movements from you, and has fallen upon Junot! This would not have happened if you had been with your advance-guard, and had directed the movements of your army from that position. Then you would have been aware of his movements, and you would have pursued him, either by going into Bohemia, or by following in his rear. You have a great deal of pretension, a certain amount of wit, a few good qualities—all ruined by your conceit. You are extremely presumptuous, and you have no knowledge whatever. If the armistice had not been concluded at this juncture, Kienmayer would have attacked you, after having driven Junot out of the running.

Cease making yourself ridiculous; send the Diplomatic Body back to Cassel. Have no baggage and no retinue. Keep one table only—your own. Make war like a young soldier, who longs for fame and glory, and try to be worthy of the rank you have gained, and of the esteem of France and of Europe, whose eyes are upon you. And have sense enough, by God, to write and speak after a proper fashion!

CXCI

TO COMTE RÉGNIER, CHIEF JUDGE AND MINISTER OF JUSTICE.

SCHÖNBRUNN, 18th July 1809.

I HAVE your letter of 11th July, which informs me of the judgment passed by my Criminal Court of the Seine, on Mons. Victor-Mériadec de Rohan, accused of having borne arms against France since 1804. I desire you will have the same thing done with regard to MM. Chasteler and d'Argenteau, who have had no French domicile for the last ten years, and against a great number of Generals in the Austrian service, whom the police will report to you, and who must be got rid of once for all. These men are still bearing arms against us.

CXCII

TO COMTE FOUCHÉ, MINISTER OF POLICE.

SCHÖNBRUNN, 20th July 1809.

I HAVE received Argenton's examination; I conclude you keep the man in secret confinement, and that you have

taken every precaution to prevent his escape. What he says
of Generals Laborde and Loison is nonsense, but what he
says of Colonel Donnadieu astonishes me. Issue a warrant
to bring up Donnadieu and Lafitte. There is something
extraordinary about all this, which is worth clearing up.
Not that I believe the Generals to be implicated, but there
must be a plot by some evil-disposed persons.

CXCIII

TO COMTE FOUCHÉ, MINISTER OF POLICE.

SCHÖNBRUNN, 24th July 1809.

THE newspapers are extremely badly edited. In the copy
of the *Gazette de France*, which I now send you, you will
see the public is given to understand that Prussia is anxious
to declare war against us, and that Russia is opposed to us.
Let the editor of the *Gazette* understand that I shall suppress it if he goes on printing such articles, and that I
have actually been upon the very point of signing the necessary order. You will also give positive orders that no
Gazette is to make any mention of the Pope. Who is the
editor of the *Gazette de France*? On what data does he
write such letters from Berlin? Pray, direct the newspapers
better. Why do they refer with emphasis to a pretended
Revolution at Bologna, in Italy? The Italian journals may
refer to that—it is their business, but the French newspapers
are not devoid of weight in Europe. The *Journal des Débats*
might very well have refrained from ascribing importance
to that incident. Generally speaking, our newspapers are
always ready to seize on anything likely to disturb public
tranquillity, and give a false idea of our position.

CXCIV

TO JEROME NAPOLEON, KING OF WESTPHALIA.

SCHÖNBRUNN, 25th July 1809.

I HAVE your letter of the 20th. The letter you have
received from me since that of the 14th will have informed
you of my position and intentions. I consider that you
have thoroughly misconducted yourself during this cam-

paign. It was no thanks to you that Junot was not well thrashed, and that Kienmayer did not advance against me with his 25,000 men; seeing that, except for the Armistice of Znaïm, I should have pursued Prince Charles to Prague.

You have ordered a warship; you have abandoned the sea, and left your Admiral without orders. You have put forward all sorts of suppositions, which have not taken in either myself, or my Minister; but one ship is a small matter, and I was overwilling to overlook that incident. I see you continue to carry on the same system : you think other people are deceived, but you take in nobody. During the whole of this campaign you have constantly been just where the enemy was not. You say the Duke of Abrantès' retreat on the Danube forced you to take up a position at Schleitz, and to cease acting on the offensive. The Duke of Abrantès' retreat was brought about by your absurd manœuvres. If you had moved to your right, as I ordered you, to join the Duke of Abrantès, if, after having driven the enemy out of Bayreuth, you had marched on Dresden, this would not have happened. If, instead of remaining three or four days in the same place, instead of being slower and more irresolute than the Austrians themselves, you had marched with the alertness and eagerness befitting your age, the enemy would not have masked his movements, and concealed them from you. This, as to your first observation ; and now, as to the second. You were at Schleitz when you received the news of my great victories, and you add that, from that time, you had no reason to fear the enemy would attack you. But you should have feared it might attack Junot; you should have feared its falling on me ; and are 25,000 men, more or less, a matter of so small importance in a battle? You should have feared the re-occupation of Dresden by that corps. Instead of all that, you break up your own, you content yourself with declaring that Kienmayer's Corps is dissolved, and finally you run away in shameful fashion, and bring disgrace on my arms, and on your young reputation.

As for the English, your cunning march on the Baltic cannot take in any one but fools. You knew very well that the English had not landed, and if they really had disembarked, what else ought you to have done, except join the Duke of Abrantès and the Saxons, and not dissolve your own corps? 3000 Saxons, 10,000 men of your own, and 7000 or 8000 belonging to the Duke of Abrantès, would have put you in a position to drive back the English; you could not do anything alone; a single victory does not decide a war. According to my calculation, I should have found you at Dresden, and following the enemy into Bohemia.[1] Your march on the Baltic was intended to conceal your return to Cassel, and your shameful desertion of Saxony.

Besides, your letters, like your Cassel *Moniteur*, are full of false suppositions. You say you retired from Schleitz because the enemy had retired into Bohemia. But no; the enemy had remained at Plauen. You should have stayed at Schleitz, have kept the Saxons with you, and have effected a junction with the Duke of Abrantès. You suppose the enemy not to have re-entered Dresden, but you know it did re-enter it, on the 14th, as soon as it became aware of your ridiculous man-œuvres. I am sorry, for your sake, that you give so little proof of talent, or even of good sense, in military matters. It is a far cry from the profession of a soldier to that of a courtier.[2] I was hardly as old as you when I had conquered all Italy, and beaten Austrian armies three times as numerous as mine. But I had no flatterers, and no Diplomatic Body in my train! I made war like a soldier, and there is no other way of making it. I did not set myself up as the Emperor's brother, nor as a King. I did everything that needed doing, to beat the enemy.

You are withdrawing the 22nd from the Oder fortresses. You do wrong, unless you replace this regiment, as I have ordered, by the 1200 French troops you have at Cassel. Mons. Reubell has ventured to give orders, and counter orders, to detachments, such as sappers, miners, etc., sent by me to the army. If this goes on I will have him arrested in the middle of your camp, and I will have him tried by a Military Court for violating my orders, and disturbing my arrangements.

As regards the future, I do not desire to disgrace you by relieving you of your command; but, nevertheless, I do not intend to risk the glory of my arms, for the sake of any foolish family considerations. One war-ship more or less

---

[1] After this word the following sentence in the rough draft is struck out, by Napoleon's own hand: ' Your tactics do not deceive me; you are too young for that.'

[2] The word ' courtier ' replaces ' satrap,' which has been struck out.

was a trifling matter, but 20,000 men more or less, well handled, may change the fate of Europe. If, therefore, you intend to continue as you have begun, surrounded by men who have never made war, such as d'Albignac, Reubell, and Fürstenstein, without a single good adviser, following your own fancy and not carrying out my orders, you may stop in your seraglio. Be assured that, as a soldier, I have no brother, and that you cannot hide the real motives of your conduct from me, under frivolous and absurd pretexts. I should be glad, so as to save you from the danger of such results, to see you make over the command of your troops to the Duke of Abrantès. You are a spoilt young fellow, although you are full of fine natural qualities. I very much fear it is hopeless to expect anything of you.

If you continue in command of your troops, you are to proceed at once to Dresden. I will send you a Chief of the Staff possessed of common sense. Mass the Saxon and Dutch troops, those of the Grand Duchy of Berg, and all those under your orders, at Dresden. Have the fortress re-armed, and put in a thorough state of defence. The Saxons will reorganise there. Withdraw the 22nd Regiment from the Oder fortresses ; but have it replaced by the 1200 French conscripts you have at Cassel. Let the Duke of Abrantès occupy Bayreuth. Let the Staff have news of you once every day. Do away with your Court and your retinue, and make war as befits a man of my name, who thirsts for glory, more than for any other thing. If hostilities are reopened, Bohemia will be the seat of war, and you will have to play an active part. If the war should not proceed, the presence of a considerable body of troops at Dresden and Bayreuth may facilitate negotiations.

As for the English, you are better placed for marching against them at Dresden, than anywhere else. Their landing cannot be prevented, but I find it difficult to believe that they will come and set themselves between Denmark and the Confederation. They have quite enough to do in Portugal. Besides, they must disembark, before we can know what we should do. The King of Holland's letter is meaningless, and I do not believe a word of it. I receive similar news from my coasts every day. Their having landed 200 men rather leads me to suppose that they do not intend to land in force, for it would be a mistake to show they intended to disembark at any particular point. If I were to pay attention to such signs as these, my troops would always be marching and countermarching, and would have to proceed to every point on the ocean, the Mediterranean, and the Adriatic. The man who could not read, and weigh the value of, reports, and took every molehill for a mountain, would have very little common sense.

CXCV

TO COMTE FOUCHÉ, MINISTER OF POLICE.

SCHÖNBRUNN, *26th July* 1809.

I SEND you a copy of the *Gazette de France*, in which you will find another article about Berlin. Give orders, on receiving this letter, to have the editor arrested and put in prison, for having caused several articles from Berlin to be inserted in his newspaper, the object of which is to cast doubt on the alliance of France with Russia, and to offend our allies. You will keep the editor in prison for a month, and you will appoint somebody else in his place. You will let me know whence these articles originate. Generally speaking, the newspapers are horribly badly managed. For the last two months, the Continent has been kept in a fright about the great English expedition. It really is as if the police did not know how to read. They attend to nothing.

CXCVI

TO MARSHAL LEFEBVRE, DUC DE DANTZIG, COMMANDING THE 7TH CORPS OF THE ARMY IN GERMANY.

SCHÖNBRUNN, *26th July* 1809.

I SEND you some intercepted letters, which will inform you as to the enemy's position in the Tyrol. You will see by them, that General Buol has only 2000 men, that there are only 600 in the Vorarlberg, and that the Tyrolese have never had more than 1200 peasants under arms. The Prince Royal's division, that of the King, Rouyer's division, that of Colonel d'Arco, and Beaumont's division, must bring you up to 18,000 or 20,000 men. I hope, then, you will soon inform me that you have beaten and dispersed the enemy, and dis-

armed the country. Every ringleader must be treated as
a hostage, and sent to the Citadel of Strasburg, and you
must make an example of the leaders, and burn the
principal villages. As for the Austrians in the Tyrol, you
must give them a certain number of hours, in which to
declare whether they intend to take advantage of the
armistice, and evacuate the Tyrol. If they refuse, you
must execute severe justice, as on men who have disobeyed
their Government.

CXCVII

TO COMTE FOUCHÉ, MINISTER OF POLICE.

SCHÖNBRUNN, 28th July 1809.

IN the *Publiciste* of the 22nd, I see an account of the
battle of Wagram, in which great praise is given to the
Prince of Ponte-Corvo, who did anything but well. Whence
does this information come, and why cannot people go by
the official news?

Have Cardinal Pacca arrested, and taken to Fenestrelle ;
he is a man who does not deserve the smallest consideration.
Have his nephew arrested likewise. Have his secretary, a
certain Cosmo Pedicini, brought to Vincennes, so that you
may obtain information from him.

CXCVIII

TO COMTE FOUCHÉ, MINISTER OF POLICE, HOLDING THE
PORTFOLIO OF THE MINISTER OF THE INTERIOR.

SCHÖNBRUNN, 28th July 1809.

I HAVE received a farrago, which you have sent me, on the
subject of the Corn trade, and which is perfectly ridiculous. I
do not know why you begin there. I wonder you did not begin
by teaching me the alphabet. It is mere political economists'
chatter. Who is there in France who objects to the Corn
trade? Who opposes exportation? Not the law of the
country. It is the English who prevent neutral nations from
entering our ports and carrying off our vessels (*sic*). These
arguments are pitiful in themselves, but they have one great
drawback—that of encouraging the commercial community

to lecture the Government, to open discussions, and disturb
men's minds. The Administration has nothing to do with
political economy. The principle of the Corn trade is un-
varying. Exportation begins as soon as there are outlets.
There is no exportation without foreign trade. This channel
for trade is blocked by England. I have endeavoured to
replace it by licences, and if these are used, the evil may be
remedied.

As far as I am concerned, I request you will not send me
such idle tales: I have no need of the twaddle, nor the
advice, of M. Dupont de Nemours, and a few merchants.

I have read the letter from the Chamber of Commerce.
You did wrong to receive it, and I regret to see the direction
you are giving to the internal government of the country.

We do not need any advice from the Chamber of Commerce, and if we did, it would not be M. de Nemours who
should bestow it. Some conversation with certain well-
informed merchants may be useful, but the deliberations
of the Chambers are invariably valueless, and have certain
serious drawbacks. The Chamber of Commerce must be
very ignorant indeed if it is unaware, (1st) that the
Americans have not raised their embargo for France; (2nd)
that I have never objected to the Americans entering my
ports. It is the English who have objected to that. The
embargo has been raised for Holland. The King thought it
his duty to accept it. I have ceased to allow the introduction
of Dutch merchandise into France, and I have called upon
him to revoke the step he has taken, as I desire France
and Holland shall act on the same principle. And certainly,
if England is willing to allow American vessels to come to
France, I shall be the first to approve her action. The
Chamber of Commerce knows nothing at all, and only
chatters theories. I beg you will not expose me to the
annoyance of receiving such memoirs. I see you have
no experience whatever of internal government. We do not
require any fresh legislation on matters of trade. France is
suffering greatly, I know, not on account of legislation, but
on account of the English blockade. This is because the
Danish, Russian, and Prussian flags, being those of England's
enemy, cannot move about, and because the Americans have
laid an embargo on their own ports, and after that have
proceeded to publish an act of impeachment.

There is no outlet. I have endeavoured to supply it by patents or licences Let me know the effect of these measures, and do not disturb the commercial mind by foolish and unseasonable discussions. There will be a world of chatter, and nothing worth saying will be said. They have not even the most elementary notion of the question.

CXCIX

TO MARSHAL LEFEBVRE, DUC DE DANTZIG, COMMANDING THE 7TH CORPS OF THE ARMY IN GERMANY.

SCHÖNBRUNN, 30*th July* 1809, 6 P.M.

I HAVE this moment received your letter, dated 5 A.M., of 28th. I see the Communes of the Taufers[1] have submitted. I am sorry you have not punished them. My intention is, that on receiving this present letter, you shall demand 150 hostages, taken from all the Tyrolese Cantons; that you shall cause at least six large villages, all through the Tyrol, and the ringleaders' houses, to be sacked and burned, and that you shall let it be known that I will put the whole country to fire and sword, if all the muskets—18,000 at the very least—are not given up to me, with as many brace of pistols, which I know to be in existence. You will have the 150 hostages taken, under good and safe escort, to the Citadel of Strasburg. When I made my armistice, I did it principally with the object of reducing the Tyrol. After what has happened at Taufers, I fear you may allow yourself to be fooled by that rabble, which will be worse than ever, the moment your back is turned. Frenchmen and Bavarians have been massacred in the Tyrol. Vengeance must be taken, and severe examples made there. As for the Austrians, I have already made my intention known to you. They must be aware of the Armistice. They are a most egregiously false set. They are in far too close relations with the Austrian headquarters. No parleying! If they do not evacuate the country promptly, have them arrested. They are mere ruffians; they gave authority for the massacres. Give orders, then, that 150 hostages are to be made over to you; that all the worst characters are to be given up, and

---

[1] In the original draft the word is 'Lowfers.'

all the guns, at all events until the number reaches 18,000.
Make a law that any house in which a gun is found, shall be
razed to the ground, and that every Tyrolese found with a
musket shall be put to death. Mercy and clemency are out
of season with these ruffians. You have power in your
hands. Strike terror! and act so that a part of your troops
may be withdrawn from the Tyrol, without any fear of its
breaking out afresh. Six large villages must be sacked and
burned, so that not a vestige of them remains, and that they
may be a monument of the vengeance wreaked on the
mountaineers. My orderly officer, L'Espinay, has taken you
my orders. I long to hear that you have not allowed yourself to be caught, and that you have not rendered my
armistice useless ; for the chief benefit I desired to draw
from it was to take advantage of the six weeks it gave me,
to reduce the Tyrol. Send columns to Brixen.

CC

TO M. BIGOT DE PRÉAMENEU, MINISTER OF
PUBLIC WORSHIP.

SCHÖNBRUNN, 2nd August 1809.

YOU will let the Bishop of Ghent know that I am
displeased with the manner in which he manages his
diocese, with his weakness, and the small amount of personal
attachment he shows me ; that since he has been made
Bishop of Ghent, the feeling among his clergy, which was
already bad, has grown worse ; that I order the Abbé
Desure, his Vicar-General, to resign and proceed to Paris ;
that he is to change his Council, and compose it of better
disposed people, and take such measures that I may never
in future have to complain of the clergy of Ghent, because if
I once put my hand to the matter, I shall punish them
severely.

CCI

TO COMTE FOUCHÉ, MINISTER OF POLICE.

SCHÖNBRUNN, 2nd August 1809.

IT is my intention that the Abbé Desure shall not continue to be Vicar-General of Ghent. I have ordered the

Bishop to change the composition of his Council; let me know what is done.

Have the editor of the Brussels *Oracle* arrested. If it is true that two Saxon women ventured to make a scene in the theatre at Aix-la-Chapelle, have them arrested and taken to prison, where they are to remain for three months.

Wesel being a fortified town, measures for changing its population must be submitted to me. My intention would be to send about one hundred families, amongst those known as being most attached to the Prussians, to a distance of twenty leagues from Wesel, and to fill their places by the families of half-pay soldiers, who will be given an increase of pay, and obliged to live and settle permanently at Wesel. There ought to be no prisoners of war in the frontier fortresses; I am surprised therefore that there should be prisoners of war at Wesel.

CCII

TO COMTE FOUCHÉ, MINISTER OF POLICE.

SCHÖNBRUNN, *2d August* 1809.

IT appears complaint is being made of the bad feeling in Belgium. Send reliable men to collect information. The authorities must be weeded out, bad characters must be arrested, and 500 or 600 suspected persons must be sent to live in Burgundy and Champagne. You must submit a proposal to me, for placing the young men of those Departments in schools, or in regiments. You are not following up this idea, and nothing will have been done by the time I get to Paris. You confine yourself to two or three families in Paris, whereas the operation should affect 2000 or 3000 persons.

CCIII

TO THE PRINCE DE NEUFCHÂTEL, MAJOR-GENERAL OF THE ARMY IN GERMANY.

SCHÖNBRUNN, *5th August* 1809.

WRITE to General Beaumont that I conclude him to have entered the Vorarlberg; that he is not to busy himself with issuing absurd proclamations, but to take measures for insuring tranquillity; that the most urgent of these is complete disarmament—not only as regards guns, pistols, and swords, but also as regards gunpowder and war material. That country must give up at least 12,000 weapons. Two hundred hostages, also, must be taken, and sent to a French citadel, and ten or twelve houses, belonging to the ringleaders, must be burnt and sacked by the troops, and all the property of these ringleaders must be sequestered, and declared confiscated.

CCIV

TO COMTE FOUCHÉ, MINISTER OF POLICE.

SCHÖNBRUNN, 6th August 1809.

I WROTE yesterday to inform you that I would give definite orders about the Pope, when I was sure of his whereabouts, and to give you directions to keep close watch on Cardinal Pacca, who is a schemer and a rogue, and to lodge him at Fenestrelle. As for the Pope's permanent residence, what objection would there be to bringing him close to Paris, and placing him, for instance, in one of my apartments at Fontainebleau? I would bring such Cardinals as are my French and Italian subjects to Paris, and leave them there in freedom. It would be an advantage to have the head of the Church in Paris, where he cannot cause any inconvenience. If he makes a sensation, that will only be a novelty. At Fontainebleau I would have him served, and waited upon, by my own people. By insensible degrees, his fanaticism would die down. Tell me your opinion of these views.

CCV

TO GENERAL CLARKE, COUNT D'HUNEBURG, MINISTER OF WAR.

SCHÖNBRUNN, 7th August 1809.

THIS morning I have seen the 11th and 12th provisional half-brigades. I have ordered them to be disembodied, and I shall incorporate them with other regiments. I remarked among them, one or two half-pay officers, whom you have employed, and whom I had dismissed. They are thorough good-for-nothings. There is one, especially, who has been constantly under arrest, ever since Strasburg. He has been

K

on half-pay since the year V. He cannot have been kept out of the army for so long, without strong reason. The army is tainted by the presence of such scamps. Send me no more half-pay officers.

CCVI

TO COMTE FOUCHÉ, MINISTER OF POLICE.

SCHÖNBRUNN, *9th August* 1809.

YOU did well to prepare the Prefects for furnishing National Guards. I wrote to you that I had ordered a levy of 30,000 men for the National Guard; this will cost me money, but I have it.

If it was the editor of the *Journal de Paris* who published the article drawn from the Berlin letters, which was copied by the *Gazette de France*, that is the editor who must be arrested.

There is a mania in Paris for making up news at random. I know persons attached to me, who go about everywhere, saying, for instance, that it is Russia who forced me to make the armistice, and all this, just to make themselves important. I am on good terms with Russia, but I never take advice from her, nor from anybody else. I can quote the person who said this. It was Regnauld. Who the devil confided that fact to him? What fools these over-important folk are!

Enclosed you will find a report on the English expedition against Naples. It supplies matter for derisive articles. As soon as they heard of the victory of Wagram, they took to flight.

If my idiots of sailors have had the sense to run into Antwerp, my squadron is safe. The English expedition will come to nothing. They will all perish from inaction and fever.

CCVII

TO COMTE FOUCHÉ, MINISTER OF POLICE.

SCHÖNBRUNN, *10th August* 1809.

I SEND you the Bishop of Namur's Charge, which seems to me written with an evil intention. Find out who drew it up.

I see by your report of the 3rd, that the Commissary-General of Police at Lyons discloses the fact that on being informed that the order for the *Te Deum*[1] on the 30th was not, according to the usual custom, to be preceded by my letter, he pointed out the omission. If this be so, you will have a conversation with Cardinal Fesch, and you will make him understand, that unless he instantly withdraws the order he has given, and causes my letter to be re-incorporated with his mandate, I shall consider him my enemy, and the enemy of the State.

Make him understand that there is nothing contrary to religion in my letter; that I do not permit any one, and him least of all, to fail in respect to the authority with which I am invested. Settle this matter with him, if you can, and let my letter appear in his mandate. You will send for Mons. Emery, who is the Cardinal's councillor, and you will speak to him in this sense: 'Either my letter is contrary to religion or it is not; and has any Bishop the right to change the sense I have given it?' I am as much of a theologian as they are, and even more. I shall not go out of my province, but I will allow nobody else to go out of theirs.

CCVIII

TO COMTE FOUCHÉ, MINISTER OF POLICE.

SCHÖNBRUNN, 11*th August* 1809.

I SEND you a letter from one of those travelling preachers. Is there no means of ridding our Departments of these vagabonds? They should be treated as spies.

CCIX

TO PRINCE BORGHESE, GOVERNOR-GENERAL OF THE TRANSALPINE DEPARTMENTS.

SCHÖNBRUNN, 13*th August* 1809.

THE Minister of Police informs me he has had Cardinal Pacca arrested, and is sending him to the Castle of Fenestrelle. You must issue orders that he is to be treated with

---

[1] For the victory of Wagram.

severity, and not to be allowed to hold communication with any one at all. Let the Commandant know he will have to answer for him with his head.

As for the Pope, the Minister is sending him to Savona, by Aix and Nice. You are at liberty to put him either at Albenga or Savona. The reason I have preferred sending him to Savona is because of the citadel, which insures his safety in any event. You will lodge him in the Bishop's house, where he will be comfortable. You will form a guard of some fifty cavalry, headed by a trusty officer, which you will keep at Savona. You will take care the fort is well provisioned, and well garrisoned by a small battalion, of 400 men. You will send the Colonel of the Gendarmerie to Savona, with seven or eight companies. The detachment of fifty cavalry will be sufficient. The Pope will be allowed to do as he likes,—to give as many benedictions as he chooses; but care must be taken, however, to prevent any unusual communication with Genoa, or with other countries. Take care that all letters written by himself, or by his suite, are sent by Turin, where you will have them opened, as well as any that may be addressed to them, so as to find out whether they contain anything harmful to the State.

CCX

TO GENERAL CLARKE, COMTE D'HUNEBURG,
MINISTER OF WAR.

Schönbrunn, 16th August 1809.

I HAVE your letters of the 9th and 10th. What I foresaw has come to pass. The King of Holland is establishing his headquarters at Bergen-op-Zoom. And the Island of Cadzand and my Provinces are left without a General. What excites my gravest displeasure is, that the King takes command of my troops without orders from me, in virtue of his quality of Constable. He must be profoundly ignorant of our Constitution, if he thinks the dignity of Constable gives him command of my troops.

That is a five-hundred-year-old anachronism. Put a stop to this absurd comedy, and send a Marshal, since General Sainte-Suzanne, who is quite capable of managing the whole thing, is precluded from doing so by the condition of his health. This step will settle everything. The King of Holland cannot command our troops; as a matter of fact, he has no right to do it, and, besides, he has not the experience. Where should he have gained it? He never commanded so much as a regiment, during the war. How can you believe that any man in France can take command of my troops without my orders? You might have conferred the command on the King of Holland in my name,—well and good; but the idea of your allowing him to assume it, is not easy to conceive. The Prince of Ponte-Corvo, Marshals Moncey and Bessières, are all well fitted for this work, —better than the King of Holland and all the Dutchmen in the world. Even General Rampon would have been better.

Who is this General Garnier whom you are sending to command a division? Is it the man who was at Toulon, and has made a map since? If so, recall him instantly; he is not fit to command a company. General Colaud must have reached Antwerp. At Metz, at Strasburg, in the 12th Military Division, and everywhere else, you have much better generals than General Garnier. My positive orders are that this General is to be relieved of every command. Do not taint my troops with such people. I have been obliged, during my inspection of the different corps, to get rid of several officers of this kind, whom you have brought back to active service.

Further, the King of Holland has enough to do at home. Let him raise his National Guard, and the 30,000 soldiers he ought to have. If several thousand English land at the Texel, or in the island of Goree, the King will march to defend Amsterdam, and you will have brought a terrible responsibility on your own head. Indeed I should have more confidence in General Rampon than in the King; and if I had chosen to give the King command of my troops, I should have appointed a General to direct him. I hope you will have received my letter of the 6th; that you will have sent off several Marshals forthwith; and that you will have saved me from the greatest danger I could have run,—that of leaving the command in the hands of the Dutch. As for my squadron, the Minister for the Navy must give orders concerning it. All this confusion passes my comprehension.

CCXI

TO ELISA NAPOLEON, GRAND DUCHESS OF TUSCANY.

SCHÖNBRUNN, 17*th August* 1809.

I HAVE received your letter. You have the right to appeal to me against my Minister's decisions, but you have no right to hinder their execution, in any way. The Ministers speak in my name. No one has any right to paralyse, or stop the execution, of the orders they transmit. Will you, therefore, be good enough to recommence the carrying out of the Minister's decision, and to revoke the prohibition you have issued? For the order you gave in this case is criminal, and, in strict law, an accusation against you might be founded on it. There is no authority in France superior to that of the Ministers. I do not intend to go deeply into the question, because even if my Minister were in the wrong, I am the only judge of that, and you had no right to put the smallest difficulty in the way of his action. Even were it for that reason alone, I approve my Minister's decision. As for the tone of his letter, I consider it correct, and my Ministers will always adhere to it, because they all know my intention in that respect, and that I should not allow them to show the smallest compliance. So do not expose yourself to these quarrels, and to such annoyance. You are a subject, and, like every other French subject, you are obliged to obey the orders of the Ministers—for a writ of Habeas Corpus, issued by the Minister of Police, would fully suffice to arrest you—and not you only, but the first Prince of the Blood. And pray what would become of the State, if the police officer who had to execute this writ believed that the order or decision of a Minister could be stopped by any other, except that of the law, or an Imperial decree? If the Chancery Department has adhered to your order, and not carried out that of the Minister, it is exceedingly blameworthy.

CCXII

TO COMTE FOUCHÉ, MINISTER OF POLICE.

SCHÖNBRUNN, 17*th August* 1809.

HEREWITH you will find a letter from Mons. Hédouville, which will show you the stupidity of the newspapers (and

particularly of the *Journal de l'Empire*) which copy reports
circulated by agents of the English, who have such persons
in all the chief commercial towns. It would be a very good
thing if you gave your attention to this subject. If one
editor is not sufficient, two or three should be appointed, to
read the despatches, and cut out everything that should not
be printed. Although we are on good terms with Russia,
the English desire we should be on bad terms with her, and
they work so hard, that they cause it to be believed, in spite
of the evidence of facts. There is a clerk in one of the
Ministerial offices in London, who writes to a dozen agents,
scattered about the chief commercial towns, and these agents
correspond with our newspapers. It is shameful that they
should still be deceived by this manœuvre, so long after it has
been unmasked. Tell them positively, that I will suppress the
paper of the first editor who is taken in by these reports,
and prints mischievous articles.

CCXIII

TO GENERAL CLARKE, COMTE D'HUNEBURG, MINISTER FOR WAR.

SCHÖNBRUNN, *18th August* 1809.

I HAVE your letter of the 11th. So now the flower of my
troops are under the orders of Dutch generals! They will
tempt my soldiers to desert, so as to enrol them in Dutch
regiments. So the Dutch Minister of War is directing the
French forces! This is glorious indeed, and mighty advantageous to France! Your letter to the King of Holland
contains false views of our national rights. Where did you
find out that I do not give you more authority during
my absence, than when I am present? I have left all my
own powers with you. Whenever anything has to be done
which exceeds the limit of the Ministerial power, I have
given orders that a Council shall be summoned at the Grand
Chancellor's house, and that you are to avail yourself of
the decision of that Council, as if I had given it myself. It
is really indispensable that our Ministers should know our
Constitution. Your idea is as singular as the belief under
which you labour, that the Constable has a right to command
my troops. According to this, I suppose I have an army of

Brabant, and France is part of Holland! It would have been quite easy to appoint the Prince of Ponte-Corvo, or Marshal Moncey, or even to leave General Rampon. Anything would have been better than to put the French army into the hands of the Dutch. The idea of sending General Rousseau and 4000 men to the Island of Walcheren, is a piece of folly, traceable to the King of Holland's inexperience. There are more troops than are wanted in the Island of Walcheren. The more people there are, the sooner Flushing will be taken, because the sooner the provisions will fail. Four thousand extra National Guards will not drive the English out of the Island of Walcheren, where they have entrenched themselves. The calculation is easy enough—4000 more mouths at Flushing, and 4000 fewer arms at Cadzand. The King of Holland knows nothing of the force at your disposal. I see he is asking you for seasoned regiments, and meanwhile, without knowing anything, he acts at random. Once more I say, General Monnet has nothing to fear, as he can always cut the dikes. The King talks of taking up the offensive again, with inferior troops. That is just what the English wish for. There is madness in it all. On the very first appearance of an English boat on his coast, my troops will be sent there.

CCXIV

TO THE COMTE DE CHAMPAGNY, MINISTER FOR
FOREIGN AFFAIRS.

SCHÖNBRUNN, 20th August 1809.

I SEND you back your courier, who does not bring you anything of interest. I have received your letter dated midnight, on the 19th. Mons. de Metternich may possibly get news from England; try to find out what he hears, and especially whether he gets English newspapers. I see no objection to your sending him the French Gazettes. All the documents relative to the descent of the English have not yet been published, because of the time spent in sending them to me. All the telegraphic despatches, reports, and other official documents, will be in the *Moniteur*, in a few days. Give him the news that, in Spain, General

Wellesley, with 30,000 English, has been thoroughly beaten, about three days' journey from Madrid, and that, as a consequence, the English will be driven into the sea. As for Flushing, I consider that expedition a piece of good fortune, because it gives me the best excuse for asking for 80,000 men (which I have done by my message of the 16th August), which 80,000 men will remain in hand after the re-embarkation of the English, which, I conclude, will have taken place before the end of the month. The Austrians must know its object better than we do. Doubtless it was to seize the squadron; but the English would appear to have false information as to Antwerp and Flushing.[1]

Let Mons. Gardanne know that his letter of the 17th August has been placed before me, and that I have found it full of faults, and ignorance of his duty. Just as an Ambassador cannot speak without orders, he cannot return without orders, more especially when the Ambassador is leaving an Embassy which has already cost me more than a million of money, and is endangering relations of such great importance, from every point of view. Thus, in any case, his return to France, without orders, would be a crime. But, as your letter of the 17th of July from Toulouse, which he quotes, contained orders to remain at his post as long as possible, it was a clear intimation that he was to stay until the Court of Persia drove him out. And, far from driving him away, the Court of Persia was in despair at his departure, and did everything it could to keep him. I cannot help perceiving that this conduct shows little zeal for my service, and is a manifest infraction of his duty. But all his despatches, indeed, are so incoherent, that it seems to me something must have gone wrong with his brain. Send me a report which will show what Frenchmen remain in Persia, and which went there with Mons. Gardanne. I send you back the Emperor of Persia's letter. Draw me up an answer, which you will send by the shortest route. You will say that I have reprimanded and disgraced General Gardanne, for having left his Court, that I have ordered my Chargé d'Affaires to return to his capital, and that I will immediately send him another Ambassador: that his letter shows me he has thoroughly understood my position, just as I have understood the

<hr />

[1] The Comte de Champagny was then at Altenburg, for the peace negotiations with Austria.

reasons which obliged him to reopen momentary and ostensible relations with the English.

Write to Mons. de St. Marsan that the Berlin Ministry still appears to be on a false scent; that those simpletons fancy the French army here does not number more than 70,000 men. Let him know the real facts, so that, if necessary, he may make them understand that the army numbers more than 300,000 men, and that the ideas at present prevailing at Berlin had better be compared with those current before the battle of Jena, when they also believed the French army had disappeared.

I desire to cultivate my relations with Persia; I consider them of great importance.

CCXV

TO COMTE FOUCHÉ, MINISTER OF POLICE.

SCHÖNBRUNN, *22nd August* 1809.

YOU ask how the Pope is to be treated at Savona. Give orders that he is to be allowed every liberty; that he is to give benedictions, and say masses, as much as he chooses; that the people are to be prevented from coming about him in too great numbers; that all arrivals are to be watched; and that no letter from, or addressed to, him, or any member of his suite, is to be allowed to go or come. Make arrangements as to this, with Mons. de Lavallette, and the Minister of Finance. See Mons. Aldini, and have the necessary measures taken in Italy. Forbid any Cardinal to come to Savona, except the Cardinal of Genoa, to whose coming there is no objection, as he belongs to the neighbourhood; but do not give this permission to any other. Have the Pope's former confessor, who is a rascal, arrested at Rome, and shut up at Fenestrelle. I have given Prince Borghese orders to send a Colonel of Gendarmes to Savona, and to keep a garrison of from 500 to 600 men in the citadel. Thanks to these precautions, the Pope will be safe, whatever happens. I am having him lodged in the Bishop's Palace, where he will be very comfortable. Write to the Prefect that he is not to let him want for anything he may wish for.

Postscript.—Write everywhere, so that it may not be mentioned in the Gazettes.

CCXVI

TO COMTE FOUCHÉ, MINISTER OF POLICE.

SCHÖNBRUNN, *2nd September* 1809.

I HAVE your letter of the 29th. Nobody can deny that General Monnet [1] has behaved like a vile coward.

The eleven Superiors-General of monastic orders, whom I have sent to Paris, must be sent to small towns.

The person who sends such mischievous reports to the King of Holland is a certain Mons. Decazes, a judge in the Inferior Court. He is, I believe, Mons. Muraire's son-in-law. There is no folly, and no absurd news, to be heard of, which the man does not write. Is this folly or spite? Put order into it.

CCXVII

TO THE COMTE DE CHAMPAGNY, MINISTER FOR FOREIGN AFFAIRS.

SCHÖNBRUNN, *4th September* 1809, 4 P.M.

I SEND you your letters. I have your report on the papers found in the Vorarlberg, and sent by the Court of Stuttgart. It shows me that there are culprits to be arrested in Switzerland, and in the Baden States. Send the necessary extracts to my Ministers in Switzerland and Baden, so that all those persons may be arrested at the same time, and satisfaction given me. Make my Minister in Switzerland understand that I shall more especially judge the feeling of the Swiss Government for me, by its behaviour with regard to this matter. Demand, at the same time, the arrest of the Bishop of St. Gall, and his monks. You will have to send my Ministers copies—not the original ones, but signed by your own hand—of all the documents, so that they may follow up the trials of all these persons.

CCXVIII

TO COMTE FOUCHÉ, MINISTER OF POLICE.

SCHÖNBRUNN, *6th September* 1809.

MARET will send you a collection of all the different kinds of bank-notes. Enclosed you will find an order on the

[1] He had surrendered Flushing.

subject. I desire you will manufacture these notes, of every amount, until you have reached 100,000,000. You must set up machinery which will turn out 10,000,000 a month. It was paper currency which enabled Austria to make war against me, and with paper money she may be able to do it again. That being so, it is my policy, both in peace and war, to destroy that paper currency, and to force Austria to come back to the metallic currency, which, by its very nature, will force her to reduce her army, and all that wild expenditure on her part, which has threatened the safety of my dominions. It is my intention that this operation shall be carried out secretly and mysteriously. Yet the object I set before me is far more a political one, than any advantageous speculation or gain. This subject is exceedingly important. There is no hope of peace in Europe, so long as the House of Austria can obtain advances of 300 or 400 millions, on the credit of its paper currency.

Send a shrewd and intelligent agent, who will come while we are here, and collect all the information necessary to give this affair the scope I desire it to have, and which will cause it to have so great an influence.

CCXIX

TO M. BIGOT DE PRÉAMENEU, MINISTER OF
PUBLIC WORSHIP.

SCHÖNBRUNN, 7th September 1809.

YOU will receive a Decree, by which I order that from the 1st July, the sum of 200,000 francs shall be paid monthly, by the Roman Consulta, to the account of your Ministry. This sum is intended to provide for the Pope's household, and for that of the Cardinals, and the Heads of Orders, who have come to France, such as Cardinal Ruffo, etc. Let me know who and what these Heads of Orders are, and give them a suitable income, which will enable them to live creditably. You will likewise order the Doria Cardinals, and, generally speaking, all Cardinals who have become French subjects, and do not reside within their bishoprics, to proceed to Paris. It is my intention that they shall all receive the 30,000 francs which I allow the French Cardinals. I have sent Mons. Salmatoris to the Pope, to organise his household. Take measures that the Holy Father shall lack nothing, and shall be fully and completely provided. Keep 100,000 francs a month for this purpose.

CCXX

TO COMTE FOUCHÉ, MINISTER OF POLICE

Schönbrunn, *12th September* 1809.

THE Prince of Ponte-Corvo, who is going to Paris, will probably have a conversation with you. You will let him know that I was displeased with his Order of the Day to the Saxons, which has a tendency to ascribe a glory to them, which is not their due—for they were in flight during the whole of the 6th; that I have been not less displeased with his Order of the Day to the National Guard, in which he says he had only 15,000 men, whereas I had 60,000 on the Scheldt; that even if he had only 10,000, it is a criminal act on a general's part, to let the enemy, and all Europe, into the secret of his numerical strength; that he has no sense of proportion; and that I have been very much dissatisfied, during the Swedish business, at his having allowed the Swedes admission, provisionally, and thus compromised me with Russia; that he receives letters from a pack of schemers in Paris; that I know he is not fool enough to believe their reports, but that the thing in itself is improper; that I cannot endure intrigue; that it is both his duty and his interest to be straightforward; that he must get rid of all this rabble, and not permit it to write to him, and that if he does not, misfortune will overtake him. The Prince of Ponte-Corvo has made a great deal of money at Hamburg; he made money too at Elbing. That brought the bad business in Poland and the battle of Eylau on to me. I am tired of schemers, and I am scandalised that a man, whom I have loaded with benefits, should lend his ear to a set of wretches whom he knows and values at their proper worth. You will tell him that he has never seen a man, nor received a letter, without my knowledge; that I am aware how little importance he attaches to it all, but that to permit such men to write to him, and to receive them, is to encourage them.

All this is a secret matter. You will make no use of these details unless the Prince of Ponte-Corvo should speak to you. If he does not, you will not say anything to him.

CCXXI

TO COMTE FOUCHÉ, MINISTER OF POLICE.

SCHÖNBRUNN, 15*th September* 1809.

I HAVE read the Pope's letter to Cardinal Caprara. As that Cardinal is a trusty person, you can have it sent to him, after having it copied.

The move from Grenoble to Savona has been harmful, as every retrograde step always is. You have not grasped my intention. It is this backward step which has kindled that fanatic's hopes. You see he would fain have us revoke the Napoleonic Code, deprive us of our liberties, and so forth. There can be no greater madness. I have already given directions, that all Superiors-General of Orders, and Cardinals who have no Bishoprics, or who do not reside within their dioceses, whether Italians, Tuscans, or Piedmontese, shall proceed to Paris. And I shall probably end the whole matter by sending for the Pope himself, and putting him in the neighbourhood of Paris. It is only proper that he should be at the centre of Christendom. For a few months, it will be looked on as a novelty, but that will soon pass.

CCXXII

TO COMTE FOUCHÉ, MINISTER OF POLICE.

SCHÖNBRUNN, 15*th September* 1809.

I SEND you a fresh report on that Mons. Decazes. After what you have told me, the simplest course will be to send him to Holland. If he is the King's spy, he can find him employment at home. The King takes these reports to be really true. He believes I do not desire peace, because I insist upon having the whole of the course of the Danube, and that irritates and vexes him.

That little rascal Decazes must have some source of information in your office. You see what he says of the Prussian Minister. I have had occasion to make this remark several times. Order him to be gone within twenty-four hours, otherwise I will have him arrested.

CCXXIII

TO COMTE FOUCHÉ, MINISTER OF POLICE.

BRÜNN, 18th September 1809.

YOU have done wrong to alarm all France, and even Piedmont, by writing everywhere to 'prepare' the National Guards. The word 'prepare' has no meaning, and the whole Empire is unnecessarily alarmed by it.

You never mention Paris to me. I do not know what this Mounted Guard can be. People say that there are sixty of them, and further, that they refuse to leave Paris. Am I to be turned into ridicule? It appears to me that you would have done well to tell me about all this. I see clearly that Rome is not in Paris, but in my good Departments. Ah! there they really are French! As Paris has been quite useless to me, it must not cause me any present anxiety, nor oblige me to endure the consequential airs of the National Guard; for that would be to give me all the drawbacks of a measure, without my having enjoyed its advantages. If it is true that those sixty young men were assured they would not have to go on active service, and that they enlisted on the faith of that assurance, they must be quietly disembodied.

CCXXIV

TO LOUIS NAPOLEON, KING OF HOLLAND.

SCHÖNBRUNN, 21st September 1809.

YOUR letter of the 8th reached me at Brünn. You speak to me of a brilliant action fought by the Dutch, to regain possession of Batz. This strikes me as being very ridiculous. The English evacuated Batz, as they will evacuate Flushing, on account of sickness. The greatest harm is done to soldiers, by heaping praises on them, which they do not deserve. Lay it down as a principle, that General Bruce's head must be cut off. That villain has imperilled the safety of my squadron and my territory. I know he has a strong backing in Holland, but I insist upon this reparation. The manner in which your Minister of War has left the Fort of Batz, and the Island of Walcheren, unprovided, is shameful.

You say, in your speeches, that it is because it was

indispensable to win on the Danube, that you have no army. I do not know what has become of the three regiments you have in Germany. What are these eight companies, and one hundred horses, that you have in Spain?

What can I say to you? That which I have told you a hundred times already. You are no king, and you do not know how to be a king! Such things would never have happened in the days of Schimmelpenninck and the Dutch Republic, which always had 40,000 men in its pay.

I have sent you back your flotilla from Boulogne, that you may keep it in the Scheldt or in your canals. You have disarmed it; you have neither Navy, nor Finances, nor Army, and you set up to be a free and independent State! All your difficulties and anxieties are the outcome of your bad administration, and of your never having listened to my advice.

Trade with England goes on in Holland, just as in times of peace, and the partisans of England triumph. I must inform you, however, that this cannot be allowed to go on. Four things are necessary to the independence of Holland : Finances, an army, a flotilla and fleet, and an absolute prohibition of any communication with England. Short of that, I shall never have peace. The Customs system ought to be the same as that of France, so that no change should be made in the Customs Legislation and Tariff except by agreement with me. The necessary measures for defending my dockyards at Antwerp must also be attended to. Batz and Zealand can certainly not be left in the hands of a nation which does not know how to defend them.

As for your protestations of attachment to my person and to France, I desire to believe in them; nevertheless, the French have never been worse treated than in Holland. I have portfolios of complaints from my shipowners, against your agents, and if you do not put a stop to the vile behaviour of your Admirals to my Flag, beware lest I put a stop to it myself. My Flag is sacred—no Dutch Admiral has a right to touch it—yet, in your waters, my privateers are stopped, and my Flag is violated.

I should desire something further. It is that you should not mention me in your public speeches; that is a mere hypocrisy, for you very well know that everything you do is opposed to my opinion, and that I have often told you I foresaw the changeableness and folly of your action would ruin your kingdom.   Do not, therefore, give any one the impression that I approve of your measures.   I have been tempted, several times, to affix notes after your speeches in the *Moniteur*, so as to make it thoroughly clear that I disapproved what you ascribed to me.   You will realise the discomfort this will cause you.   I beg, then, that you will neither speak of me, nor of France.   It is a constant regret to me, that I have given you a kingdom in which you have only used the palladium of my name to serve my enemies, and to do all the mischief possible to my system, and to France.

I thank you for the interest you take in my health.   I should not think it very sincere, if I were to seek its proof in your speeches, in which you strive to tarnish my glory— if that were possible to a man like you, who has done nothing at all.   The packet you sent me the day after that speech is altogether like you, and a type of your ordinary behaviour. I do not know, indeed, what stories people choose to tell about my health ;—it has never been better.

Postscript.—I see a speech in the *Moniteur*, in which you say your Guards have saved Antwerp (that is to say, abandoned it in the moment of danger), and that the expedition was easy to foresee.   Why, then, did you go to Aix-la-Chapelle, instead of going to make an inspection of your coasts, arming the fort of Batz, throwing 6000 men into the Island of Walcheren, and raising 12,000 in your dominions? If you had foreseen the expedition, why were not the 200 launches or gunboats I sent you hurried into the Scheldt? It really is pitiful, that a man who governs a State with such ineptitude, should also make such unreasonable statements.   Your indictment, and that of your government, are in your own speech.   How can any man make game or Europe, and show so little respect for the name he bears, as to assert in public, ' I foresaw the expedition, but I took no means to oppose it!' You say you have no army, because you have 4000 bad troops in Hanover, where they have covered themselves with glory, by pillaging the North of Germany.   It was your duty, since your genius was so great, to provision your forts, to have 200 gunboats in the Scheldt, and to raise troops to oppose the English invasion.   You have no wise counsellor about you.   All day long you are writing nonsense—that's the word—contradictions and mis-constructions.   I see you told the Amsterdam burghers that their real duty was to protect their town against sharpers, and immoral women ; while it is well known that they refused to march for the defence of their country !   I should not mention all this to you, but that you implicate my name in it.   You give it to be understood that the Dutch have done everything, and are exceedingly energetic.   Yes ; they are very energetic in the smuggling trade !   That poor Dutch nation is much to be pitied.   Its sufferings arise from the instability of your character, and the folly of your measures.   I repeat once more, it is my will that you shall never speak of me, directly or indirectly, in your harangues, and that they shall never refer either to my affairs, or to my name.

CCXXV

TO COMTE FOUCHÉ, MINISTER OF POLICE.

SCHÖNBRUNN, 23rd *September* 1809.

MARET is sending you what you ask for.   I repeat that, whether in peace or in war, I attach the greatest importance to having one or two hundred millions' worth of notes.   This is a political operation.   Once the House of Austria is shorn of its paper currency, it will not be able to make war against me.   You can set up the workshops where you please—in the Castle of Vincennes, for instance, from which the troops would be withdrawn, and which no one would be allowed to enter.   This stringent rule would be accounted for by the presence of State prisoners.   Or you can put them in any other place you choose.   But it is urgent and important that your closest attention should be given to this matter. If I had destroyed that paper money, I should not have had this war.

CCXXVI

TO THE COMTE DE CHAMPAGNY, MINISTER FOR
FOREIGN AFFAIRS.

SCHÖNBRUNN, 8th *October* 1809.

FIND out from Bourrienne why he has accepted a portrait of the King of Westphalia without my orders.   Write him orders to send back that portrait instantly.   No Minister is to receive a present from a Sovereign without my permission. Inquire, at the same time, why he has not informed me of the financial negotiations which the Court of Cassel is carrying on at Hamburg. You will send him a special courier to fetch his answer, and clear this matter up. Let him hear of my displeasure at his having allowed the Postmaster at Hamburg to write to Denmark, about the correspondence with Sweden, without your authority. And, in short, make him clearly understand that I insist on knowing everything, and that I shall hold him responsible for everything he does not tell me.

Inform Reinhard that if the King employs H—— he is to ask for his passports, and let it be known that he has orders to make a positive declaration that I will not permit such a rascal to remain about the King. Tell him to take steps to have the French Custom-houses protected on the Osnabrück side; this is a measure which I take against England, as Protector of the Confederation.

Write to Switzerland that the man Testa Ferrata, the Nuncio's brother, is to be arrested, or at all events turned out of Switzerland.

Inform Prince Kourakin that I have give orders that the twenty-two Finnish prisoners of war, whom he claims as subjects of the Russian Empire, are to be given up to him, and that the Minister of War has orders to that effect.

CCXXVII

TO GENERAL CLARKE, COMTE D'HUNEBURG,
MINISTER OF WAR.

SCHÖNBRUNN, 10th October 1809.

SEND the enclosed newspaper extracts to Spain. The French troops there are very much enfeebled. This comes from the Orders of the Day, and proclamations, which asserted that the enemy's strength exceeded ours, three or four times over. By dint of asserting our own inferiority over and over again, we end, quite naturally, by reckoning Marshal Soult's troops at 8000 men, those of Marshal Mortier at 10,000, and so on. You will therefore write to the King, that the art of war consists in exaggerating one's own strength, - and underrating that of the enemy. He, on the contrary, exalts the enemy's forces, and depreciates his own.

CCXXVIII

TO GENERAL CLARKE, DUC DE FELTRE, MINISTER OF WAR.

MUNICH, 21*st October* 1809.

CAPTAIN D'ARGENTON of the Dragoons, who is accused of treason, and of holding communication with the enemy, should be arraigned before a Military Court; you will have this order carried out, unless the Minister of Police opposes it, in the hope he may be able to get still more information out of the man.

CCXXIX

TO M. FOUCHÉ, DUC D'OTRANTE, MINISTER OF POLICE.

FONTAINEBLEAU, 26*th October* 1809.

GIVE orders forthwith, that the priest Desmasures, now on his way to Savona to see the Pope, is to be arrested after he has seen the Holy Father. His papers will be sent to you, and his person conveyed to the Castle of Compiano in the Duchy of Parma, where he will be kept in secret confinement, without any possibility of holding correspondence with any one.

CCXXX

TO THE PRINCE BORGHESE, GOVERNOR-GENERAL OF THE TRANSALPINE DEPARTMENTS.

FONTAINEBLEAU, 26*th October* 1809.

I HAVE your letter of 12th October. You must write Sal-matoris that he is not to rush into foolish expense for the Pope; that, on the contrary, I should wish a large economy made on the 1,200,000 frances set apart for his support, so that if the Pope should have to travel, whether to go to Paris, or to any other point in France, there may be a reserve fund for this expenditure.

CCXXXI

TO MARSHAL BESSIÈRES, DUC D'ISTRIE, COMMANDING THE ARMY OF THE NORTH.

PARIS, *20th November* 1809.

I AM pained to observe that you do not proceed with the necessary firmness. You have the chief command, and you ought to overcome all difficulties. There are guns at Lillo, at Antwerp, at Bergen-op-Zoom, at Breda, and at Batz. You have fifteen or sixteen companies of gunners, but to get these you must withdraw every one you have on the defensive. These sixteen companies must make up 900 men. It is clear that if you want to line Antwerp, and all the banks of the Scheldt, with men and war material, as though the enemy were on the offensive, you will not come to any result at all. Counting the Dutch, you have 30,000 men, apart from 30,000 National Guards, who can protect your rear, and occupy Breda, Bergen-op-Zoom, and all the Dutch fortresses. With your flotilla, you should be able to land 30,000 men in one day. You hold command of all the Dutch fortresses and troops, of my fleet, my arsenals, and my troops. Everything you do will be well done, provided you win, and that quickly. Act swiftly and vigorously, without 'buts,' and 'ifs,' and 'fors.' Instead of writing to the Minister of War, give orders, and let me soon hear that the Sloe is rid of the enemy. The special affection I bear you has induced me to give you a chance of winning this glory. Be firm, show wisdom and decision. If there are any evil-disposed persons in the Dutch army, have them arrested. If the King hinders you, don't listen to him. Overcome all obstacles. The only thing I should blame in you would be pusillanimity or irresolution. I shall sanction everything that is vigorous, spirited, and politic.

CCXXXII

TO GENERAL CLARKE, DUC DE FELTRE, MINISTER OF WAR.

PARIS, *9th December* 1809.

I HAVE your report touching that wretch Argenton. I have nothing to say, except that the reporter must draw up his articles of impeachment, without regard to anything but justice.

CCXXXIII

TO M. DE CHAMPAGNY, DUC DE CADORE,
MINISTER FOR FOREIGN AFFAIRS.

TRIANON, 17th *December* 1809.

I THINK it is necessary that you should send a courier to-day to the Duke of Vicenza, to bring him the *Moniteur*.[1] You will point out that it must make the necessity for a prompt and decisive answer on his part, clear enough. You will answer him that it is not true that Prince Galitzin's letter was shown to any one at all; that when the word Poland is used in any document, it is by a mistake on the part of the employés, who do not mean any harm; that I have informed the Prince of Neufchâtel of my displeasure at his having allowed this word to appear in the Military Convention; that these delicate shades can hardly fail sometimes to escape the notice of the employés; that I was glad to have it intimated, in the speech delivered by the Minister of the Interior to the Legislative Body, that the acquisitions in Galicia were not a political, but an accidental matter; that the Emperor Alexander has perceived how I have settled the question of Moldavia and Wallachia, at the very moment in which I received news of Prince Bagration's reverses; that I have helped on the peace with Sweden; and that the sentence in my speech, already mentioned, will procure him peace with the Porte. What more could I do?

You will tell him that Mons. Ledoulx' conduct is madness, and that I am ordering him to return to Paris to account for it. [You will in fact transmit this order to him. I shall be glad to have information about the condition of the country from the Consul. He will leave his Chancellor behind him.] You will further inform the Duke of Vicenza that if the presence of a French Consul at Bucharest is an inconvenience, he shall be removed.

The Duke of Vicenza will not fail to tell Mons. de Romanzoff that, all Frenchmen being born with the idea that France must protect the Porte, there are certain things which depend on the Protocol, and on circumstances, and that I cannot publicly proclaim the fact that I am abandoning Turkey; and that my speech leaves no doubt as to the

---

[1] Containing the Decree of Divorce between Napoleon and Josephine.

union of Moldavia and Wallachia. The Duke of Vicenza, who has the Protocols of the Altenburg Conference, must point out to Mons. de Romanzoff, that, during these conferences, we never showed any desire to have Galicia ; that we have made a separate question of that, and that Austria, on the contrary, would have given it to us altogether.

CCXXXIV

TO PRINCE CAMBACÉRÈS, GRAND CHANCELLOR OF THE EMPIRE.

TRIANON, *22nd December* 1809.

OUR brother, the King of Holland, having requested us to permit him to separate from his wife, Queen Hortense, we have thought proper to seek the opinion of the Family Council, both as to the request itself, and as to the measures to be taken to arrange everything relative to the respective interests of the parties. We therefore cause this letter to be sent to you, so that you may convoke the Family Council, which will be held in the Throne Room at the Tuileries. The Council will be presided over by yourself. Our brother, the King of Westphalia, is nominated to take part in it, and the Duke of Conegliano will be called as Senior Marshal of the Empire. The further composition of the Family Council will follow the rule prescribed by the Thirty-fourth Article of the Family Statute.

CCXXXV

TO M. FOUCHÉ, DUC D'OTRANTE, MINISTER OF POLICE.

TRIANON, *24th December* 1809.

SEND General du Châtelet, the two brothers Clauvès-Briant, and Major D'Assonville, of the Department of Jemappes, orders to proceed to Paris. You will inform them that my intention is that they shall not continue to live in Belgium, and that they are to select a residence forty leagues from Mons. You will suggest to me that their children and cousins should be at once taken, and placed in a *Lycée* or in a regiment.

Write to Venice that Mme Cassini is to be arrested, and let it be known that whoever has recourse to foreign influence will be treated in the same manner. I do not intend that Mons. Cassini shall leave Fenestrelle on any pretence whatsoever. The villain lost all right to my protection when he appealed to foreign influence.

CCXXXVI

TO M. FOUCHÉ, DUC D'OTRANTE, MINISTER OF POLICE.

PARIS, 27th December 1809.

I SEND you a summary of your statistics about the Belgian families. Send me the draft of a Decree—the provisions of which you will see in the notes I have added—to the effect that those persons who might do harm to the Government by their fortune, or their connections, are to be obliged to come and live in Paris, and that, in other cases, the children are to be sent to St. Cyr, or to St. Germain. Have the same thing drawn up for all the conquered countries which have lately been added to France.

CCXXXVII

TO M. DE CHAMPAGNY, DUC DE CADORE, MINISTER FOR FOREIGN AFFAIRS.

PARIS, 30th December 1809.

PUT the strongest pressure on the King of Naples, and make him understand that if measures are not taken to pay his debts, and if he does not fulfil all his engagements, I shall exact payment by main force; that his kingdom is always costing me money, and that I am furious at not being paid what I am owed.

CCXXXVIII

TO M. DE CHAMPAGNY, DUC DE CADORE, MINISTER FOR FOREIGN AFFAIRS.

PARIS, 17th January 1810.

I SEND you back your report about Rome. It strikes me as being weak, and contains some doubtful assertions. When you say that the entry of the troops into the March of Ancona was not an act of hostility, you put yourself in the wrong, and bring forward questions which would startle Europe. The style is not sufficiently business-like ; what I want is hard reasoning, not picturesqueness. I will ask you, therefore, to remodel this report, and return it to me. Generally speaking, the report has no divisions or plan, and leaves no impression on the mind after it has been read.

CCXXXIX

TO M. FOUCHÉ, DUC D'OTRANTE, MINISTER OF POLICE.

PARIS, 21st January 1810.

ORDER Mons. d'Oultremont, of the Department of the Ourthe, to come to Paris ; when he arrives, you will inform him that he is to remain there, until you have made him aware of my intentions.

You will also order Mons. Van-der-Leyen, of Krefeld, in the Department of the Roër, to proceed to Paris. You will tell him to reside there until further orders ; and that unless his two sons, who are at Leipsic and Frankfort, have been brought back to France, and placed, according to their ages, in a *Lycée* or some other establishment, within six months, I will have his property confiscated.

You will order Mons. Chasteler, of the Department of the Dyle, to come to Paris. When he appears before you, you will inform him that I intend he shall take up his residence elsewhere than in Belgium—as, for instance, in one of the towns in Old Flanders, or in Champagne.

You will give the same order to Mons. Ribaucourt, of the Dyle, to Messrs. Jacques and Philippe Desprès, Vermoesand, Van de Werke, Van-Praët, Glys, and to Mme d'Oultremont, of the Department of the Deux-Nèthes.

You will be careful not to have more than two of these people sent for from their Departments, at a time, and to leave an interval of a fortnight or three weeks between the dates of their departure, so that this measure may not appear forced and extraordinary, but merely a regular administrative step.

A person who has been described to me as being rich does not appear on your list. Let me have a report about this.

CCXL

TO M. DE CHAMPAGNY, DUC DE CADORE, MINISTER FOR FOREIGN AFFAIRS.

PARIS, 24*th January* 1810.

I HAVE asked you for a report on American affairs. It is necessary, before all things, that you should write to America, in cipher, to ask that another Minister may be sent to Paris, and to bring formal complaint against this one, who is perfectly useless. Meanwhile, until I can send a new Minister to America, send a secondary agent, who can act as Secretary of Legation. He will sail on an American schooner and will carry your despatches; he will also be the bearer of the American Minister's letter about the sequestration of St. Sebastian, and your reply, in which you will once more develop my ideas on that subject. All this should be done without delay.

CCXLI

TO M. DE CHAMPAGNY, DUC DE CADORE, MINISTER FOR FOREIGN AFFAIRS.

PARIS, 27*th January* 1810.

SEND for the Dutch Minister this evening before midnight. You will inform him that my troops have entered Breda and Bergen-op-Zoom, but that the authorities have behaved badly, which has obliged me to take severe measures; that I hear the Dutch troops are moving towards Holland; that there seems to be an intention to take up a hostile position; that I have just given orders to bring up the troops I have at Düsseldorf and Hamburg, by forced marches; that the King's meaning has yet to be made clear, that he will be responsible for the blood that will be spilt, and that this misfortune will not be long delayed; that after I had received the Duke of Reggio's packet, I gave orders to my Minister of War to communicate that Marshal's despatches to the King; that I have created an army in Brabant, and have placed the Dutch troops under the Duke of Reggio's orders; that if the King desires to avoid misfortune and bloodshed, he must instantly send orders to his troops to quit the hostile position they have taken up ; that the first soldier or civilian who opposes force with force, in the countries between the Meuse and the Scheldt, will be put to the sword, and that the King will be responsible for the blood that will flow, and for the consequent misfortunes to Holland.

CCXLII

TO M. DE RÉMUSAT, PREFECT OF THE POLICE.

PARIS, 13th February 1810.

As the opera, 'The Death of Abel,' is ready mounted, I consent to its being played ; but in future I intend no opera shall be given without my order. If the last management has left the new one my written permission, it will be in order, not otherwise. The former management deferred to me, not only as to receiving works, but as to selecting them. Generally speaking, I disapprove of the production of any work founded on Holy Scripture. These subjects should be left to the Church. The Chamberlain who has charge of the theatrical business will immediately make this known to the authors, so that they may devote themselves to other subjects. The Ballet of 'Autumnus and Pomona' is a cold and tasteless allegory. That of the 'Rape of the Sabines' is historic and more suitable. Only mythological and historical ballets are to be given—never anything allegorical. I desire four ballets may be produced this year. If Gardel is not in a position to do it, you are to find other persons who will. Besides 'The Death of Abel,' I should desire another historical ballet, more apposite to present circumstances than the 'Rape of the Sabines.'

CCXLIII

TO M. DE CHAMPAGNY, DUC DE CADORE,
MINISTER FOR FOREIGN AFFAIRS.

PARIS, 18th February 1810.

INFORM my Ambassador at Madrid that I have given orders that the four provinces, Catalonia, Arragon, Biscay, and Navarre, are to form four governments ; that I have given the fullest powers to the Generals commanding there, and that I have desired the revenues of these four Governments shall be paid into the Army Chest. Ask the Prince of Neufchâtel to give you my Decree; you will send it to Mons. Laforest, and you will commission him to inform the King's Ministers that this is my will, that Spain has quite sufficient resources to bear this expense—a fact I cannot doubt, more especially when I consider his wild expenditure.[1] You will let my Minister know, by a cipher letter, that his correspondence must become more active; that I intend to incorporate the left bank of the Ebro, and perhaps even the whole country up to the Douro,[2] with France; that he must take care that no one touches the property belonging to the sentenced families, and that no member of these families must be permitted to return; that if this question were put forward in any treaty or capitulation, he must oppose it, and protest against it; that I will not consent to ratify any pardon that may be thus extended, and that wherever my troops lay hands on such persons, they will be put to the sword. And further, that he must take a more active part; must speak to the King's Ministers, and point out that rewards have been bestowed on Frenchmen whose only merit consists in having followed the King; that the money thus bestowed is a loss to the common stock; that the Spanish war is costing me several hundred millions of money, and that instead of being repaid for the enormous expense I have had, I have the pain of seeing him squandering Spanish moneys on his favourites. You will send Mons. Laforest to-morrow's *Moniteur*, so that he may see my principles as to the French Princes, and that I have the right, when they forget the ties which bind them to France, to recall them, or to force them to act primarily in the interests of their country.[3]

CCXLIV

TO M. FOUCHÉ, DUC D'OTRANTE, MINISTER OF POLICE.

PARIS, 18*th February* 1810.

I CANNOT be otherwise than displeased with the tone of the newspapers. Who gave the *Gazette de France* leave to

---

[1] The word 'wild' was struck out of the draft by the Emperor.
[2] Here Napoleon has erased the following sentence in the draft: 'That the constant talk which goes on about integrity displeases me; that those who do it cast down the glove and defy me; that this is impolitic on their part.'
[3] This last phrase was struck out of the draft.

say that MM. Léon de Beauvau, de Noailles, and de Mortemart, are soon to travel to Germany on a mission? What is the meaning of this? I remark upon it because I have long noticed that the newspapers are mixing themselves up with what does not concern them, and filling their columns with nothing but doubtful news.

CCXLV

TO MME DE LA ROCHEFOUCAULD, LADY OF HONOUR TO THE EMPRESS JOSEPHINE.

PARIS, 24*th February* 1810.

MADAME,—I have been satisfied with the manner in which you have performed your duty as Lady of Honour, in my Palace. I regret, and yet I cannot but approve, the feeling which causes you to desire not to fill the position of Lady of Honour in the new Household. But I should be sorry if that inspired you with the smallest doubt of my feeling for you, for I should wish to give you proofs of my satisfaction, and to be especially agreeable to you, on every opportunity.

CCXLVI

TO M. DE CHAMPAGNY, DUC DE CADORE, MINISTER FOR FOREIGN AFFAIRS.

PARIS, 26*th February* 1810.

I DESIRE you will submit to me, in the course of the day, the carefully prepared draft of a circular to be addressed to my Ministers and Consuls, in which you will give the true motive of my alliance with Austria. This circular is not to be printed, but my Ministers will base their language on it.

In it you will say, that one of the principal means used by the English to rekindle the war on the Continent has been the supposition of my intention to overthrow all dynasties. Circumstances having placed me in a position to choose a Consort, I have desired to deprive them of that dangerous pretext for disturbing the nations and sowing discord which has steeped Europe in blood. Nothing appeared to me more likely to calm the general anxiety, than my request for the hand of an Austrian Archduchess. The brilliant and lofty qualities of the Archduchess Marie Louise, of which I had been specially informed, have enabled me to act in conformity with my policy. The request for her hand having been made, and acceded to by the Emperor of Austria, I sent the Prince of Neufchâtel to make my formal proposal, and to be present as witness at the marriage, which will take place at Vienna, on the 6th of March, when an Archduke will act as my proxy. I have been very glad to take advantage of this opportunity to unite two great nations, and prove my esteem for the Austrian nation, and the inhabitants of the town of Vienna. You will add that I desire they will suit their language to the bonds of kinship which unite me to the House of Austria, without, however, saying anything to diminish my close alliance with the Emperor of Russia. You will write specially to my Ministers at Stuttgart, Munich, and Carlsruhe, to let them know the itinerary of the Empress's journey, and give them detailed instructions as to the etiquette to be followed when she passes through the various Courts. There is no use in going by what was done in my case, for I only passed through when I was travelling on business, and I never concerned myself at all with etiquette. I had so much to think of, that I set no store by anything of the kind. But the Empress's case is different. The manner of the Empress's reception must be clearly settled, and also the question of whether she is to pay a visit to the Queens, while she is at Munich and Stuttgart. My intention is that the course followed with regard to her, shall be such as would formerly have been taken respecting the Empress of Germany.

CCXLVII

TO M. DE CHAMPAGNY, DUC DE CADORE, MINISTER FOR FOREIGN AFFAIRS.

PARIS, *2nd March* 1810.

SEND a note to the Minister of Baden to inform him that I am grieved to see that Prince Louis has recovered his influence at Carlsruhe; that the Catholics are subjected to vexatious treatment; that officers who have not fought on our side, or who have served against us, are promoted, to the prejudice of those who have fought under my orders ; that I desire this deliberate attempt to displease me may be put a stop to ; that the Baden Cabinet's behaviour is unworthy of an ally ; that I shall take the part of the troops who fought through the Polish, Prussian, and Austrian campaigns with me ; that I insist that Prince Louis shall retire from the States of Baden ; that he is at the bottom of all the mischief ; that he is to leave the country instantly, and that if he does not, I will have him arrested, and shut up in a French fortress, where he shall expiate all his crimes.

Write to my Minister to say, and make it known far and wide, that I insist that appointments shall be equally divided between Protestants and Catholics, that promotion shall be given to the soldiers who served with my troops, and not to new-comers, and that I even request the new-comers may be got rid of.

CCXLVIII

TO M. FOUCHÉ, DUC D'OTRANTE, MINISTER OF POLICE.

PARIS, 12th March 1810.

I FREQUENTLY complain of the newspapers, but I do not believe the orders given them are ever sufficiently positive. This is what you should write to the editors :—

The editors are never to publish any news as to what I have done, drawn either from foreign newspapers or foreign correspondents. There is no difficulty about this. If a foreign newspaper says I have been to the Comédie Française, the French newspapers are not to repeat the fact ; if they say I have made a treaty, published such or such an edict, it is not to be repeated—for a matter relating to the Government should not come from abroad. Thus, if this rule were followed, one-half of the complaints to which the newspapers now give rise would disappear. It is ridiculous that it should be from a German newspaper that people hear I have sent Gobelins tapestry to the Emperor of Austria. The journalist who draws such a piece of intelligence from a German newspaper must clearly be a simpleton, and no justification can be offered for him.

CCXLIX

TO M. DE CHAMPAGNY, DUC DE CADORE,
MINISTER FOR FOREIGN AFFAIRS.

PARIS, 3rd April 1810.

I DESIRE that the present made to Mons. de Metternich should be of the same value as that made to the Prince of Neufchâtel : he must therefore receive a similar medallion. I approve of the present you suggest for the Prince of Schwartzenberg. I desire these gifts may be presented with as little delay as possible. I think Prince Trauttmansdorff, who already has my portrait, would rather receive some Gobelin tapestries or a fine toilet service (*nécessaire*). Prince Schwartzenberg, who has a great house, might perhaps prefer an ordinary portrait, worth about 16,000 francs, and a porcelain *nécessaire*, to the value of 30,000 francs. Count Metternich might perhaps also prefer a handsome porcelain *nécessaire*, in which case you would give him a portrait of the ordinary value. Have hints given on this subject.

CCL

TO PRINCE EUGÈNE NAPOLEON, VICEROY OF ITALY.

PARIS, 3rd April 1810.

I HEAR Cardinal Oppizoni was not present at my marriage. He ought to have been there, in his triple quality of Cardinal, Senator, and Bishop of one of my chief towns.

You will send for him, and you will inform him that he is to send in his resignation as Archbishop of Bologna, before the evening.

You will make him aware of all the indignation I feel at the shameful conduct of a man whom I have loaded with benefits, whom I have made Cardinal, Archbishop, and Senator, whom I have protected, and whose infamous debaucheries I concealed, by intervening with my authority, and interrupting the course of criminal proceedings at Bologna. You will be careful to send his resignation by the evening express, and to see that the Chapter forthwith appoints suitable Vicars.

You will not fail to make him feel that there must be no hesitation, and that he could not possibly desire to remain Archbishop in spite of me, after the failure in duty of which he has been guilty.

CCLI

TO M. FOUCHÉ, DUC D'OTRANTE, MINISTER OF POLICE.

COMPIÈGNE, 14*th April* 1810.

HEREWITH you will find the letter written me by Prince Ferdinand. Make me a report on the whole of this business, in a sense which will fit it for publication in the *Moniteur.* Is the arrest of the person in question so little known, that he may be supposed to have been arrested at Valençay? I should like you to put in your report, that the person arrested at Valençay is at Vincennes; that he had been charged with a mission from the English to the Princes; that he had attempted to carry it out, and that Prince Ferdinand gave me warning. At the end of this report the details of the fête given by the Princes, at Valençay, in honour of my marriage, should be inserted. The business, presented in this fashion, will have the best possible effect in Europe. The Princes might be left in the belief that it is they who brought about the English agent's arrest. I shall answer Prince Ferdinand in a letter which may also be inserted in the *Moniteur.* You will feel the necessity of drawing up a letter to the Governor of Valençay, and two examinations, one at Valençay and the other here, in which he will give his name, etc. Arrange all this in whatever way is most likely to impose upon the English.

I desire you will let me have all this to-morrow, for I wish it to be printed in the *Moniteur* on Monday or Tuesday.

All that will then remain for you to do, is to keep the English agent in the closest confinement, so that he can have no outside communication whatever, and to renew the strictest orders against his being given pens, ink, or paper.

CCLII

TO M. DE CHAMPAGNY, DUC DE CADORE, MINISTER FOR FOREIGN AFFAIRS.

COMPIÈGNE, 24th April 1810.

I SEND you some remarks on the Russian counter proposal. You will form these into a Note, which you will submit to me, when it is drawn up. When you send this Note to Mons. Kourakin, you will inform him that I will not alter these terms; that, after all, this is an explanation which I am good enough to give, and nothing else; that I am displeased with my Ambassador for not having weighed his words more carefully; that on words, honour between nations, even as honour between individuals, depends; that this demand on Russia's part appears to me utterly unreasonable, and that I vainly seek to discover to what it is attributable.

It is necessary that you should write to Mons. de Caulaincourt, and send him an accurate and methodical reply to his despatch of the 8th March. Let him know how completely the items of your instructions have been misunderstood. What! could it follow that because you had given him authority to sign anything which reassured Russia, he was to contract engagements concerning which he did not know my will? Should he not have understood that he was only authorised to reassure Russia as far as I, and events of my making, were concerned. The mistake he has made is a gross one. He has misunderstood his instructions, and failed to discern the limit of his powers. You must work out this in the most detailed manner.

CCLIII

TO M. FOUCHÉ, DUC D'OTRANTE, MINISTER OF POLICE.

COMPIÈGNE, 24th April 1810.

Is it true that engravings are being published with the title of 'Joséphine Beauharnais *née* La Pagerie'? If this is true, have the prints seized, and let the engravers be punished.

CCLIV

TO GENERAL CLARKE, DUC DE FELTRE,
MINISTER OF WAR.

COMPIÈGNE, 26th April 1810.

I THINK General Duhesme must be given leave to come to Paris. You will hear him, and give me an account of all he says. The General has rendered me great services. His honour is sorely compromised. If he is innocent, he must be cleared instantly ; if he is guilty he must lose his head on the scaffold. Appoint somebody to hear the General, and also to hear my Consul, and the agents I had at Barcelona. Ask the Duke of Castiglione for positive assertions and proofs. That general officer would have done far better to be fighting at the head of his troops, instead of staying at Barcelona to bring this affair into prominence, and react on a country where Frenchmen have so many enemies. I send you General Duhesme's memorandum, which I have not read. Make yourself acquainted with it, and report to me on it.

CCLV

TO PRINCE EUGÈNE NAPOLEON, VICEROY OF ITALY.

COMPIÈGNE, 26th April 1810.

I HAVE your letter, dated midnight on the 25th April, containing one from the Empress. Herewith you will find my answer.

See Cambacérès about Tascher's marriage. I desire it may take place as speedily as possible. I will keep all my promises about it.

As for the other Tascher, I take no interest in him. He has failed too completely in his duty to me for me to take any trouble about him. The little blackguard doffed the French cockade at Madrid, without giving me notice, simply because he fell in love, and completely forgot all the duty he owed me, especially before that occasion. Let him do what he likes, and marry whom he chooses. I do not care a jot. I shall not concern myself with the matter at all. I do not mention the subject to the Empress, but you know my views, and I shall never alter them. I believe the young man to be giddy-headed, and bad-tempered. I send you the King of Spain's letter. I consent to whatever the Empress does, but I will not confer any mark of my regard on a person who has behaved ill to me.

I am very glad indeed the Empress likes Navarre. I am giving orders to have 300,000 francs, which I owe her for 1810, and 300,000 more, for 1811, advanced to her. She will then only have the 2,000,000 from the Public Treasury yet to come in.

I should have no objection, if she has not already spent the 100,000 francs I gave for carrying on the work at Malmaison, to its being suspended, and the money laid out at Navarre. This would very nearly make up the million the Empress asked for. I very much approve of her plan of spending everything at Navarre. She is free to go and take the waters wherever she likes, and even to come back to Paris, after the season for taking them is over. As I start for Antwerp to-morrow, I do not see so much objection to her going to the baths of Aix-la-Chapelle. The only one I could make, would be against her returning to places where I had been with her. I would rather she went to other waters, where she has been without me, such as those of Plombières, Vichy, Bourbonne, Aix-en-Provence, etc.; but if the Aix-la-Chapelle waters are those which suit her best, I will make no objection whatever. What I desire, above all other things, is that she should make herself easy, and not allow herself to be excited and disturbed by Paris gossip.

CCLVI

TO LOUIS NAPOLEON, KING OF HOLLAND.

OSTEND, *20th May* 1810.

I HAVE your letter of 16th May. In our mutual position, we should always speak frankly. You know I have frequently read documents of yours, which were not written with the intention of my seeing them. I know all your most secret arrangements, and nothing you tell me, in a contradictory sense, will be of any avail. You need not speak of your feelings, nor of your childhood. Experience has taught me the truth about all that. Holland is in an unpleasant position —that I know. I can quite conceive your desiring to get

NEW LETTERS OF NAPOLEON I   181

out of it. But I am surprised you should appeal to me for assistance. It is not I who can do anything in the matter; it is you, and you only. When you so behave as to convince the Dutch that you act on my inspiration, that every step and every feeling of yours agrees with mine, then you will be loved and esteemed, and you will acquire the credit necessary for the re-constitution of Holland. The Dutch illusion on this subject is still some support to you. Your journey to Paris, your return, and that of the Queen, and other reasonable grounds, make your people still believe that you may possibly return to my system, and my manner of looking at things. But you alone can confirm these hopes, and remove the smallest doubt on the subject. There is not an action of yours, which your fat Dutchmen do not appraise, just as they appraise a matter of credit, or of trade; so they know very well what they have to expect. When friendship with France, and with myself, entitles a man to be well received at your Court, the whole of Holland will notice it, the whole of Holland will begin to breathe, the whole of Holland will find itself in a natural position. This depends on you alone. You have done nothing towards it, since your return. Do you wish to know what the result of your conduct will be? Your subjects will feel themselves tossed backwards and forwards, between England and France. They will not know what to hope or to desire. They will cast themselves into the arms of France, and clamour to be incorporated with her, as a refuge from all this uncertainty and whimsicality. Your Government would fain be paternal, but it is only weak. I have found nothing but the most in-coherent kind of administration in Brabant and Zealand. Even in Zealand itself, which is so thoroughly Dutch, they are glad to be attached to a great country, and to be saved from a vacillation which the people find it impossible to understand. Do you think the letter you have had written to Mollerus, and your assurance of the affection you bear him, at the very moment when you are dismissing him, will add to your consideration in the country? Do not deceive yourself! Every one knows that apart from me, you have no credit, and that without me, you are nothing at all. If then, the example you had under your eyes at Paris, if your knowledge of my character—which is to go straight towards my object, without being stopped by any consideration—

have not altered nor enlightened you, what can I do? I can do without Holland, for I hold the waters of the Meuse and the Rhine, down to their mouths. But Holland cannot do without my protection. If the country, governed by one of my brothers, and looking to me only for salvation, does not see my image in him—if, when you speak, it is not I who speak—you destroy all confidence in your administration —you shatter your own sceptre. Believe me, nobody is taken in. Do you desire to tread the path of political safety? Then love France, and love my glory; that is the only way to serve the King of Holland. Under a king, the Dutch have lost the advantages of a free government. You may have been a haven to them, but you have destroyed this haven with a light heart. You have dotted it with reefs.

Do you know why you were a haven for Holland? Because you were the Covenant of an eternal union with France —the bond which made her interests mine; and Holland, which, through you, became a portion of my Empire, was my beloved province too, because I had bestowed it on a Prince who was almost a son to me.

If you had been what you should, I should take as much interest in Holland as in France, and the prosperity of that country would be as near my heart as that of France. Most assuredly I believed myself, when I set you on the throne of Holland, to be filling it with a French citizen, as devoted to the greatness of France, and the interests of the mother country, as I was myself. If you had followed up this plan of conduct, you would now be reigning over six millions of subjects. I should have made the throne of Holland a pedestal, on which I would have set Hamburg, Osnabrück, and a part of Northern Germany. This would have been the nucleus of a nation which should have thrown the German mind still further out of its orbit, and that is the first object of my policy. But far from doing this, you have followed a diametrically opposite course, and I have been obliged to forbid your presence in France, and to take possession of part of your country.

You never say a word in Council, you never confide anything to any one, that is not known and turned against you, and that does not stultify you. For, to the Dutch mind, you are nothing but a Frenchman, who has only been amongst them for four years. All they see in you, is me, and the

advantage of being protected from the thieves and inferior
agitators who have worried them, ever since the Conquest.
The moment you prove yourself a bad Frenchman, you
become less to them than a Prince of Orange, to whose
family they owe their rank as a nation, and a long continu-
ance of prosperity and glory. It is clear, to the Dutch mind,
that your estrangement from France has cost them what
they would not have lost under Schimmelpenninck, nor under
a Prince of Orange. Before all things, be a Frenchman, and
the Emperor's brother, and then, you may be sure, you are
in the path of the true interests of Holland. But why has
all this happened? Fate is against you, and you are incor-
rigible. Already you would fain dismiss the few Frenchmen
remaining with you. Neither counsel, nor advice, nor affection, should be bestowed on you—nothing but threats and
main force. What is the meaning of these prayers, and
mysterious fasts, you have ordered? Louis, you have no
desire to reign for long! Your every action reveals your
inmost sentiments, even more clearly than your private letters.
Hearken to a wiser man than yourself: return from the path
on to which you have strayed! Be thoroughly and heartily
French, otherwise your subjects will drive you out, and you
will quit Holland,—the laughing-stock of the Dutch, and the
object of their pity. Good sense and policy are necessary
to the government of States,—not sour unhealthy bile.

CCLVII

TO M. FOUCHÉ, DUC D'OTRANTE, MINISTER OF POLICE.

LILLE, 23rd May 1810.

IT is my intention that no French officer in the Austrian,
or Russian, or any other foreign service, shall enter France
under any pretext whatsoever—neither on leave, nor with
a passport, nor on business. Any who present themselves
for that purpose, must be stopped on the frontier. No
exception of any kind is to be made. Write on this subject
to all Prefects in Belgium, Tuscany, and Piedmont, and even
to all former Prefects. I will not have any of these officers
in France. I will not tolerate the idea of any Frenchman
taking military service with a foreign Power. I am very
angry that leave was given to M. La Roche-Aymon. He

has done me a great deal of harm at the Court of Prussia. It was he who put the idea of taking this measure into my head. My intention is, that he shall be arrested, taken to Vincennes, placed in solitary confinement, and the seals put on his papers.

Have your Police Registers searched, to find out whether they bear the names of Belgians or Frenchmen in foreign services; they must not return to France. But I do not object to those who desire to take advantage of the Amnesty doing so.

CCLVIII

TO LOUIS NAPOLEON, KING OF HOLLAND.

LILLE, *23rd May* 1810.

AT the very moment when you are making me the very finest protestations, I learn that my Ambassador's people have been ill treated. I intend that the persons who have been so guilty towards me shall be given up, so that the punishment I shall wreak on them may serve as a warning. Mons. Serurier has given me an account of the manner in which you behaved at the Diplomatic audience. In consequence of this, I will have no Dutch Ambassador here: Admiral Verhuell, who is at Paris, has orders to be gone in twenty-four hours. I will have no more talking and vowing. It is high time for me to know whether you intend to bring Holland to misery, and cause the ruin of your country, by your follies. I will not have you send a Minister to Austria. I will not have you dismiss the Frenchmen in your service. I will not keep an Ambassador in Holland any longer. The Secretary of Legation, who remains there as Chargé d'Affaires, will inform you of my intentions. I do not choose to expose an Ambassador to such insult in future. I will have nothing but a Chargé d'Affaires. As it was the Russian Ambassador's master who placed you on your throne, it is quite natural that you should follow his advice. Write me no more of your customary twaddle; three years, now, it has been going on, and every instant proves its falsehood!

Autograph Postscript.—This is the last letter I shall ever write you in my life.

CCLIX

TO THE PRINCE DE NEUFCHÂTEL, MAJOR-GENERAL OF THE ARMY IN SPAIN.

LILLE, 23rd May 1810.

WRITE to Marshal Oudinot that I am very much displeased with the behaviour of the inhabitants of Amsterdam,
and that, within a very short time, I shall be obliged to send
fresh troops into Holland.   Desire the Marshal to keep his
eye on everything that happens, both in Amsterdam, and
all over the country.   My intention is that he shall have no
intercourse with the King, and that he shall not allow any
officer of his army to have any either.

CCLX

TO GENERAL SAVARY, DUC DE ROVIGO, MINISTER OF POLICE.

ST. CLOUD, 6th June 1810.

THE Ouvrard business is growing serious ; it must be sifted
to the bottom.   Have him taken to Vincennes.   You will
send for the Governor ; you will employ a few trustworthy
gendarmes, and you will take every measure, in fact, to
prevent his holding communication with any one.   Bring
me the report of the examination of Desmarest, and
d'Hauterive, to-morrow morning.   You will not allow
Ouvrard to hold any further communication with the last
named, whose mission is now closed.

As the people belonging to the Ministry of Police do not
appear to me to possess the independence necessary for
pushing forward this business, I shall have the examinations
conducted by Mounier, my Private Secretary, so as to make
the matter more impressive, and obtain full and clear knowledge of everything that happens.

The great point is that he should be put into solitary
confinement in Vincennes, and that henceforward he
should see no one.   A more important State criminal has
never existed.

CCLXI

TO M. DE CHAMPAGNY, DUC DE CADORE, MINISTER FOR FOREIGN AFFAIRS.

St. Cloud, *9th June* 1810.

INFORM Mons. Serurier that there is no question of my troops occupying Amsterdam—that is not my intention; that he must not, therefore, alarm the Dutch with this idea, but that he is to make a declaration that, on the very first appearance of any preparation which can be considered as an insult to France, he has orders to ask for his passports, and leave Holland, and that his Majesty will look on any hostile attitude which reflects on the dignity of France, as a declaration of war. You will direct the Chargé d'Affaires to keep the quarrel open, and to insist on reparation which will wash out the outrage on my Ambassador. And he will add, that if full satisfaction is not given, the King must renounce all future hope of my friendship and protection.

CCLXII

TO GENERAL SAVARY, DUC DE ROVIGO, MINISTER OF POLICE.

St. Cloud, *24th June* 1810.

GIVE orders that all English people who are in Paris, or within thirty leagues of the residence of the Court, are to depart. The Minister of War will inform them as to the towns in which they may reside. In future, no English person is to come to Paris, nor reside there.

CCLXIII

TO M. DE CHAMPAGNY, DUC DE CADORE, MINISTER FOR FOREIGN AFFAIRS.

St. Cloud, *24th June* 1810.

ENCLOSED you will find samples of the licences granted by the King of Holland. You will write to my Chargé d'Affaires, to demand that these licences shall be considered null and void, and suppressed, as being in contravention of the treaty made with me. At the same time, he will point out the absurdity of their style, and the senselessness of speaking of emperors and kings in such a manner, in any document.

In the correspondence, I notice a letter from Mons. Gohier, dated 15th June, as to the injustice of the Dutch Government, which keeps back funds due to my privateers. Write my Chargé d'Affaires by the same packet, that unless my privateers instantly receive the money belonging to them, I shall order it to be taken, by main force, out of the Dutch Treasury. Let him say clearly, that I am not going to endure anything more from the Dutch; that they had better behave straightforwardly, and have done with all this chicanery and deceitful behaviour.

CCLXIV

TO GENERAL CLARKE, DUC DE FELTRE, MINISTER OF WAR.

ST. CLOUD, *6th June* 1810.

THE Irish Battalion which has been in Spain, has recruited a great number of English prisoners of war, who have since deserted. The Irish Regiment has thus lost, in this present year, more than 1000 English recruits, who have deserted. Let the recruiting authorities of this regiment know of my displeasure at their having accepted English recruits.

CCLXV

TO GENERAL SAVARY, DUC DE ROVIGO, MINISTER OF POLICE.

ST. CLOUD, *29th June* 1810.

SEND Réal to the Duke of Otranto's house. He will remove the seals affixed by the Prefect of Police. He will make inquiries about Mme Dillon and other correspondences of that kind. When that has been done, the Duke of Otranto can depart.

CCLXVI

TO M. DE CHAMPAGNY, DUC DE CADORE, MINISTER FOR FOREIGN AFFAIRS.

ST. CLOUD, *June* 29, 1810.

I RETURN your St. Petersburg letters, which were brought by my Orderly Officer, Watteville. I desire you will send an express to-morrow to the Duke of Vicenza. You will begin by entering into a very full dissertation on the prosperous state of France, and of our manufactures. You will point out the falsehood of the imputation that we carry on commerce with England; and you will say that its only foundation rests on the fact that we granted a passage to a few vessels, laden with corn.

(2nd) You will inform him that we have not written to Lord Wellesley, who therefore cannot have said that, and that if he had, it would have been a lie.

(3rd) That Austria has made no overture of any kind to England, and that Count Metternich has taken no step of that nature.

(4th) That neither has any overture been made by Holland; that the Duke of Otranto alone, on his own responsibility, and without the Emperor's approbation, put Ouvrard, a purveyor, and a certain Fagan, a relation of Lord Wellesley's, into communication with the Minister, not so much for purposes of negotiation, as to carry on a matter of espionage; that when the Emperor heard it, he dismissed the Duke of Otranto from the Ministry of Police; that the English therefore boast falsely, when they boast of having received overtures; that the negotiations for exchanging prisoners are still being carried on; that the English are in a very bad way, and that they are not so little inclined to listen to peace proposals, as they give themselves out to be; that they are in great disorder and confusion; and that the folly with which they are pushing forward the war in Portugal, where they have not 30,000 men, will bring some catastrophe upon them; that Spanish affairs are going on satisfactorily.

You will also inform the Duke of Vicenza that I have had an explanation with Prince Kourakin, with regard to the Convention; that we do not know what Mons. de Romanzoff means by our estrangement, and our subsequent reconciliation with them; that our course has always been steady and straightforward ; that we are in no way bound to Austria ; that people must imbue themselves with the conviction that nothing in the world would induce me to sign a document of a dishonourable nature ; that, consequently, to sign the words ' Poland will not be re-established,' would be more than to acknowledge the partition, it would be blasting my own character, and that I am ready to alter the Convention.

You must have a long conversation, in the same sense, with Prince Kourakin.

(1st) You must formally certify the fact that you have never written to Lord Wellesley, that there has never been any open negotiation ; and you will point out the absurdity of such an idea.

(2nd) You will tell him I am distressed to notice that Mons. de Romanzoff credits the news circulated by the English Gazettes. That they never mention a reverse or a negotiation without his believing it. That Austria has made no overture, and has sent no one to England.

You will make him aware that he should write to his Court in this sense, and that when in doubt, he should apply to you, this being the only way in which he can protect his Court from the mischievous reports with which it is flooded.

CCLXVII

TO M. FOUCHÉ, DUC D'OTRANTE.

St. Cloud, 1st July 1810.

MONS. LE DUC D'OTRANTE, your services can no longer be acceptable to me. You would do well to start within twenty-four hours, to take up your residence in the district for which you are Senator. This letter having no other object, I pray God to have you in his safe and holy keeping.

CCLXVIII

TO M. SAVARY, DUC DE ROVIGO, MINISTER OF POLICE.

St. Cloud, 1st July 1810.

ENCLOSED you will find a letter for the Duke of Otranto. You will have it delivered to him during the day. My intention is that he shall retire to his Senatorship. If, however, he should have planned a journey through the kingdoms of Naples and Italy, I should not oppose it, but in that case he would have to furnish you with his itinerary. You will let him know that if he does not travel, I wish him to retire to Nice. I need not tell you, that as he retires as an exile, into his Senatorship, he is not to exercise any influence, or to receive any honours within it. You will take care that my order is executed, and ·that he starts before the twenty-four hours have run out.

CCLXIX

TO M. SAVARY, DUC DE ROVIGO, MINISTER OF POLICE.

St. Cloud, 3rd July 1810.

If what your report of 1st July states, concerning the Antwerp Béguines, is true, you must have three or four of the chief ones arrested, and put in the gaol at Vilvorde, and at the same time, several of the Vicars, or Priests, who direct them, must be arrested, and shut up at Fenestrelle.

CCLXX

TO GENERAL CLARKE, DUC DE FELTRE, MINISTER OF WAR.

St. Cloud, 3rd July 1810.

GIVE orders to the Duc of Reggio, that as soon as he has entered Amsterdam, he is to have all the cannon, mounted on the lines of that town, which might be used against me in future, quietly sent away to France. All guns placed there with the intention of using them in revolt, shall be sent to France.

CCLXXI

TO COMTE BIGOT DE PRÉAMENEU, MINISTER OF PUBLIC WORSHIP.

Rambouillet, 13th July 1810.

I HAVE carefully read your report of 10th June, and the documents attached to it. It would be far too much to establish institutions for 6000 orphan girls in France. What should we do with this great number, when they reach the age of twenty-one?

It therefore appears to me more convenient, merely to open six houses, within the ancient boundaries of France, of which that at Paris would be the principal, each to contain 600 orphans. These orphans would, in the first instance, be children whose fathers had died on the field of battle, or belonged to the Legion of Honour. Taking 600 to be the total number, I would pay 400 francs each for 300, and 200 francs for the other 300. Thus they would cost me 180,000 francs. I would charge this sum on the landed property of the Legion of Honour which would pay the pensions. The six houses would be arranged in such a manner, that each should be able to receive an equal number of paying inmates, so that the education of 1200 orphan girls would thus be provided for. I have consequently modified the plan you laid before me. I have placed these houses under the protection of the Princess who is at the head of the establishments of Ecouen and St. Denis, as all the institutions will be connected with each other.

I desire to establish other institutions, under the Ursuline rule, though not bearing that name, the number of which, including Holland, may reach fifty or sixty, and which should be able to receive about 5000 pupils. Two thousand five hundred of these scholars will have 300 francs a year, or half scholarships, and their parents will pay another 300 francs. This would cost 750,000 francs. For the other 2500 pupils I would give 500 francs, which would bring my total expenditure up to 2,000,000. I should provide for this, partly through the Legion of Honour, and partly by endowment. Five thousand extra paying pupils may be received, and this would give us 10,000 girls, distributed between forty or sixty institutions. In the course of this week, you will submit the draft regulations for the formation of these institutions.

The six houses for the education of these orphans will form an institution specially attached to the Legion of Honour, whose orphans will be placed there.

TO THE COMTE DE MONTALIVET, MINISTER OF THE INTERIOR.

RAMBOUILLET, 16*th July* 1810.

I HAVE decided on the system of our trade with the Americans, and I conclude you will lay the thirty permits for the cotton trade before me, at the Council. If there should be any difficulty as to the necessary association with factories, you can dispense with that. You may content yourself with the promise, which may or may not be worth anything. But I see no objection to your proceeding further. When these thirty permits are exhausted, you will issue thirty more, so as to have some sixty or eighty persons licensed for the American trade. By this means, my factories will be fully supplied with cotton.

The corn trade in France is forbidden, as a measure of public safety. As soon as I am satisfied about the harvest, I shall re-open my ports, and exportation will be allowed along the whole frontier. I conclude that at the present time, in those places where the export of corn is permitted, no ship is allowed to sail without a licence, and that, as my Decree provides, no ship is allowed to sail as an adventurer. If I should be mistaken, you must revise the law, so as positively to forbid this, and prevent any ship from sailing for the merchant trade, without being licensed.

I suppose you will submit the licences for Bordeaux, La Rochelle, and those ports from which exportation is allowed, for my signature, to-morrow,—so that trade may not be checked; and I suppose you will also submit the licences for the Mediterranean ports, so that trade with the Levant and Africa may be carried on.

Having thus provided for the most pressing needs of the export trade of the Empire, we must attend to that of the Allied Countries. Submit the draft of a Decree which will set forth the arguments on both sides, and will grant licences for Hamburg and Bremen. According to these licences, the ships actually belonging to that country, and no others, will be sent away laden with corn: you will let me know whether these ports contain much wheat. They will be sent to the port of Dunkirk, with Customs permits. These ships, properly numbered and registered, like those in the American trade, and each bearing on its licence a sentence in cipher (which the Consul will also mention in a letter to Paris) can go to England, anchor there, and unload their corn. But (1) the return cargo must be timber, or matters needful for my fleet, which must be landed at Dunkirk. (2) At Dunkirk a fresh cargo must be shipped, of wine, silk stuffs, and other French goods, which must be discharged at Hamburg; (3) the licence must be paid for at so much per ton, and I desire the charge shall be a heavy one, quite equal to the double duty imposed in France on exported wheat, so that I may draw considerable benefit from it. This course will bring me three advantages :—(1) Heavy navigating dues; (2) the exportation of French goods; (3) timber, tar, and other supplies which my navy may require. I shall follow the same course for Dantzig. This will rejoice the heart of Poland, which country is overflowing.

Hamburg and Bremen are the outlets of the Elbe and Weser, as Dantzig is that of the Vistula. I shall thus be able to lay a heavy duty on these ports, supply my Navy with Northern timber, and gain very advantageous results.

From the date of the issue of my edict, no vessel will sail from Hamburg, Bremen, or Lübeck without a licence.

This Decree, of which you will bring me the rough draft, will be to the effect :—

(1) That the ships may put in at Dunkirk or Nantes.

(2) That part of their cargo must be in timber.

(3) That they are to carry a certain proportion of wines and goods, produced and manufactured in France, out of this country.

(4) That there are to be French Custom-house officials at Hamburg, Bremen, and Lübeck, who will send out the ships, with licences and permits, number them, notify their sailings to the Director-General of Customs, and take the further precautions usual in the American trade.

As to Italy, I will grant licences for exporting corn from Venice and Ancona. This corn may go out of its way, and be taken to Malta, and even to England. Apart from the corn trade, I will allow the exportation of cheese, and other products, grown in Italy. My Consuls will take the same precautions for these ships as for the others. Those which go to England must call and discharge cargo at Nantes,

N

on their way back. Those going to Malta must return by Genoa, Toulon, or Marseilles. Permission will be given for the exportation (either direct, or by Venice and Ancona) of cloth, silk fabrics, and other raw and manufactured goods, both French and Italian. And I shall also authorise the issue of licences for the export of oil and cottons, on board Neapolitan boats. The origin of the cotton goods would have to be certified, and the vessels would have to load with French merchandise, in my ports.

You will perceive that this huge system will help to feed my ports, will make this trade an exceptional one, and will bring me in a considerable revenue. The plan is therefore advantageous, from every point of view. It replies to the English Naval tax by a Continental one, it pays back injustice with injustice, and answers one arbitrary act with another. Thus it is no piece of folly which I here under-take.

CCLXXIII

TO PRINCE LEBRUN, GRAND TREASURER OF THE EMPIRE, THE EMPEROR'S LIEUTENANT-GENERAL IN HOLLAND.

St. Cloud, 17th July 1810, midnight.

I HAVE your letter of the 14th, and was glad to hear of your arrival, and the good reception given you at Amsterdam.

It is my intention to keep the Palace at Amsterdam in its present state, and not to have any furniture sold or removed. I am giving orders to Comte Daru to proceed thither; there will be no difficulty about your being lodged in it. It would not do to strip it of furniture. I keep it for myself, and expect to go there in six weeks or two months.

Let the Palace servants know I keep them on, at their old wages.

Both men and horses belong to me.

Comte Daru will make all arrangements as soon as he arrives. You will settle with him that the horses you need shall be placed at your disposal, without your having to buy any.

Send the King's two young private secretaries to me, in Paris, with all the King's private papers, found in his study or elsewhere, duly sealed up. When I have them at St.

Cloud, I will settle what is to be done with them. You will also send everything that belonged to the King, before he ascended the throne, to Paris.

Write Dr. Latour that I not only give him permission to join the King, but that I even desire him to do so; that the Prince is still dear to me; that I shall be glad to think he will remain with him, and take care of him; and that I shall look upon all service he may bestow on him, as a personal service to myself.

I think the title of *Moniteur* is not suitable for the *Gazette d'Amsterdam*, because such a title presupposes the paper to be an official one. Call it the *Courrier d'Amsterdam*.

It is not the present Finance Minister whom I have sent for to Paris, it is the old one. The new Minister must be left in his stead, to see to the collecting of the revenue. However, give no counter orders.

When I asked you to appoint a Police Commissary, I did not intend to appoint either Gohier or Noël, but a Dutch-man. Look about for a man who is attached to France; there are many who have long been so.

I have settled that a deputation from the Legislative Body is to proceed to Paris, and I have since ordered you to add a deputation from the Council of State. This Commission will make arrangements here, about matters relating to the various debts—that on the hospitals, the communes, the mortmain; meanwhile everything must be reduced by two-thirds. This is not an absolute settlement, but it is better than nothing. As regards the money borrowed by the King, that can only be settled in Paris, with the Council. The whole question is reduced to this,—that only one-third of everything is to be paid. When I have full information, I will settle about the rest.

CCLXXIV

TO GENERAL SAVARY, DUC DE ROVIGO,
MINISTER OF POLICE.

St. Cloud, *20th July* 1810.

I SEND you back your statement, with notes in my own hand; I am heartily sorry I set several people at liberty on the occasion of my marriage. I was not then aware of all Mons. Fouché's intrigues. The person who proposed I should set some of these people free, must have desired to betray me.

I see, on the list of persons removed to a distance from Paris, several whose position the police have ventured to mitigate. You will recall these orders. The police has no right to make any alteration in arrangements I have made.

CCLXXV

TO GENERAL SAVARY, DUC DE ROVIGO,
MINISTER OF POLICE.

TRIANON, 4th August 1810.

HEREWITH you will find a letter from General Morand, and another from the Russian Chargé d'Affaires at Cagliari.

You will write to General Miollis, to express my displeasure at his allowing vessels to sail from Civita Vecchia without my leave. You will give him orders that no more are to be allowed to leave the Roman ports in future, and that the ship which has gone to Sardinia, is to be seized when she returns.

You will inform General Miollis that he is to watch the Senator Lucien, who appears to be keeping up correspondence with enemies of the State; that he is to let him go on, and that if he should actually take steps to embark, and give himself up to the English, he is to be arrested; that I confide this secret to his fidelity and zeal. He will watch the Senator Lucien as long as he remains in the neighbourhood of Rome, but he will have him arrested the moment he sets foot on board ship.

You will make arrangements with the naval authorities for seizing the vessel which has gone to Cagliari, when she returns, taking possession of the ship's papers, and having the seals affixed, arresting the captain and crew, and having them sent to Paris. Write straight to the Police Commissary at Civita Vecchia.

CCLXXVI

TO GENERAL CLARKE, DUC DE FELTRE,
MINISTER OF WAR.

TRIANON, 8th August 1810.

I HAVE your letter regarding Madame d'Orléans. Her letter astonishes me; I thought she was at Palermo. She did go there for her son's marriage; I think I hold proof of that. I cannot understand why she is at Barcelona. Let me have some light on the subject.

CCLXXVII

TO M. DE CHAMPAGNY, DUC DE CADORE,
MINISTER FOR FOREIGN AFFAIRS.

TRIANON, 18th August 1810.

WRITE to General Rapp, and inform him of my displeasure, first of all, because he had no business to give an official dinner; secondly, because he ought to have given the Russian Consul precedence over the Consul of Prussia, and every other; and lastly, because it would have been far simpler to have invited no one but his own officers to dinner.

Tell him I am specially displeased with his letter, because it fails in courtesy to a great Power, which is allied with France. I desire you will let Caulaincourt know of my displeasure, when you write to him. You will also go and see Mons. de Kourakin, and make him aware of it. Tell him I was on the point of recalling General Rapp; that, however wrong any Russian Consul had been, no letter should ever have been written in such a tone, and that the act was that of a madman.

CCLXXVIII

TO PRINCE LEBRUN, GRAND TREASURER OF THE EMPIRE,
THE EMPEROR'S LIEUTENANT-GENERAL IN HOLLAND.

TRIANON, 11th August 1810.

I HAVE your letter of 8th August. As the King's papers, and his secretaries, are in Paris, he cannot have them.

The private secretaries have taken the oath of allegiance. I have given orders to Mons. Daru to send his wardrobe to Paris. I do not intend you to correspond with him. Nor do I intend him to hold any correspondence with Holland.

Mons. Bylandt will remain in Holland. I do not intend him to leave it. The Comptroller of the Crown Property is to cease to act, altogether. No agent is to correspond with any one but me.

I have your letter about the Castle of Loo. I am in no hurry to give it away. I shall keep the Castle for the present. I have no inclination to give away either the house of the French Minister, or the King's Palaces. A fit of generosity was on you when you wrote me that letter.

I do not know why vessels belonging to the United States sail from Dutch ports, without my leave; they go to England. As for the ship for Batavia, let it start as soon as possible.

Have the Titles Office established by the King suppressed by Decree, and declare it broken up. Send all the documents to Mons. Pasquier in Paris; all those who require them must apply to him. You will announce that all endowments are revoked. The King had no right to give away what did not belong to him, whether Crown lands, or State property.

CCLXXIX

TO GENERAL SAVARY, DUC DE ROVIGO, MINISTER OF POLICE.

St. Cloud, 21st *August* 1810.

I THINK no notice should be taken of the Duke of Otranto. I believe he is returning to his Senatorship. You must write to him to do so.

CCLXXX

TO COMTE BIGOT DE PRÉAMENEU, MINISTER OF PUBLIC WORSHIP.

St. Cloud, 22nd *August* 1810.

I SEE you have 500 contumacious priests at Parma. That must be rather too large a number for Parma. You might leave 200 of them at Parma, and send 200 to Bologna. Speak about this to Aldini. The priests will be very comfortable at Bologna.

CCLXXXI

TO M. DE CHAMPAGNY, DUC DE CADORE, MINISTER FOR FOREIGN AFFAIRS.

ST. CLOUD, *20th August* 1810.

REPLY to Mons. Bourgoing, that I am very glad he has not been in Bohemia, and that he has not had any meeting with the King [of Holland]; that I disapprove of what he has written and said, and that I desire he will take no further part in this business. If the Comte de Saint Leu consults him, he will give him no reply whatever. He will let him do as he chooses, and not interfere in any way.

CCLXXXII

TO GENERAL SAVARY, DUC DE ROVIGO, MINISTER OF POLICE.

ST. CLOUD, *31st August* 1810.

SEND me a report about General Rousseau, an officer in the Austrian service, who is at Brussels. Who authorised his coming there? Who gave him passports? He must be denounced to the Chief Judge, and a report must be sent to me. Before you make me that report, you will remove the fellow from Belgium, and have him sent to Valenciennes, until I have decided what is to be done with him.

The Chief Judge will revise the sentence, and submit it to the Court of Appeal. In a general way, let no passports for Belgium be given to Belgians qualified by the Treaty of Campo Formio, unless they take advantage of the amnesty. Write about this to Comte Otto, at Vienna. I will not have these Belgians, nor those in the Austrian service, who come on six months' furlough. There is an amnesty; they can take advantage of it if they choose. If any come, send them forty leagues away from Belgium, and make me an individual report as to what should be done with them.

CCLXXXIII

TO M. DE CHAMPAGNY, DUC DE CADORE,
MINISTER FOR FOREIGN AFFAIRS.

St. Cloud, 5*th September* 1810.

I HAVE just read your report, which I enclose, and I think, notwithstanding, that ever since the 15th August, Mons. Billiot has conducted himself very ill. Generally speaking, I cannot approve of this Consul's. tone. It has been the custom, from time immemorial, that whenever a General Officer of the Consul's nation, invested with the command, was present where the Consul was stationed, the Consul should show him all proper respect and consideration, help him with all his knowledge and information, and never raise any barrier, nor set up any authority, against him.

CCLXXXIV

TO MARSHAL BERNADOTTE, PRINCE DE PONTE-CORVO,
PRINCE ROYAL ELECT OF SWEDEN.

St. Cloud, 10*th September* 1810.

[*This letter was published in the Correspondence, No. 16,890. Instead of the last phrase, the original draft bore the following paragraph, which the Emperor afterwards struck out.*]

These letters patent give you authority to become a Swede ; one clause only has been added, to the effect that you, personally, cannot bear arms against France. This restriction is in conformity with the Constitution of the Empire ; it agrees with your own inclination, and is not, indeed, opposed to the duty of the throne you are about to ascend, which can never, except in utter madness, be at war with France.

CCLXXXV

TO THE PRINCE DE NEUFCHÂTEL, MAJOR-GENERAL OF
THE ARMY IN SPAIN.

St. Cloud, 16*th September* 1810.

STRONG complaints of General Kellermann reach me from all quarters. Send an officer to make him aware of my displeasure at the vexatious acts committed in his Government, and ask him for a categorical statement of all the contributions he has levied. Everything, even to the liberation of prisoners, is sold in that Government, and this occurs in other places,—even at Valladolid. You will inform him that I hold him responsible for abuses so hurtful to the wellbeing and interests of the army. You will let him know that I have asked for a report on the subject, that the officer you send has orders to bring back his reply, and that I expect he will report to you, that he has caused the persons guilty of such crimes to be arrested, and tried by court-martial. You will tell him that if he does not punish these horrible abuses I shall believe he protects them (as public rumour asserts), and that there are more robberies committed in his Government, than in any other in Spain.

CCLXXXVI

TO THE PRINCE DE NEUFCHÂTEL, MAJOR-GENERAL OF
THE ARMY IN SPAIN.

ST. CLOUD, 16th September 1810.

LET General Drouet know that serious complaints are brought against General Barthélemy at Santander ; that I intend he shall be dismissed, and replaced by another General, and that an inquiry shall be held as to the embezzlement committed. The same thing is to be done with regard to General Avril. Write him, also, that great complaints are made of General d'Agoult's nephew ; that it is urgently necessary that severe examples should be made ; that corruption is carried to such lengths, that the freedom of prisoners is sold ; and that I desire he will be most energetic in his inquiries. Embezzlement is also going on in the province of Biscay. Desire him to seize the stores of Colonial merchandise, cotton goods, coffee, sugar, etc., on the French frontier of Biscay, and Navarre. All these goods are intended to be smuggled into France.

CCLXXXVII

TO PRINCE LEBRUN, GRAND TREASURER OF THE EMPIRE, THE EMPEROR'S LIEUTENANT-GENERAL IN SPAIN.

ST. CLOUD, 19*th September* 1810.

I HAVE your letters of the 16th, and that of the Director of Customs at Amsterdam. You might have sent my Decree into East Friesland without delaying six days. A courier would have conveyed it there in twenty-four hours. My Decree was founded on your letters, and on the claims of the Dutch. It seemed to me absurd that, after I had given them such immense advantages, they should request me to put off the dates of payment—that is to say, that I should let them wait till their correspondents in England sent them funds; for the goods they have in Holland are not their own, they only have them on commission, and on current account. Since receiving information on the subject from London, I am half sorry I did not confiscate them all.

The Minister of Finance is giving orders to facilitate the payments. By payment, we mean an undertaking to pay—then no blame can be attached, if the sums cannot be levied.

I am sorry the Dutch mind should be full of terror. Make them aware that I am not King Louis, and that I know how to insure obedience to my orders. There must be no listening to improper claims.

I do not know how a man of your experience can believe these people are terrified, because they cannot pay. Terror is only for those who have no means of paying. Well then, let such persons make a declaration that the goods do not belong to them.

CCLXXXVIII

TO PRINCE LEBRUN, GRAND TREASURER OF THE EMPIRE, THE EMPEROR'S LIEUTENANT-GENERAL IN HOLLAND.[1]

PARIS, 25*th September* 1810.

YOU speak of the complaints of the inhabitants of Amsterdam; of their alarm and discontent. Do these

[1] This letter was printed in the *Correspondence*, No. 16,497, but Napoleon cut out all the end. We now give it as it was originally drafted.

Dutchmen take me for their Grand Pensionary Barnevelt?
I do not understand such language. I shall do what is best
for the good of my Empire, and the clamour of the madmen
who will insist on knowing what is right better than I do, only
fills me with scorn. Really, one would fancy you had never
known me! At all events, you must have swiftly forgotten me!
I have not undertaken the government of Holland to consult
the populace of Amsterdam, and do as other people like.
The French nation has been willing, at various times, to put
its trust in me. Who knows it better than you? I hope the
Dutch will be good enough to show me the same respect.
If any one speaks in a different tone before you, you must
use language which befits my Lieutenant-General. 'The
Emperor is doing that which is best for the good of his
Empire, and whatever he plans, he sets his whole soul upon.'
The silly talk you credit seems all the more pitiable to me,
because I spend my time, here, amongst the most enlightened
men in the country, and I consult no interests but theirs.
Let this, then, be the last occasion on which such remarks are
heard in your presence.

CCLXXXIX

TO PRINCE LEBRUN, GRAND TREASURER OF THE EMPIRE, THE EMPEROR'S LIEUTENANT-GENERAL IN HOLLAND.

FONTAINEBLEAU, *26th September* 1810.

I HAVE your letter of the 20th. The Minister Secretary of
State sends you the Decree I have issued. [You will see I
am far from approving of your conduct.][1] What is the object
of showing any special interest in the family of a man killed
in an insurrection of which he was a member? Was it right
of you to cause one of my Customs officials, who had been
wounded in the performance of his duty, to be arrested?
[My Decree will inform you of my will.] The inhabitants of
Amsterdam must know [that I am not afraid of them, that I
am strong enough to break up any plots, and] that I am
stronger than the smugglers. Your duty is to give the law
active assistance, and not to let yourself be overawed by a
few smugglers. Any other behaviour would mean ruin. You

---

[1] The passages in brackets have been struck out of the draft.

will not lead the populace by coaxing it. Call together the magistrates and the municipal authorities [and make them aware of my intentions]. They themselves should point out the hidden stores; there are many remaining. You must start on the principle that I mean to know them all ; that my Custom-house officers must be supported, and that if the Amsterdam magistrates desire to escape the discomforts consequent on a different line of conduct, they must cause domiciliary visits to be made, and must discover the whereabouts of the forbidden merchandise. Energy is what is wanted. No people which begins by revolt can justify itself. My Customs officers have been ill-treated, stones have been cast at them ; it would be a terrible thing for those men, and a disgrace to the Administration, if it forsook them. The burghers do wrong when they resist armed force. The reason given for running down Custom-house officials is quite inadmissible. You will soon see them casting stones at my Customs officers as a matter of honour, and honest principle ! If the Superintendent of the Customs employed a person of bad character, complaint might fairly be made, but that was no reason for rising in rebellion. The fault, therefore, rests entirely with the town. Make the magistrates aware of my views, and inform them, that if they desire to deserve my favour, and to avoid the occupation of their town by 30,000 of my soldiers, they had better obey me. I will have it thus— do you understand ? and you will let them know it clearly.

CCXC

TO COMTE LAPLACE, CHANCELLOR OF THE SENATE.

FONTAINEBLEAU, 27th September 1810.

I WRITE this letter to inform you that the name of M. Lucien Buonaparte is no longer to appear on the list of Senators. He has been absent five years from the territories of the Empire, and when Rome was added to these, he left this country to cross the seas, and retired to America. He has thus resigned his Senatorial duties and dignity. As President of the Senate, we are bound to consider this resignation complete.

When the will of the French nation raised us to the Imperial Throne, we had a right to the co-operation of all

those who, like him, owed us a special duty. But he had
given himself over to a shameful passion for a woman, whose
manner of life had raised an insurmountable barrier between
herself and all decency, and we decided that he could not be
included in our hereditary line.   Whereas our brothers were
raised, by us, to a rank befitting their birth, and the interests
of our Crown, he remained a private individual.   When, in
later times, we had to overcome great perils, and struggle
with all Europe leagued against us, his duty should have
recalled him to our side, and we had a right to claim the
service of the talents Heaven had given him. He has always
been deaf to our call, and he has sought refuge, at last,
outside the Empire, under the protection of Powers which he
knew had but scant affection for our throne, and has thus
made his renunciation of his duty to ourselves, the Senate,
and his country more utterly irrevocable.   He has asked the
Minister of Police for passports for himself, and the object of
his guilty passion, and he has gone far from the Empire,
which he had no right to leave without special authority.   It
is necessary to the peace and tranquillity of the State, that
he should not only cease to be a member of any political
body in France, but that neither he, nor his children, should
ever return to our Empire.

We have written you this fully detailed letter, because it
is our intention that it shall be transcribed, under this day's
date, in the records of the Senate, and the copy signed, on
the record, by yourself and the other officers of the Senate.
It is likewise our intention that this letter shall remain secret,
and not be given publicity, until a suitable and opportune
moment, when such publicity may serve the interest of our
subjects, and of posterity.

CCXCI

TO GENERAL SAVARY, DUC DE ROVIGO,
MINISTER OF POLICE.

FONTAINEBLEAU, 28th September 1810.

I HAVE sent you back Mme de Staël's book. Has she
any right to call herself a Baroness? Did she take this
title in the books she has published up to the present?
Have the passage about the Duke of Brunswick suppressed,

and also three-fourths of the passages in which she extols England. That unlucky enthusiasm of hers has done mischief enough already.

CCXCII

TO GENERAL CLARKE, DUC DE FELTRE, MINISTER OF WAR.

FONTAINEBLEAU, *2nd October* 1810.

YOU will answer the Duke of Reggio that my intention is that he shall turn all his activity to breaking up the mobs. Tell him that no excuse can be made for them ; that I have found fault with the Prince Grand Treasurer's views on the subject ; that the populace always puts itself in the wrong when it resists the military ; that the Custom-house officers are part of the military ; and that, far from being discouraged, they should be supported and backed up.

The Duke of Reggio must make the Amsterdam populace understand that no mercy will be shown it. Every soul who is taken in the act of firing on the military is to be tried by court-martial, and summarily executed.

CCXCIII

TO JEROME NAPOLEON, KING OF WESTPHALIA.

FONTAINEBLEAU, *4th October* 1810.

I HEAR from every quarter that my troops are exceedingly uncomfortable in Westphalia. They have no pay, they receive no civility from the inhabitants, and their rations have been considerably reduced. Good God ! will you let me have an end of this ?

CCXCIV

TO COMTE MOLLIEN, MINISTER OF THE PUBLIC EXCHEQUER.

FONTAINEBLEAU, *5th October* 1810.

I AM informed that the pay of my Minister at Munich has been seized [by his creditors]. It is my intention that no notice shall be taken of any opposing claim. I do not give my Ambassadors an income for their own use, but for the purpose of representing me.

CCXCV

TO M. DE CHAMPAGNY, DUC DE CADORE,
MINISTER FOR FOREIGN AFFAIRS.

FONTAINEBLEAU, 7*th October* 1810.

HAVE newspaper articles published about the late King of Sweden, so as to let people know the fact that he has been stopped on the Russian frontier, and to show up all the wild follies he has committed.

CCXCVI

TO M. DE CHAMPAGNY, DUC DE CADORE, MINISTER FOR
FOREIGN AFFAIRS.

FONTAINEBLEAU, 12*th October* 1810.

YOU will write the letter, of which I send you a draft, to the Duke of Santa Fè :—

Draft of an Answer to be sent by the Minister for Foreign Affairs to the Spanish Ambassador, the Duke of Santa Fè.

SIR,—I have read the document written by the Minister, Urquijo. This document ascribes terms to me, which I have never used, and does not, on the other hand, quote one word of what I did say, when I sought, in conversation with you, for the possible reasons for the apparent coolness between the two Courts.

You will allow me, sir, to send you back the document, the nature of which, as it appears to me, makes it more fit to figure in an English pamphlet, than to be placed on the shelves of my Ministry.

If the French Generals behaved ill during the time when the King was at the head of the army of the Emperor, his brother, why did he not have them arrested, and brought before a military tribunal ? If any cause for complaint still exists, why is not a clear and exact statement of the subjects of such complaint sent to the Major-General ? You must feel that shafts levelled against Generals,—without authority, without proofs, and in a kind of pamphlet, every sentence of which breathes bitterness and irritation,—can hardly be considered as a business document. I have not been able to submit it to the Emperor, but I shall make it my business to lay anything before his Majesty, which may be sensibly written, by cool-headed persons, and supported by facts warranting an inquiry.

CCXCVII

TO THE COMTE DE MONTALIVET, MINISTER OF
THE INTERIOR.

FONTAINEBLEAU, 13th October 1810.

FALSE reports are too easily put about by evil-disposed and idle persons, under the influence of England, and even by means of echoes from foreign newspapers. There are certain objections to contradictions in our own newspapers, and besides, such a course is not always sufficiently dignified. I beg you will send the Prefects a weekly circular, to make them aware of the real truth as to current reports, and thus direct their opinions and language. You will order them to keep your despatches to themselves, and to make use of them in every way which may influence the public opinion of their Department.

I should wish the objects of your circular to be—first, to make known our system against England; that it is not want of money which dictates these measures to the Government, but the desire to harm England, and that the advantage of this system has been proved by experience. Second, to make known the prosperous condition of French finances. This year's revenue amounts to over 800 millions, as is proved by the accounts of the Ministers of Finance, and of the Public Exchequer, which will shortly be published. This proves the absurdity of the reports spread in certain Departments, as to the creation of a paper currency, of mortgages, of new taxes, and even of contributions to be levied on the Funds—the authors of which would fain apply the disastrous measures taken in Austria, Russia, Prussia, and England, to France.

The third point of the circular should refer to the affairs of Spain. The French armies there are in the best possible condition, and abundantly supplied. The army of Andalusia, which occupies Seville, Grenada, etc., has more than 90,000 men fit for active service, under the orders of Marshals the Dukes of Belluna and Treviso, Count Sebastiani and the Duke of Dalmatia; the army of Portugal, under the orders of the Prince of Essling, the Dukes of Elchingen and Abrantès, and Count Régnier, has more than 70,000 men under arms. It has seized Ciudad-Rodrigo and Almeida, and was face to face, on the 24th, with the English army, which it had forced to retire for ten marches, and which seemed to be falling back on its vessels. A battle was imminent, and the English were reinforcing their army, which amounted, possibly, to some 36,000 men.

You will say that the reports circulated against the Duke of Abrantès are calumnious and false, that the General in question is winning the greatest distinction, and that the most perfect harmony reigns amongst the various Generals; that Aragon, which was the most disturbed of all the Spanish Provinces, is now the most submissive; that General Suchet, who has a fine army, numbering 40,000 men, is besieging Tortosa and threatening Valencia; that, the Duke of Tarento having moved towards Tarragona, a few armed bands have taken advantage of his absence to gather about his rear, and violate certain parts of the Pyrenean frontier; that other strong bodies of French troops occupy Navarre, the Asturias, Biscay, and other provinces; that a few smugglers, and the remnants of the Spanish army, have formed themselves into bands, which seize travellers—hardly to be wondered at in such a large country as Spain,—but that, on the whole, things are going very well indeed.

If the chief functionaries of the Departments are thus warned, every week, against the false rumours which are rife, their tone will be steady, and this will react on Paris itself. You will submit these letters to me at the business sitting.

CCXCVIII

TO GENERAL SAVARY, DUC DE ROVIGO,
MINISTER OF POLICE.

FONTAINEBLEAU, 14th October 1810.

You have sent me three reports on the newspapers, two of them to-day, and one some days ago. These reports are

O

not clear, and do not give me a sufficient idea of the condition of things.

I request (1st) that you will submit to me everything I have done, for several years past, as to the newspapers, and the orders issued by the Minister of Police, when the newspapers were laid under contribution, and editors appointed to them; (2ndly) that you will make me a very full report on MM. Bertin de Vaux. I have an idea that the MM. Bertin have been proved to be in correspondence with England, that their newspaper was founded with English money, and that they have always been hostile to the Government. I desire you will furnish me with all the proofs you must hold against them, so that I may be thoroughly informed. For if I find my opinion of them is correct, it is my intention not only to forbid them holding their newspaper property, without giving them any compensation, but also to deprive them of all right to print, and to send them fifty leagues away from Paris. It would be too scandalous, indeed, if such schemers—enemies of the State, and in the pay of the foreigner—should continue to exercise any literary influence.

CCXCIX

TO M. DE CHAMPAGNY, DUC DE CADORE, MINISTER FOR FOREIGN AFFAIRS.

FONTAINEBLEAU, 16*th October* 1810.

YOU will send Mons. Malchus back his Note, and you will answer him very much in these terms:—

'I cannot accept the Note you send me, since the King of Westphalia declares himself freed from a Treaty he made with France. The consequence of such a liberation would be incalculable. Nothing but a singular want of thought could have led the Westphalian Ministry to issue such an order. The Treaty of Paris must be carried out to the very letter. The Cassel Cabinet must be aware that treaties made with the Emperor are not to be trifled with, and that all engagements made, must be faithfully kept.'

In the course of your explanation with Mons. Malchus, you will make him aware that the pay due to my troops in Westphalia must be promptly paid, up to the present date; that the King had no business to form camps, and be in such a hurry to raise a Westphalian army, on which he cannot depend, and to spend large sums on internal affairs ; that the refusal of the Court to pay my troops would be exceedingly disadvantageous to Westphalia, which country would be no longer considered, by France, as being bound to her by Treaty. Write to Mons. Reinhard on the subject. Make them understand that if my Decree as to English merchandise is applied to the Hanoverian towns, very considerable sums of money will be procured ; that Brunswick is full of such merchandise, and more especially of colonial goods.

Inform Mons. Reinhard, for his guidance, that the King's correspondence is of no importance, for that I never answer him on any business matter, and that Reinhard may consider himself quite certain on this point.

CCC

TO GENERAL SAVARY, DUC DE ROVIGO,
MINISTER OF POLICE.

FONTAINEBLEAU, 17th October 1810.

A GREAT many foolish rumours are rife in Paris, but that which most needs your attention, and which must be put a stop to by every means, without allowing it the credit of a printed contradiction, is one of a supposed marriage between Prince Ferdinand and an Austrian Princess. I suppose this story to be put about by a certain Laborie, and by the other members of a gang connected with the Bertins. Your report of yesterday mentions this Laborie, in connection with Mme de Staël's book.[1] No more reference must be made to that book, nor to that worthless woman, but you must watch the Laborie gang, and report to me.

CCCI

TO GENERAL SAVARY, DUC DE ROVIGO
MINISTER OF POLICE.

FONTAINEBLEAU, 18th October 1810.

YOU can release Tavera, the skipper, and his crew, whom you had arrested in connection with the Senator Lucien's

---

[1] *De l'Allemagne*, all the copies of which book had been seized at the book-sellers', and destroyed.

business. It would be well to keep all the documents relating to that affair, in due form.

A positive answer must be required from General Miollis, as to why he allowed the Senator Lucien to embark, and why the ship *Hercules* sailed without my leave. Send him these questions, which he will do well to answer.

CCCII

TO JOACHIM NAPOLEON, KING OF NAPLES.

FONTAINEBLEAU, 18*th October* 1810.

I HAVE your letter of 9th October. I desire you will send part of your flotilla to Brindisi and Otranto, to facilitate the passage to, and communication with, Corfu. The duty on silk and cloth may be established in your kingdom, on condition that you forbid the entrance of the silks and cloths of other countries. Desire your Minister to come to an understanding on this subject, with the Duke of Cadore. Competition is the only thing to be feared. If you only get them from France, it is little matter whether you impose a duty or not.

You must now be aware how great a fault you committed when you sent the ship *Hercules* to Lucien, since the poor wretch is a prisoner in the hands of the English at Malta. As I did not send him the ship, it was because I did not wish him to start. The Queen will tell you how extremely displeased I have been by this. Be more circumspect in future, and do not interfere in matters which do not concern you.

CCCIII

TO GENERAL SAVARY, DUC DE ROVIGO,
MINISTER OF POLICE.

FONTAINEBLEAU, 20*th October* 1810.

IN the *Gazette de France* I see an article about a Minister of the Spanish Junta to the United States, in which Ferdinand VII. is referred to. Who gave the *Gazette de France* authority to insert so mischievous an article? Inform the *Gazette de France* that the first time such an article is copied, the paper will be suppressed.

CCCIV

TO M. DE CHAMPAGNY, DUC DE CADORE, MINISTER FOR FOREIGN AFFAIRS.

FONTAINEBLEAU, 21st October 1810.

HEREWITH you will find a letter from General Rapp. Here is my decision, which you will communicate to the Prussian Minister. I demand that all these ships[1] shall be allowed to enter the Prussian ports, and then confiscated; that agents of the two Courts shall make an independent valuation of the cargoes; that the confiscated property shall be mine, but that the amount of the contributions due by Prussia, shall be included in the sum confiscated.

CCCV

TO GENERAL SAVARY, DUC DE ROVIGO, MINISTER OF POLICE.

FONTAINEBLEAU, 25th October 1810.

I SEE, by your Police Report, that the blocks of a will of Louis XVI., which was being printed for a certain Bonneville, a dealer in engravings, have been seized in the house of one Farge (No. 2, Cloitre Saint Benoit). Have these two persons arrested. Write to the Director of the Censure Department to have their charter revoked, and that they are never to be allowed either to print books, or sell engravings, again; then you will have them shut up in a State prison, until the millennium. When the Censorship was instituted, provision was made for depriving any handful of wretches who might attempt to disturb the public peace, of all right either to print or sell books. Send me a statement of the book-sellers and printers who are known to be evilly inclined, and cannot be depended upon, so that I may revoke their licence. Follow this up vigorously; it is time to make an end of it. There can be no greater crime than that committed by these people.

---

[1] Vessels laden with English merchandise.

CCCVI

TO M. DE CHAMPAGNY, DUC DE CADORE, MINISTER FOR FOREIGN AFFAIRS.

FONTAINEBLEAU, *8th November* 1810.

I AM assured I have signed a decree appointing Mons. Billiot, formerly Consul at Stettin, to be Consul at Riga. If this is true, the appointment is an error on my part. I have never had any intention of appointing that Consul anywhere, so long as his business with General Liébert has not come to an end. On the contrary, I have sent for General Liébert to Paris, to clear up the dispute. You will therefore submit another name to me for the Riga Consulship. I cannot have thought, when I signed Mons. Billiot's appointment, that he was the man whom I had just put under examination as to a contentious matter. It would have been well to await the end of this inquiry, before submitting the nomination to me.

CCCVII

TO M. DE CHAMPAGNY, DUC DE CADORE, MINISTER FOR FOREIGN AFFAIRS.

FONTAINEBLEAU, *9th November* 1810.

YOU will answer the letter from my Minister at Cassel, dated 31st October, thus:—That the King and his Ministers are constantly making fresh vows, but that they always do just as they choose; that I have told the King, over and over again, that he ought not to have cuirassier regiments, because that branch of the service costs too much money, and the native horses are not adapted for it; that besides, it suited me better to have lancers, and light cavalry, which would be more useful to me, and that, in short, this would have been an immense economy; that the King of Westphalia has taken no notice of this advice— that he is playing at soldiers, and raising regiments of every kind; that as for the recruiting of the troops in Catalonia, I will send no more Westphalians thither, to swell the enemy's bands; that of all the German soldiers, they are the least to be depended upon; that in consequence of an old-standing hatred, arising from the fact of these troops having always served with the English, they have more satisfaction in fighting against us, than any others ; that when I sent 18,000 men into Westphalia, I did it partly with the object of preventing the King from having too many troops, and officers, who might turn against me ; that Bavaria, Saxony, and Hesse Darmstadt, being old-established countries, are sure of their troops' fidelity, and that even the Princes of those countries do not amuse themselves by creating new corps, but leave their troops to rest in peace ; that I will not have any cuirassiers ; that it is a great act of folly to increase troops, whom there is no means of supporting, and which cannot be depended upon ; but that, indeed, I take no interest in the matter, so long as the engagements made with me are kept, and my troops given both their back pay, and that which is now due.

Inform Herr von Wintzingerode, by a Note, that no person has any right to inspect my troops ; that my army returns should suffice, so long as the number of troops does not exceed that fixed by treaty ; that Westphalia is only dealing in pettifogging trifles ; that this is the way to set things astray ; that, besides, the treaty does not say that the 18,000 men were to be paid if they were present ; that if that had been so, I ought to have insisted on their being paid from the very day on which they should have entered Westphalia ; that no person in the Westphalian army has the command of my troops ; and that I have censured the Generals who allowed my troops to be inspected, without my orders. You will write to the Prince of Eckmühl to inform him of my intentions.

CCCVIII

TO GENERAL SAVARY, DUC DE ROVIGO,
MINISTER OF POLICE.

FONTAINEBLEAU, 14th November 1810.

I SEE the *Journal de l'Empire* denominates the new Archbishop of Paris, 'Administrator of the Diocese.' Let the editor know that he should not have ventured to use such a title, with reference to Cardinal Maury. The Cardinal is Archbishop of Paris, and must always be described as such.

I will not permit him to be called by any other name, and I conclude the Cardinal himself neither accepts, nor assumes, any other title. The newspapers should be the very first to recognise what is recognised by the Government. Everything continues to show that this *Journal de l'Empire* is badly managed.

CCCIX

TO GENERAL SAVARY, DUC DE ROVIGO, MINISTER OF POLICE.

PARIS, 21*st November* 1810.

THE Pope continues to keep up a very mischievous correspondence. The most explicit orders must be given to reduce it. No letter must reach him except through the Prefect.

CCCX

TO THE COMTE DE LAVALLETTE, DIRECTOR-GENERAL OF THE POSTAL SERVICE.

PARIS, 28*th November* 1810.

GIVE orders that all letters written by the Pope, or by the members of his household, and all those sent to the Pope, or to his household, are to be forwarded to Paris.

CCCXI

TO GENERAL SAVARY, DUC DE ROVIGO, MINISTER OF POLICE.

PARIS, 28*th November* 1810.

MEASURES must be taken to prevent any letter from reaching the Pope, and to get possession of all those he writes. For this purpose, you must be very sure of the postmaster at Savona. If you are not quite sure of him, it might be well to change him. I am ordering the Bishop of Savona to proceed to Paris. If there are any intriguing people about the Pope, they should be removed, and even searched, if there is any reason to suspect they have letters about them.

CCCXII

TO PRINCE BORGHESE, GOVERNOR-GENERAL OF THE
TRANSALPINE DEPARTMENTS.

PARIS, 31st December 1810.

I HAVE received the report you sent me. The Minister of Police will send you the Decree I have issued. I send you a copy in case of delay. Give the Chief of the Police instant orders to take measures for the arrest of the Vicar-General and Canons [of Asti] named in the Decree, to have them taken to Fenestrelle, and have the seals affixed to their papers. You will call the Chapter together, to receive the notification of my Decree, and of the suppression of the five prebends. You must take care that nothing is put upon Bishop Dejean, so as to save him from all odium.

The Chapter will be informed that my first impulse was to suppress it altogether, and to merge its property in the Crown, but that I came to the conclusion I ought not to charge the Chapter with the punishment earned by a few ill-disposed persons; yet, that if it does not behave itself better in future, I shall be driven to that extreme measure.

Take care that the agent sent to arrest the Canons arrives at eight o'clock in the evening, and that they are seized, and sent away to Fenestrelle, under good escort, before the town knows anything about it. The notification of my Decree, and the summoning of the Chapter, will not take place till twenty-four hours later.

CCCXIII

TO GENERAL SAVARY, DUC DE ROVIGO,
MINISTER OF POLICE.

PARIS, 31st December 1810.

SEND orders by to-night's express, to the Chief of Police, at Turin, that he is to take the necessary steps for having Dani, the Vicar-General, and the three Canons, Curione, Cavalleri, and Barberi, arrested, and taken with post-horses to Fenestrelle, before any one at Asti can be aware of it. You will have their papers sealed up. Give orders that not only the persons mentioned in my Decree, but any others who may misconduct themselves, or are known as being amongst the worst disposed, are to be arrested. You will order them to be examined, and kept in solitary confinement at Fenestrelle. The Chief of the Police will lay informations against these persons, as being guilty of intrigues against the safety of the State. You will send me a report of the examinations, and a further report on the proceedings; meanwhile, give stringent orders to prevent their communicating with any one. You will write to the Register Office, to seize the property of the suppressed canonries.

CCCXIV

TO COMTE BIGOT DE PRÉAMENEU, MINISTER OF PUBLIC WORSHIP.

PARIS, 1st January 1811.

YOU will give orders to General Miollis, that if, at any future time, he should have to arrest any priests, he is to send them to Civita Vecchia, where they are to be put on board a brig. When a score of them have been thus collected, they will be sent to Corsica, where they will be kept together. Let me know how many there now are at Piacenza, and at Pinerolo, and whether the youngest and worst disposed could not be got rid of, by sending them to Corsica.

CCCXV

TO PRINCE BORGHESE, GOVERNOR-GENERAL OF THE TRANSALPINE DEPARTMENTS.

PARIS, 1st January 1811.

As the Pope has been misbehaving himself at Savona, I desire you will give orders that the carriages I had placed at his disposal should be sent back to Turin, and that his household expenses should not be allowed to exceed 12,000 to 15,000 francs a year. Make sure that no letters are received at Savona, nor sent from there; that the Pope has no secret correspondence, and no intercourse with any one but the Prefect.

Send me a list of the people about the Pope. If some of them, especially those who do most writing for him, can be removed, the result will be very beneficial. Everything he does is full of poison. It is therefore desirable to limit him to his own pen, and to get rid of this pack of fellows who write for him.

Generally speaking, I beg you will give the Governor strict commands to keep the most stringent order, to see that none of the servants carry out letters, and to have them closely watched. The Chief of the Police should have some agent in the Pope's household, who would find out through what secret channel the letters pass, and would supply information as to what goes on in the house.

You will have seen what I have done about Asti. Have the Pope told, that he does very wrong to preach disturbance, and stir up disorder, in Christendom, and that if he thinks I am likely to be frightened by such wild folly on his part, he is mistaken.

CCCXVI

TO ELISA NAPOLEON, GRAND DUCHESS OF TUSCANY.

PARIS, 1st January 1811.

I AM displeased at your allowing the Florence Chapter, and other priests, to receive letters from the Pope, and at their not bringing them to you, with the seals unbroken, when they do receive them. You must have any of the Canons who have received such letters, arrested, and sent to fortresses, because they had no right to receive them without showing them to the Council of State.

Take the strongest and most active measures to prevent the flame of sedition, which the Pope is kindling everywhere, from reaching Tuscany.

CCCXVII

TO GENERAL SAVARY, DUC DE ROVIGO, MINISTER OF POLICE.

PARIS, 2nd January 1811.

THE Florence Chapter has sent two ecclesiastics, one of whom is Signor Mancini, nephew of the Bishop of Fiesole, to meet the Archbishop of Florence, and notify him that the Chapter cannot recognise him. Send orders, by this evening's express, that these two ecclesiastics are to be arrested, that the seals are to be put on their papers, and that they are to be taken to Fenestrelle, whether they are at Piacenza, have turned back towards Bologna, or are at Florence.

Issue warrants of arrest against Canons Mozzi, Gentile, and Berto. Have their papers sealed up, and send them to Fenestrelle. Have a Florence lawyer, of the name of Valentini, arrested, and put the seals on his papers. Have Corboli, a vicar, arrested also. Send all these warrants to the Grand Duchess, because she may have taken steps, and there must be no confusion. All this must be done in a determined way. Those persons who have caused the Pope's so-called brief to be read out, without laying it before the Government, must be arrested, and lastly, give the Grand Duchess, the Prefect of the Arno, and Archbishop Osmond, my orders, that this last is to be recognised as Archbishop, and that, if the Chapter should be recalcitrant, the Grand Duchess must suppress it, and have the seals affixed to all its property. Write to the Grand Duchess, that the principal culprits are those persons who have laid a letter they had no business to receive, before the Chapter.

CCCXVIII

TO PRINCE BORGHESE, GOVERNOR-GENERAL OF THE TRANSALPINE DEPARTMENTS.

PARIS, *2nd January* 1811.

YOU have set no watch upon the Pope, and the consequence is, that he corresponds with any one he chooses. I gave you orders yesterday, and I repeat them to-day, to deprive the Pope of all means of correspondence, and even, should that become necessary, to shut him up in the Citadel of Savona. Have such of his servants as are known to have passed out his letters, or helped him in his work of preaching disorder and insubordination, forthwith arrested.

CCCXIX

TO PRINCE BORGHESE, GOVERNOR-GENERAL OF THE TRANSALPINE DEPARTMENTS.

PARIS, 2nd January 1811.

THE Pope is stirring up disorder everywhere. I have written you orders to withdraw all external signs of respect, to send the carriages with which he was provided back to Turin, and to reduce his household expenses so that they may not amount to more than 12,000 or 15,000 francs a year. I have given orders that the Bishop of Savona is to be summoned to Paris; that his papers are to be sealed up, and put into safe hands, so as to find out what intrigue is being carried on through that channel. I have written you that all suspected persons, and those who helped the Pope to write so much, must be removed from his neighbourhood, for he is sending whole sheets of diatribes in all directions; that it is even necessary to have the servants you suspect replaced by foreigners, and not to allow any outside communication, and that if he writes letters, they must be sent to the Minister of Public Worship; that the Prefect is the only person who must be allowed to see him.

I have made you aware of my intention as regards Asti. I conclude that the papers containing the key to this intrigue have been seized. I have been obliged to dismiss a Vicar-General, in whose possession letters from the Pope were found. The Pope must be told by the Prefect, that as he abuses his liberty by sowing discord in every direction, he can only be looked on as the enemy of the Empire, and the State.

CCCXX

TO GENERAL SAVARY, DUC DE ROVIGO, MINISTER OF POLICE.

PARIS, 3rd January 1811.

As the Pope has probably written to the Chapter of Aix, in Provence, you will send a special courier to the Sub-Prefect, or to the Police Commissary at Marseilles, or, if you have no confidence in these persons, to the Prefect, with orders to send suddenly for the Vicars-General, and ask them for the letters from Savona, and the correspondence arising out of them. No attention is to be paid to their excuses, and they are not to be set at liberty, until that letter is given up, for they most certainly have received it.

CCCXXI

TO THE PRINCE DE NEUFCHÂTEL, MAJOR-GENERAL OF THE ARMY IN SPAIN.

PARIS, *4th January* 1811.

YOU will see news from Portugal in to-morrow's *Moniteur*. The English make great game of General Gardanne. That simpleton was not more than three leagues from the French troops on the Zezere.

You will find the whole despatch. Send it to General Drouet, and give him orders to send the General, who seems an arch idiot, back to France. Send to-morrow's *Moniteur* all down the road, and send some to Madrid, as well.

CCCXXII

TO PRINCE BORGHESE, GOVERNOR-GENERAL OF THE TRANSALPINE DEPARTMENTS.

PARIS, *6th January* 1811.

THE Pope has taken advantage of the liberty I have allowed him at Savona, to sow rebellion and disorder amongst my subjects. I had been satisfied [until the great question of the Canonical Institution had been settled[1]] to allow the Bishops whom I had appointed, to govern in the name of the Chapter, and as Vicars Capitular, according to the maxims of the Church, and to the example of Louis XIV. and other European Sovereigns.

Nevertheless the Pope [inspired by the disorderly spirit so characteristic of him] has contrived, by means of sly and seditious intrigue, to communicate briefs, contrary to the laws of the Empire, to the Chapters of Paris, Florence, and Asti [and contrary indeed to the laws of the rest of

---

[1] The passages in brackets were struck out by the Emperor, in the original draft.

Europe, the Sovereigns of which continent, feeling the necessity of defending themselves against the peevish action of the Popes, had forbidden any communication with the Chapters without their own permission.   The Pope is all the more wrong in this matter, because, even according to the Ultramontanes, he has no right to alter the decisions of a Chapter while the diocese is vacant, and this is yet far more opposed to the liberties of the Gallican Church.]

As I desire to protect my subjects from the rage and fury of this ignorant and peevish old man, I hereby order you to notify him, that he is forbidden to communicate with any Church of mine, or any of my subjects, on pain of the punishment consequent on his disobedience, and theirs.

You will remove all suspicious persons from the Pope's household.   You will only leave the number of persons necessary to wait on him, and you will not permit any one of any kind to visit him.   You will take steps to increase the garrison of Savona.   You will take care to have all the Pope's papers, books, and documents taken from him, and you will have them sent to Paris.   If the Pope should indulge in any extravagant behaviour, you will have him shut up in the Citadel of Savona, which you will have taken care to provision, and furnish with all necessaries, beforehand.

Take steps to have these orders carried out.   The Prefect, or some other person, will be desired to send him the notification [in writing], and to tell him [that I no longer recognise him as Pope, and] that a man who preaches rebellion, and whose whole soul is full of hatred and malice, ceases to be the mouthpiece of the Church.

You will realise the importance of these measures.   I have sent an officer of Gendarmes to Savona.   It will be easy for you to select some thirty old Gendarmes from the Legion, and confide the carrying out of the orders to them.   [The time for tacking has gone by!]   As nothing will teach the Pope sense, he shall see that I am strong enough to do as my predecessors did before me, and depose a Pope.

The examination of the Pope's papers must be skilfully done.   You will leave him no paper, nor pens, nor ink, nor any means of writing.   You will give him a few French servants, and you will remove the unsatisfactory ones.   Besides this, the people of his household can be forbidden to go out.

CCCXXIII

TO ELISA NAPOLEON, GRAND DUCHESS OF TUSCANY.

PARIS, 8*th January* 1811.

I HAVE your letter of 28th December. You did quite right to have Canon Muzzi arrested. The island of Elba too, appears to me a very well chosen spot. You will send the dissident priests there, taking care not to let them remain at Porto-Ferrajo nor at Porto-Longone, but to send them into the villages. I conclude you will have forbidden the lawyer Valentini to correspond with the Pope. You must also have those members of the Chapter who misconduct themselves arrested. Indeed, the Chapter, which numbers thirty-six members, may very well be reduced to twenty. I suppose you have received the Pope's brief, sent to the Chapter, which has just been sent to me. It is the very height of ignorance and absurdity.

CCCXXIV

TO GENERAL SAVARY, DUC DE ROVIGO, MINISTER OF POLICE.

PARIS, 15*th January* 1811.

THE Abbé Reboul, formerly Almoner to Mesdames, came from Trieste, and brought the Pope's Bull to Paris, with him. This man writes a great deal, lives on the fifth story, and appears very fanatical. He goes every evening to see Mme Séguier's mother. This person must have a watch set upon him, so as to find out where he lives, and whom he sees. After having tracked him for several days, you will have him arrested, outside his house, just at the very time when his papers are being seized. His arrest should throw some light on this intrigue. This Abbé Reboul sees a great deal of the Curé of St. Roch.

Mme Séguier, the wife of the Chief President, is exceedingly religious. A great many questions relating to the present condition of the clergy are discussed in her house. If you introduce some person into this circle, he will hear many things, which will enable us to find out a great deal about this affair. Mme Séguier has read the Pope's message. This watching must be done very circumspectly, and the only use you must make of the hint I give you, is to have an eye upon the house. The matter is of some importance, because it may enable the police to make discoveries, which may be of interest.

CCCXXV

TO PRINCE BORGHESE, GOVERNOR-GENERAL OF THE TRANSALPINE DEPARTMENTS.

PARIS, 15th January 1811.

I HAVE your letter of 9th January. I am glad to observe you have taken the steps I prescribed, to prevent the Pope distilling his poison into the Empire. The sum of 15,000 francs is perhaps too small. I give you liberty to arrange matters, so that he shall not suffer, and to raise his expenditure to 100,000 or 150,000 francs. Do not allow him any external sign of consideration, but furnish him with an abundance of all necessaries, so that no one may be able to suppose him to be in any discomfort.

I conclude the Bishop of Savona has started for Paris, and that you have had all the Pope's papers seized.

CCCXXVI

TO GENERAL SAVARY, DUC DE ROVIGO, MINISTER OF POLICE.

PARIS, 20th January 1811.

I SEND you the Prefect of Montenotte's confidential report on the persons composing the Pope's household, and on their various characters. You can leave the Pope his doctor, Porta ; his steward, Palmieri ; Campa, his florist ; Targhini, his cook ; and Cotogni, his footman. You will have Ceccarini, his surgeon ; Soglia, his chaplain ; Moiraghi and Morelli, his valets de chambre ; Bertoni, a footman, and Petroncini, Monsignor Doria's man-servant, arrested. If the Pope needs one or two more servants, you will take Frenchmen, and persons on whom you can rely. You will be careful that all the persons I have just mentioned to you, as to be removed

P

from Savona, should start simultaneously, at midnight, without seeing the Pope. You will give directions that their papers shall be seized and sent to you ; they must have preserved some important documents. All these people, with the exception of those who are to be sent to Paris, can be sent to Fenestrelle. You will take care to keep them in solitary confinement for five or six months, before you set them at liberty, so that they may have been a long time separated from the Pope, before they return to general society. You will have them cross-examined when they get to Fenestrelle ; something about the intrigues which have been carried on will be got out of them. Monsignor Doria will also depart without seeing the Pope. He will be taken with post-horses to Naples, *via* Ancona, and he is to live there with his sister. You will advise him to be wise, and you will write the King of Naples to that effect. As for Porta, and the other persons you leave with the Pope, you must make them clearly understand that the smallest intrigue with the outside world will be severely punished, and that their very lives will be endangered.

You will reiterate my orders to the Prefect of Montenotte and the Commandant of the Gendarmerie, that the Pope is not to be allowed to correspond with any one, that all the approaches to Savona, and all inns, are to be closely watched, and that all suspicious characters are to be secured. It would even be well to watch the places frequented by the servants who are to remain about the Pope, and, on the slightest misbehaviour on their part, to confine them within the house, and sequester them altogether.

CCCXXVII

TO COMTE DARU, CHIEF COMPTROLLER OF THE EMPEROR'S HOUSEHOLD.

PARIS, *22nd January* 1811.

I HAD given orders to sequestrate St. Leu. My intention is that you shall send for Queen Hortense's man of business, and have that place made over to him, so that the Queen may have the full enjoyment of it, and make what arrangements she chooses there.

CCCXXVIII

TO GENERAL SAVARY, DUC DE ROVIGO,
MINISTER OF POLICE.

PARIS, 10*th February* 1811.

IT would be well to stop all letters coming from England
on licensed ships, and to have them carefully examined.
They nearly all of them contain important matter. I do
not refer to the letters sent to England. I conclude no more
of these go, as I have laid an embargo on the French ports.
Have an explanation on this subject with your Police Commissaries at Ostend, in Holland, and at other ports. The
only possible communication with England is through Morlaix, and letters cannot pass except through your hands. I
especially desire that all letters referring to the condition of
trade may be laid before me.

CCCXXIX

TO COMTE DE MONTALIVET, MINISTER OF
THE INTERIOR.

PARIS, 21*st February* 1811.

YOU must instruct the Prefect of Geneva that he is never
to see Madame de Staël at all, that he is to keep that
scheming woman within reasonable bounds, and apply his
mind to making Geneva thoroughly French.

CCCXXX

TO M. DE CHAMPAGNY, DUC DE CADORE,
MINISTER FOR FOREIGN AFFAIRS.

PARIS, 3*rd March* 1811.

I RETURN your draft letter to the Duke of Vicenza. It
seems to me that a few passages should be added, to inform
him that I shall not declare war on account of the Ukase
and the Tariff, but that I shall hold myself in readiness to
resist the effects of the bad spirit which inspired this action,
and that I shall only make war if Russia intends to be
reconciled with England. The Duke of Vicenza must dis-
avow any measure supposed to have been taken prior to

the Ukase. I have myself told Mons. de Czernitschef that
since I have been made aware of the Ukase, I have raised
the conscription, which step will cost me a hundred millions
this year.   You will inform the Duke of Vicenza that I am
sending 10,000 Poles to reinforce the Dantzig garrison, and
that I am pushing forward a regiment of cavalry, and another
of infantry, to garrison Stettin.   As these movements will
be very late in taking place, the Duke of Vicenza should be
informed of them, so that when they are mentioned to him,
he may reassure the St. Petersburg Cabinet.   In the first
place, he will say that this fortress must be prepared against
an English attack, and there can be no harm, at last, in
saying openly that, under present circumstances, so important
a fortified town must be secured.

CCCXXXI

TO GENERAL SAVARY, DUC DE ROVIGO,
MINISTER OF POLICE.

PARIS, 14*th March* 1811.

HAVE all the works of art, and other property, belonging
to the Senator Lucien, either in Rome or elsewhere, sequestrated, so that it may not fall a prey to the English.   You
will request Mons. Campi to hand you a declaration on the
subject.

CCCXXXII

TO GENERAL SAVARY, DUC DE ROVIGO,
MINISTER OF POLICE.

PARIS, 16*th March* 1811.

THERE is a printing-press in Mons. de Chevreuse's house
at Dampierre.   My intention is that you shall have it seized.
There is a governess in the family, an Englishwoman, and
four bad priests, who direct the children's education.   There
is no objection to Mons. de Chevreuse having a governess
and priests in his house ; but the governess must not be an
Englishwoman, nor the priests evil-disposed persons.   I
think, before you do anything in the matter, you should
verify these facts and report to me.   When you have made
your report, I will give you definite orders.

CCCXXXIII

TO GENERAL SAVARY, DUC DE ROVIGO,
MINISTER OF POLICE.

PARIS, 18*th March* 1811.

I SEND you a letter from General Molitor. Let the Grand Treasurer know that the measures taken are too feeble, that the students and townsmen of Utrecht, who have insulted the patrols, must be arrested forthwith, and tried by a military court.

CCCXXXIV

TO PRINCE LEBRUN, GRAND TREASURER OF THE EMPIRE,
THE EMPEROR'S LIEUTENANT-GENERAL IN HOLLAND.

PARIS, 18*th March* 1811.

YOU do not mention the constant riots at Amsterdam, nor the steps you take to put them down. General Molitor's correspondence with the Minister of War is full of these events. It strikes me, that instead of concealing such crimes against my troops, which encourage the rabble, you should take measures to punish them.

CCCXXXV

TO PRINCE LEBRUN, GRAND TREASURER OF THE EMPIRE,
THE EMPEROR'S LIEUTENANT-GENERAL IN HOLLAND.

PARIS, 18*th March* 1811.

I DESIRE you will call together the General commanding the Division, the Colonel in command of the Gendarmerie, the Chief of the Police, and the Comptrollers of the Finances, and of the Department of the Interior, and deliberate with them, in Council, as to what is to be done to insure the peace of Amsterdam. There is no doubt that you have nothing to fear from the moneyed classes, but there are a great number of vagabonds in the town. These people must be arrested, given over to the naval authorities, placed in asylums for mendicants, or employed in labour of some kind. These four courses, taken together, would confer all sorts of advantages, and give the populace occupation. Another course would be to open a military court, and make a severe example of the first person who stirred. As these vagrants do exist, they must be kept in order.

CCCXXXVI

TO GENERAL SAVARY, DUC DE ROVIGO, MINISTER OF POLICE.

PARIS, 14*th April* 1811.

I COULD not read, without indignation, the article in the *Journal de l'Empire*, of the 12th of this month, which is evidently intended to cast ridicule on one of the Emperor of Russia's aides-de-camp, with whom I had had several hours' conversation the previous evening, and who had brought me a letter from his master. It is my intention that Mons. Esmenard, the censor, shall be discharged from your offices, and sent forty leagues away from Paris, and that Mons. Etienne shall be suspended from his duty for a fortnight.

CCCXXXVII

TO GENERAL SAVARY, DUC DE ROVIGO, MINISTER OF POLICE.

PARIS, 14*th April* 1811.

MM. FRANÇOIS, Gautier, Materban, and Rodier, are four priests who reside at La Rochelle, and who are reported as being dissidents, and enemies of the Government.

Mons. Doucin is the leader of the dissident priests in the Lower Charente and the Vendée, whither he frequently travels. He resides in the Commune of Dampierre, near La Rochelle.

At Fontenay, MM. Girard, Moulin, and Henri, who live partly at Pissotte and sometimes at Gros-Noyer, are priests of the same kidney.

At Herbiers, one Buffart, who is generally in the Commune of La Verrerie, is in the same position.

The same thing applies to the former Curé of Livière, a man of the name of Viaud, who lives at La Chapelle Largeau, and to a certain Tissier, living at Courlay.

I should wish all these people to be arrested at once, the seals put upon their papers, and they themselves brought, without any one knowing where they are, either to Vincennes, or to some other State prison. All their papers should be sent to Paris, where they must be examined.

But the arrest of these persons is no light matter—all these priests are instruments of civil strife, who have confederates in all directions. You must not trust either the Prefects, or the Justices of the Peace, nor the local gendarmes, but you must employ Paris police agents, and good picked non-commissioned officers of the Gendarmerie, who will proceed simultaneously to all the places where these priests are to be found, and seize their persons.

This business will have to be very carefully managed, or it will fail; so great is the cunning of these fellows, so far-reaching their ramifications, and so numerous their hiding-places. You must take your measures so as to seize them all at once, and not miss a single one—otherwise it would be better to do nothing at all.

CCCXXXVIII

TO PRINCE LEBRUN, GRAND TREASURER OF THE EMPIRE, THE EMPEROR'S LIEUTENANT-GENERAL IN HOLLAND.

PARIS, 17th April 1811.

I HAVE been distressed by the decisions you have taken. The fewer proclamations you issue, the less fuss you will make, and the better that will be. They echo all over Europe, and produce the worst effect possible. What is the use of rushing into print? It would be far simpler to let the military commander seize the guilty persons, assemble a court-martial, and have them sentenced;—that could have been done without any writing. These pompous proclamations take nobody in, and are a sign of weakness. In my opinion, they have the drawback of investing things with importance, which are really not serious enough to make it necessary to mention them. Steady severity is what is wanted at Amsterdam.

I hear you have kept back the guns applied for by the Minister of War. What does it matter whether they are paid for, or not? Let those guns be on the road to Wesel and Liège, according to the Minister of War's order, twenty-four hours after you have received this letter. The matter of payment is quite a secondary one.

CCCXXXIX

TO GENERAL SAVARY, DUC DE ROVIGO, MINISTER OF POLICE.

St. Cloud, 21*st April* 1811.

I SEND you a letter from the Grand Treasurer. This is a very serious business. You must send a senior police agent, with a sufficient number of armed men. The 500 sailors who have banded themselves together, must be arrested, and sent to France.

Who is the General in command of that Department? Who commands the Gendarmerie? How comes it that they have taken no steps to put down this rabble? Give orders that three of the worst mutineers are to be publicly executed, and that the rest of the 500 are to be sent back to my ports in France. I conclude you have reports from the Police Commissary, who is there.

CCCXL

TO M. MARET, DUC DE BASSANO, MINISTER FOR FOREIGN AFFAIRS.

St. Cloud, 24*th April* 1811.

I send the documents about the Queen of Etruria. You will ask the police for the originals. It will be well for you to send some one to lay them before King Charles, at Marseilles, and before the Princes, at Valençay, so as to make them aware of the follies committed by their daughter and sister. You will also send some one to the Princess, to inquire what can have driven her to such excesses, and to inform her that she is perfectly free to proceed to any country she may choose; that I might punish her, but, after this instance of her ingratitude, I can take no further interest whatever in her. It will be well to have a short memorandum written upon these documents, which may be shown to the Austrian Ambassador, and the Saxon and Bavarian Ministers, and make them aware that I have had the Queen informed she can depart if she chooses.

CCCXLI

TO PRINCE LEBRUN, GRAND TREASURER OF THE EMPIRE, THE EMPEROR'S LIEUTENANT-GENERAL IN HOLLAND.

ST. CLOUD, *3rd May* 1811.

I HAVE your letter of 30th April.   Is this Mons. Lemosy a clever man?   How old is he?   Can he be depended upon?

The Prefect of Emden is a very weak man.   I shall await Comte Réal's report before making a decision.   It is my intention that the 500 men who formed the mob which beat the Prefect, shall all be sent to France, and forced to serve in my ports.   Write in that sense to State Councillor Réal.   I will have no joking on this subject.   The Prefect represents me, and those persons who have taken no interest in the matter are guilty in it.   Would you not have me return my thanks to the two towns[1] because they were so kind as to allow themselves to be disarmed, when my troops arrived? The houses of the persons who have taken to flight must be burnt, their relations arrested, their goods confiscated, and they themselves condemned to death by default, in a military court.   It is necessary to have several of the most guilty shot.   Send a copy of my letter to State Councillor Réal. Blood and chastisement alone can wash out the insult offered to the Government.

CCCXLII

TO GENERAL SAVARY, DUC DE ROVIGO, MINISTER OF POLICE.

ST. CLOUD, *3rd May* 1811.

WRITE to Réal to repeat my orders to him.   My intention is, that the 500 sailors who took part in the affair at Aurich, on the 11th March, shall be arrested and brought to France, to serve at Toulon, Brest, and Lorient ; that several shall be brought before a military court and shot ; that the most guilty of those who have fled, shall be sentenced to death by default, their fathers, mothers, wives, brothers, and sisters imprisoned, their houses burnt, and their goods

---

[1] The towns of Emden and Aurich, where the riots had taken place.

sequestrated.   The crime committed is a monstrous one.
The Prefect, who is the chief civil magistrate, has been
beaten.   I have no notion of sharing the Grand Treasurer's
weakness, and that of the local administration.   Let Réal
take measures to insure this.

CCCXLIII

TO GENERAL SAVARY, DUC DE ROVIGO,
MINISTER OF POLICE.

ST. CLOUD, 7*th May* 1811.

THE Spanish Princes are making excursions on horseback.   Plans are being made to carry them off, and they will
be so carried off.   You must take measures to stop these rides,
and even to prevent the presence of a single saddle-horse in
the establishment.   The persons responsible for their safety
must be very imprudent.

Who is a certain Schmidt who is about the Princes?

CCCXLIV

TO PRINCE LEBRUN, GRAND TREASURER OF THE EMPIRE,
THE EMPEROR'S LIEUTENANT-GENERAL IN HOLLAND.

ST. CLOUD, 12*th May* 1811.

I HEAR you have altered your late decision, on the occasion
of the riots in Amsterdam, and that you brought the persons
implicated in the affair before the civil Courts.   Let me
know the reason of this step.   You may have taken the
initiative in a moment of confusion, but this particular course
having been disapproved by me, you cannot return to it
without my consent.   I cannot understand this vacillation.
Severe examples should have been made at Amsterdam.
They would have prevented what has happened at Rotterdam.

CCCXLV

TO MARSHAL DAVOUT, PRINCE D'ECKMÜHL, COMMANDER-
IN-CHIEF OF THE ARMY IN GERMANY.

RAMBOUILLET, 17*th May* 1811.

I HAVE your letter of 12th May.   I am glad to see you
are going to arrest a large number of English agents.   Show

no mercy.   Keep these people in prison, and if there are any prominent agents among them, have them shot.

Write to Mons. de Saint-Marsan, that he is to demand the arrest of the Berlin and Königsberg merchants who are implicated in this correspondence.   Write to Cassel to have the Brunswick merchants arrested, and take steps to have those belonging to Swedish Pomerania seized.   We must strike terror into these smugglers.

I have given directions that the General in command of the Ems Oriental is to be warned to obey your orders, yet, in ordinary administrative matters, you had better leave him under the orders of the General of his Division.

CCCXLVI

TO PRINCE LEBRUN, GRAND TREASURER OF THE EMPIRE, THE EMPEROR'S LIEUTENANT-GENERAL IN HOLLAND.

RAMBOUILLET, 20th May 1811.

IT is my intention that the measures I have prescribed shall be taken, in all their strictness and integrity, in the Department of the Ems Oriental.   Similar steps will be necessary at Amsterdam and Rotterdam.   It is indispensable that honest and well-intentioned people should be protected, and led by kindly treatment ; but the rabble must be driven by terror.   The way in which things are going on at Amsterdam, and Rotterdam, is disastrous.   Sedition-mongers go unpunished, and, in the end, they will have to be suppressed by fire and sword.   And further, I cannot leave my armies in the interior of the country for ever.

You have a right to take measures, in a moment of pressure, but once such measures have been ratified by me, you have no right to revoke them.   The rioters at Amsterdam and Rotterdam must therefore be sentenced by military courts.

CCCXLVII

TO GENERAL SAVARY, DUC DE ROVIGO, MINISTER OF POLICE.

CAEN, 24th May 1811.

I HAVE informed the Duke of Bassano of my intentions with regard to the Queen of Etruria, and have desired him to

transmit them to you. I see two English frigates have
appeared before Nice. Let me know how soon it will be
possible to have the agents in this intrigue brought before
a military tribunal, the Princess shut up in some Roman
convent, and her son given up to King Charles.

CCCXLVIII

TO M. MARET, DUC DE BASSANO, MINISTER FOR
FOREIGN AFFAIRS.

CAEN, 26th May 1811, 4 A.M.

As news has come from Spain, I desire you will not have
the extract from the English Gazettes, which I sent you
some four hours ago, inserted in the *Moniteur*. All you
will do is to have a letter written, nominally from London,
for the minor newspapers, which will assert that the English
are very much alarmed, that they thought they had come to
the end of the war, but that war is breaking out on all sides.

CCCXLIX

TO M. MARET, DUC DE BASSANO, MINISTER FOR
FOREIGN AFFAIRS.

ALENÇON, 1st June 1811.

I HAVE your letter of 30th May. I do not understand
about this decoration set with diamonds, sent to the King of
Rome. Was this done when the Dauphin was born? or on
what other occasions in Europe? Send me a word of
explanation on the subject.

The Grand Cordon of the Order of St. Leopold, given to
Comte Beauharnais, is explicable, as he is a gentleman-in-
waiting on the Empress, and that conferred on Comte
Regnaud is explained, by his position as State Secretary to
the Imperial family; but as regards that given to Comte
Sémonville, I don't see what it has to do with Comte
Sémonville? I do not take kindly to the idea.

CCCL

TO M. MARET, DUC DE BASSANO, MINISTER FOR FOREIGN AFFAIRS.

St. Cloud, 13th June 1811.

I WISH you to ask for an account of the money brought in by the trade certificates, issued at Hamburg by Mons. Bourrienne, with the duty he has levied, and the sum it has amounted to. It is my intention that he should account for it accurately, and that 75 per cent. of the duty he has levied shall be paid into the Treasury of the Ministry for Foreign Affairs, to pay for finishing the Ministerial residence.

CCCLI

TO GENERAL SAVARY, DUC DE ROVIGO, MINISTER OF POLICE.

St. Cloud, 22nd June 1811.

I HAVE been interested in reading the alphabetical statement of the [French and Belgian] officers in the Austrian service. I return it to you. You must have it made out for each Department, send it to the Prefects for them to report, and have the property of these persons sequestrated, without delay. You must warn the Registry Department, so that it may cause all property and inheritances that may fall due to them, to be seized.

CCCLII

TO PRINCE LEBRUN, GRAND TREASURER OF THE EMPIRE, THE EMPEROR'S LIEUTENANT-GENERAL IN HOLLAND.

St. Cloud, 22nd June 1811.

I HAVE been interested in seeing the result of the military inquiries, and that three men have been sentenced to death and executed. There is no other way of overawing the mob.

CCCLIII

TO PRINCE LEBRUN, GRAND TREASURER OF THE EMPIRE, THE EMPEROR'S LIEUTENANT-GENERAL IN HOLLAND.

ST. CLOUD, 29th June 1811.

THE police did wrong to hold any communication with England. I am giving it orders to cease doing so. I will have no communication between Holland and England, on any pretext whatsoever. That of obtaining military information is quite inadmissible. We have a well organised, specially arranged, correspondence, on the Normandy coast, which is quite sufficient to keep us informed of what goes on in England. There is no necessity that Holland should interfere in the matter. Take effectual measures to have this stopped, and give orders in the Custom-house that no such intercourse is to be allowed.

CCCLIV

TO MARSHAL DAVOUT, PRINCE D'ECKMÜHL, IN CHIEF COMMAND OF THE ARMY IN GERMANY.

ST. CLOUD, 5th July 1811.

I HAVE carefully read the minutes of the sitting of the Council of the 18th of June, and I notice that to General Liébert's inquiry as to whether colonial produce from Gothenburg is to be admitted, the Council replied in the negative, 'because Sweden does not belong to the Continental system.' This answer seems to me a strange one, and I therefore write to give you the clear bearings of these questions. Colonial merchandise and produce, coming from Sweden, Prussia, or any other place whatsoever, must be seized and confiscated, because it originally comes from England. Send orders to this effect, and see they are adhered to. This should direct your action as to Dantzig. I conclude my line of Custom-houses has been established on the land side, and that no colonial produce can get through. In consequence of a mistake, Saxony and Westphalia had allowed colonial merchandise from Prussia to enter their country, and had recognised the duty paid in Prussia. But Westphalia and Saxony have changed their procedure. Turn your special attention to this subject, which is of paramount importance. Every article of colonial produce must be stopped, unless it has paid duty to you.

You must quietly stop all communication with Gothenburg. For this purpose, all packets, going and coming, must be delayed twelve or fifteen days. The letters must be read, and everything for England must be suppressed.

Whenever you are in doubt, write to me, for that gives me an opportunity of explaining my views. Send spies to find out if there is any colonial produce in Holstein, and if the Danes propose to go on receiving it. Speak plainly to the Danish agents, and take measures to have all the produce confiscated.

I expect satisfaction for the insult offered my flag at Stralsund. I shall perhaps decide on giving you orders to occupy Pomerania. You will desire your agents, at the same time, to seize all the colonial merchandise to be found there.

CCCLV

TO CARDINAL FESCH, GRAND ALMONER.

TRIANON, 12*th July* 1811.

THE extreme displeasure caused me by the Bishops of Ghent and of Troyes, on account of their constant misconduct, which has obliged me to request the police to keep special watch upon them, induces me to write you this letter, to inform you that I have removed them from the list of officers attached to my Household. You will no longer consider them my Almoners.

CCCLVI

TO COMTE DE MONTALIVET, MINISTER OF THE INTERIOR.

TRIANON, 19*th July* 1811.

IT is necessary for you to give the Director-General of the Department of Literature orders not to allow any work on ecclesiastical affairs to be printed. The great art in such matters is never to mention them. I have been distressed by the pamphlets which have appeared on such subjects. And to back up my intention, you must prevent people from writing such things.

TO GENERAL COMTE BERTRAND, GOVERNOR-GENERAL OF THE ILLYRIAN PROVINCES.

TRIANON, *22nd July* 1811.

I HAVE received your letter about the province of Cattaro, dated Laybach, 1st July. Appoint a good Sub-Delegate; send a good Military Commander : both these measures are within your duty. Have the strictest order kept, and bring back those who have got out of hand, to their duty. Have all contributions paid up, both arrears and those now due. The presence of one or two battalions, for a couple of months, will suffice for that. Have the same imposts levied at Ragusa, as throughout the rest of your Government. Send a Greek Bishop to Cattaro, and forbid all correspondence with the Bishop of Montenegro, on pain of death. Make a few examples, and arrest any priests he may have appointed. Send a good officer of Gendarmes; you have power to make over the police duty to the Commandant. Let me hear, within a month, that you have seen to everything. Far away as you are, you have extraordinary powers ; everything referred to in your letter, should have been done already.

TO GENERAL COMTE HULLIN, GOVERNOR OF THE CASTLE OF VINCENNES.

ST. CLOUD, *25th July* 1811.

I HAVE received the sentences passed on Cifenti and Sassi della Tosa. You will have the first-named—a rascally spy—executed. I will permit the commutation of Sassi della Tosa's sentence ; but you will have him taken to the place of execution, and after Cifenti has suffered, just as Sassi della Tosa is about to mount the scaffold, you will cause the page bearing the reprieve to make his appearance. But I intend Sassi shall have the full example of the punishment of his crime before his eyes.

CCCLIX

TO M. MARET, DUC DE BASSANO, MINISTER FOR FOREIGN AFFAIRS.

ST. CLOUD, 26th July 1811.

I SEND back your documents about Princess Marie-Louise's business.[1] I do not wish to write to King Charles on the subject, but it is necessary he should be informed of it by you, or by the police, through a person of some importance. There is an old Spanish Colonel here, who is attached to them, and whom you might send to Marseilles for this purpose.

CCCLX

TO GENERAL SAVARY, DUC DE ROVIGO, MINISTER OF POLICE.

ST. CLOUD, 26th July 1811.

I DESIRE you will notify the sentence of the Commission to the Queen of Etruria. You will have her carried off that very day, and taken with all speed, by carriage, to Rome. She is to have nobody with her, but her maid and her daughter. Her papers will be seized, and sent to the Ministry. She will be placed in the convent in which a Princess of the Bourbon family already is. Her daughter and her maid will remain with her. Her son will be sent to Marseilles. Have the contents of the documents communicated to the Spanish Princes.

CCCLXI

TO GENERAL SAVARY, DUC DE ROVIGO, MINISTER OF POLICE.

ST. CLOUD, 27th July 1811.

I SEND you the Trappist Fathers' letters. The affair had already been mentioned to me. Have the Superior arrested, and shut up in a State prison. Have the seals put on the property of the monastery, and have the Trappist community broken up, so that no more may be heard of them.

[1] The Queen of Etruria.

Q

Take their habits away from them, and inform the Prefect that the monastery is dissolved. There is a Trappist monastery in the Forest of Sénart. Find out what is going on there, so that if it shares the sentiments of this other one, I may have it suppressed.

CCCLXII

TO M. MARET, DUC DE BASSANO, MINISTER FOR FOREIGN AFFAIRS.

ST. CLOUD, 29*th July* 1811.

SEND orders to my Minister at Cassel, to proceed to the Brunswick Fair, taking agents and brokers with him, to watch what happens there. Before he starts, he will signify, to M. de Fürstenstein, my intention that all English goods found there shall be confiscated, without any regard to Prussian certificates. Mention this also to M. de Wintzingerode. My Minister will stay at Brunswick as long as the Fair lasts.

CCCLXIII

TO GENERAL SAVARY, DUC DE ROVIGO, MINISTER OF POLICE.

ST. CLOUD, 29*th July* 1811.

IF Mons. Lestrange has not been arrested before he entered Switzerland, write to my Minister to have him arrested at Friburg, and at the same time, to seize all his papers.

You will have received my Decree that the Superior of the Cervara convent is to be shot, and the monks imprisoned. If those in the Forest of Sénart are Trappists, have the seals put on their house. I have revoked the gifts I bestowed on them. Those at Mont Genèvre and at . . .[2] are in the same case. I conclude the military court will do justice on the Superior, who has dared to preach sedition. The Trappists have a house at the Calvaire. They have set up three crosses, a thing worthy of the most barbarous mountaineers. Have the seals put on their house. I am assured they have other establishments in Paris.

---

[1] Illegible word.

CCCLXIV

TO GENERAL CLARKE, DUC DE FELTRE,
MINISTER OF WAR.

St. Cloud, 30th July 1811.

EXPRESS my displeasure at General Cæsar Berthier's having had the priests, deported to Corsica, to dine with him. This is an impropriety. He must not ill-treat them, indeed, but he must not ask them to dinner, nor go to any house where they are invited. Such conduct is inconsistent.

CCCLXV

TO GENERAL SAVARY, DUC DE ROVIGO,
MINISTER OF POLICE.

St. Cloud, 1st August 1811.

THE Trappists at Cervara might be sent to the Island of Capraja. It will suffice to deprive them of their habit, give them ordinary frocks, and lodge them in the tower at Capraja.

CCCLXVI

TO GENERAL SAVARY, DUC DE ROVIGO,
MINISTER OF POLICE.

St. Cloud, 4th August 1811.

COMTE LAVALLETTE has just informed me of your decision to re-open correspondence with England, so that all letters sent to the police, no matter what ship brings them, will be sent back to the postal authorities to be taxed. The Berlin Decree is explicit : every letter sent to, or out of, England must be burnt. Have this Decree strictly carried out, and do not follow up your decision in any way. Repeat your orders to the Police Commissaries as to the strict execution of my Decree. Forbid the licensed ships to carry any letters; the only one they are to have, is that authorising the ship to sail.

As for the prisoners' letters, they, too, must be burnt,

unless they pass the Morlaix Challenge.   In that case, they will be sent to the police, if they only refer to matters unconnected with politics, and even then, the thing must be done quietly, and as a concession.   Prisoners writing to their families about themselves may, as a concession, send letters by Morlaix, but as a matter of principle, all letters coming from England must be burnt.   This is the Berlin Decree.   Its terms are positive.

CCCLXVII

TO GENERAL CLARKE, DUC DE FELTRE, MINISTER FOR FOREIGN AFFAIRS.

St. Cloud, 4th August 1811.

I AM informed that a great number of refractory conscripts are confined in the Citadel of the Ile de Ré, and that they are dying from overcrowding.   I do not see why they should not be allowed to move about the town.   The Island itself must be guarded by the Custom-house authorities, and besides, I will not have men shut up in a manner detrimental to their health.   Send an officer to verify these facts, and remedy them.   I get a large number of fine conscripts in those islands.   They must be well cared for.

CCCLXVIII

TO M. MARET, DUC DE BASSANO, MINISTER FOR FOREIGN AFFAIRS.

St. Cloud, 5th August 1811.

THERE is no object in M. de Moustier's being in the Queen of Sweden's company.   There is no doubt whatever, that if he cannot avoid meeting her, and is obliged to address her, he must call her 'Your Majesty.'   The title is hers, because, if the position itself is lost, the title, according to custom, remains.   A Dowager Queen keeps the title of Majesty.   If Gustavus Adolphus should return to the country, he must avoid seeing him.

CCCLXIX

TO GENERAL CLARKE, DUC DE FELTRE,
MINISTER OF WAR.

PARIS, 15*th August* 1811.

I HAVE a letter you have sent me, from General Puthod, which proves that officer's want of sense and capacity. Recall him forthwith. You have doubtless suspended him from duty. Give him leave to go home, and point out to him the indecency, and want of principle, evident in his letter. He has no right to arrest any French citizen, much less one of the Emperor's officers, travelling through his command. General Nansouty's commission, and all the other proofs of his quality, put forward by Mortemart, were ample evidence of his rank as an orderly officer. This officer carried no orders to General Puthod, and had nothing to say to him. His sole mission was to look on, and observe ; but General Puthod had no right to arrest him, just as he would have no right to arrest the meanest French drummer passing through his command.

General Hogendorp, on the contrary, is travelling for an avowed object, which gives him a command in the Division, and it is quite right that his position should be formally notified, and that the General of the Division should be informed as to his mission. This is always done when an aide-de-camp takes up command of a flying column, or any other duty which involves his being employed in a Division.

CCCLXX

TO GENERAL SAVARY, DUC DE ROVIGO,
MINISTER OF POLICE.

ST. CLOUD, 20*th August* 1811.

I HAVE been assured that the Spanish Crown diamonds have been carried off by Frenchmen, and that they could be tracked, if certain jewellers' shops, especially those which supply the Court of Naples, were searched. Follow this up skilfully, so as to get at the truth.

CCCLXXI

TO GENERAL SAVARY, DUC DE ROVIGO, MINISTER OF POLICE.

St. Cloud, *22nd August* 1811.

WHEN the Duke of Otranto was dismissed from the Ministry, I gave orders that he was to retire to a distance from Paris. A year having now gone by, you can inform him that he is at liberty to come and spend the autumn at his country house.

CCCLXXII

TO M. MARET, DUC DE BASSANO, MINISTER FOR FOREIGN AFFAIRS.

St. Cloud, *24th August* 1811.

WRITE in cipher to Comte Laforest, that he is to see the King of Spain, and inform him, that having reason to believe that from fifteen to eighteen millions' worth of diamonds had been stolen by certain persons from the Spanish Crown jewels, and having learnt that a certain Aymé was implicated in the matter, I have had the man arrested and imprisoned, until he shall have confessed all he knows of the business; that he has already acknowledged having seen very fine diamonds, and amongst other jewels the *Perla peregrina*; that when King Charles left Madrid, these jewels were left there under the care of five Spaniards; that I request these five Spaniards may be examined, and the report of their examination sent to Paris; that the said Aymé has told us that the *Perla peregrina* passed into the hands of a jeweller who is now at Naples; that I have ordered my Minister at Naples to have this jeweller questioned, and to collect everything which may throw light upon this subject, my intention being that the fifteen or eighteen millions' worth of diamonds shall be found, and their value sent to the King, as such help will be of essential use to him in present circumstances; that very valuable articles were stolen from the house of the Prince of Peace; that investigation must be made, that this will be done in France also, and that very considerable sums of money will be recovered.

You will write in cipher to Baron Durand, that he is to have the Neapolitan Court jeweller, who is now in Naples, and in whose possession the pearl was seen, questioned; and to cause inquiry to be made as to what has become of this pearl, and of the other Spanish Crown jewels; that he is to carry on all his inquiries with the utmost secrecy, and that in the present position of Spain, it is necessary to recover these valuables.

CCCLXXIII

TO COMTE MOLLIEN, MINISTER OF THE PUBLIC EXCHEQUER.

COMPIÈGNE, *3rd September* 1811.

I SEND you a letter from Hamburg, with reference to Mons. Bourrienne. I beg you will have a summary made of it, for me. Collect your information without the police being aware of it, because Mons. Bourrienne is well acquainted with the workings of the police. Try to find out about this address—

'Madame Jouannet,
No. 6 Cloître St. Médéric,
Paris,'[1]

who lives there, and what it all means? Is it customary for you to have your accountants arrested, and their papers seized, without appealing to the police?

CCCLXXIV

TO M. RÉGNIER, DUC DE MASSA, CHIEF JUDGE, AND MINISTER OF JUSTICE.

COMPIÈGNE, *3rd September* 1811.

THE Mayor of Cahors, and the recruiting captain of the Department of the Lot, are accused of dishonesty, in connection with the conscription. They are said to have received more than 300,000 francs, within the last six years. Give the Imperial Procurator orders to open an inquiry on the subject—an official one, and of the strictest nature.

[1] On the same day an order was issued to the Director-General of the Postal Service to lay hands on all letters directed to Mme Jouannet.

CCCLXXV

TO M. RÉGNIER, DUC DE MASSA, CHIEF JUDGE, AND MINISTER OF JUSTICE.

COMPIÈGNE, *6th September* 1811.

ALL American ships captured in the Baltic are our lawful prizes, for they all sail under English convoy. The Decree must run, that they have been taken and confiscated, as being under English convoy. They really are English in disguise. Have all this business settled on the spot; there can be no doubt about the matter.

Let me know the number of American ships taken elsewhere than in the Baltic, by what privateers they have been captured, the place of their capture, and the ports in which they now lie, so that everything may be settled at once.

There is no difficulty whatever as regards the Baltic, and I intend that before the 10th September, the Prize Committee shall have made them over to the privateers.

CCCLXXVI

TO GENERAL CLARKE, DUC DE FELTRE, MINISTER OF WAR.

COMPIÈGNE, *7th September* 1811.

I AM astonished that a man of honour, like General D——, should desire to marry the daughter of a notary who has been disgraced, and driven out of the professional body. The very idea is dishonouring. If the General should persist in such a choice, he must be turned out of the artillery.

CCCLXXVII

TO MARSHAL BESSIÈRES, DUC D'ISTRIE, COMMANDING THE IMPERIAL GUARD.

COMPIÈGNE, *11th September* 1811.

THIS report is ridiculous. A crime, which is a disgrace to my Guard, has been committed. Either the regiment will take its own measures to discover the culprits, or, if they are not given up within a week, I shall reduce it to a regiment of the line. The *Chef d'Escadron* had no right to sell hay, in order to buy straw, without an order from the Minister of War. Officers and non-commissioned officers will all be put under arrest, and if, within a week, I do not know everything, just as it happened, I shall send the whole regiment back to the line.

Who is this *Chef d'Escadron*? Where has he served?

CCCLXXVIII

TO GENERAL SAVARY, DUC DE ROVIGO,
MINISTER OF POLICE.

COMPIÈGNE, 12th September 1811.

HAVE the wife of Gallet, the pilot who is in the English service, arrested, and have that sailor written to, that, unless he comes back to France, or proceeds to some neutral country, so that we may be sure he is not serving the English, she and her children will be put in prison, into a dark cell, on bread and water. Extend this measure to the wives and children of all pilots in the English service. Submit a Decree on the subject to me, and have full inquiry made, as to the pilots on board enemies' ships.

CCCLXXIX

TO GENERAL SAVARY, DUC DE ROVIGO,
MINISTER OF POLICE.

ANTWERP, 30th September 1811.

THERE must be no alteration in the course followed by persons about the Pope, at Savona. No stranger is to come to Savona, and there is to be no communication between Savona and the other parts of the Empire. But for that, I should have to begin again in a fortnight, which would cause a shock.

CCCLXXX

TO GENERAL SAVARY, DUC DE ROVIGO,
MINISTER OF POLICE.

ANTWERP, 30*th September* 1811.

YOU are not to mix yourself up with the Queen of Naples' concerns. Let her do as she chooses. The less you talk to her the better; conversation with her must be mischievous, because you are ignorant of my objects. You will therefore show her all proper respect, and you will keep quiet. Generally speaking, all diplomatic conversations are very harmful. You had one with Campochiaro—what good did it do? It would have been far better to have had none at all, or only the very slightest. Let this be a rule to you, —the less you talk with Foreign Ministers, and the fewer Ambassadors you have at your table, the better.

I think I have already informed you, that you did wrong to write to Switzerland, about the Comte de Gottorp. You do not know my intentions; I have not informed you of them; and you have therefore exposed yourself to the danger of giving my Minister instructions opposed to those sent him by the Minister for Foreign Affairs. Once the Comte de Gottorp was outside France, he was no business of yours. You might have warned the Minister for Foreign Affairs, but you should not have taken anything upon yourself. When a Minister meddles with what does not concern him, he upsets the whole Administration. It is not regular for you to give a single instruction to my Ministers abroad.

I know that Mme de Chevreuse has passed through Paris. I cannot conceive how my orders—which are that the lady in question is to remain forty leagues away from Paris—have been disobeyed, nor how you can have permitted such an oversight. I desire this may not happen again. I have made you aware that my system, as regards the exiles, is to take no more notice of them, and not to confer importance on them, by perpetual interference in their business.

As for the licences, I am heartily convinced you are taken in by schemers. This is the tendency of my Ministers, whenever they have to do with agents of this sort, who are a

disgrace to the Administration.   The whole system must be
given up, for, carried on as it is, it offers more drawbacks
than advantages.

I have received the report you have sent me, from the
Police Commissary at Boulogne, as to Dunkirk.   I have
never come across so loquacious and bumptious a man as
this Commissary.   He has been with me for over an hour,
teaching me all about finance, exchange, general administration,—and wrong at every point.   Such an official is very
far removed from a Villiers, and from police agents of the
real sort.   Loquacity and presumption are qualities the very
reverse of those necessary to a good Police Commissary.   I
believe he is zealous, indeed, but he does his work badly.
The smugglers are not watched at Dunkirk, they are increasing in the town.   It is this Commissary's duty to keep order,
but he chattered some story to me,—I know not what,—
to explain that my orders on this point ought not to be
executed.   So stupid is this Commissary, that when I was
anchored at Boulogne, he allowed the smugglers to go out of
Wimereux.   When I remonstrated he said very foolish things
to me.   Give orders that no smuggler is to leave Wimereux,
without warning Rear-Admiral Baste.   The Police Commissary at Boulogne has a great deal of power.   He should
be a man who unites great prudence with great dexterity,—
very different qualities from those possessed by the present
Commissary.

The Police Commissary at Flushing is, I think, related to
Réal.   He is very young, and every one agrees that his lack
of knowledge and activity renders him perfectly useless.

Stir up the police in Paris; order is very badly kept, and
the public is beginning to notice the loss of Dubois' activity.
Women of bad character crowd the public squares, and fresh
houses of ill-fame have been opened.   Put a stop to the bold-
ness of these wretched creatures, and take steps to diminish
the evil, instead of allowing it to increase.   Do not leave
Pasquier in ignorance of the fact, that public report in Paris
has it, that the police does not keep such good order as it did
under his predecessor.   You need not tell him this as my
opinion, for that would discourage a magistrate for whom I
have a regard; at the same time, you must warn him, so
that he may use more energetic measures.

CCCLXXXI

TO GENERAL SAVARY, DUC DE ROVIGO,
MINISTER OF POLICE.

UTRECHT, *7th October* 1811.

I SEE by the *Gazette de France*, that the Emperor has promoted a conscript, whose wife came and cast herself at his feet, to the rank of officer. This is so silly, that I do not know how the editor of the newspaper can have printed it.

CCCLXXXII

TO GENERAL SAVARY, DUC DE ROVIGO,
MINISTER OF POLICE.

UTRECHT, *7th October* 1811.

YOU are to give the Prefect of Montenotte, and the Commandant of Gendarmerie at Savona, the following instructions :—

As soon as the deputation of Bishops has departed, the Prefect will notify the Cardinals that I leave them at Savona, on condition that they administer no business, keep up no correspondence, and give no information as to anything touching the spiritual affairs of Europe ; that they are only to write to their families, to give them news of themselves, and that all letters as to Bulls, Dispensations, etc., are to be made over to the Prefect, until this business is concluded ; that the smallest transgression will be a crime, and will bring them misfortune. It would be well, indeed, that the Prefect, and the officer commanding the Gendarmerie, should act accordingly, for until everything is wound up, nothing is changed, and the same watch must be kept upon the Pope, both from without, and from within.

CCCLXXXIII

TO COMTE DE MONTALIVET, MINISTER OF
THE INTERIOR.

AMSTERDAM, *20th October* 1811.

I SEND you back the report of the sitting of the Victualling Council. The increase in the price of bread is regrettable, unless it results from the high price of wheat; flour being really only a secondary matter.   Before putting up the price of bread, which it would be advisable to delay, it is my intention that the bakers shall be given a bounty on every sack of flour they may buy, or have bought, since the 20th October.   This bounty will be fixed by the Council at every sitting.   It must not exceed five francs on each sack already bought, or which may be bought, after the day of the sitting. So that at the end of November, the same quantity of flour there may be in hand as now.   You will note that I say each sack of flour which the bakers may buy, or have bought, after the 20th of October, and reckoning from what was in hand on that day.   Note, too, that I do not mean to give a bonus to the bakers on the batches of bread they bake, for that would be an imposition, indemnifying them for the flour they have bought cheap, without giving any guarantee for their replacing it.   Thus, for instance, if the bakers buy their flour for sixty-nine francs, they can sell the loaf for four sous. Whether it is worth seventy-two francs on the 20th October, or seventy-four francs on the 25th, we shall give five francs bounty on every sack the baker may have bought.   The baker can lay in a good store, as no sack will cost him more than sixty-nine francs, even if he pays seventy-four.

You will point out to the Council, that I have not chosen to fix a basis, and say, for instance, that the bounty is to be whatever the flour is worth, over sixty-nine francs, because then it would be to the baker's interest to drive up average prices.   But the Council, having this latitude, can so indemnify the bakers, that it will be to their interest to lay up a store, at this opportune moment.   Supposing the bakers to buy 40,000 sacks of flour, it will cost us some 150,000 or 200,000 francs, which will save the people of Paris from a rise in the price of bread, and which will put me in a position to make some definite decision at the end of November, when Martinmas will be over, and the new corn will be on the market.

I choose the 20th, and not the 25th, of October, for my starting-point, because I calculate that my decision should reach Paris on the 22nd, that the Council will consider it on the 23rd, and that the Prefect of Police can pay the bakers the bounty for whatever they have bought, during these four days, which is preferable to insurances, etc.   He will tell the bakers, that he will give them the same bounty, every day, for every sack of corn they buy. As I have placed two millions in the Sinking Fund, at Comte Maret's disposal, he will advance 100,000 francs out of this sum. And indeed, as soon as I know what the cost has been, I will credit you with the necessary funds.

Postscript.—The Council will keep all its deliberations secret, and the Prefect of Police, only, will distribute the money, and that secretly.

CCCLXXXIV

TO M. GAUDIN, DUC DE GAÉTE, MINISTER OF FINANCE.

AMSTERDAM, *23rd October* 1811.

HAVE all property at Rome, palaces and other belongings, formerly in the possession of the King of Naples, sequestrated. The only thing I gave the King of Naples, was the pictures in the Farnese Palace. This property is, therefore, mine, and the Crown Property Office ought never to have given it up. It must be offered for sale, at once, and the price it brings incorporated with the public property of this country. All persons employed by the King of Naples, for the management of this property, must be discharged.

CCCLXXXV

TO MARSHAL DAVOUT, PRINCE D'ECKMÜHL, IN CHIEF COMMAND OF THE ARMY IN GERMANY.

ROTTERDAM, *26th October* 1811.

IT is quite true that Prince Augustus has gone to Basle, and thence to Erfürt. The truth is, the Prince is over head and ears in love with Mme Récamier. He has even given her a promise of marriage. She, who is no fool, laughs at it, and makes game of him. She did not keep her engagement to meet him at Basle. So you see politics have very little to do with it all. The young man is senseless and rudderless—a great grief, I am told, to the Prussian Royal Family.

CCCLXXXVI

TO COMTE MOLLIEN, MINISTER OF THE PUBLIC EXCHEQUER.

WESEL, 1st November 1811.

THE Crown Treasury has advanced several hundred thousand francs, which Mons. Pierlot owed the Empress Josephine and Queen Hortense. I desire to know when the liquidation of Mons. Pierlot's property will permit of the reimbursement of the Crown Treasury.

You will do well to send privately for the Empress Josephine's Comptroller, and make him aware that nothing will be paid over to him, unless proof is furnished that there are no debts; and, as I will have no shilly-shallying on the subject, this must be guaranteed on the Comptroller's own property. You will therefore notify the Comptroller, that from the 1st of January next, no payment will be made, either in your office, or by the Crown Treasury, until he has given an undertaking that no debts exist, and made his own property responsible for the fact. I have information that the expenditure in that household is exceedingly careless. You will therefore see the Comptroller, and put yourself in possession of all facts regarding money matters; for it is absurd that instead of saving two millions of money, as the Empress should have done, she should have more debts to be paid. It will be easy for you to find out the truth about this, from the Comptroller, and to make him understand that he himself might be seriously compromised.

Take an opportunity of seeing the Empress Josephine yourself, and give her to understand, that I trust her household will be managed with more economy, and that if any debts are left outstanding, she will incur my sovereign displeasure. The Empress Louise has only 100,000 crowns; she pays everything every week; she does without gowns, and denies herself, so as never to owe money.

My intention is, then, that from the 1st of January, no payment shall be made for the Empress Josephine's household, without a certificate from her Comptroller, to the effect that she has no debts. Look into her budget for 1811, and that prepared for 1812. It should not amount to more than a million. If too many horses are kept, some of them must be put down. The Empress Josephine, who has children and grandchildren, ought to economise, and so be of some use to them, instead of running into debt.

I desire you will not make any more payments to Queen Hortense, either on account of her appanage, or for wood-felling, without asking my permission. Confer with her Comptroller too, so that her household may be properly managed, and that she may not only keep out of debt, but regulate her expenditure in a fitting manner.

CCCLXXXVII

TO GENERAL CLARKE, DUC DE FELTRE,
MINISTER OF WAR.

St. Cloud, *16th November* 1811.

I HAVE already informed you of my intention that a banner should be sent to each army division, with an inscription on one side running, 'The Emperor Napoleon to such and such a regiment,' and on the other side, the battles in which the regiment has taken part, such as Ulm, Austerlitz, Jena, Friedland, Eckmühl, Essling, Wagram, and Madrid. This banner must be about the same size as that affixed to the eagles. Most of the eagles have lost theirs; they can be renewed every two or three years, without any great expense. Have the sketch for this banner made, and draw up the detail of what is to be put for each regiment.

A definite order must be issued, about the pike to be carried by the two ensigns, whose duty it is to escort and defend the eagle. The pike must be a strong one, with which the standard may be defended, independently of the brace of pistols each of these officers wears on his breast.

Finally, I desire each battalion shall have a guidon without any emblem or inscription. It will be a pole, carrying a piece of stuff, of one colour for the first battalion, of another for the second, another for the third, and another for the fourth, so that the number of the battalion may be easily recognised merely by the colour of the flag.

There will be one eagle to each cavalry regiment. I request you will turn your attention to all this. The custom has been very much neglected in various corps. It must be re-established.

CCCLXXXVIII

TO M. MARET, DUC DE BASSANO, MINISTER FOR FOREIGN AFFAIRS.

ST. CLOUD, 18*th November* 1811.

MAKE a complaint to the Mecklenburg Chargé d'Affaires, of the way in which things are going on in that country, and the bad feeling of the press. Write to Mons. Desaugiers that I blame his weakness, and that at the very first fresh offence, he is to write to the Prince d'Eckmühl, who will have the journalist arrested, and severely punished. He must have an explanation in this sense, with the Prince of Mecklenburg.

Write to Bavaria to point out the absurdity of not arresting Dr. Schneider, and of allowing him to hang about the frontiers of Switzerland, and the importance of taking advantage of the folly committed by the man, when he returned to his country, to seize his person, and keep him in prison.

Arrange with the Minister for the Navy as to the answer to be sent to Naples, about the ships. The idea of selling ships cannot be entertained; but Neapolitan crews might be received on board three French ships, which might be replaced by Neapolitan vessels. These, though belonging to France, would fly the Neapolitan flag.

CCCLXXXIX

TO GENERAL SAVARY, DUC DE ROVIGO, MINISTER OF POLICE.

ST. CLOUD, 21*st November* 1811.

SEE the Minister of Public Worship, and desire him to inform the three Bishops of Ghent, Tournay, and Troyes, that they no longer possess my confidence. The Minister of Public Worship will send some one to them, to demand their resignation of their Bishoprics. As soon as these resignations have been sent, by letter, to the Minister of Public Worship, my intention is that you shall oblige the Prelates to start secretly, and at night, for points sixty leagues from Paris, and from their dioceses. You will inform me as to the places of residence you may choose for them, so that I may approve them.

R

CCCXC

TO GENERAL SAVARY, DUC DE ROVIGO,
MINISTER OF POLICE.

ST. CLOUD, *24th November* 1811.

HEREWITH you will find a Decree, which declares a certain number of *Curiali* beyond the pale of the civil law. Have them deported to Corsica, and take care that all their goods, furniture, and houses, are confiscated and sequestered. These people must be out of Rome twenty-four hours after the receipt of this Decree, and the thing must be done swiftly and quietly.

CCCXCI

TO GENERAL SAVARY, DUC DE ROVIGO,
MINISTER OF POLICE.

ST. CLOUD, *30th November* 1811.

IT is my intention to set the Bishop of Troyes at liberty, and keep him under surveillance, in a commune in one of the safest parts of France—in Alsace or Normandy. Consult the Bishop, as to the town to which he would like to retire; my intention being to place him in a small commune. You will report to me, so that I may give you further orders.

CCCXCII

TO GENERAL SAVARY, DUC DE ROVIGO,
MINISTER OF POLICE.

ST. CLOUD, *30th November* 1811.

WHAT is the meaning of this courier whom Princess Pauline has sent to Soissons? Find out about it.

CCCXCIII

TO QUEEN JULIE OF SPAIN.

PARIS, *4th December* 1811.

I AM informed that the King of Spain is continuing, with a lavishness very ill suited to his position, to give salaries to persons in Paris, who do nothing for him, and this because I continue to pay him his income of a million a year, as a French Prince. So long as you remain in Paris, I intend the Minister of Finance shall pay that million over to you, but I desire that all salaries to persons in Paris, who render you no actual service, may be suppressed. I am assured that 50,000 crowns are thus unnecessarily expended, and they would be very much better employed, if they were sent to Madrid, to the King, seeing that he is asking for money on every possible occasion.

CCCXCIV

TO COMTE MONTALIVET, MINISTER OF THE
INTERIOR.

PARIS, 9th December 1811.

INFORM the Prefect of the Deux-Nèthes[1] of my displeasure with his ridiculous behaviour at the ceremony on the 2nd. Instead of proceeding to the house of the General in command, and accompanying him, he went straight to the Church, unknown to anybody, so that there was a regular scene. . . . Make the Prefect understand that obedience to the laws can never disgrace him ; that, further, he owed some consideration to a General holding so important a command as that of Antwerp, who had been maimed, and lost an arm, on the field of battle ; that the only result of such behaviour must be to disturb the harmony between civilians and the military—which has not earned the right of being being despised and ill treated in any country, and least of all in France.

CCCXCV

TO JEROME NAPOLEON, KING OF WESTPHALIA.

PARIS, 10th December 1811.

I HAVE your letter of 5th December. I only notice two facts in it : (1st) That the Hanoverian and Magdeburg proprietors are leaving their houses, to avoid paying the heavy additional charges you have laid on them. (2nd) That

<hr>

[1] Mons. de Voyer d'Argenson.

you do not think you can be sure of your army, and warn me not to reckon on it.

As to the first point, it does not concern me. I have constantly advised you, as a matter of principle, to keep down the enemies of France, not to allow them to become over confident, and, by showing a greater amount of confidence in the Generals commanding at Magdeburg, to insure the safety of that important fortress ; and, in short, to manage the whole finance system of Westphalia, which is the worst governed State in the Confederation, consistently and economically.

As regards the second point, it is what I have never ceased telling you since the day you ascended the throne. A small number of troops, and these well chosen, and a more economical administration, would have served yourself, and the common cause, far better.

When you have facts to lay before me, I shall always be glad to be informed of them, but when, on the contrary, you desire to draw me fancy pictures, I will ask you to spare me them. You tell me nothing new, when you tell me your administrative system is a bad one.

CCCXCVI

TO GENERAL SAVARY, DUC DE ROVIGO,
MINISTER OF POLICE.

PARIS, 10th December 1811.

HAVE the Bishop of Troyes removed at night, and taken, with post-horses, to Falaise, without passing through Paris. You will let the officer in command of the Gendarmerie know that he has to keep an eye on his behaviour. You will ask him to give his word of honour not to go two leagues beyond Falaise, without your authority. Have the Bishop of Tournay removed in the same manner, and send him to one of the small communes in the diocese of Orleans. It must not be the chief commune.

In the same way, you will take the Bishop of Ghent, and send him to a small commune in the diocese of Dijon. Make them all give their word that they will stay quietly in these communes, without having any correspondence with their dioceses, or mixing themselves up with ecclesiastical affairs.

CCCXCVII

TO COMTE DE LAVALLETTE, DIRECTOR OF THE POSTAL SERVICE.

PARIS, 25*th December* 1811.

I AM sorry you should have allowed Princess Pauline's letter to the Comte de St. Leu[1] to pass, for you know all such letters are read abroad, and Europe is thus admitted into the family secrets.

I desire you will stop all the family letters to the Comte de St. Leu, and all the letters from the Comte de St. Leu to his family. The advantage of this will be, that they will correspond by every private opportunity, and that their letters will not be read.

CCCXCVIII

TO M. MARET, DUC DE BASSANO, MINISTER FOR FOREIGN AFFAIRS.

PARIS, 26*th January* 1812.

I HAVE dismissed Mons. Tassoni, my Italian Chargé d'Affaires at Naples. I am summoning him to Paris, to give an account of his conduct. Find out about this Chargé d'Affaires; he has behaved so ill, that I have dismissed him. It was not his place to remain neutral, in a business which affected the dignity of my Crown. If, apart from this, he should be found to have been in communication with Maghella, or any other person, I intend to make a severe example of him.

As regards this Neapolitan business, I conclude it to be clearly understood, that Dolgorouki will not be received at Court, nor recognised as Minister; that you have warned Baron Durand of my intentions, and that he would leave Naples, if any other course were followed. My Ministers must be pre-eminent at Naples, as in all the other States of the Confederation,—because I am their Suzerain.

[1] Louis Napoleon, ex-King of Holland.

CCCXCIX

TO M. MARET, DUC DE BASSANO, MINISTER FOR
FOREIGN AFFAIRS.

PARIS, 9*th February* 1812.

I BEG you will make my Minister at Cassel acquainted with the Decree which provides that every insult to my soldiers, in the territory held by the Grande Armée, shall be laid before a military court, for sentence. I conclude you have received this Decree ; let it also be communicated to Mons. de St. Marsan.

My Minister at Cassel must let it be known, that I am exceedingly displeased with the town of Brunswick, and that the very next time the town is guilty of an offence, I shall put it beyond the pale of my protection, and have so severe an example made of it, that the posterity of the inhabitants will remember it, a hundred years hence.

CCCC

TO M. MARET, DUC DE BASSANO, MINISTER FOR
FOREIGN AFFAIRS.

PARIS, 29*th February* 1812.

WRITE to my Minister at Naples, that I have recalled Maghella, who performed the duties of Minister of Police at Naples, and that he must let it be known that he must leave Naples, to return to France, within forty-eight hours, on pain of arrest. . . . You will not conceal from Baron Durand, that Maghella is accused of intriguing against the safety of the Empire, and that he had an understanding with the English, to stir up a rising of so-called patriots, in Italy. He will not mention this to him, but he must speak very decidedly, and Maghella must instantly depart from Naples.

CCCCI

TO JEROME NAPOLEON, KING OF WESTPHALIA.

WILNA, 4*th July* 1812.

I HAVE received your packet sent from Grodno, at four o'clock yesterday afternoon. I was exceedingly glad of its arrival, as I hoped you would have sent the Major-General news of Bagration's Corps, of the direction in which Prince Poniatowski had pursued it, and of the movements of troops in Volhynia. What was my astonishment at learning that all the Major-General had received, was a complaint of a General!

I can only express my dissatisfaction at the small amount of information I have from you. I neither know the number of Bagration's Divisions, nor their names, nor where he was, nor what information you obtained at Grodno, nor what you are doing. I have five or six columns in motion, to intercept Bagration's march. I cannot think you have so neglected your duty, as not to have pursued him, the very next morning. I hope, at all events, that Prince Poniatowski has followed him, with the whole of the 5th Corps. My operations are stopped, for want of information from Grodno. I have had none since the 30th. The Chief of your Staff does not write; Prince Poniatowski does not write. It is impossible to make war in this fashion! You never think nor speak of anything but trifles, and I am distressed to see how thoroughly small-minded you are. If General Vandamme has committed acts of brigandage, you did well to send him to the rear, but in present circumstances the question is such a secondary one, that I regret you have not sent me information which might have been of service to me, nor explained your position, by your courier.

I do not know why Prince Poniatowski does not correspond with the Major-General, twice a day. I certainly ordered him to do so.

Postscript.—You are jeopardising the whole success of the campaign, on the right ; it is not possible to carry on the war in this way.

CCCCII

TO MONS. MARET, DUC DE BASSANO, MINISTER FOR FOREIGN AFFAIRS.

Moscow, 5*th October* 1812.

I RETURN these despatches. It seems to me extraordinary that the person in question should have ventured to take this upon him. I cannot help acknowledging that the thing is well and cleverly written, but I do not know the man well enough to be able to rely on what he says, for indeed, a person of that kind might have invented the whole thing, to give himself credit.   I think I recollect his being employed, some ten or twelve years ago, at the English Admiralty Courts, and that he obtained the release of a dozen ships at Hamburg, which he had given back, and on which he received several hundred thousand francs.   That being so, it would not be according to my usual custom, to give him powers to act as a Commissary for Exchange, but I do not object to your employing him as a secret agent, and sending him back to London, to negotiate any kind of business.   The simplest way of discharging my obligation to him, is to pay him. I therefore think you should send for him to Wilna, and have a long conversation with him, after which you should send him back to England, by Sweden, Denmark, or any other route.

As to the root of the question, I may decide to send a French Commissary to London—for I will have no English Commissary in France.   The agent might, therefore, be commissioned to say, that if they choose to give him passports to admit a French Commissary, he will pass them through.   Only it must be clearly understood that I will not abandon the principle of simultaneous exchange.

CCCCIII

TO MONS. MARET, DUC DE BASSANO, MINISTER FOR FOREIGN AFFAIRS.

DOUBROWNA, 18*th November* 1812.

FOR the last five days I have had no express.   I hear the enemy entered Minsk on the 16th.   Where then was Prince Schwartzenberg?   I know not!   The Duke of Belluna had not done anything by the 16th.

Since the last letter I wrote you, our position has been damaged.   Frost, and bitter cold, of sixteen degrees, have killed almost all our horses—30,000 of them.   We have been forced to burn more than 300 pieces of artillery, and an immense number of ammunition-chests.   In consequence of the cold, the number of men left behind has greatly increased. The Cossacks have taken advantage of our absolute lack of cavalry and artillery, to harass us, and cut our communications, so that I am somewhat uneasy about Marshal Ney, who remained behind, with 3000 men, to blow up Smolensk. Apart from that, a few days' rest and good food, and above all, horses and artillery stores, will set us on our feet. The enemy has the advantage over us, in its habit of, and experience in, moving on ice, and this gives it an immense superiority in winter. Where we cannot get an ammunition-waggon, or a gun, up the smallest ravine, without losing twelve to fifteen horses, and wasting twelve to fifteen hours, they, with their · skates, and other specially made contrivances, move it more quickly than if there was no ice.

Send news of us to Paris. See what artillery we can get at Kowno and Wilna, and write to Dantzig, that all the ammunition-waggons and campaigning vehicles there are to be got ready to send to us. Find out, too, what is to be had at Modlin, and the other fortresses in the Grand Duchy.

CCCCIV

TO JEROME NAPOLEON, KING OF WESTPHALIA.

PARIS, 23rd December 1812.

I HAVE your letter. I believe it is more necessary for you to be in your kingdom, at this moment, than in Paris. No troops of the Westphalian army remain with the Grande Armée, and everything seems to point to a struggle next spring. Let me know what you have sent, to fill up your ranks, what you can do to complete your artillery and cavalry, and, to conclude, what you are in a position to do, towards provisioning, and thoroughly arming, Magdeburg, against any event. A perusal of the reports, and news you may have received, direct from the Grande Armée, may have informed you that it has had to take up its winter quarters on the Vistula, after having undergone considerable losses.

CCCCV

TO PRINCESS STEPHANIE, GRAND DUCHESS OF BADEN.

PARIS, 29th December 1812.

MY daughter, I have your letter of 20th December. You cannot doubt the share I have taken in the loss which has befallen you. But you have courage and good sense, and I trust the year now about to begin, will bring you some reason for consolation.

CCCCVI

TO GENERAL SAVARY, DUC DE ROVIGO, MINISTER OF POLICE.

PARIS, *8th January* 1813.

I DESIRE you will send for M. Thurot, and ask him by what right, and what authority, he sends me drafts of decrees, and memoirs of every kind. Chance has thrown his last into my hands. I had not seen the preceding ones, for my Secretaries, and very properly, throw them into the fire. The liberty taken by this individual, who enters into correspondence with me, without permission, strikes me as being very impertinent. Let him know that he is to put a stop to it. He is an ill-conditioned fellow, with whom I will have nothing whatever to do.

CCCCVII

TO COMTE DEFERMON, COMPTROLLER-GENERAL OF THE STATE PROPERTY EXTRAORDINARY.

FONTAINEBLEAU, 24*th January* 1813.

IT is my intention that the son of the King of Naples shall not be invested with the principality of Ponte-Corvo, until he has taken the oath of fidelity to me in person. Keep back my Decree and retain possession of the Principality. Speak to the Grand Chancellor so that the Titles Office may not grant investiture.

CCCCVIII

TO COMTE BIGOT DE PRÉAMENEU, MINISTER OF PUBLIC WORSHIP.

FONTAINEBLEAU, 24*th January* 1813.

I HAVE ordered General Henry to move with his flying columns, in pursuit of the robbers who have taken refuge in the woods and are committing excesses. Write to the Bishops in the Mayenne, and the Sarthe, that, without printing anything, they are to write to their Curés, to back up the military, by giving information, and causing it to be given. The Bishops must see General Henry, so as to give him all possible information. Send me a list of the most active and influential priests in those localities.

CCCCIX

TO GENERAL SAVARY, DUC DE ROVIGO,
MINISTER OF POLICE.

FONTAINEBLEAU, 24th January 1813.

I SEE that one of the Imperial Crowns in the Third Military Division has been damaged. The culprits have pleaded, indeed, that they were drunk, but this is no sufficient excuse. Have two of them arrested instantly, brought before a court-martial, and shot within twenty-four hours. You will then assure the Police Commissaries and Prefects that large numbers of troops are proceeding to the Elbe, and that a body of 30,000 men will always be kept in the 32nd Division, to insure the public peace. You must take hostages for the worst Cantons.

CCCCX

TO GENERAL CLARKE, DUC DE FELTRE,
MINISTER OF WAR.

FONTAINEBLEAU, 24th January 1813.

WRITE to General St. Cyr, that I am dissatisfied with the small amount of activity and vigour he is at present displaying. All persons who have committed excesses, and stirred up rebellion, either by setting up any rallying signal for the crowd, or by exciting it against the French, or the Government, must be brought before a military tribunal, and instantly shot. Two or three examples are indispensable, and must be made.

Write to General Lauriston, that while he is with the 32nd Military Division, he must keep the populace down, and try to make some examples. Some attempts at sedition have already taken place. Any insult offered the French, any attempt to resist authority, any setting up of a rallying point, must be punished with the death penalty, and by martial law. One of the Imperial Crowns in the 32nd Division has been broken. The culprits assert they were drunk. Drunk or not, two men must be shot. Write the same thing to General St. Cyr. Let the two men who have committed this offence be instantly arrested and shot. It is indispensable that some examples should be made in the country. Let them be made forthwith.

CCCCXI

TO ELISA NAPOLEON, GRAND DUCHESS OF TUSCANY.

FONTAINEBLEAU, 25th January 1813.

I HAVE just concluded a Concordat with the Pope. I send you a copy of it. You will be good enough to keep it to yourself, and not let any one whatever know of it. When the news begins to spread at Florence, you can announce it in the newspapers, in an article which you will write yourself, and which, nevertheless, will have no appearance of coming from an official source. You will mention the news as a rumour. The Pope intends to settle at Avignon.

CCCCXII

TO GENERAL SAVARY, DUC DE ROVIGO,
MINISTER OF POLICE.

FONTAINEBLEAU, 26th January 1813.

YOU will receive a Decree, by which I order the formation of a flying column at Le Mans. General Henry, who commands it, should be there to-morrow, and as the troops are already at Blois, Vendôme, and Cherbourg, he will be able to begin operations at once. I am desiring the Minister of War to remit him funds, both for secret expenses and for gratuities.

Send a few intelligent and practical police agents down into that country. Let them look about among the former Chouans. Police Commissaries, Mayors, Sub-Prefects and Prefects, must march, whenever necessary, with the National Guard, to scour the woods, and make an end of these wretches.

See General Henry before his departure, and tell him to keep constantly moving, and direct his columns carefully. I conclude he will be at Le Mans to-morrow.

CCCCXIII

TO PRINCESS PAULINE BORGHESE.

FONTAINEBLEAU, 27*th January* 1813.

I HAVE your letter of 20th January. I am distressed to notice how bad your health is. You would have done better to come to Paris, than to have allowed yourself to be sent from place to place, by doctors who hope to do you good. You would have done better to go to Nice, than to Hyères. I see no objection to your going to that town.·

CCCCXIV

TO GENERAL SAVARY, DUC DE ROVIGO, MINISTER OF POLICE.

PARIS, 28*th January* 1813.

I BEG you will address all the idle tales from Vienna you are sending me, to the Duke of Bassano. I have no time to read them, and all they do is to charge my memory with useless matter. The Duke of Bassano, who has nothing else to think of, may assess the value of this information, by comparing it with what other he may have.

The man who writes to you from Vienna is a blackguard, who picks it all up in the streets ; nevertheless, it may be worth sending to the Duke of Bassano.

CCCCXV

TO GENERAL CLARKE, DUC DE FELTRE, MINISTER OF WAR.

PARIS, 28*th January* 1813.

SEND orders, by express, to General Brenier, commanding the 25th Military Division, to send 1200 infantry, and fifty cavalry, under the command of a Brigadier-General, to Ronsdorf, in the district of Elberfeld, in the Grand Duchy of Berg, to disarm the district, and scatter the mob collected there ; to arrest the chief culprits, have them instantly tried by court-martial, and six of them shot ; to take hostages, and, if the ringleaders should have taken flight, to have their houses burned.

General Brenier is to write to Düsseldorf, to the Minister of the Grand Duchy, who will send 300 or 400 men to join his Brigade. If the troops first despatched should not be sufficient, General Brenier himself will march, with a stronger Brigade.

As a large number of troops must be massed at Wesel, and as they would only be turned two or three marches out of their way, he might even, with General Lauriston's permission, employ one or two regiments belonging to the Corps of Observation on the Elbe, in this operation.

Inform Count Roederer, my Minister-Secretary of State in the Grand Duchy, of these steps, so that he may give orders as to all concerted measures in the Grand Duchy. If General Lauriston is still at Wesel, General Brenier will submit everything for his approbation.

The chief point is, that six of the ringleaders must be shot, hostages taken, and a severe example made, so as to overawe all the ill-disposed persons in those countries.

CCCCXVI

TO PRINCE EUGÈNE NAPOLEON, VICEROY OF ITALY, IN CHIEF COMMAND OF THE GRANDE ARMÉE.

PARIS, 28th January 1813.

I HAVE your letter of 21st January. You can dismiss the Duke of Abrantès—that will be one encumbrance the less for the army ; and indeed he is a man who would not be of the slightest use to you. Let him know that he is no longer employed with the army.

CCCCXVII

TO GENERAL DUROC, DUC DE FRIOUL, GRAND MARSHAL OF THE PALACE.

PARIS, 3rd February 1813.

I SEND you a letter from Denon. You must make him understand that he must not send these trifles to me. Let him send them to the Duke of Cadore, who will lay them before me at a convenient moment. When I receive such letters, together with other important papers, all I can do is to throw them into the fire.

CCCCXVIII

TO VICE-ADMIRAL GANTEAUME.

PARIS, 6th February 1813.

I HAVE received your letter. I have ordered Comte Defermon to advance you all your income, up to the 1st January 1813. I have desired the Minister of the Navy to allow you a gratuity of 30,000 francs out of the Treasury of the Invalides, and I have told La Bouillerie to remit you a sum of 20,000 francs out of the funds of the State Property Extraordinary. I am very glad to have given you this proof of my satisfaction.

CCCCXIX

TO GENERAL CLARKE, DUC DE FELTRE, MINISTER OF WAR.

PARIS, 18th February 1813.

YOU will answer General Vignolles that our political relations with Austria are of the most amicable description ; that all the alarming reports rife in Italy are put about by the English, on all the coasts and corners of the Empire. You would do well to write in this sense to all commanding officers of Military Divisions on the sea-board, to make them aware of these tactics on the part of the English.

CCCCXX

TO M. GAUDIN, DUC DE GAÉTE, MINISTER OF FINANCE.

TRIANON, 19th March 1813.

I HAVE your letter, and I perceive, with the greatest surprise, that State Councillor Chaban has left his post [1] without orders. The State Councillor has behaved very ill in this matter. He first of all took refuge at Altona, he parleyed with the Danes, and then left his post without orders. Let him know that he must take steps to be gone to-morrow, before midday ; he will proceed to Wesel, and thence to

---

[1] At Hamburg.

the headquarters of the Division, where he will take up his duties again. As the Prefect remained at Bremen, he could have stayed there too ; and besides, large numbers of troops are moving in that direction.

Postscript.—It will suffice if Comte Chaban has started before the morning of the 21st.

CCCCXXI

TO GENERAL SAVARY, DUC DE ROVIGO, MINISTER OF POLICE.

TRIANON, 19*th March* 1813.

I AM assured that certain letters from Langeron, which assert that Louis XVIII. desired him to take the greatest care of the prisoners, are being circulated in Parisian society. You do not keep a close enough watch on the Faubourg St. Germain, and the Bourbon coteries. If there is the smallest truth in this report, you will have all Langeron's relations sent forty leagues from Paris.

CCCCXXII

TO GENERAL CLARKE, DUC DE FELTRE, MINISTER OF WAR.

TRIANON, 20*th March* 1813.

I SEE, by your report of the 19th, that the King of Naples owes you 450,000 francs for guns. Have nine bills drawn, of 50,000 francs each, the first payable on the 5th April, and the eight others successively, three days after each other, so that all of them shall be paid before the month of May. Write to the Neapolitan Minister of War, to the effect that these bills are the manufacturer's account, that he has placed the sum to his account at his own banker's, and have the bills drawn by some Paris banker. By this means you will get the debt paid. It will be necessary for you to inform the Duke of Bassano of this step, as well as my Minister at Naples.

CCCCXXIII

TO PRINCE LEBRUN, GRAND TREASURER OF THE EMPIRE AND GOVERNOR-GENERAL OF THE DUTCH DEPART-MENTS.

TRIANON, *22nd March* 1813.

THERE is a report here, that your daughters and your nieces are leaving Amsterdam, and throwing all Holland into a state of alarm. I cannot credit such a piece of imprudence. Take care that no French man or woman leaves Amsterdam, and that no sign of anxiety is betrayed.

CCCCXXIV

TO GENERAL SAVARY, DUC DE ROVIGO, MINISTER OF POLICE.

PARIS, *23rd March* 1813.

ORDER the wife of the Commissary-General of Police at Amsterdam, to return immediately, and make the Commissary aware of it. Send the Commissary at Antwerp orders to proceed to Gorcum, and make all the women go back. This is the way to spread alarm all over the country. It is a strange thing that the Police Commissary should be the first to show bad feeling.

CCCCXXV

TO M. MARET, DUC DE BASSANO, MINISTER FOR FOREIGN AFFAIRS.

PARIS, *24th March* 1813.

I SEND back your notes on Sweden. The document is so badly drawn up that it must be done over again. Make it over to Comte d'Hauterive, and let this chaos of documents be cleared up, so that we may know what should, and what should not, be printed.

S

CCCCXXVI

TO COMTE BIGOT DE PRÉAMENEU, MINISTER OF PUBLIC WORSHIP.

PARIS, 25*th March* 1813.

I THINK that, for to-day, we must content ourselves with sending the Decree, which allows the priests a month, to Corsica, to Bologna, Piacenza, and all other places where priests are detained in custody, so that they may be informed of it.

You will let the Bishops know, that as several of them have made representations to the effect that their presence was necessary in their dioceses, on account of the Easter solemnities, His Majesty has recognised the force of their reasoning, and authorises them to return, so as to be there before Holy Week. You will except the Bishops of Nantes and of Trèves, Councillors of State—their presence being necessary at the Council Board. These steps appear to me sufficient for the present.

CCCCXXVII

TO MARSHAL KELLERMANN, DUC DE VALMY, COMMANDING THE 5TH, 25TH, AND 26TH MILITARY DIVISIONS.

PARIS, 27*th March* 1813.

I HAVE your letter of the 24th. I am as much displeased with your son as I am pleased with you. This is not the moment when any man of spirit should put forward pretensions; however, out of consideration for you, I will give him employment, if he wishes to serve.

CCCCXXVIII

TO GENERAL SAVARY, DUC DE ROVIGO, MINISTER OF POLICE.

PARIS, 30*th March* 1813.

I HAVE your letter. I confess I could not help being very much astonished by the play yesterday [*L'Intrigante*].

I do not refer to the platitudes and silly remarks which the author so constantly pours forth—all that was addressed to the pit. But I had a right to expect that the Minister of Police would not have allowed the Court to be handled in so dull and silly a fashion. The author is said to be a well-disposed person. In that case, he is a proof of the adage, that it is better to have spiteful enemies, than foolish friends. Never have people been allowed, in any country, so to depreciate the Court. If it had not been for its clumsiness, and lack of talent, the play would have had a most mischievous effect on public opinion. What surprises me most of all, is that it should be a man who is earning 80,000 francs a year, in your offices, who takes it into his head to court popularity in this fashion. Put a stop to the performances of this wretched comedy, and alter the composition of your Board of Censors. No one but simpletons, or ill-disposed persons, would have approved such a play.

CCCCXXIX

TO GENERAL CLARKE, DUC DE FELTRE,
MINISTER OF WAR.

PARIS, 31*st March* 1813.

THE Viceroy informs me that General Reynier has started without leave, and I see by the Travellers' Report at Mayence, that he has just arrived in that town. Send an officer to meet him, with orders that he is to turn back at once. Make him aware of my displeasure at his having left his post, without leave from the Viceroy, who has made a complaint to me on the subject. Your officer will tell him that if he pushes forward, and does not at once return to his post, he will be arrested.

You are to have General Loison put under arrest at once, and you will then have him questioned as to the reasons he has to offer, in excuse for having left his post. You will ask him why he was not at the head of his Division when it came upon the enemy at Wilna—a fact which caused the loss of that fine Division.

CCCCXXX

TO GENERAL SAVARY, DUC DE ROVIGO,
MINISTER OF POLICE.

PARIS, *2nd April* 1813.

HERE follows the course to be followed at Fontainebleau. You will begin by sending an intelligent Police Commissary there, whom you will provide with every facility for surveillance, and whom you will take care to make known to the officer in command of the Gendarmerie, and to the Mayor of the town. You will give orders that no stranger is to be admitted to Fontainebleau ; no sisters of charity, nor any religious folk whatever,—on the principle that the faithful must only address the Pope through their Bishops, and that they had, therefore, better apply to their Bishops. You will give orders to the Adjutant of the Palace, Lagorse, that he is not to allow any man or woman to be present at the Pope's mass, nor even any ecclesiastic whatsoever, except the Cardinals and the four Bishops, whom I have commissioned to look after the business of Public Worship,—if they should attempt to be present. He must make it known, in conversation, that our principle is, that the Pope can only bestow the blessing of the Church upon the faithful through the Bishops.

You will commission the Adjutant of the Palace to wait on each of the Cardinals, one after the other, and inform them, that as they have done nothing during the two months they have been gathered together, and have not chosen to attend to the welfare of the Church, but rather appear to have tried to take advantage of their meeting, to disturb matters, I only allow them to remain at Fontainebleau on condition that they interfere in nothing at all, write no letter, and remain, in fact, in a state of stagnation, paying their court to the Holy Father, and meditating on the evil influence they have had on Church affairs ; that the slightest transgression in this respect, the shortest letter written to Italy, would not only make them objects of suspicion to the Emperor, but would imperil their liberty. You will desire the Adjutant to report each visit, and the hints he will have given each Cardinal, in writing, and in separate letters.

You will give orders that Cardinal di Pietro is to be

carried off secretly, at night, that all his papers are to be seized, and that he himself is to be conducted to some small town in Burgundy, far removed from all traffic, and there he is to stay, under surveillance. On the following morning, the Adjutant of the Palace will have the Pope informed, through Cardinals Consalvi and Pacca, that Cardinal di Pietro has been removed, in consequence of his having intrigued for the transmission of briefs, and because he is one of the principal causes of nothing having been as yet arranged with the Pope, and, in fine, because the man is an enemy to the State. He will have the same thing signified to the Bishop of Edessa, and to the doctor. He will tell the sisters of charity that they are to stay quietly at home.

You will have informed the Adjutant that he must refrain from saying anything about the letter, whether he has delivered it or not, and that he must not enter into any discussion. He must confine himself to this one and only answer,—that as they will do nothing for religion, they must at all events do nothing against the State.

I am ordering the Minister for Public Worship to send him the *Bulletins des Lois*, containing the three Decrees on the Concordat, and its execution. He will allow these documents to fall into the Cardinals' hands.

CCCCXXXI

TO GENERAL CLARKE, DUC DE FELTRE, MINISTER OF WAR.

St. Cloud, *8th April* 1813.

HAVE the inquiry into General Loison's conduct proceeded with. It is time to make an example. The greatest insubordination exists among the Generals ; it is affecting the lives of my soldiers, and the glory of my arms.

Make General Loison answer the following questions :—

Did he receive information at Königsberg that he had been placed in command of the 34th Division?

Did he consequently make a bargain to buy horses and teams for his artillery ?

Did he get orders to start with the Division ?

Why did he allow it to start without him ?

May not the breaking up of this Division at Oszmiana, where it was left to bivouac in the open, and exposed to the danger of death from cold, be laid at his door, as a consequence of his neglect of duty?

Was he not responsible for the Division the moment he was appointed to command it? and had he any right, once it had marched against the enemy, to leave it and stay in comfortable headquarters?

Let the minor newspapers announce that General Loison, who left the army without leave, has been put under arrest, and that General Pamphile Lacroix, who forsook his post, has been arrested, and will be tried with all the severity of martial law.

CCCCXXXII

TO GENERAL CLARKE, DUC DE FELTRE,
MINISTER OF WAR.

ST. CLOUD, *8th April* 1813.

LET the Comte de Valmy know, that in consideration of his father's services, and of the regard I have for the Marshal, and also for his own personal services at Marengo, I have forgotten many follies; that I am willing even to forget this one too ; but that I hope his good behaviour and good feeling will at last make him worthy of the name he bears. Give him orders to proceed to Mayence, where he will be employed according to circumstances.

CCCCXXXIII

TO GENERAL CLARKE, DUC DE FELTRE,
MINISTER OF WAR.

ST. CLOUD, *14th April* 1813.

I RETURN you the documents relating to General Loison. You will express my displeasure to him. Make him aware that I have read his answers very attentively, and that they are very far from justifying him. Tell him, that once his Division had reached Kowno, it was before the enemy, and that, from that moment, he should have marched, if not with the leading battalions, at all events with the bulk of his troops ; that I therefore still think the loss of the Division

confided to his care, must be attributed to him ; that, in spite
of this, I am willing not to forget the service he has rendered
me on other occasions, but that I hope this will be a lesson
to him, and that he will come to a better understanding of
the importance of the duty of a General commanding a
Division, for which he is answerable.   Give orders for him to
be released from arrest, and let him be at his own home
within twenty-four hours.   You will then let him know
his ultimate destination.

CCCCXXXIV

TO PRINCE CAMBACÉRÈS, GRAND CHANCELLOR OF
THE EMPIRE.

MAYENCE, 19th April 1813.

I HAVE your letter of 16th April.
I think it is most absurd that a reprieve should be suggested for a man of the name of Sala, who went over to the
enemy.   There can be neither reprieve nor mercy, for such
an offence.   Express my dissatisfaction on the subject to
the Minister of War.
I am equally surprised that this Minister should have
used the telegraph, to desire General Delmas to join the
army.   This is the way to ruin people.   The General had
given me cause for complaint.   I have made a concession,
in present circumstances, to his urgent request, but it is
perfect madness to use the telegraph to tell him to rejoin,
just as if he were a saviour who was being sent to the army.
The Minister of War lacks tact, and so I complain of these
blunders to you.
I must make you aware that when the Regent begins to
sign, I do not intend her to sign promotions and military appointments to any rank above those of *Chef d'Escadron* and
Chef de Bataillon, and I do not desire she should sign the
appointment of any sub-lieutenant, except in the case of
cadets leaving St. Cyr, or St. Germain, or former sergeants,
nominated by their regiments.   All appointments in favour
of young men of family must be referred to me.   I desire
you will take particular care that no Irishman, foreign
émigré, or youth who has not yet served in the army, should
be included in the appointments submitted for Her Majesty's

signature. Warn the Minister of War that all these must be included in a special report, to be submitted to me; the Empress is only to sign things in the ordinary course of business; that is to say, matters not presenting any difficulty. If you do not pay attention to this, the Minister will end by tainting the army, and to such an extent, that I shall be obliged to withdraw my confidence from him.

CCCCXXXV

TO BARON DE SERRA, MINISTER-PLENIPOTENTIARY TO THE KING OF SAXONY.

MAYENCE, 20*th April* 1813.

I CAN only express my extreme displeasure at your having sent my orderly officer, Lauriston, back without an answer. You know the King of Saxony has 1800 cavalry, of whom I stand in so much need, and you say nothing at all. Your sluggishness is beyond belief. Ask categorically whether they will send the cavalry, and in that case let it be despatched either to Würtzburg, or to General Bertrand at Coburg. You must let it be known that I should consider a refusal as the beginning of a change of system. I should not have expected it of the King, after what I have done for that Court. As for you, it is beyond all conception that you should have carried your forgetfulness of propriety to such a point, as to allow Baron Lauriston to depart without an answer. Do not keep this courier more than twelve hours, and send me back a statement of the strength of the cavalry, by him. General Bertrand is only at Coburg, and the cavalry will be very useful to him.

I send you the letter I am writing to the King. If, during the interval which has elapsed, the King should have agreed to my request, and sent his cavalry off, you will not give him my letter. If, on the contrary, nothing has yet been done, you will seal my letter, and give it to him, and you will appear to ignore its contents.

I conclude the King will also have given orders to General Thielmann, at Torgau, so that, as soon as communication is reopened, General Régnier may reassume the command of the troops, and that I may dispose of them, as well as of the garrison, according as I think necessary.

You must have heard of my departure from Paris on the
17th. I am surprised at your not having at once sent me a
courier to Mayence, to inform me of every fresh thing which
has happened. If such a courier had been sent off on the
18th, he should be with me to-day.

Write to Mons. de Mercy that the Prince de la Moskowa
has arrived at Weimar, that my headquarters are being
moved to Erfurt, and that everything is in motion. For I
wish him to press a request that General de Wrede should
take command of the Bavarian troops, if he is in a fit condition to do so, and that such instructions should be given
to commanding officers, as will insure their unrestricted
obedience to my orders.

I desire you will send me a daily courier, to inform me
of everything which comes to your knowledge, either by
Bohemia, through the Saxons, or Bavarians. Your couriers
will pass through Würtzburg, and will find out my whereabouts from my Minister.

Postscript.—Thinking better of it, I prefer sending my
aide-de-camp, Flahaut, who will be the bearer of my letter
to the King, and of my letter to you.

CCCCXXXVI

TO BARON REINHARD, MINISTER-PLENIPOTENTIARY TO THE KING OF WESTPHALIA.

MAYENCE, *20th April* 1813.

I HAVE your letter, dated 11 o'clock on the evening of the
18th, with a postscript added at 6 o'clock, on the morning of
the 19th. I desire you will keep me informed of everything
that happens, drawing a careful distinction between rumours
and reports, and what appears to you reliable information.

The Prince de la Moskowa reached Erfurt on the evening
of the 17th, and should have occupied Weimar on the 18th.
I myself expect to be at Eisenach immediately.

I cannot understand how the enemy can make any serious
attempt on Cassel; this must be mere fancy, or the work of
partisans.

Take advantage of the circumstance, to make the King
understand the insanity of his present position; that if, at
this moment, he had a guard of 600 French cavalry, 3000

French infantry, and one or two companies of French artillery, he would be lord of his own kingdom, and safe from all attack. The King of Spain and the King of Naples have taken good care to have this. I myself kept a French guard in my Kingdom of Italy, until the spirit of the Italian army became so excellent that this precaution was unnecessary, and besides, I was not living in the kingdom. The King's possession of the government is disputed by the former Sovereigns, and has, indeed, never been recognised by one of the principal great Powers,—England. How comes it that, under such circumstances, he did not take the course I recommended to him (in itself so politic), of getting together a reliable bodyguard which would never betray him. I think the mistake may easily be repaired, as soon as time permits, but a certain amount of precious time has been already lost. If it had been done six years ago, the Westphalian guard would be a magnificent body of men, instead of which, it will now have to be made up of conscripts. Yet better late than never! The King of Westphalia will never be certain of his throne all his life long ; for even if England should make peace, and recognise him, it would again refuse to do so, if a fresh war were to break out.

The Kings of France had Swiss guards, because their French subjects were too often Burgundians or Armagnacs. Foreign guards have been employed in every country in the world, and certainly the King of Westphalia's circumstances specially called for one. The King's great fault is his ignorance of the history and principles of politics, and the rash manner in which he behaves. Here is the result— though he has an army of from 15,000 to 20,000 men, he is on the brink of being driven out of his capital, by two or three squadrons of, probably, inferior troops. Who could have been surprised at the King's raising a French guard ? There was even a moment when I felt inclined to insist upon it, for the sake of the dignity of my family ; but I was prevented from doing so by the false idea instilled into the King, that such a course would weaken his own independence. As if independence were not a fact, rather than a right !

I desire you will cultivate these notions, and that the King may at last emerge from his present ridiculous position, and place himself under the protection of good French troops.

CCCCXXXVII

TO GENERAL CLARKE, DUC DE FELTRE,
MINISTER OF WAR.

BORNA, 5*th May* 1813.

WRITE and repeat your orders to the King of Spain, so that if the English really have withdrawn their troops, he may advance to the frontiers of Portugal, and threaten that country. Tell him I am distressed to notice that he does the very contrary of what he has been told to do, so that while I leave my troops in Spain, the English are able to withdraw theirs ; and that such action is an absolute betrayal of French interests.

CCCCXXXVIII

TO MARIE LOUISE, EMPRESS-QUEEN, AND REGENT.

COLDITZ, 6*th May* 1813.

WRITE the enclosed letter to the Minister of Public Worship.

'*To the Minister of Public Worship.*

'I send you a circular which I desire you will transmit to the Bishops. Be good enough to insure its reaching them without delay.'

Circular to the French Bishops.

'The victory won by the Emperor and King, our very dear husband and Sovereign, on the field of Lützen, must be considered a special mark of the Divine protection. We desire you, on receipt of the present letter, to arrange with the proper persons, that a *Te Deum* may be sung, and thanks offered to the God of Armies, and you will add what prayers you deem most suitable, to call down the Divine protection on our arms, and above all for the preservation of the sacred person of the Emperor, whom may God shield from every danger! His safety is as necessary to the welfare of Europe, and of the Empire, as to that of religion, which he has raised up, and which he is called upon to confirm and strengthen. He is its sincerest and truest protector.'

CCCCXXXIX

TO THE PRINCE DE NEUFCHÂTEL, MAJOR-GENERAL OF
THE GRANDE ARMÉE.

WALDHEIM, 7th May 1813.

SEND an officer to Bremen, to inform the Prince d'Eckmühl of the events which have just occurred ; and that we
shall probably be at Dresden to-morrow ; that the Prince de
la Moskowa is about to cross the Elbe, and march on Berlin.
It is indispensable that the Prince d'Eckmühl should move
on Hamburg, seize that town, and forthwith send General
Vandamme into Mecklenburg. This is the course he must
take.

He will at once arrest all subjects of the Town of Hamburg, who have taken service under the title of 'Senators
of Hamburg.' He will bring them before a court-martial ;
he will have the five worst culprits shot, and he will send
the rest, under strong escort, to France, where they will be
detained in a State prison. He will have their property
sequestrated, and declare it confiscated. The Crown will
take possession of all houses, landed property, etc.

He will have the whole town disarmed. He will have the
officers of the Hanseatic Legion shot, and he will send all
persons who have enlisted in that corps to France, to the
galleys.

As soon as my troops have reached Schwerin, he will
endeavour, without saying a word, to lay hands on the
Prince and his family, and will send them to France, to
a State prison. These Dukes have been traitors to the
Confederation. Their Ministers will be treated in the same
way.

He will not permit any hostile act against the Swedes, so
long as they remain in Pomerania, and undertake to remain
quiet.

He will draw up a proscription list of 500 of the richest
and most ill-behaved persons, belonging to the 32nd
Military Division ; he will have them arrested, and will have
their property sequestrated ; it will be taken over by the
Crown. This measure is particularly necessary in Oldenburg.

He will mulct the towns of Hamburg and Lübeck, in a
sum of fifty millions. He will take steps to have this

contribution assessed in such a manner as to insure its prompt payment.

He will have the whole country disarmed, and will have all gendarmes, gunners, coastguardsmen, and officers, soldiers, or officials, who have behaved as traitors, arrested. Their goods must be confiscated. Let him especially remember those Hamburg families which have behaved ill, and whose intentions are evil. The landed proprietors must be turned out, or we shall never be sure of the country.

He must have the fortress of Hamburg armed ; he must have drawbridges made to the gates, place guns on the ramparts, raise the parapets, and make a citadel on the Harburg side, in which four or five thousand men may be out of reach of the populace, and safe from all attack. He will also have Lüneburg armed, so that it may be secured against sudden attack, and he will reorganise Cuxhaven.

All these measures are indispensable, and the Government must not be allowed to modify any one of them. The Prince d'Eckmühl must declare these my express orders, and must act, in due time and place, with the necessary caution. All known ringleaders of rebellion are to be shot, or sent to the galleys.

As to Mecklenburg, my general view is, that the Princes of that country have forfeited the Emperor's protection ; but you must not allow this to become apparent, and I shall probably have time to give orders. As the Prince d'Eckmühl may not be aware of these arrangements, he may, in the first instance, promise anything he is asked, under the sole reservation of the Emperor's approval being obtained. When that approbation is received, everything will be in order.

You will observe this letter is in cipher.

Hamburg being in a state of siege, the Prince d'Eckmühl will appoint a strong commanding officer to keep order. He will send General Vandamme forward, with his headquarters, but he will spare the General, for such warriors are growing rare. Write to General Vandamme, that I am well pleased with his conduct at Bremen, and that I intend to give him a good command : that, meanwhile, he must second the Prince d'Eckmühl by every means in his power ; that I shall be obliged to him for doing so, and shall take due account of what he does in this respect.

CCCCXL

TO PRINCE CAMBACÉRÈS, GRAND CHANCELLOR OF
THE EMPIRE.

DRESDEN, 11*th May* 1813.

I HAVE your letter of the 5th. It would be quite natural that the Bishops should take the oath to the Regent. It will also be quite natural for the Regent to grant the usual sum for the expense of establishment, to the Bishops.

I beg you will send me a memorandum as to replacing the Chief Judge, if that should become necessary. Have inquiries made in all the Law Courts; we shall need a man of very great talent.

I conclude the Minister of War never inserts any official news of the army in Spain, in the *Moniteur*, without first submitting it to the Regency. Such news, however, had better appear as being extracted from the Minister of War's letters, that being the natural course, and a different form having been adopted for news from the Grande Armée, only because I myself command it. It is none the less necessary that the Regent should have the first knowledge of the news, and should judge whether it is to be printed or not; for there may, from time to time, be some objection to the manner in which it is drawn up.

CCCCXLI

TO M. MARET, DUC DE BASSANO, MINISTER FOR
FOREIGN AFFAIRS.

NEUMARKT, 1*st June* 1813.

I HAVE your letter; the only thing to do is to gain time. In the first place, constantly on horseback as I am, and probably at Breslau, I cannot have received the letter yet. By this excuse, you will gain two or three days. The armistice is now in course of negotiation; I do not know if it will be carried through. If it should be concluded, I will let you know at once.

I conclude Mons. de Stadion keeps his Court very well informed as to all this business. You had better say nothing about it to Count Bubna. You can tell him, that it was by no fault of mine that the battle of Würtschen took place ; that I had proposed to send the Duke of Vicenza to attempt overtures for an armistice, without, however, making any positive proposal,—because such proposals, on the eve of a battle, are always looked on as a symptom of inferiority. Make that clear, so that it may come out in his correspondence with Vienna. Try, too, to discover whether he has no other proposals to make, than those already made. It seems to me, that if those were his only ones, he would not have been so much disturbed by his instructions having fallen into the enemy's hands ; for I think he hardly could have received any which would have been more agreeable to the Russian Cabinet. Give him details of the battle of Würtschen, so that he may send them on, and try to get at the bottom of all his instructions. I propose to avoid seeing him. If the armistice is not concluded, the circumstances of the war will be sufficient justification for this. If it is concluded, I shall send you back to Dresden, where I shall be supposed to come, and whither I shall not go.

You might try, very delicately, to find out what benefits this peace would be likely to bring me ; for, to make it appear honourable, it must bring me something. You must try to make him speak. If you can get nothing out of him, you must fall back on generalities, and the common ground of what can be done against England.

Have you news from Denmark, or from the Hamburg side ?

CCCCXLII

TO M. MARET, DUC DE BASSANO, MINISTER FOR FOREIGN AFFAIRS.

NEUMARKT, 2nd June 1813.

As I desire to write to you in cipher, I shall be very concise.

We must gain time, and to gain time without displeasing Austria, we must use the same language we have used for the last six months—that we can do everything, if Austria is our ally. Metternich asserts that the alliance still continues, and proposes to negotiate a treaty to replace the secret articles, which, on his own authority, he declared annulled. Work on this, beat about the bush, and gain time on this head.

Look through the treaty of alliance, to find the articles Austria desires to preserve. Does she desire to preserve the integrity of the Empire? the mutual guarantee of the two States? the article as to the integrity of the Ottoman Empire? You can embroider on this canvas for the next two months, and find matter for despatching twenty couriers.

The armistice is in process of negotiation. If it does not come into force I should wish you to proceed to Dresden, so as to be in a position suitable to a Minister, holding so many documents, and keeping up intercourse with so many quarters.

I will write to you to-morrow.

CCCCXLIII

TO MARSHAL DAVOUT, PRINCE D'ECKMÜHL, COMMANDING THE GRANDE ARMÉE.

BUNZLAU, *7th June* 1813.

I NEED not tell you that you are to disarm the inhabitants [of Hamburg], to seize all muskets, swords, guns, and powder, to make domiciliary visits wherever necessary, and to utilise everything for the defence of the town. Nor need I tell you that you are to press all the sailors, up to three or four thousand, and send them to France; that you are to press all bad characters, and send them to France, also, to be enrolled in the 127th, 128th, and 129th regiments. You will thus clear the town of five or six thousand men, and the hand of justice will be heavy on the rabble, which, it appears, could hardly have behaved worse. As regards other arrangements, I refer you to the Major-General's letter, dated 7th May.

CCCCXLIV

TO JEROME NAPOLEON, KING OF WESTPHALIA.

DRESDEN, *10th June* 1813.

BROTHER,—I notice with the greatest astonishment, in a letter written by you to General Dombrowski, to change that General's route, that you assert you write by my order, and according to my instructions; and thus fail in your duty to yourself and to me. Such behaviour, which I will not define, is too objectionable to be endured by me. The first time you venture to express such a supposition, I will have a paragraph inserted in the General Order of the Day, to the effect that nothing you write is to be attended to. It is not that I do not think it quite natural, under the circumstances, that you should request commanding officers to alter their route, as you did in the case of General Teste; but it is contrary to the welfare and the honour of my service, for you to assert you do so in my name, and thus annul my order. Such a proceeding might disturb the progress of my armies. It is a complete falsification, which no other person would have ventured on.

CCCCXLV

TO M. MARET, DUC DE BASSANO, MINISTER FOR FOREIGN AFFAIRS.

DRESDEN, 17th June 1813.

PRESENT a note to Mons. de Kaas, to inform him that I am having a list of absentees (which is the same thing as émigrés) drawn up, to include all persons who have left the 32nd Military Division; that many of these have taken refuge in the King of Denmark's dominions, and that I desire the King will send all such persons out of Holstein.

I do not contend that they must not be received in Norway and in Zealand, but I desire they may not remain in the neighbourhood of Hamburg. All those who are not ill-disposed, and have not taken part in the riots, can return to Hamburg; but those who took any active part in the disturbances must, at least, retire to a distance from that town. Send an express to Baron Alquier, to inform him of my intentions.

CCCCXLVI

TO GENERAL SAVARY, DUC DE ROVIGO, MINISTER OF POLICE.

DRESDEN, 18th June 1813.

I HAVE your letter.

It is my intention that Hamburg shall be treated with great severity. The various Decrees you have received will

T

give you proof of this. I desire all proprietors, and all guilty persons, may be driven out, so that all property in that Military Division may change hands. The Prince d'Eckmühl is therefore only carrying out my orders, and you, instead of thwarting him, must help him, by every means in your power. The cackling of the Paris bankers matters very little to me. I am having Hamburg fortified. I am having a naval arsenal established there. Within a few months it will be one of my strongest fortresses. I intend to keep a standing force of 15,000 men there.

As for Mons. d'A——, I do not know him. But I am inclined to think him not over scrupulously honest, seeing he sends sums of 60,000 francs to his wife, in Paris, for her to buy property in Normandy. As regards his influence on military matters, the fault lies with the Generals, who should not listen to the arguments of a man who knows nothing about war, much less consult him.

Generally speaking, the police does not do good service; it accepts all the false rumours that come from London, and dins them into the General's ears. The Antwerp Commissary never does anything else. All these police reports mean nothing, and, luckily, do no harm when they are sent to me, but Generals who have no habit of command, and no steadiness of mind, take them for official documents. They mind what they are told, and act accordingly, to clear their own responsibility. Forbid the Commissaries of Hamburg and Antwerp, as well as the Commissary at Amsterdam, to give this sort of information to the military authorities. They are all three duped by the English, who purposely spread reports of steps they have no real intention of taking.

CCCCXLVII

TO PRINCE CAMBACÉRÈS, GRAND CHANCELLOR OF
THE EMPIRE.

DRESDEN, 18th June 1813.

THE Minister of Police, in his reports [with which, generally speaking, I am very well satisfied, owing to the many details they contain, and the frequent proofs of zeal they furnish], seems to desire to incline me to peace. This can have no result, and it wounds me, because it gives rise to the supposition that I am not peacefully inclined. I desire peace, but not a peace which would force me to take up arms again within three months, and would dishonour me. I know my own financial position, and the condition of the Empire, better than he does, and therefore he has nothing to say to me on the subject. Make him aware of the impropriety of his behaviour. I am no blusterer, I do not make a trade of war, and no one is more pacific than I am. But my decision on this subject will be ruled solely by my sense of what a solemn matter this peace is, by my desire that it may last, and by the general situation of my Empire.

CCCCXLVIII

TO THE PRINCE DE NEUFCHÂTEL, MAJOR-GENERAL OF THE GRANDE ARMÉE.

DRESDEN, 18th June 1813.

HERE is a very extraordinary article out of the *Journal de Leipsic*. Send it to the officer in command, that he may get an explanation of it. Let him have the gazetteer arrested on the spot, brought before a court-martial, and shot, if there is the smallest evidence of evil intention.

CCCCXLIX

TO VICE-ADMIRAL DUC DECRÈS, MINISTER OF THE NAVY.

DRESDEN, 24th June 1813.

ADMIRAL WILLAUMEZ does not possess my confidence. I do not wish to employ him. I would rather try the last promoted post-captain, and make promotions like that of Baudin, which at all events leave me a certain amount of hope.

I see no difficulty about your recalling Admiral Lhermite from the Elbe, and Admiral Duperré from Venice, and replacing both of them by post-captains. You must send me no Dutchmen to Hamburg ; you must send me Frenchmen, to act in concert with other Frenchmen. Rear-Admiral Petit being dead, I desire you will submit the name of one of your best post-captains to fill his place.

To conclude : if the Dutch Rear-Admiral should be at Toulon, where his rank would give him a right to be second

in command, I think it would be well that the Chief of the
Staff, or the Naval Prefect, should have a sealed letter from
you, appointing the most distinguished of the French Rear-
Admirals Vice-Admiral.

Give a little promotion to a few young men.

Vice-Admiral Allemand would perhaps do well at Venice,
if that place were to be besieged. He has the requisite
energy for taking measures to defend the lagoons. Let me
know your opinion on this subject.

CCCCL

TO PRINCE CAMBACÉRÈS, GRAND CHANCELLOR OF
THE EMPIRE.

DRESDEN, 30*th June* 1813.

I HAVE your letter of 23rd June. All this gossip about
peace, among the Ministers, is doing me the greatest possible
harm; for everything is known, and I have seen more than
twenty letters from foreign Ministers, to their own countries,
stating, that in Paris peace is desired at any price, and
that my Ministers are writing to me daily, to that effect.
In this way, peace may be made impossible, and the chief
fault lies with the Minister of Police. Instead of this pacific
talk, a somewhat warlike tone should be assumed. People
in Paris are very much mistaken, if they think peace
depends upon me. The enemy's pretensions are excessive,
and I know very well, that a peace not in conformity with
French opinion concerning the strength of the Empire, would
be very ill received by every one.

CCCCLI

TO GENERAL SAVARY, DUC DE ROVIGO,
MINISTER OF POLICE.

DRESDEN, 30*th June* 1813.

YOU will inform Mons. Bourrienne that he is to break off
all correspondence, on any pretence whatsoever, with Hamburg; for that the first time he writes about, or concerns himself, directly or indirectly, with Hamburg affairs, I will have
him arrested, and I will make him disgorge everything he
has stolen from that city.

CCCCLII

TO JOSEPH NAPOLEON, KING OF SPAIN.

DRESDEN, 1st July 1813.

I HAVE thought proper to appoint Marshal the Duke of Dalmatia my Lieutenant-General, in chief command of my armies in Spain and in the Pyrenees. Make over the command to him. I desire you personally will remain, according to circumstances, at Burgos, Vittoria, St. Sebastian, Pampeluna, or Bayonne, until I further inform you of my intentions. You will put your Guards, and all armed Spaniards, under the command of the Duke of Dalmatia; and I desire you will not concern yourself in any way with the affairs of my army.

CCCCLIII

TO PRINCE CAMBACÉRÈS, GRAND CHANCELLOR OF THE EMPIRE.

DRESDEN, 1st July 1813.

I HAVE letters from the Minister of War, enclosing General Foy's letter of the 22nd. The Minister of War will make known my intentions to you.

I am sending the Duke of Dalmatia to Spain, with the rank of my Lieutenant-General; but he will be under the orders of the Regency, and will report himself to the Minister of War.

As for the King of Spain, my intention is that he shall remain at Pampeluna, St. Sebastian, or Bayonne, and there await my orders. In any case, I do not intend him to come to Paris, nor that any high dignitary, Minister, Senator, or Councillor of State, shall see him, until I have informed him of my intentions. If he should have crossed the Loire, you will arrange with the Ministers of War and Police, to do whatever is most proper, without worrying the Empress with details. The King should not cross the Loire without my orders; but if he should actually have crossed it, he must proceed to Morfontaine, in the most profound *incognito*, and neither he, nor any officer of his household, must go from that place to Paris, to disturb the government of the Regency. You will settle with the Minister of Police as to who should be sent, to inform the King of my intentions. You might select Roederer, or any other person whom the King is accustomed to see ; but however that may be, you must employ the utmost secrecy in carrying out my orders. Generally speaking, I desire any communication to the King of Spain may be made to him through the Minister of War, and not through the Minister of Police.   On receipt of this present letter, you will send for the Ministers of War and of Police, and you will give them their letters, impressing on them, at the same time, the necessity of keeping the most perfect silence about the whole matter.

If the King should have recovered his advantage, and reoccupied Vittoria, you will take all the more care to spare his feelings.   I presuppose that Senator Roederer, or any other person in the King's confidence, might be sent to convince him that I had been obliged, by present circum-stances, and my opinion of his military powers, to confer the command of the army on a General who possessed my confidence.

I also send you a letter for the King of Spain ; you will give it, or not, to the Duke of Dalmatia, according as it may seem necessary to the Minister of War.   I desire the Duke of Dalmatia may not deliver it, unless it should appear impossible to do otherwise.   It seems to me that an exten-sion of the Decree, and a letter from the Minister, should be sufficient.

See that the Minister of Police does not interfere in any-thing, except the matter of surveillance, and that the Minister of War writes nothing to the King of Spain but that which the circumstances of the war make it necessary for him to know, so that everything may be carried out with the utmost possible moderation.

CCCCLIV

TO PRINCE CAMBACÉRÈS, GRAND CHANCELLOR OF
THE EMPIRE.

DRESDEN, 1st July 1813.

I WROTE to you, two hours ago, with regard to Spanish affairs.   I have sent you all the letters, so that you may manage the business as circumstances may direct.   The

question rests on two hypotheses : either the King has been
beaten, or the position of things has improved.   If the King
has been beaten, he cannot remain at Pampeluna, and if there
is any fear of his returning, it will be necessary to send him
some one, from whom you will not conceal the fact that,
considering the bad spirit he has shown in Spain, I fear
his presence would sow discord, which might cause trouble
to the Regency.   If the King should have won a victory,
and been able to retrieve matters, my intention would still
be unchanged.   I should desire him to leave the army, which
he is quite incapable of leading, to allow the Duke of Dalmatia to take command, and to remain, himself, at Vittoria.

CCCCLV

TO GENERAL CLARKE, DUC DE FELTRE,
MINISTER OF WAR.

DRESDEN, 1st July 1813.

THE Duke of Dalmatia starts this day for Paris.   He will
go with you to see the Grand Chancellor ; he will not remain,
altogether, more than twelve hours in Paris, and will go on
his way thence to Bayonne, to take over the command of
the armies in Spain, with the title of my Lieutenant-General.
He will, none the less, in spite of his being my Major-General,
be under your orders, and those of the Regency, and he will
report everything concerning his command to you.   Write
to the King of Spain to make over the command to him, and
to put his Guards, and all his Spanish troops, under his orders.
I have complete confidence in the Duke of Dalmatia.   He
will have full powers, and will be authorised to organise
everything as he sees fit.

The King will remain, according to circumstances, at Burgos,
St. Sebastian, or Bayonne, but he is not to go to Paris, under
any pretext whatsoever.   If he should have already reached
Bayonne, he is to stop there ; but if, by chance, he should
have already got beyond that town, he must proceed *incognito*
to Morfontaine, and there live, without seeing anybody whatsoever.   My intention is that you should not mention all
this to the Empress.   Nothing will be put in the newspapers,
and nobody must know where he is.   In a word, I desire

you will take every means of preventing his coming to Paris ; but if he should reach Morfontaine, he must neither see the Empress, nor any one else, nor receive any visitors, and no State arrangements must be disturbed. Send a confidential officer to make him aware of my intentions ; you will go to the Queen yourself. Employ Count Roederer, or any other person, to make him understand what my will is, with all proper regard and consideration.

It is my intention that no Spanish officer about the King of Spain, etc., shall cross the Garonne. All the refugees will be collected in some town, such as Agen or Auch, which you will select, after having consulted the Grand Chancellor, and the Minister of Police.

All the follies which have taken place in Spain are the result of the mistaken consideration I have shown the King, who not only does not know how to command an army, but does not even know his own value sufficiently to leave the military command alone. I am not yet sufficiently informed as to the state of things, but, short of an absolute necessity, and for purposes of frontier defence, you must not make any alteration in the orders I have given for the march of the troops. If the worst comes to the worst, I will defend my frontiers. If the Duke of Dalmatia should think proper to dismiss Marshal Jourdan, he will remain åt Bayonne, awaiting my orders. I need not tell you to have Bayonne, and the other frontier fortresses, armed, and provisioned.

Everything regarding the King is extremely secret, and even the Duke of Dalmatia himself is to know nothing of it.

CCCCLVI

TO GENERAL SAVARY, DUC DE ROVIGO, MINISTER OF POLICE.

DRESDEN, 1st July 1813.

THE Grand Chancellor and the Minister of War will make you aware of my intentions as to the King of Spain. Take pains to have them carried out considerately, but, at the same time, with all necessary decision. There are plenty of persons in Paris, who might be employed to inform the King of my intentions.

Give orders that no provincial, or Parisian, newspaper, is to mention Spanish affairs, or the King of Spain.

If the King should have left Pampeluna, St. Sebastian, or Bayonne, without my orders, and if he should have crossed the Loire,—which would be contrary to my intention,—he must instantly, without sleeping in Paris, retire to Morfontaine, there to remain until I have made known my orders, and that without any attention being attracted.

CCCCLVII

TO GENERAL CLARKE, DUC DE FELTRE,
MINISTER OF WAR.

DRESDEN, *3rd July* 1813.

I HAVE your letter of the 28th. I do not understand the Spanish business yet. I do not know whether it is a battle that we have lost, nor what troops were present, nor where the King and the army now are. I conclude the Duke of Dalmatia will have left Paris, when you receive this letter. I confess it is difficult to understand that such things should happen, with an army like that in Spain. I can only ascribe them to the excessive ineptitude of the King, and of Jourdan.

CCCCLVIII

TO GENERAL SAVARY, DUC DE ROVIGO,
MINISTER OF POLICE.

DRESDEN, *3rd July* 1813.

I HAVE received the news sent you by the Bayonne Commissary. It is hard to imagine anything so inconceivable as what is now going on in Spain. The King could have collected 100,000 picked men ; they might have beaten the whole of England. The Duke of Dalmatia must have passed through. I hope he will retrieve matters. ·

CCCCLIX

TO GENERAL CLARKE, DUC DE FELTRE,
MINISTER OF WAR.

DRESDEN, *6th July* 1813.

YOU will see, by the enclosed despatch from Consul Seguier, that the poor Duke of Abrantès is almost out of his mind. I am writing to the Viceroy to give him orders to retire to his home in Burgundy. The capital must not be vexed by such a sight. Give his wife notice, so that she may go and meet him, and remain in Burgundy with him. I will consider as to who is to replace him, and meanwhile, the Comptroller will perform all administrative functions. I have ordered a superior officer, or a general, to be sent to command the country.

CCCCLX

TO MARSHAL DAVOUT, PRINCE D'ECKMÜIIL, COMMANDING THE 13TH CORPS OF THE GRANDE ARMÉE.

DRESDEN, 9th July 1813.

A DEPUTATION from Hamburg has waited on Comte Daru, and the Master of the Horse, to request an audience of me. I have refused to receive it, until the forty-eight millions are fully paid, and I have ordered it to leave Dresden in the course of the day.

I think it right to make you aware of my intentions on this occasion. I mean to have the full forty-eight millions, without reducing them by a single sou. It appears that these gentlemen assert, in the memorandum they have brought with them, that they do not possess forty millions. This is my reply: So long as the forty millions still owing are not paid, all warehouses will remain under sequestration, —for I suppose you have placed, and kept, all the great warehouses, and even the shops, under sequestration. This measure must even be extended to the large warehouses in the Second Military Division, to all buildings used for commercial purposes, and all dwelling-houses, which will be held for my benefit. All these buildings and dwelling-houses will belong to me; the merchandise also will belong to me, and will be sent to France, or to other places in Germany, for sale. Now there is certainly more than forty-eight millions' worth of merchandise in Hamburg, and besides that, there is the land itself, which is worth a good deal more than a hundred millions, and which, if necessary, I will have awarded to the Crown.

I have ordered Comte Daru to answer in this sense, and you yourself must take the same tone.

The crime they have committed—of rebellion and felony—

has deprived them of all their property, and all their civil rights. The war contribution is their ransom. They have paid ten millions in money, and ten millions in merchandise. Make them sign bonds for another ten millions, and they will still owe eighteen millions. They can easily raise a loan on their own security, as they have done before. They have credit in every market, they can very well draw ten millions' worth of bills on exchange. This will complete their payment. In consideration of the payment, I will release their goods from sequestration, I will restore their civil rights, and each man will regain possession of his property.

As to the Amnesty, you know very well I have given you *carte blanche.* I make no difficulties on that head. I would far rather make them pay ; it is much the best way of punishing them. You must try and reach the rabble, and make it bear part of the war-tax, by doubling or quadrupling the poll-tax, and that on doors and windows, by increasing the *Octroi* duty, and that on the sales in the wine-shops. This would only bring in two or three millions, but it is well to strike at the lower class too, and let it see we are not afraid of it. It must also be touched by taking as many men as possible, and sending them to serve with the troops in France, and also by laying hands on all the firebrands, and sending them to the galleys, or to French prisons.

CCCCLXI

TO PRINCE CAMBACÉRÈS, GRAND CHANCELLOR OF THE EMPIRE.

WITTENBURG, 11th July 1813.

I HAVE your letter of 6th June.

I have no information, as yet, as to the position of my armies in Spain, nor any details concerning them. I have ordered the Minister of War to suspend Marshal Jourdan, to send him to his country residence, and keep him there till he has accounted for what has happened. I have also desired the Minister to demand an account from the Officers Commanding-in-chief, from the Commanding Officers of Engineers and Artillery, and from the Paymaster-General.

I have found fault with the Minister of War, for having been complimentary in his letter to the King of Spain. I

may have sufficient consideration not to admit the public
into the secret of my extreme displeasure ; but it is ridiculous, and improper, that the Prince should not be made clearly
aware that it is to him I ascribe the fault of everything that
has happened in Spain, for the last five years.   He has not
shown either military talent, or care in government.   I
therefore desire you will inform the Minister, that the Prince
must not deceive himself as to my opinion with regard to him.
He did not know how to command himself, and he has
committed the great fault, in my eyes, of not leaving the
command to those who knew how to use it.

Put pressure on my Ministers of War, and Army Administration, to make them show a little more energy.   It is
perfect madness to have recrossed the Bidassoa.

I am writing to the Minister of War that, as there may be
objections to the King of Spain's presence at Bayonne, my
intention is that he should proceed, *incognito*, to Morfontaine,
and be supposed to be remaining there, until further orders
from me.   This would put an end to all difficulties.

CCCCLXII

TO GENERAL CLARKE, DUC DE FELTRE,
MINISTER OF WAR.

WITTENBURG, 11*th July* 1813.

I AM as full of surprise, as of indignation, at having no information as to the position of my armies in Spain.   I am
still unaware of the reason why no junction was effected with
General Clausel.   I do not know how many men we lost,
and I have received no account of the battle.   Express my
displeasure to Marshal Jourdan, suspend him from his
functions, and give him orders to retire to his country-house,
where he will remain, suspended and without pay, until he
has accounted to me for the campaign.   His first duty was to
put you in possession of facts, and send you an account of
the battle.   Desire each General-in-chief, also, to send you a
report, and make the King aware of my displeasure at his
not having sent me one, and at his not having informed me
of the reasons which led him to abandon General Clausel.

Answer the Duke of Dalmatia, that there is no special
salary attached to the rank of my Lieutenant-General, that

he will have his Marshal's pay, and the 10,000 francs a month for official entertainments, which no one but himself is allowed ; that my present position necessitates the greatest economy. Tell him it is impossible for me to take any measure. I have not the slightest idea. I do not know the amount of our losses ; I do not know the circumstances of the battle. Once more, order every officer in chief command to send in his report, under the severest penalty. I understand the Duke of Dalmatia's dislike to the King's remaining at Bayonne. My opinion is, that the best course will be for the Prince to retire, without delay, to Morfontaine, in the strictest *incognito*, and without any one being aware of the fact.

I am not very well pleased with the letter you have written the King. I see too many compliments in it. When a man's inept folly has cost me an army, I may indeed show him sufficient consideration not to take the public into my confidence, but it is hardly an occasion on which to pay him compliments. On the contrary, the whole fault of this lies with the King, who does not know how to command, who has sent in no reports, and has given us no means of looking after the army. It would be well for you to take steps to have my view of matters made known to the King, and all about him. His behaviour has never ceased bringing misfortune upon my army, for the last five years ; it is time to make an end of it. It appears they have blown up the bridge over the Bidassoa. There is a world of folly and cowardice in all this. Let Reille know of my displeasure ; tell him I cannot recognise him. Generally speaking, they are all behaving like cowardly women.

CCCCLXIII

TO M. MARET, DUC DE BASSANO, MINISTER FOR FOREIGN AFFAIRS.

MAGDEBURG, 12*th July* 1813.

AFTER having been anxious about General Clausel, who was forsaken, in such a ridiculous fashion, by the other armies, we have heard he has moved towards Saragossa, where he arrived on the 30th, without having been molested. I write you this for your guidance.

It will be well for you to write a circular to all my Ministers, to guide their utterances as to Spanish affairs. You will tell them, that in consequence of the concentration of all our armies in Spain, to form a reserve, to be drawn on as occasion makes it necessary, the Northern Army has moved from Pampeluna on Aragon, and the others, upon the outlets of Biscay and Navarre; that the English, noticing these operations, have taken advantage of them to press us closely, and that a somewhat brisk engagement took place on the 21st, at Vittoria, in which both sides lost equally; that the army has carried out the movement, and reached the appointed place of junction: but that the enemy seized about a hundred guns and military waggons, which were left without teams at Vittoria,—the remains of the immense number in Spain and Madrid at the time of the evacuation; and that it is these which the English are trying to pass off as artillery with full teams, captured on the battle-field.

CCCCLXIV

TO M. MARET, DUC DE BASSANO, MINISTER FOR
FOREIGN AFFAIRS.

DRESDEN, 15th July 1813.

I SEND an intercepted letter for your guidance. It would be well for you to drop a word to Baron Reinhard, for such indiscretions might have the drawback of embroiling us with the Swedish nation, and causing the King of Sweden to think we desire to dethrone him, which is very far from my intention, ill as he has behaved to me. People would do very much better not to concern themselves with my policy. You will say we know about this, by the talk it is making everywhere, and that everybody believes the King of West-phalia is commissioned to make overtures. You will further add, that there is something ridiculous about this reception of a former Sovereign at Cassel, while the former Sovereigns of Brunswick and Hesse are still alive. There is an incon-sistency about the whole proceeding, of which all foreigners are keenly aware.

CCCCLXV

TO PRINCE CAMBACÉRÈS, GRAND CHANCELLOR OF THE EMPIRE.

DRESDEN, 16th July 1813.

THIS letter starts on the 16th: it will reach you on the 20th. I desire the Empress may start on the 22nd, so as to be at Mayence on the 23rd, or 24th. I shall go to meet her there.

She will bring with her the Duchess,[1] two ladies-in-waiting, two red serving-women, two black serving-women [*deux femmes rouges, deux femmes noires*], the Prefect of the Palace, two chamberlains, two equerries (one of whom will start twenty-four hours in advance, and go to Metz, so as to divide the journey), four pages (who will be distributed along the road, so as to spare the boys' strength), her private secretary, if he is well enough, and her doctor. Besides these, she will bring kitchen people, so that her table may be properly served,—for I shall bring nothing with me, and the German kings and princes may come to see her. It will not, however, be necessary to bring the silver gilt service.

Comte Caffarelli will travel with the Empress, to look after her escorts.

The Empress will spend the first night in the house of the Prefect of Châlons, the next, in the house of the Prefect at Metz, and the third, at Mayence. Notice of her journey will be given in these three towns, so that all proper honours may be paid her.

The first part of her travelling cortège will consist of four carriages, and the second and third, of four each,—twelve carriages in all. The escorts will be furnished, as far as possible, by the military authorities along the road. The gendarmes on the route will also be under arms, and in full dress. Full regulation ceremony will be observed. The General commanding each Division will accompany her through his Division.

On the day of her departure you will have the following notice inserted in the *Moniteur*: ' Her Majesty the Empress-Queen and Regent has proceeded to Mayence, to spend a

---

[1] The Duchess of Montebello, lady-in-waiting.

week there, in the hope of seeing His Majesty the Emperor. Her Majesty will spend to-night [the 22nd] at Châlons, to-morrow night [the 23rd] at Metz, and will be at Mayence on the 24th. Her Majesty will return early in August.'

You will let me know the day of the Empress's departure, and the day and hour of her arrival at Mayence, by telegraph. I will arrange my own departure accordingly. If the Ministers had anything pressing to say to me, which made them desire a personal conference, they might take advantage of my stay at Mayence, where I expect to be from the 23rd to the 1st August ; and come there to meet me.

CCCCLXVI

TO MARSHAL DAVOUT, PRINCE D'ECKMÜHL, COMMAND-
ING THE 13TH CORPS OF THE GRANDE ARMÉE.

DRESDEN, 16th July 1813.

I HAVE authorised you, by my letter of this day,[1] to arrange the war-tax with the Hamburg merchants, so as to have ten millions paid down, and twenty millions in bills, payable within ten months, between October 1813, and the 1st of August 1814. Each bill to be for one hundred thousand francs, and to be considered, if we choose, as a note payable by the Bank. Each bill to bear the date of payment. These two hundred bills should be delivered to the Treasury before the end of August.

By this means, thirty millions will be paid off. Of the eighteen millions remaining, fifteen may be paid in necessaries for the army, and three millions, by requisitions within the 32nd Division.

I approve your appointing a Commission to receive these necessaries. I approve your including the value of the houses in the fifteen millions payable in goods. I approve of your accepting no manufactured articles. As Comte Chaban points out, manufacture costs money, and the town cannot be called upon to give more than the raw material, as it is warehoused. I think this answers Comte Chaban's memorandum. You will therefore make the necessary changes in the requisitions for which I have given orders.

---

[1] We do not give this letter, as all its details are more fully reproduced in the one now before the reader.

You will cut out (1st) all manufactured goods, and (2nd) anything the town does not possess. Send me a fresh detail of the requisition for the fifteen millions.

After corn, wine, rice, brandy, vinegar, salted meat, cows and bullocks, cheese, salted fish,—all of them necessary for army and siege supply, either for the town of Hamburg, or for Magdeburg—there are the necessary articles for clothing and equipping the men : cloth, kerseymere, linens, boot and shoe leather, saddle and harness leather, felt for shakos ; and besides, there are saddle and draught horses, medicines of every kind, wood and iron—for the artillery and army waggons ; sail-cloth, hemp, timber, masts, and spars, for the navy. Of course you will not include anything belonging either to Russians or Prussians. To all these objects of immediate utility to the army, you will add the value of those houses about to be pulled down, and those which are to be used for naval and military purposes. You must be careful, however, to leave out the houses of absentees, or of men who are not in the country, and to remember the law that the value of these houses is not to exceed three or four millions. You may thus close this business of the war-tax, by an agreement with Comte Chaban, and the merchants. As for the draft of the Amnesty Decree, I have authorised you to grant it. Have it made public.

I do not think it correct that you should serve on the Commission with your subordinates ; but you will give orders for its formation, according to the rules of Article II. The Commission will submit its conclusions to you, and you will decide. All the other Articles will do. You have my authority to settle them. Get this business finished ; the chief point is to lose no time about making up our minds.

CCCCLXVII

TO THE PRINCE DE NEUFCHÂTEL, MAJOR-GENERAL OF THE GRANDE ARMÉE.

DRESDEN, 19th July 1813.

I BEG you will select four officers who have been wounded, exceedingly clever men, who know German ; you will send two to the waters of Toplitz, and two to those of Carlsbad. They will receive extra pay. They will remain at these

U

places, to act as spies, and report everything that occurs. They will be supposed to be taking the waters for their own benefit.

TO PRINCE CAMBACÉRÈS, GRAND CHANCELLOR OF THE EMPIRE.

DRESDEN, 20th July 1813.

I HAVE your letter. I let you know, from Wittenberg, that it was my intention that the King should retire to Morfontaine, and there remain, in strict *incognito*. I do not intend you to see him. If he should ask for an interview, you will reply I have forbidden it. I do not intend him to see any of my Ministers. If he should ask to see them, the same answer must be given. The President of the Senate, the Ministers of the State, and the Presidents of Sections, are not to see him. You will inform the King, in the most positive manner, that my intention is that he shall not see any one, until after my return.

He has just written me a letter, in which he makes accusations against the Minister of War, and every one else. The whole fault is his. The English report shows, clearly enough, how incapably the army was led. There never was anything like it, in the world, before. The King is not, of course, a soldier, but he is responsible for his own immorality, and the greatest immorality that can be committed is, to exercise a profession of which you know nothing. If there was one man lacking to that army, that man was a General, and if there was one man too many in its ranks, that man was the King. So I will have no jesting on the subject. If you were to show weakness, and not make my intentions clearly known, the King would receive visitors; he would become the centre of a network of intrigues; and that would drive me to the necessity of arresting him,—for my patience is worn out. I have found fault with the letter written him by the Minister of War, because the King would easily be taken in by it. He must be made aware of my real feelings, and be convinced, that if he does not fall in with them, the Minister of Police has orders to arrest him. This is absolutely the only way of restraining him.

I am surprised, after what I wrote to you, that you should have had any further doubt as to how you should behave to the King. The whole arrangement is only to be provisional. It is therefore very natural that he should remain in the country, and rest himself, until I can bring him to account for his bad conduct. I do not know what you have desired Roederer to tell him, but, if you have not spoken frankly, and shown him my letters, you will have missed your aim. I hear Roederer is coming to me. I am very glad of it. I shall be able to tell him all my mind, and that I do not any longer intend to risk the success of my undertakings, out of consideration for simpletons, who are neither soldiers, nor politicians, nor administrators.

CCCCLXIX

TO GENERAL SAVARY, DUC DE ROVIGO, MINISTER OF POLICE.

DRESDEN, 20th July 1813.

I THINK I have informed you of my positive intention that the King of Spain shall not go to Paris, nor even near it. He is to stay at Morfontaine. If he were to come to Paris, or to St. Cloud, you would take measures to have him arrested, and he must not be left in ignorance of that. My intention is, that no one belonging to my household, no high dignitary, none of my Ministers, no President of any Section of the Council of State, nor the President of the Senate, shall see him ; and that, in fact, he is to remain in the most complete *incognito*, until I arrive. He may only receive his wife, Madame, his own family, a few of his intimate friends among the Spaniards, and Roederer,—but that without attracting any remark. As you will have seen by the English newspapers, the misfortunes in Spain are all the greater, because of their absurdity. That is England's own opinion of them. But this is no disgrace to the army. The army in Spain had a General too little, and a King too much. When I look at it closely, I cannot help seeing that the fault is mine. If, as it occurred to me to do, just as I was leaving Paris, I had sent the Duke of Dalmatia back to Valladolid, to take up the command, this would not have happened. Of course you must not allow anything to be printed about the Prince ; but yet it is necessary he should know this is my opinion, and should not be able to deceive himself upon the subject.

CCCCLXX

TO FREDERICK, KING OF WURTEMBERG.

DRESDEN, *22nd July* 1813.

SIRE AND MY BROTHER.—I have received your Majesty's letter of 16th July. I share the grief this second freak of your son's must cause your Majesty. It is sad, that after having done so much for your family, your Majesty should be so poorly rewarded. Your Majesty must find some source of consolation, at least, in the thought of your son's youth, and his lively passions.

CCCCLXXI

TO ELISA NAPOLEON, GRAND DUCHESS OF TUSCANY.

MAYENCE, *22nd July* 1813.

I AM surprised to notice that opposition is being offered to a parish priest, appointed by the Bishop, in Florence. Take the most vigorous measures to put down this religious resistance, at the very outset. Send all persons guilty of it to the island of Elba.

CCCCLXXII

TO GENERAL SAVARY, DUC DE ROVIGO, MINISTER OF POLICE.

MAYENCE, *29th July* 1813.

LET the minor newspapers publish all that is known about Mons. Anstett, the Russian Plenipotentiary at Prague. He belongs to Strasburg, and the details, which will show he is a Frenchman, and of very low extraction, will prove how little the Russians, who make such an extraordinary selection, really desire peace.

CCCCLXXIII

TO GENERAL CLARKE, DUC DE FELTRE, MINISTER OF WAR.

MAYENCE, 31st July 1813.

GIVE orders that all wives of generals, officers, and Government employés, and all women of bad character, including those dressed up as men, who have come from Spain, and are now at Bayonne, and in the Departments of the Landes, and the Basses Pyrénées, are instantly to be sent back across the Garonne, and that, forty-eight hours after the issue of the order you will cause the officer commanding the Division to publish on this subject, all those who have not obeyed, are to be arrested by the civil and military authorities, and taken to their homes. The loose women will be confined in the Salpêtrière. You will take care that the wives of the three Generals, G——, F——, and V—— , are not only sent back across the Garonne, but straight to their own homes.

CCCCLXXIV

TO THE PRINCE DE NEUFCHÂTEL, MAJOR-GENERAL OF THE GRANDE ARMÉE.

MAYENCE, 31st July 1813.

WRITE to the Marshals and Generals commanding Corps, to the Governors of Dresden and Magdeburg, the Commandant at Würtzburg, etc., that under present circumstances, the Emperor's fête will be kept on the 10th of August. For this purpose I order a gratuity of twenty sous, for every non-commissioned officer and private. The Marshals will take measures to have the gratuity paid over on the 9th. This sum will provide extra fare. Double rations of bread, rice, brandy, and meat, will be issued to the troops.

I desire the Marshals will issue orders, that each General of Division is to invite all the officers of his Division, together, to his table. Each Marshal will himself preside at the table of the Division with which he is present. For this purpose I grant six francs a head, in addition to the double rations. The total sum will be given to each Marshal, who will have it placed at the disposal of the various Generals of Division.

I also desire a *Te Deum* may be sung in every camp, that there may be great illuminations at night, that the artillery may let off fireworks, and that, in fact, each Marshal may do everything suitable to the celebration of a day so dear to Frenchmen, to cheer the soldiers, and impress the allied nations. The allied troops will receive the same gratuity as the rest.

The officers' repast should take place in the open air, and at the same hour as the soldiers'. The toasts will be honoured with salutes of 100 guns. In the allied countries, the local authorities and principal inhabitants will be invited, and even in hostile countries, the authorities, and such of the chief inhabitants as have given satisfaction, may be invited. Wherever that is possible, the General will give a ball.

At Dresden, the Imperial Guard will give a great ball to the whole town. In the evening there will be manœuvres, and instead of cartridges, fireworks will be used; this will have a better effect.

The military operations, and the close of the armistice, which may take place on the 10th, are my reasons for advancing the celebration from the 15th, to the 10th.

At Frankfort, Hanau, Fulda, Cassel, and in the 32nd Military Division (except at Hamburg), the fête will not be kept till 15th August, when it will be celebrated at Wesel, Mayence, and in the rest of France; these towns are therefore not included in this day's Order.

CCCCLXXV

TO GENERAL CLARKE, DUC DE FELTRE,
MINISTER OF WAR.

MAYENCE, *1st August* 1813.

IT would be well to give the public an account of the Spanish business. Nothing must be said, either of the Vittoria business, or of the King. The first notice you will insert in the *Moniteur*, will run as follows: 'His Majesty has appointed the Duke of Dalmatia his Lieutenant-General, in command of his armies in Spain. The Marshal took command on the 12th, and instantly made arrangements to march against the English, who were be-

sieging Pampeluna and St. Sebastian.'   After that you will
have General Rey's first letter, about the assault of St.
Sebastian, inserted, and then the letters about such events as
took place on the 25th, 26th, and 27th.   It will be well for
you to make some addition to the number of prisoners and
guns taken, not on account of France, but on that of Europe.
As I am having General Rey's letter published in the
Journal de Francfort, and as I have made alterations of this
kind in it, I send you back the original, with my alterations,
so that it may appear in the *Moniteur*, in the same form.

CCCCLXXVI

TO GENERAL SAVARY, DUC DE ROVIGO,
MINISTER OF POLICE.

DRESDEN, 6th August 1813.

THE Minister of Public Worship has sent me his report
on the Seminarists at Ghent.   These are my intentions; see
they are exactly adhered to.

You will have the Director of the Seminary, who professes
such bad principles, arrested, and confined in a State prison,
without anybody being aware of his whereabouts.

You will have all the Seminarists, over eighteen years of
age, seized, and taken to Wesel, whence they will be sent to
Magdeburg.   They will be given military clothing; General
Lemarois will enrol them in the regiments at Magdeburg,
and make them do military duty.   They cannot become
priests now.

All the Seminarists below eighteen years of age, you will
have arrested, and taken to the best Seminaries in old France,
dividing them up, so that there shall only be one in each
Seminary, and desiring the Directors to instil good principles
into them.

Give orders, too, that these Ghent Seminarists are to be
replaced by an equal number, drawn from good French
Seminaries, and already fairly well instructed in the principles
of the Gallican Church.   And see the Seminary has a good
Director.

I have no time to write about this to the Minister of Public

Worship; let him know the contents of my letter, and take measures in concert with him.

I do not know whether it is at Tournay, or elsewhere, that the Béguines are misbehaving themselves. Have them turned out of the town.

CCCCLXXVII

TO GENERAL SAVARY, DUC DE ROVIGO, MINISTER OF POLICE.

DRESDEN, *7th August* 1813.

I HAVE your letter of 2nd August. I am really distressed by what you write me about poor Junot. He forfeited my esteem during the last campaign; but that did not prevent my still feeling a regard for him. He has regained my esteem now, for I see his cowardice, then, was already caused by his illness. I approve all the proposals you submit to me. See the Grand Chancellor, to whom I am writing. There will be no difficulty about placing the two young girls at Ecouen. You do not tell me the two children's ages.

Speak to the Grand Chancellor, too, about the Duchess of Istria, and find out what will have to be done to settle her affairs. I intend to help her also.

CCCCLXXVIII

TO GENERAL SAVARY, DUC DE ROVIGO, MINISTER OF POLICE.

DRESDEN, *7th August* 1813.

I APPROVE of your making an arrangement with the Duchess d'Abrantès, as to some country-house, whither she shall retire, and live in future. You will inform her that as, being the wife of the Governor of Paris, she has chosen to misbehave herself, and so to embroil her family affairs, that she has ruined herself, and brought her children to starvation, it is time for me to put an end to this state of things, and for her to drop out of public notice.

CCCCLXXIX

TO GENERAL SAVARY, DUC DE ROVIGO,
MINISTER OF POLICE.

DRESDEN, 7*th August* 1813.

I SEE an article about Mons. Anstett, in the *Journal de l'Empire*, the terms of which are rather too emphatic. All that was necessary, was to state who his parents were, what he himself has done, and to say he has always been looked on as an agent of the English, from whom he has received a salary.

CCCCLXXX

TO GENERAL CLARKE, DUC DE FELTRE,
MINISTER OF WAR.

DRESDEN, 7*th August* 1813.

LET Marshal Jourdan be allowed to retire, and let me hear no more of him. Let all his aides-de-camp be employed elsewhere, and sent to join the army for duty. Do the same thing with all the officers about the King, whom he has not kept with him. I think I have already written to ask you what rank they can be given, on going back to duty.

CCCCLXXXI

TO GENERAL SAVARY, DUC DE ROVIGO,
MINISTER OF POLICE.

DRESDEN, 11*th August* 1813.

THE Duke of Otranto, who has just travelled through all the Austrian States, tells me the surest way to strike at that Power, in the event of a war, will be to affect its paper currency, on which all its armaments depend.

CCCCLXXXII

TO COMTE DE RÉMUSAT, FIRST CHAMBERLAIN, SUPERINTENDENT OF THEATRES.

DRESDEN, *12th August* 1813.

I SEND you a statement of the gratuities I will allow the actors of the Comédie Française who travelled to Dresden. This statement reaches a total of 111,500 francs ; you will have the gratuities paid out of the Treasury of Theatres.

Mons. Fleury	10,000 francs.
„ Talma	8,000 „
MM. Desprez, St. Prix, St. Phal, Baptiste Cadet, Armand, and Vigny . .	6,000 „
„ Michot, Thénard, Michelot . .	4,000 „
Mons. Barbier, ...	3,000 „
Mlle Mars	10,000 „
„ Georges	8,000 „
Mlles Emilie Contat and Bourgoin . .	6,000 „
„ Thénard and Mézeray . . .	4,000 „
Mons. Maignien	2,000 „
MM. Fréchot, Colson, Combes, Bouillon, and Mongellas	500 „

CCCCLXXXIII

TO PRINCE CAMBACÉRÈS, GRAND CHANCELLOR OF THE EMPIRE.

DRESDEN, *14th August* 1813.

YOU will find, enclosed, a confidential letter, with reference to the verdict of the Brussels Court of Assize, which I am sending to the Chief Judge. You will send for the Minister, and hand him the letter yourself. You will also send for the Minister of Police, so that before my intention is made public, the accused persons may have been re-arrested, and the jurymen who are implicated, seized. My letter will not be inserted in the *Moniteur*, and the Decree submitted to the Senate, until three or four days afterwards. I authorise you to appoint the members of the Secret Council, and take the initiative in the whole of this business. The Minister of Police will be one of the members of the Secret Council. Extraordinary circumstances necessitate extraordinary measures, and they are provided for in our Constitution.

CCCCLXXXIV

TO GENERAL SAVARY, DUC DE ROVIGO,
MINISTER OF POLICE.

DRESDEN, 14th August 1813.

GIVE orders for the arrest of all the Canons and members of the Tournay Chapter. See the Minister of the Exchequer, and have their salaries instantly stopped. Give orders that the Tournay Seminarists, under eighteen years of age, are to be scattered through the seminaries in old France, and that those over eighteen, are to be forthwith taken to Wesel, whence they will be sent to Magdeburg. Give orders that the Rectors and Professors of the Tournay Seminary are to be obliged to take the oath insisted on in France, before the Revolution, to teach the four points of doctrine of the Gallican Church. Let all this be done without a hitch, without scandal, and let the delinquents be sent to a State prison. Especially, and before anything else is done, let Goes, the head of the Chapter, and Constant, both of whom signed the resolution of the Chapter (an absolute act of rebellion), be arrested. Arrange so as to have the Canons all arrested at once; you can send the three most guilty to a State prison. As for the rest, whom I conclude to be aged men, and simpletons, they can be lodged in Seminaries, but in the very heart of old France.

Inform me as to the behaviour of the town of Tournay in this matter. If the town has behaved ill, the seat of the Bishopric must be removed to some other French town, or the diocese must be suppressed. If it is necessary, send 250 gendarmes, mounted and on foot, into the Department of Jemappes.

CCCCLXXXV

TO GENERAL SAVARY, DUC DE ROVIGO,
MINISTER OF POLICE.

DRESDEN, 14th August 1813.

GENERAL MOREAU has certainly reached Berlin. It would be well for you to make sure of the whereabouts of Adjutant-General Hulot, and even to take possession of his person. He applied for his pension about a month ago, probably in order to go and join General Moreau.

CCCCLXXXVI

TO THE COMTESSE DE MONTESQUIOU, GOVERNESS
TO THE KING OF ROME.[1]

DRESDEN, 14*th August* 1813.

I HAVE your letter, and the King's, of the 9th. I think the King makes very good rhymes, and, more especially, that his rhymes express very true feelings. I will leave it to the Empress to provide the King with toys.

CCCCLXXXVII

TO THE PRINCE DE NEUFCHÂTEL, MAJOR-GENERAL
OF THE GRANDE ARMÉE.

DRESDEN, 29*th August* 1813.

I DO not approve of your sending Adjutant-General Galbois to the King of Naples. I do not see why you should inform the King of Naples as to my communications with the Austrians. Your letter is an improper one, and serves no good purpose. Send Adjutant-General Galbois to the Duke of Ragusa.

In your letter to the Adjutant-General, I find the following words: 'That he will recognise my liberal arrangements.' This is an improper phrase. Do I owe him any explanation of my intentions? The people who draw up your letters do it very ill.

CCCCLXXXVIII

TO MARSHAL GOUVION ST. CYR, COMMANDING THE
4TH CORPS OF THE GRANDE ARMÉE.

DRESDEN, 1*st September* 1813.

THE Duke of Tarento has allowed himself to be driven back on Görlitz. I may possibly be obliged to march on Bautzen to-morrow, or the day after. You will therefore promptly occupy all the defensive positions, so that the Duke of Ragusa, and my Guard, may be free to march with me, in that direction.

That unhappy Vandamme, who seems to have killed himself, had not a sentinel on the mountains, nor a reserve

[1] The King of Rome was then two and half years old.

anywhere. He plunged into a deep valley, without attempting to send out a single scout. If he had only kept four battalions, and four guns, in reserve, on the heights, this misfortune would not have occurred. I had given him positive orders to entrench himself on the heights, to encamp his troops on them, and only to send isolated parties of men into Bohemia, to worry the enemy, and collect news. Apart from the men belonging to his corps, who have reached you, many have arrived, and are still arriving, at Dresden.

CCCCLXXXIX

TO GENERAL COMTE FRIANT, COLONEL COMMANDING THE INFANTRY GRENADIERS OF THE IMPERIAL GUARD.

DRESDEN, 3rd September 1813.

IF you move along the Bautzen road, you will find a great number of stragglers and marauders from the 3rd, 5th, and 11th Corps, who have thrown their weapons away. My intention is that you should drive them all back to Bautzen, whither muskets are being taken for them. Send out patrols on the right and left of the high-road, and drive me back all this rabble, with the butt-ends of your guns.

CCCCXC

TO THE PRINCE DE NEUFCHÂTEL, MAJOR-GENERAL OF THE GRANDE ARMÉE.

DRESDEN, 4th October 1813.

HEREWITH you will find the reports of General Chastel and General Reiset. Inform General Chastel of my displeasure at his behaviour, and order him to return forthwith to the bank of the river. I had a right to expect more zeal for my service, from any General of Division. Why did he not instantly send an officer to the Headquarter Staff, and another to General Souham, to warn them the enemy had crossed? How could he carry caution to such lengths as to think his safety compromised, when the enemy had not yet begun their bridge? I do not really know what terms to apply to such cowardly and careless conduct. Write to the Duke of Ragusa, that if the enemy has really thrown a bridge across the river at Mühlberg, he must instantly march and destroy it. Give General Reiset orders to return to his post. Write to General Souham, that if the enemy has thrown a bridge across at Mühlberg, he must move upon it with Ricard's and Delmar's Divisions, and his reserve Artillery, drive the enemy back upon the right bank, and destroy the bridge. Make him understand this operation is of urgent importance. You will also order General Chastel to return to his post.

CCCCXCI

TO PRINCE CAMBACÉRÈS, GRAND CHANCELLOR OF THE EMPIRE.

ERFURT, 23rd October 1813.

I CANNOT understand this restriction on the publication of the speeches made in the Senate, under pretence that they must first be seen here. The pretext is absurd. The Regent has quite sufficient judgment to decide whether they contain anything objectionable. It is too late now to publish them. This fashion of doing business, in such times as these, does no good, and even does harm.

CCCCXCII

TO THE COMTESSE DE MONTESQUIOU, GOVERNESS TO THE KING OF ROME.

MAYENCE, 3rd November 1813.

I HAVE your letter of 29th October. I am glad to see that the little King's fall has done him no harm. I hear so much praise of him, that my longing to see him, and my obligation to you, are both increased.

CCCCXCIII

TO PRINCE CAMBACÉRÈS, GRAND CHANCELLOR OF THE EMPIRE.

MAYENCE, 5th November 1813.

I SEND you a letter from King Louis, which appears to me that of a madman. I conclude the Prince has not gone to

Paris. If he should come there as a French Prince, it is my intention to forget all his follies, everything he has caused to be printed, and to receive him. If he should come as King of Holland, and still persist in pursuing that chimera, he cannot be received. If he should have committed the folly of coming, no visits are to be paid him, and he must remain in retirement with Madame, at Pont. Above all, the Empress must not see him.

CCCCXCIV

TO PRINCE CAMBACÉRÈS, GRAND CHANCELLOR OF THE EMPIRE.

MAYENCE, 6th November 1813.

I SEND you an unsealed letter to Madame; you will read it, and seal it, and you will confer with Madame about it.

If Louis comes as a French Prince, he will write me to that effect, and as soon as you have his letter, he can be presented to the Empress, and can enjoy the income of his appanage.

But if Madame can do nothing with him, and he is only coming to disturb my peace, and put forward the wild plan suggested to him by Austria, and by the enemies of France, I expect Madame, who, up till now, has never done me any service with her sons, will induce him to depart, and let me hear no more of him. If, forty-eight hours after this present attempt, Louis is still in Paris, and has not affirmed that he comes as a French Prince, you will proceed to his residence, with the Vice-Grand Elector, the President of the Senate, the Chief Judge, and the Secretary of the Imperial family, and you will call upon him to acknowledge the laws of the Empire, to remain in France as a French Prince, and to recognise the Decree which joins Holland to France. If he refuses, a formal report will be drawn up, and immediately afterwards, he will be arrested, and taken, *incognito*, to the Castle of Compiègne.

Hold a small council, with the Prince of Benevento, the President of the Senate, the Chief Judge, and Count Regnaud. Show them the King's letter to me, mine to Madame, and this present letter. It is horrible that he should choose this moment to come and insult me, and tear my heart, by forcing me to act severely. But it is my fate to see myself

perpetually betrayed by the frightful ingratitude of the men
on whom I have showered most benefits, and more especially
by this one, for whose education I denied myself everything,
even absolute necessaries, when I was only twenty. You
know that the libels he published against me were printed
and underlined by Austria, after the declaration of war, as
though to blacken my character, and increase the enmity
which broke out in all quarters.

It is my most positive intention, as soon as Louis shall
have declared that he does not acknowledge the Decree, and
has thus placed himself in rebellion against the laws of the
State, to declare he has forfeited all his rights to the throne.
You understand that I do not even insist on this declaration
of the gratitude of Holland, if he will make your official
inquiry unnecessary, and will assert, in a letter written to
me, that he comes as a French Prince, to rally round the
throne, and offer his right arm to defend his country.

CCCCXCV

TO MADAME MÈRE.

MAYENCE, 6th November 1813.

MADAME, AND VERY DEAR MOTHER,—I learn by telegraph
that Louis has arrived at your house. I send you a copy of
the letter he has written me.

If Louis is coming as a French Prince, to rally round the
throne, he will find a welcome from me, and oblivion of the
past. I brought him up in childhood, and loaded him with
kindness. My reward has been the libels with which he has
chosen to fill every Court in Europe. Yet, once again, I
will forgive him ; you know I never harbour spite. But if
Louis, as his letter leads me to fear, comes to claim Holland,
he will place me under the painful necessity (1st) of dealing
severely with him ; (2nd) of doing so permanently, for I
should be obliged to send him a formal summons through
the Grand Chancellor, and in presence of the Prince Vice-
Grand Elector, the President of the Senate, the Chief Judge,
and the Family Secretary, and if he does not acknowledge
the laws of the Empire, he will forthwith be declared a
rebel.

He shows very little generosity in thus causing me fresh trouble, and obliging me to proceed with severity, at a moment when I have so much on my hands, and when my heart needs consolation, and not fresh anguish.

Holland is a French country, and will be so for ever. The law of the State has thus appointed it, and no human effort can take it away. I appeal to you, then, if Louis is coming primed with the same wild fancies as before, to save me the pain of having him arrested as a rebel subject, to induce him to leave Paris, and to live quietly, and unknown, in some corner of Italy. He was in Switzerland; why did he leave it?

In spite of all the proofs of hatred he has given me, I cannot believe him to be so wicked, and such an enemy to his children, as to desire, in present circumstances, when the whole of Europe is rising up against me, and when my heart is wrung by so much trouble, to cause me the additional distress of obliging me to proceed against him.

I close with a repetition of my assurance, that if, on the contrary, he comes simply as a French Prince, to rally round the throne, which is in danger, and to defend the interests of his country, his family, and his children, I will forgive all the past, I will never mention it to him, and I will welcome him, not as remembering his conduct during the past ten years, but as recollecting the affection I had for him in his childhood.

CCCCXCVI

TO PRINCE CAMBACÉRÈS, GRAND CHANCELLOR OF THE EMPIRE.

MAYENCE, *6th November* 1813.

THE King of Westphalia has had the property of Stains bought for him. I believe this step is contrary to the Family Statutes, and beg you to make sure. I fancy they contain an article providing that no property can be acquired in France, by any Prince of the family occupying a foreign throne, without my permission. If I am not mistaken as to this, order the Chief Judge to send for the notary who drew up the deed of purchase, to make him aware of the provisions of the Statute, and to have the sale annulled.

X

I have ordered the King of Westphalia to proceed to Aix-la-Chapelle. I am shocked that when all private citizens are sacrificing themselves for the defence of their country, a King, who is losing his throne, should be so tactless as to choose such a moment to buy property, and to look as if he were only thinking of his private interests.

I have informed the King of Westphalia that I intend the Queen shall go and join him.

CCCCXCVII

TO M. MARET, DUC DE BASSANO, MINISTER FOR
FOREIGN AFFAIRS.

St. Cloud, 12th *November* 1813.

THINKING over the best way of pushing forward Spanish affairs, I have thought it well to desire Comte Laforest, who is near Tours, to start for Valençay. He will go there *incognito*, with only one servant, and as unpretentious a carriage as possible. He will take a Spanish name, and will remain at the Castle of Valençay in the strictest *incognito*. Comte Laforest will bring the Prince of the Asturias the enclosed letter from me, of which you will send him a copy; you will make him thoroughly aware of my intentions.

The chief point is (1st) to find out the three Princes' state of mind, and to make sure, directly or indirectly, whether they have had any news. They can scarcely have failed to hear something. (2nd) To find out in what persons they have confidence. They must have some adviser. Comte Laforest will let them know that General San Carlos is coming to Paris, and will suggest Canon Escoïquiz, or any other person, to them.

It is of the greatest importance that no one should know he is Comte Laforest. Even the French officer in command of the place must not know it. Comte Laforest will bring him a letter from the Minister of Police, under some subaltern title, something like Police Commissary. He will travel under that name. Draw up his instructions instantly, and come and submit them to me.

CCCCXCVIII

TO FERDINAND, PRINCE OF THE ASTURIAS.

St. Cloud, *12th November* 1813.

Cousin,—The present policy of my Empire makes me desire that affairs in Spain should be brought to a settlement. England is fomenting anarchy, Jacobinism, and the overthrowal of the Monarchy and the Nobility, with the object of establishing a Republic in the country. I cannot fail to be affected by the destruction of a nation so close to my own dominions, and with which I have so many naval interests in common. I therefore desire to remove every pretext for English influence, and to re-establish those bonds of friendship and neighbourliness, which have so long existed between the two nations. I send Mons. le Comte Laforest to your Royal Highness, under an assumed name. You may rely on everything he says to you. I desire your Royal Highness will be convinced of the feelings of esteem and regard I entertain for your Royal Highness.

CCCCXCIX

TO M. MARET, DUC DE BASSANO, MINISTER FOR FOREIGN AFFAIRS.

St. Cloud, *19th November* 1813.

When the Treaty is made with Prince Ferdinand, it will be necessary to provide for a pension for King Charles and the Queen. This pension must be about equal in amount to that I insured to them by Treaty. You must also insure them, and all the Spaniards in their service, the right to live in France, or where else they choose.

D

TO GENERAL SAVARY, DUC DE ROVIGO, MINISTER OF POLICE.

Paris, *6th December* 1813.

Disturbance is being fomented in Belgium, where England would be glad to see a rising. I have ordered the

Minister of War to send General Henry to Bruges, with a
hundred picked gendarmes.   He will be supported by fifteen
hundred men of the National Guard, who are coming from
Cherbourg, and will be under his orders.   He will, first of all,
force all refractory conscripts and deserters to go back to
duty.   He will take all necessary steps, in all directions, for
arresting all persons suspected of being agents of the enemy.
I have also given orders that General Saunier is to proceed,
with a flying column, to the Departments of the Deux-Nèthes
and the Bouches-de-L'Escaut.   But these measures are not
sufficient.   Some senior Police Agents, and even one official of
high rank, should proceed to Belgium, to provide for present
necessities.   There are certain arrests which must be made.
There can be no doubt that a great many English agents
are in that country.   The flying columns must hold courts-
martial, which will mete out swift justice on evil-disposed
persons, and on defaulters who make any resistance.   Arrange
with the Ministers of War, and of the Interior, as to what
measures you should submit to me for Belgium.   You will
meet at the house of the senior Minister.   Hold your
meeting to-morrow, and bring me the result at our business
sitting on Wednesday.

DI

TO DUC CHARLES DE PLAISANCE, GOVERNOR OF ANTWERP.

PARIS, 16th December 1813.

I HAVE recalled General Decaen ; he seems quite to have
lost his head.   His evacuation of Willemstadt is an unheard-
of thing.   The troops on board the flotilla alone, would have
been sufficient to hold the fortress, which is defended by
the floods.   This General appears to have no knowledge
whatsoever of localities, and gives his orders without consulting the Engineer Officers.   You will send somebody to
take his place.   I have given orders that he is to be brought
before a Court of Inquiry, for having evacuated a fortified
town, fully armed and provisioned, without orders on the
subject.   I look on the evacuation of this fortress as the
greatest misfortune that has happened to us.   As soon
as General Roguet is in a position to do so, he must try to
retake Breda, and to re-open communications with Gorcum.

Breda was not armed, nor looked on as a fortified place, and I do not consider its evacuation as so guilty an act; but none the less, it was a shameful one. Four hundred muskets and 700 sick were left there. People must really have lost their heads.

General Molitor is near Bois-le-Duc, and the Duke of Tarento is in communication with him. I have no further hope of our being able to re-capture Willemstadt, which is almost impregnable, once the dykes are cut. It will serve as the base of all the enemy's operations. You must now think very seriously about Bergen-op-Zoom. Pour in supplies by every channel, and get the garrison together; troops must be coming in every moment. The General in command there, is said to be a man of considerable merit; order him to defend his fortress to the last extremity. It appears that the National Guard from the Pas-de-Calais is proceeding to Flushing, and that more than three quarters of it is there already. Order General Gilly to issue arms and clothing to it. He can do as he thinks best. Let him take everything he needs, and give bills in return. Let him get supplies for a year into Flushing, taking everything he can find in the island, for the purpose. Hurry on the supplies for Antwerp, but do not lose your head like General Decaen. Antwerp is impregnable, and more than a hundred thousand men will be on that portion of our frontier before the 15th January. Have Bois-le-Duc armed and provisioned. If you can get back into Breda, have that fort armed with guns taken from Antwerp. As we have lost Willemstadt, it is important for us to have Breda. Burn the first village within your reach which puts on the Orange cockade, and publish an Order of the Day, to the effect that the first person found wearing such a cockade will be shot.

DII

TO KING LOUIS.

PARIS, *4th* or *5th January* 1814.

I HAVE received your two letters, and am grieved to learn you have come to Paris without my leave. You are no longer King of Holland, since you have resigned, and I have joined that country to France. The territories of the Empire

are being invaded, and all Europe is in arms against me.
Do you desire to come as a French Prince, and Constable of
the Empire, and rally round the throne? I will receive you,
you shall be my subject, and, as such, you will enjoy my
friendship, and do what in you lies to improve matters. In
that case, you must nourish proper feelings towards myself,
the Empress, and the King of Rome.

If, on the contrary, you persist in your notion of being a
King and a Dutchman, you must retire to a distance of
forty leagues from Paris. I will have no confusion of
positions, no third party. If you agree, write me a letter
which I can have printed.

DIII

TO KING JOSEPH.

PARIS, 7th *January* 1814.

I HAVE your letter.[1] It is too complex in its nature to
suit my present position. Here is the question, in a sentence : ·
France is invaded, all Europe has taken up arms against
France, and more especially against me. I do not need your
resignation, because I do not want Spain for myself, nor
do I want to have it at my disposal; but neither will I
concern myself with the affairs of that country, except for
the purpose of obtaining peace there, and making my army
available for use.

What do you mean to do? Do you desire to rally to the
throne as a French Prince? You have my affection, and
your appanage, and you will be my subject, as a Prince of
the Blood. In that case, you must do as I do, speak out
clearly, write me a plain letter, which I can have printed,
receive all authority from me, and prove your zeal for me
and for the King of Rome, and your friendly feeling for
the Empress's Regency.

Is this impossible to you? Have you not sufficient good
sense to do it? Then you must retire to some country-
house, forty leagues from Paris, and live there in obscurity.
If I live, you will dwell there in peace. If I die, you will
be killed, or arrested. You will be useless to me, to the
family, to your daughters, to France ; but you will do me no

---

[1] Joseph, seeing France in imminent danger of invasion, had written to place
himself at the Emperor's disposal.

harm, and cause me no inconvenience.   Choose promptly,
and make up your mind.   All feelings of sentiment or enmity
are vain, and out of season.[1]

DIV

TO GENERAL SAVARY, DUC DE ROVIGO, MINISTER OF POLICE.

PARIS, 13*th January* 1814.

YOU will send, early this morning, for the architect in
charge at Stains.   You will ask him for details of all work,
of every kind, which is being done there, and·you will give
him orders to dismiss all the men, and have no more work,
of any sort, done there.   You will send for the King of
Westphalia's man of business, who looks after Stains.   You
will tell him I have ordered all work to be stopped, that
nobody is to be admitted, and the house closed, and that if
there is the slightest disobedience, the place will be laid
under sequestration, as no foreign Prince or King can acquire
property in France without my permission.

You will further inform the King's man of business (but
he should be a Frenchman, and not a foreigner) that it is
necessary for him to remain quietly at Compiègne, and not
go two leagues away from that place ; that it is a scandal, in
present circumstances, that nothing should be seen, in all
directions, but his cooks and his liveries, going hither and
thither.

You will have him told this, by some Frenchman in whom
he has confidence, and you will desire this Frenchman to
make him thoroughly understand that nobody transgresses
my orders without paying for it.

DV

TO M. DE CAULAINCOURT, DUC DE VICENCE, MINISTER FOR FOREIGN AFFAIRS.

PARIS, 19*th January* 1814.

MONS. LA BESNARDIÈRE must have informed you of my
intentions as to an armistice.

[1] The Baron du Casse has published three letters from King Joseph, to
Napoleon and to King Louis, which serve as a commentary on, and explanation of, this letter, and show the circumstances under which it was written.

I have your letter of the 17th. In spite of the importance of the circumstances which might detain me in Paris, I am about to start for Châlons. I think that if you have no letter from M. de Metternich on the 20th (that is, twelve days after the receipt of his answer, and a week after Lord Castlereagh's arrival), there will be very little to hope for, and you will then be at liberty to come and join me.

The Duke of Belluna's conduct has been dreadful. I am sending the Prince of Neufchâtel there. The Duke of Belluna might easily have remained on the Meurthe.

It seems the King of Naples has very nearly concluded his treaty. It has been negotiated by the Austrian General, Neipperg, assisted by an English officer, with whom the King treated, without his showing any powers from his Government, and even without his having recognised him as King. These gentlemen, as occurs in such circumstances, seeing the outburst of joy roused by their presence at Naples, and the influence their appearance had on public opinion, are said to have imposed very severe conditions, against which the King was still struggling. I think the clause which might interest Austria, in connection with the conditions of the armistice, is that as to the cession of Palmanova, and Venice—for she seems to intend to keep possession of the Adige.

DVI

TO GENERAL SAVARY, DUC DE ROVIGO, MINISTER OF POLICE.

PARIS, *21st January* 1814.

LET the Pope start to-night (21st to 22nd), before five o'clock in the morning, for Savona. The Bishop of Edessa will travel in his carriage with him. The Adjutant of the Palace will conduct him to Savona. The servants will go in another carriage, which you will be careful to keep sufficiently far behind, to avoid drawing attention to the Pope's journey. The carriages will cross the Rhone at Pont-St.-Esprit, and will go to Savona by Nice, on pretext of avoiding the mountains. The Adjutant of the Palace will say he is taking him to Rome, having received orders to let him burst on that place, like a clap of thunder. When the Pope reaches Savona, he will be treated in the same way as when he was there before.

Consult, in the course of the day, with the Minister of Public Worship, and let me have a statement of the Cardinals' names, and whither each should be sent. I conclude they might be sent to Provence, to the Genoese Riviera, and into the country about Montpellier and Nismes. As soon as I have approved the list, you will make arrangements for them to start, during the night of the 22nd, all of them accompanied by Gendarmerie officers, so that Fontainebleau and the neighbourhood may be cleared of all these ecclesiastics. It will be as well that none of them should know where the others are going, and that you should cause them to travel by different roads.

DVII

TO PRINCE CAMBACÉRÈS, GRAND CHANCELLOR OF
THE EMPIRE.

TROYES, 6th February 1814.

I HAVE your letter of the 4th. Monges lost his head, from the beginning to the end of his mission. He is too hot-headed a man to be employed about any business.

DVIII

TO KING JOSEPH, THE EMPEROR'S LIEUTENANT-
GENERAL IN PARIS.

NOGENT-SUR-SEINE, 21st February 1814.

THESE are my intentions with reference to the King of Westphalia. I give him authority to wear the uniform of the Grenadiers of my Guard, which permission I extend to all French Princes. (You will inform King Louis of this ; it is absurd for him to go on wearing a Dutch uniform.) The King will dismiss all his Westphalian household. The members of it will be at liberty to return to their own country, or to remain in France. The King will at once submit the names of two or three aides-de-camp, one or two equerries, and one or two chamberlains, all Frenchmen, and of two or three French ladies, to be with the Queen, to me, for my appointment. The Queen will put off appointing her lady-in-waiting till some future time. All the Westphalian pages will be placed in *Lycées*, and will wear *Lycée* uniform. I shall pay their expenses. One-third of their number will be sent to the Versailles *Lycée*, one-third to the Rouen *Lycée*, and one-third to the Paris *Lycée*.

Immediately afterwards, the King and Queen will be presented to the Empress, and I shall give the King permission to inhabit Cardinal Fesch's house (which, it appears, belongs to him), and to establish his household in it. The King and Queen will continue to bear the title of King and Queen of Westphalia; but no Westphalian will remain in their service.

And when all this is done, the King will join my head-quarters, whence I intend sending him to Lyons, to take over command of the town, the Department, and the army, —provided, however, he gives me his promise always to be with the outposts, to keep no royal state, have no luxury, and not more than fifteen horses, to bivouac with his men, and not allow a shot to be fired, without his being the first to expose himself to danger.

I am writing to the Minister of War, and will have his orders sent him. So as not to lose time, he might send off his establishment to Lyons, viz., a light carriage for himself, a cook's waggon, four canteen mules, and two sets of saddle-horses, six in each; only one cook, and one valet-de-chambre, and two or three serving-men, Frenchmen every one of them. He must choose good aides-de-camp; let them be officers who have seen active service, who know how to command troops, and not inexperienced fellows, like Verdun, and Brugnères, and others of that kidney. He must be able to lay his hand on them at once, too. And, to conclude, you had better see the Minister of War, an d onsult about choosing him his staff.

DIX

TO GENERAL SAVARY, DUC DE ROVIGO,
MINISTER OF POLICE.

NOGENT-SUR-SEINE, *22nd February* 1814.

I HAVE your letter. I cannot accept your excuse. Your language is not worthy of a Minister. When I appointed that committee I placed it under your orders. You, therefore, are responsible. In your hands everything becomes a difficulty, whereas, to a Minister of Police, everything should be easy.

DX

TO THE COMTESSE DE MONTESQUIOU, GOVERNESS TO THE KING OF ROME.

BÉZU-ST.-GERMAIN, *4th March* 1814.

I HAVE received the letter you wrote me. I think that under present circumstances you should not correspond with the Queen of Naples, nor give her any news of my son.

I have been pained to hear of the stories reported of Mme Anatole and the Duchess of Padua ; but the only way not to confirm them, is not to ascribe any importance to them. Such stories are soon put about, with regard to pretty women—but their very absurdity makes them incredible.

The Duchess of Padua ought not to have left Paris. In such critical times, a lady-in-waiting's duty is to be near the Empress. Many have failed in this duty. All sense of propriety, and of what honour demands, seems to me to have entirely passed out of memory, in France.

DXI

TO BARON DE LA BOUILLERIE, GENERAL COMPTROLLER TO THE CROWN.

REIMS, *14th March* 1814.

YOUR answer to the King was quite right. My intention is that you should not make any advance, without an order from me, or, in case of urgent necessity, the signature of the Regent, who is in sole authority during my absence, and who alone holds my complete confidence.

DXII

TO PRINCE CAMBACÉRÈS, GRAND CHANCELLOR OF THE EMPIRE.

REIMS, *16th March* 1814.

I HAVE your three letters. Nobody has been slandered to me ; for all I know of the matter, I know through a letter from Méneval, which was followed, six hours afterwards, by one from the Empress. I am convinced these mad projects would never have been confided to you beforehand, for people would have been sure you would have disapproved of them.

The Minister of Police wears me out with his petty passions. I do not know a smaller-minded or more partial man. He shares all his wife's little spites. She has a grudge against the Duchess of Montebello, and all day long he keeps writing to me against the Duchess! He meddles with all sorts of wretched things he should have nothing to do with, instead of watching the Mayors who are misconducting themselves, and keeping his eye on important State matters.

DXIII

TO KING JOSEPH, THE EMPEROR'S LIEUTENANT-GENERAL IN PARIS.

FONTAINEBLEAU, 2nd April 1814.

I HAVE desired the Grand Marshal to write to you as to the necessity of clearing Blois. Let the King of Westphalia go to Brittany, or towards Bourges.

I think Madame would do well to go and see her daughter at Nice, and Queen Julie, and your children, had better move near Marseilles.

The Princess of Neufchâtel, and the wives of the Marshals, must go to their country-houses.

It will be natural that King Louis, who has always sought to live in hot countries, should go to Montpellier.

It is necessary to have as few people as possible on the Loire, and everybody must get settled without causing more talk than can be avoided. There always is talk among the inhabitants about any colony that emigrates.

The road to Provence is clear now, and it may not be so some of these days.

In your report of the Ministers, you do not mention the Minister of Police. Has he arrived? I do not know if the Minister of War has his cipher. There is none with you, and therefore, for lack of a cipher, I cannot write to you about important matters.

Desire every one to observe the strictest secrecy.

THE HUNDRED DAYS

DXIV

TO KING JOSEPH.

PARIS, *25th March* 1815.

I HAVE ordered the Master of the Horse to place forty carriage-horses, and, if possible, a few carriages, at your disposal. This will set up your Stable Department.

Speaking generally, you must organise your household on a modest scale. In our present financial condition, I do not expect to be able to give you more than a million for this year. Next year, of course, your income will reach the two millions.

There will be no objection to your spending a few months in the Elysée Palace. But as the Tuileries are uninhabitable in the summer, I may want it for myself. See if the house I have bought from Talleyrand would suit you. The Duchesse de Bourbon is in it at this moment, but you can ask to see the plans, and that Princess is going to a country-house on the Loire. You can also look at the house near the Courts of Justice, which the Prince de Condé occupied.

I am told the Duchesse d'Angoulême, and the Princes, have bought houses. If that is so, you can take your choice. I do not know whether you have any furniture left, but I will give you a certain amount out of the Crown stores, to furnish your house.

There is also the Palais Royal. To sum it all up, I desire you will not lay out anything this year on horses, furniture, or housebuilding.

DXV

TO MARSHAL DAVOUT, PRINCE D'ECKMÜHL, MINISTER OF WAR.

PARIS, *26th March* 1815.

My intention is, that you should have the Dukes of Ragusa, Castiglione, Reggio, and Belluna, and Comte St. Cyr, removed from the list of Marshals. A retiring pension, the amount of which you will submit for my approbation, will be granted the Dukes of Belluna and Reggio, and Marshal St. Cyr. You, on your part, will have to see they do not come near Paris. You will submit to me, as soon as possible, the list of Lieutenant-Generals and Brigadier-Generals, which must now be pretty considerable. You will also submit a report on the Colonels-in-Chief, so that I may restore those who have not become unworthy of it, to their former position.

DXVI

TO COMTE DEFERMON, PRESIDENT OF THE FINANCE SECTION OF THE COUNCIL OF STATE.

PARIS, *27th March* 1815.

I REQUEST you will call the Council together, and submit the draft of a law, inflicting penalties on all persons who, after the publication of the said law, shall continue to wear the white cockade, to act in the King's name, or to belong to corps of volunteers, or any others. This law must, as present circumstances demand, be stringent and vigorous, so as to touch the people on their tenderest point.

DXVII

TO PRINCE CAMBACÉRÈS, GRAND CHANCELLOR OF THE EMPIRE, IN CHARGE OF THE MINISTRY OF JUSTICE.

PARIS, *13th April* 1815.

APPOINT a commission of reliable magistrates, to break the seals, and inventory the papers, found in the house of the Prince of Benevento, and of the other persons whom the Lyons Decree has deprived of the benefit of the amnesty. I am assured that important documents will be found. Appoint men on whom you can rely.

DXVIII

TO MARSHAL DAVOUT, PRINCE D'ECKMÜHL, MINISTER OF WAR.

PARIS, *13th April* 1815.

WRITE by special express to General Grouchy, that he must have received the letter I sent him, direct, through the telegraph, and which appeared in yesterday's *Moniteur* ; that he must make the Duc d'Angoulême sign a promise to have the Crown diamonds returned, and never to bear arms against France ; and that he is to notify to him the Decrees which condemn him to death, as a member of the Bourbon family, if he should re-enter France. General Grouchy must take back any money which has been drawn from the Public Funds, and let him go.

The intercepted letters show that the Prince of Essling is not behaving very well. Yet we must await the result of his measures. Send the Marshal orders to proceed to Paris.

I believe I have cashiered General d'Aultanne. Let me know to what part of the country he belongs. He will be sent back to his own neighbourhood ; there is no use in his coming to Paris. I have also cashiered General de Loverdo ; he must not come to Paris, nor must General Monnier come here, but, as he belongs to Avignon, he must not be left there. He might be sent somewhere near Grenoble, under surveillance.

Fresh Generals must be sent to the 8th Division, and none of the present ones must be left with it. I conclude I have cashiered General Ernouf ; he must not come to Paris ; send him to some small commune, under surveillance.

Generals Gilly and Merle are exceedingly well spoken of. They may be successfully employed in the country where they now are, and so may Rivaud and Morin, the Gendarmerie officers, who were put in prison by the Princes.

DXIX

TO M. FOUCHÉ, DUC D'OTRANTE, MINISTER OF POLICE.

PARIS, 14*th April* 1815.

I SEND you a letter from General Fressinet. If Dambray has not made his submission, by the time this present order reaches you, you will issue a warrant for his arrest, and have him taken to Vincennes. Write to the Prefect of Rouen that he is to take measures to keep down the *émigrés*, and make a clearance of the men who are known to have been attached to the old régime. If Dambray does make his submission, you will remove him from Normandy, and send him into Burgundy, under surveillance.

DXX

TO M. DE CAULAINCOURT, DUC DE VICENCE, MINISTER. FOR FOREIGN AFFAIRS.

PARIS, *27th April* 1815.

I DESIRE you will draw me up a report, to be read at the Ministerial Council on Saturday, and printed in Sunday's *Moniteur*. This report will set forth the communications we have made to England, and the answers received; those we have made to Switzerland, with. the answers; all we know about the Allies' plans; our correspondence with the King of Naples, the advantage which should accrue to us therefrom, and all we know as to his operations. This report must be clear and truthful; it will be drawn up with two objects :—

The first, to inform the nation as to the situation, and to hint what we have learned of the enemy's arrangements, and of their avowed plan for dividing and weakening France. You will not fail to remark, that we have printed all their Notes, and that they have not printed one of ours; that the Powers who desire to make war against us, can only do so, by deceiving the nations as to our real position; that we do not desire to deceive any one, and are anxious to make the whole truth known.

The second object will be, to point out that people are fond of representing us as living, like the men of '93, in a state of the most complete anarchy; and that this was one of the chief reasons which induced us to institute, by virtue of a fourth plebiscite, that true liberty, without anarchy, which is indispensable to the internal happiness of the nation, and need not alarm any other Power.

You will realise the importance of this report, with its double object. Work at it, so that it may appear in Sunday's *Moniteur*.

DXXI

TO M. GAUDIN, DUC DE GAÉTE, MINISTER OF FINANCE.

PARIS, *1st May* 1815.

I SEND you a summary of the finances of the Condé family. I desire you will bring me a statement of those of the Orleans family, and of that of the King, etc., on Wednesday, so that we may take steps to reassure their creditors.

DXXII

TO PRINCE CAMBACÉRÈS, GRAND CHANCELLOR OF THE EMPIRE, IN CHARGE OF THE MINISTRY OF JUSTICE.

PARIS, 2nd May 1815.

YOU have a notoriously evil-disposed man in your offices. My intention is that to-morrow (Wednesday), you shall bring me a statement of the persons to be discharged, both from the Ministry of Justice, and from the offices of the Council of State. If you do not make these alterations, I shall be obliged to make them myself, and that would be an unlucky step, for I might make mistakes, and once I had made up my mind, I should not alter anything that had been done.[1]

DXXIII

TO MARSHAL DAVOUT, PRINCE D'ECKMÜHL, MINISTER OF WAR.

PARIS, 2nd May 1815.

REPLY to Marshal Grouchy that it is not true that the Allies have asked for a passage through Switzerland, and over the Simplon, for their troops. Neither is it true that the King of Naples was beaten on the 15th. He gained a very distinct advantage on the 18th, at Cesena, and has retired in good order.

The last news of Marmont tells us he is at Ghent, so he is probably not commanding the Piedmontese troops.

DXXIV

TO M. FOUCHÉ, DUC D'OTRANTE, MINISTER OF POLICE.

PARIS, 3rd May 1815.

THE Duc de Berri's aide-de-camp, Mons. de Lévis, has been in Paris for the last two days. He is living at No. 2 Rue Neuve du Luxembourg. Try to have him arrested, so as to get possession of his papers.

---

[1] A similar letter was written to the Minister of the Interior; the last sentence was struck out of the draft by the Emperor himself.

DXXV

TO VICE-ADMIRAL DUC DECRÈS, MINISTER OF THE NAVY.

PARIS, 5*th* *May* 1815.

YOU will tell Captain Moncabrié that a letter has been found amongst Mons. de Blacas' papers, in which he describes the conversation he had with me at Fréjus, to Mons. Malouet; that his description is perfectly correct, and couched in friendly terms, and that I was pleased with it.

DXXVI

TO M. FOUCHÉ, DUC D'OTRANTE, MINISTER OF POLICE.

PARIS, 5*th* *May* 1815.

IT is asserted that Mons. Fouache, the ex-Sub-Prefect of Havre, is encouraging a gathering of two hundred soldiers recalled to duty, who are collecting round Havre. Order this Fouache to come to Paris, and if the action imputed to him is true, have him arrested.

There is also said to be a gathering of the nobility at Blangy, in the Seine-Inférieure, at the house of a Mons. de Calonne. What are they doing there?

It is also reported that a great number of persons go to the house of a certain Demoiselle Mache, at Rouen, bringing money with them.

DXXVII

TO MARSHAL DAVOUT, PRINCE D'ECKMÜHL,
MINISTER OF WAR.

PARIS, 5*th* *May* 1815.

SEND orders that Colonel de Vence, who is at Rouen, and who is keeping up a correspondence with his former regiment, is to be arrested on the spot, and taken to the Abbaye.

DXXVIII

TO MARSHAL DAVOUT, PRINCE D'ECKMÜIL,
MINISTER OF WAR.

PARIS, 11*th* *May* 1815.

I REQUEST you will submit to me, during the day, a list of all the general and senior officers in the King's household,

whom I have consented to take back into the army. I have
no intention of revoking this decision. But with regard to
those who have obtained promotion while in the King's
household, you will submit me the draft of a Decree, to annul
such promotion—my intention being only to give them com-
missions in the rank they held before the end of April 1814.
Those persons who refuse to engage in their former rank,
will be cashiered.

I hear General Montmarie is still in Paris, because, he
says, I have not confirmed his Lieutenant-General's appointment. These gentlemen overtax my good-nature. I will
not ratify any promotion given by the King, in his household. I do quite enough, when I wipe out the disfavour
with which I must regard those persons who entered the
King's household at all, and admit them to the rank they
held in 1814.

DXXIX

TO M. FOUCHÉ, DUC D'OTRANTE, MINISTER OF POLICE.

Paris, 13th May 1815.

IT appears that Mathieu Montmorency is the Comte de
Lille's principal agent in the Vendée, and that he is the
mainspring there, at the present moment. You must issue a
writ of Habeas Corpus against him, and have him prosecuted,
as a promoter of civil war. Either he will come, or he will
not come. If he does not, he will be condemned in default,
and all his property will be laid under sequestration.

DXXX

TO MARSHAL DAVOUT, PRINCE D'ECKMÜHL,
MINISTER OF WAR.

Paris, 13th May 1815.

As the 43rd Regiment has joined the force in the
Vendée, this regiment, with 500 gendarmes and 300 men of
the naval force, must put General Delaborde in a position
to allow all the line troops, of which we are in such great
need, to move away to the army.

Give orders to the Chief Inspector of Gendarmerie, to send
the rest of his 1st Battalion to Angers, so that there may be

500 gendarmes there, as soon as possible. Give orders that these 500 men, with 100 of the local gendarmes, 1000 men of the 43rd Regiment, and the 300 men of the naval troops—at least 1800 men in all,—are to be divided into three flying columns, of 600 men each. Each column is to be placed under the orders of a General, or Senior Officer, and these will arrange all operations between them. If the country is well covered by these columns, all seditious movements should be stifled. They must find out whether the Duc de Bourbon is there, or not, and give orders to the chief personages in the country, whose conduct does not appear to be reliable,—and even to d'Autichamps,—to proceed to Paris. You may also desire General Delaborde to fill up the 3rd, 4th, and 5th Battalions of the 43rd Regiment, with retired soldiers, who do not wish to leave the country ; giving them an assurance that this regiment, which is intended to insure the peace of the locality, will not be employed elsewhere. By this means, he will at once have five battalions, instead of two. As the dépôt is at Rochefort, he might even bring over a skeleton battalion from Nantes.

DXXXI

TO M. FOUCHÉ, DUC D'OTRANTE, MINISTER OF POLICE.

PARIS, 15*th May* 1815.

GIVE orders that the parish priests of Meudon and St. Cloud are at once to leave their commune, and be sent, under surveillance, to a place forty leagues from Paris. These two priests will, further, be dismissed. They are very dangerous men, whose presence cannot be permitted where I live.

DXXXII

TO M. FOUCHÉ, DUC D'OTRANTE, MINISTER OF POLICE.

PARIS, 16*th May* 1815.

I AM assured that on the 15th, the Sub-Prefect of Nogent-le-Rotrou had a proclamation from Louis XVIII. affixed to the church door, and that there has been a great deal of disturbance in that Commune. Give me an account of this matter.

DXXXIII

TO MARSHAL DAVOUT, PRINCE D'ECKMÜIIL, MINISTER OF WAR.

PARIS, 18*th May* 1815.

You will receive the Decree declaring Marseilles in a state of siege. Desire Marshal Brune to put General Verdier in command of the town. Give him orders to parade his troops at an opportune moment, to have the Decree secretly printed, and to give his instructions to General Verdier, who will publish his proclamation, disarm the National Guard, reorganise a new one, and have twenty-five or thirty of the principal leaders of the Royalist party taken to Fort Samalgue, all at the same moment. Desire him to take all the steps circumstances may render necessary.

DXXXIV

TO COMTE RÉAL, PREFECT OF POLICE.

PARIS, 19*th May* 1815.

It appears that Mons. Bresson de Valensolles, who was the Marshal's agent at Vienna, went abroad a week ago. You will realise the importance of this communication. See about verifying how, and by what road, he went.

A certain Lagarde, who was in Russia, spent the night at Langres, forty-eight hours ago. He was on his way to Paris, where he must have arrived. News might be had of him from Ouvrard, who appears to have some connection with him. It will be necessary to find out, without attracting any notice, whether he is here, and, if he has not come, to take steps to seize his papers before he arrives.

DXXXV

TO MARSHAL DAVOUT, PRINCE D'ECKMÜIIL, MINISTER OF WAR.

PARIS, 20*th May* 1815.

Authorise General Delaborde to keep the 6th Regiment of the line, as well as the 43rd. He must form flying columns, made up of the Gendarmerie, and of troops of the line. Authorise him to have a military court attached to them, and to have every man who is taken with arms in his hands, shot. And give him permission to send all persons who appear to him suspicious, into Champagne, Burgundy, and Dauphiné, and to have all persons who promote armed gatherings, arrested.

Order General Delaborde to collect his forces, to proceed to Mons. La Rochejaquelein's house, and raze it to the ground. He will have all his property placed under sequestration. The Province of Vendée will recognise, in this vigorous action, a renewal of the misfortunes which overwhelmed it ten years ago.

A Proclamation will point to it, as the beginning of the fresh disasters the Province will have to undergo, and which may yet be avoided.

DXXXVI

TO COMTE MOLLIEN, MINISTER OF THE PUBLIC
EXCHEQUER.

PARIS, *23rd May* 1815.

BY virtue of my Decree of 3rd May, the Exchequer owes the Empress Josephine, the Princes Joseph, Louis, Jerome, Princess Hortense, and her children, 3,965,955 francs 93 centimes, and the Emperor 8,680,622 francs 25 centimes— total, 12,646,578 francs 18 centimes. The Princes and the Crown are in equal need of these funds, to pay arrears of expenditure. Yet the Exchequer finds it impossible to pay them off. This has made me resolve to effect a payment through the Crown Exchequer, in bills issued for the purchase of National Forests. Choose lots worth a million each, in various Departments. My intention is that these bills shall be negotiated in payment of the arrears of debt. I am desiring the Crown Comptroller to see you about the matter. I wish the whole business to be concluded in the course of this week.[1]

---

[1] A similar letter was sent to Mons. de Montalivet, Comptroller to the Crown.

DXXXVII

TO M. FOUCHÉ, DUC D'OTRANTE, MINISTER OF POLICE.

PARIS, 25*th* *May* 1815.

SEND an agent to Noyon. Public meetings are held there, at which Royalists openly proclaim themselves. Your agent will remain there several days, without being known, and will then report to you as to the ringleaders, who must be arrested, or removed to a distance. The Ghent Proclamations are posted at Noyon.

Give orders that the ex-Mayor of Givet, and a certain Longueil, are to leave Givet, and go to a distance. Send them to live, under surveillance, in some small town in Burgundy.

DXXXVIII

TO MARSHAL DAVOUT, PRINCE D'ECKMÜHL, MINISTER OF WAR.

PARIS, 25*th* *May* 1815.

I SEND you back General Delaborde's correspondence. He seems still to be following a dangerous course.

The town of Nantes does not require the help of the 15th Regiment. The town, with its population of 60,000 souls, cannot allow the enemy to capture it.

Repeat orders by special express :

(1st) That he is to mass the 15th, 25th, and 26th Regiments, and all his Gendarmes, and place these troops under General Corbineau's orders.

(2nd) To recall all small detachments, whether at Fontevrauld or any other place.

(3rd) As the Young Guard will reach him to-morrow, he will form a third column, under the orders of General Brayer. Thus he will have General Travot's column, General Corbineau's column, and General Brayer's column. He will add all the Cavalry and Gendarmes he has. He will leave General Charpentier at Nantes, where he will form a fourth column; and as soon as they are ready, these four columns will march, keeping touch, so as to be able to support each other. General Corbineau will be in command until General Lamarque arrives. Give orders for the thorough organisation of the National Guard, at Saumur and Angers, where the populace is well disposed. It is of importance that it should be provided with weapons.

You must set a price on the heads of La Rochejaquelein, d'Autichamps, and the other leaders. Arrange your march so as to reach their family properties, and destroy their country-houses. The Generals must issue proclamations, and must make the Prefects do the same, to enlighten the minds of the population of the Vendée. They must announce that large numbers of troops are approaching. Make General Travot aware of my satisfaction. General Lamarque is about to start. Give him the same instructions. The chief point is that he should always keep his troops together, so as to avoid all chance of failure. Nantes, Saumur, and Angers must defend themselves, and he need not do more than garrison the castles, in those towns. The officers you have appointed have not yet started; yet it is very important that somebody should be there, to look after the preparations for defence, and stir up the communes.

DXXXIX

TO GENERAL COMTE DROUOT, ASSISTANT MILITARY
SURGEON OF THE IMPERIAL GUARD.

PARIS, 25th May 1815.

I HAVE written you several times, regarding my intention that the Young Guard shall be enlisted through recruiting offices, established in the different military quarters; that the officers commanding battalions shall draw up the recruiting placards, and that they shall proceed, with drummers, to the different public squares, and there read the said placards aloud. This may not answer, but I think it will procure you several thousand men.

DXL

TO GENERAL COMTE LEMAROIS, COMMANDING THE
15TH MILITARY DIVISION, AT ROUEN.

PARIS, 25th May 1815.

I HAVE your letter of 20th May. Send me the names of all the worst finance officials, but try not to make any

mistakes; I shall dismiss them. Let me have details about
the Duchâtel family, and let them know that if their behaviour does not improve, I shall dismiss them all. Send
me also a statement of the Generals who must be changed.
Speaking generally, you are too vague in your remarks.

You must have received the Decree whereby I appoint
a Superior Committee of Order over which you will preside.
Clear your Departments of everything which can bring harm.
It is of urgent importance that you should send off your
battalions of the National Guard to Dunkirk. Send the
old soldiers you are recalling to Paris; it will be an excuse
for getting them away.

I have sent you new Prefects. Concert measures with
them, and with the Superior Committee. Have minutes
kept of your deliberations; and everything you ask shall
be done. Alter the feeling of that fair Province, in the
population of which so much good exists.

DXLI

TO M. FOUCHÉ, DUC D'OTRANTE, MINISTER OF POLICE

PARIS, 29th May 1815.

I SEND you a letter from the Prefect of the Sarthe. Make
him aware of my displeasure. This is not worthy of the
Police Commissary of Boulogne. How has he allowed events
thus to come upon him unawares, without having taken a
single step, or even organised one battalion of the National
Guard, all through his Department, to protect it? His conduct stamps him a very poor administrator, or else a fool.

DXLII

TO M. FOUCHÉ, DUC D'OTRANTE, MINISTER OF POLICE.

PARIS, 1st June 1815.

THE disarming of Marseilles seems to have brought the
Revolutionary Party in that town back to life; and if none
but reliable men are enrolled in the National Guard, we
shall have their assistance in keeping down the evil-disposed
section.

I see Bordeaux still goes on very badly. Take the same

steps for disarming the Bordeaux National Guard,—doing the same thing there as at Marseilles, and re-organising the Guard, with none but the faithful men belonging to the town. They will suffice to keep down the malcontents. Desire the Committee of Order to arrest all persons who held commands under the King, and to have all volunteers who enrolled for the Duchesse d'Angoulême arrested, and sent to serve in the army.

The same course should be followed at Toulon and Montauban : the National Guard must be disarmed, and reconstituted with men who are friendly to the Revolution. These four operations should change the whole face of the south of France.

Make me a report about Lille. What is the strength of the National Guard in that town, and would it not be well to disarm it ? Steps would be taken, later, for raising another. It seems to me too great an imprudence to leave arms in the hands of a disaffected National Guard.

DXLIII

TO VICE-ADMIRAL DUC DECRÈS, MINISTER OF THE NAVY.

PARIS, 1st June 1815.

YOU will receive a Decree to provide men for the Artillery of the Guard. Select them out of the three battalions now in Paris, and draft them into the Guard to-morrow. You will fill their places with conscripts, and men from the naval ports.

You have suggested my bringing five companies of gunners to Paris, to be composed of a hundred cadets, who would be treated as soldiers—each company to be commanded by a captain, and midshipmen. The whole battalion under a post-captain. I think the idea a very good one. Give them orders to come to Paris. Select the post-captain who is to command them, and, when you have given the necessary orders, submit me the draft of a Decree, to sanction the formation of this new corps.

If you have boatswains and chief boatswains, in my pay, who are not actually employed, you might form them into a similar Artillery battalion.

Give orders to the 133 Artillery officers on half-pay, to proceed to the Northern fortresses, to those in Alsace, and to those on the Meuse. Send to the Minister of War, to find out the number to be sent to each fortress, and their rank, and distribute them accordingly.

You have suggested my raising a battalion of midshipmen. I should also wish to raise one of gunners, numbering 500 men—that is, five companies. I should bring them to Paris. They will be commanded by naval officers of superior rank, and the chief command of the battalion will be given to a Rear-Admiral. How much would it cost?

I should also like to organise the retired naval officers, living in their own homes at Marseilles, Nantes, and Bordeaux, into companies of 100 men each. This would have a great effect on public feeling in those towns. You must know how many unemployed naval officers there are in these towns, and how much this arrangement would cost me.

DXLIV

TO MARSHAL SOULT, DUC DE DALMATIE.

PARIS, 3rd June 1815.

I THINK you may, to avoid exciting remark in the army, assert, without any inconsistency, that the Bourbons' flight from French territory, their appeal to strangers to restore them to their throne, and the will of the whole nation, have broken all engagements made with them. Without this sentence, I think the Order of the Day might do you a mischief amongst suspicious persons.

DXLV

TO KING JOSEPH.

PHILIPPEVILLE, 19th June 1815.

ALL is not lost. I suppose that by collecting all my forces, I shall still have a hundred and fifty thousand men remaining. The federated troops, and the best of the National Guard, will furnish me a hundred thousand men ; and the dépôt battalions fifty thousand more. Thus I shall have three hundred thousand soldiers, with whom I can at

once oppose the enemy. I will horse my Artillery with
carriage-horses. I will raise a hundred thousand conscripts.
I will arm them with muskets taken from the Royalists, and
from the ill-disposed members of the National Guard. I will
raise the whole of Dauphiné, the Lyonnais, and Burgundy,
I will overwhelm the enemy. But the people must help me,
and not bewilder me. I am going to Laon. I shall doubtless
find people there. I have no news of Grouchy. If he has
not been taken, as I fear, I may have fifty thousand men within
three days. With them, I can keep the enemy engaged, and
give France, and Paris, time to do their duty. The Austrians
march slowly, the Prussians are afraid of the peasants, and
dare not advance too fast ; everything may yet be retrieved.
Write me what effect this horrible piece of bad luck has pro-.
duced in the Chamber. I believe the deputies will feel
convinced that their duty, in this crowning moment, is to
rally round me, and save France. Pave the way, so that
they may support me worthily. Above all, let them show
courage and decision !

INDEX

ABBAYE, prison of the, 338.

Abrantès, Portugal, 66.

—— Duke of. *See* Junot.

Agen, Lot-et-Garonne, letter dated thence, 100.

Agoult, d', General, 201.

Ahab, king of Israel, 43.

Aix, Bouches du Rhône: the Pope's letter to the Chapter, 221; mineral waters of Aix, 180.

—— Archbishop of, Monsignor Champion de Cicé, 119.

Aix-la-Chapelle, 144, 161; the Empress Josephine to take the mineral waters there (1810), 180.

Albany, Madame d', 128.

Albert, the Archduke, 130.

Albignac, Mons. d', 138.

Alcantara, Portugal, 67.

Aldini, Minister and Secretary of State in the Kingdom of Italy: measures to be taken by him during the Pope's residence at Savona, 154.

Alençon, Orne, letter dated from that town, 236.

Alexander I., Emperor of Russia, his troops at Corfu well treated by the French, 46. *See* Russia.

Alexandria, Egypt, 13, 16.

Algarves, 54.

Ali Pacha, 91.

Allemand, Vice-Admiral, 292.

Almeida, Portugal, 65, 66, 71.

Alquier, Baron, 7.

Ambassadors, French, their salary not to be seized, 206.

—— foreign, their correspondence to be examined, 75.

America, United States of: M. de Champagny ordered to request the Minister from that country may be recalled, 170; trade arrangements concluded by the Emperor, 192; American vessels captured in the Baltic to be retained as sailing under English convoy (September 1811), 248.

Amsterdam, Holland: Marmont goes there to negotiate a loan, 6; the French Ambassador's servants ill treated by the populace (May 1810), 184; the cannon found there to be sent to France, 190; Napoleon keeps the Palace for his own use, 194; discontent and complaint amongst the townsmen, a riot against Custom-house officers (Sept. 1810), 202-204; steps to be taken to insure peace in the town, vagrants to be arrested (March 1811), 229, 230; disturbance (May 1811), stringent measures ordered, 234, 235; letters dated from Amsterdam, 252-254; reference to the town, 149, 162.

Anarchists, 93, 94.

Ancona, the Legations united to the Kingdom of Italy (May 1808), 87; licences granted for that port, 193.

Andalusia. *See* Army of Andalusia.

Andréossy, General Count: letter to him, as Governor of Vienna, 128; measures to be taken to keep order in Vienna and put down attempted revolts (June 1809), 128-131; referred to, 114.

Angers, Maine-et-Loire, gendarmes to be sent there (13th May 1815), 339.

Anglican Church, persecution of the Irish Catholics, 41.

Angoulême, Duc d', 334, 335.

—— Duchesse d', 333.

Anstett, Mons., Russian Plenipotentiary at Prague, 308, 313.

Antonio, Infant Don, 77, 84, 86. *See* Ferdinand.

Antwerp, Belgium: ships arriving in the port, and giving themselves out as American, to be seized, 56, 57; smugglers, 89; importance of defending the dockyards, 160; the town abandoned by King Louis' guard when the English landed (1809), 161; Bessières to take cannon from Antwerp (1809), 165; arrest of Béguines (1810), 190; verdict of the Brussels Court of Assize on the

Antwerp Octroi case (August 1813), 314; armament of the fortress, 325; letters dated from Antwerp, 249, 250; reference to the town, 149, 153.

Aragon, 209.

Aranda de Duero, letter dated thence, 108.

Araujo, Mons. d', 11, 12, 14, 17.

Arberg, Mons. d', 123.

Arco, Mons. d', Colonel in the Bavarian army, 139.

Arezzo, Tuscany, 108.

Argenson, Mons. de Voyer d', Prefect of the Deux-Nèthes, reprimanded for failing in deference to a General, 259.

Argenton, Mons. d', Adjutant-Major of Dragoons, his treachery and trial, 131, 132, 133, 134, 164, 165.

Argus, newspaper, 68.

Armand, actor, gratuity allotted him, 314.

Army, 'Grande Armée,' or 'Armée d'Allemagne': troops withdrawn from Germany, to be sent to Spain (Aug. 1808), effective strength of troops left in Germany, 102; reinforcements provided by conscription, 103; mistakes made by King Jerome, 134, 135-139; Marshal Lefebvre in the Tyrol, 139, 140; various operations (Aug. 1809), 144, 145; strength of the army, 154; the Russian campaign, 262, 263, 264, 265; severe measures to be applied to Germany, 267-269; Davout marches on Hamburg, 284; the Emperor's fête-day to be kept by the army, 309, 310; orders sent to Gouvion St. Cyr, 316, 317.

—— of Andalusia, its effective strength (Oct. 1810), 209.

—— of Batavia, 6.

—— of Egypt, assistance to be sent it from Spain, 7-9.

—— of Spain: concentration of troops (March 1808), 71, 72; troops are not to be scattered, 83; various military operations and movements (July 1808), 100, 101; operations ordered (Sept. 1808), 104, 105; the English defeated, 112; various operations (Jan. 1809), 114, 115; strength of Mortier's and Soult's corps, 163; peculation, 200, 201; positions occupied and effective strength (Oct. 1810), 209; General Gardanne's mistakes, 222; the defeat at Vittoria; Soult the Emperor's

Lieutenant in Spain (1813), 293-296; all wives of generals and officers to be sent back across the Garonne, 309.

Army of Italy, the Emperor wishes to raise it to 100,000 men (Sept. 1808), 103.

—— of the North, Bessières placed in command (Nov. 1809), measures he is to take, 165.

—— of the West, 1, 3, 4.

—— of Portugal, ordered to march on Lisbon, 53-55; assistance it might furnish in case of certain events in Spain, 67, 71; its effective strength (1810), 209.

—— of the Pyrenees, 6.

—— of the Rhine, its victories, 8.

—— Bavarian, Bavarian troops with the Grande Armée (1813), 281.

—— Spanish: Spanish troops support Junot's expedition into Portugal, 55, 67; orders to Murat to write and advise the Generals commanding the Spanish army to trust the Emperor, 82; Murat to take command (April 1808), 84.

—— Dutch. *See* Holland.

—— Portuguese, steps to be taken with regard to it at the time of Junot's conquest of the country, 66.

—— Westphalian: French troops not to be placed under Westphalian officers, 91; cuirassier regiment raised by the King, 214; must be reformed after the Russian campaign, 265; its fidelity not to be counted on, 281, 282.

Arrest of persons suspected or accused of crime, 57, 58, 89, 99, 144, 184, 231, 241, 242, 337, 338, 339, 346.

Artillery, guns and artillery waggons burnt during the Russian campaign, 257; Naval cadets and midshipmen to be formed in the companies of gunners (May 1815), 346, 347.

Assonville, Major d', 167.

Asti, Italy, the Vicar-General and five Canons arrested, 217, 218, 219, 221.

Asturias, Prince of the. *See* Ferdinand VII.

Augereau, General Marshal, and Duke of Castiglione: letter addressed to him when in command of the army in Batavia, 6; he is to be asked to report on General Duhesme's behaviour (April 1810), 179; struck off the list of Marshals (March 1815), 333.

Augusta, Princess of Bavaria: letter to be sent by her to the Bavarian States-General on the subject of their wedding present to her, 27.

Aultanne, General d', 335.

Aurich, Ems Oriental, sailors revolt (May 1811), 233.

Austerlitz, battle of, 20, 132.

Austria : its position after Austerlitz, 30 ; must be forced to drive away the English Ambassador, 46, 47 ; recognises Joseph as King of Spain, 101 ; the German Princes and great land-owners in the Austrian service recalled within the confines of the Rhenish Confederation, 116, 117, 118, 119 ; sequestration of the property of those who refuse, 124, 125 ; spy system to be organised in Austria, 118 ; Napoleon forges Viennese bank-notes to ruin Austrian credit and make war impossible, 155, 156, 162, 313 ; the motives of his Austrian alliance (Feb. 1810), 173, 174 ; no overture made by Austria to England (June 1810), 188 ; the property of French and Belgian officers in Austria sequestrated, June 1811, 237 ; the negotiations to be delayed (June 1813), 287, 288 ; Fouché advises the Emperor to strike at the Austrian paper currency, 313 ; possible Austrian conditions for concluding an armistice (Jan. 1814), 328.

Austria, Marie Louise of, Empress of the French. See Marie Louise.

Autichamps, Mons. d', ordered to proceed to Paris (May 13th, 1815), 340 ; a price set on his head, 344.

Avignon, Vaucluse, 95, 122.

Avril, General, peculation during his command in Spain, 201.

Aymé, Mons., and the Spanish crown jewels, 246.

Azara, Mons., Spanish ambassador in France, 11, 17, 18.

BACHER, Mons., 119.

Badajos, Spain, 67.

—— Treaty of, 16.

Baden, Grand Duchy of : complaint to be made concerning the conduct of Prince Louis, and the vexatious treatment of Catholics and of troops which have served with the French (March 1810), 174, 175.

Baden, Prince Louis of, complaints of his conduct, Napoleon demands he shall leave Baden territory, 174, 175.

—— Margravine of, 30.

—— Stephanie de Beauharnais, Princess of, letters addressed to her, 30.

Bagration, Prince, Moldavian campaign, 166 ; Russian campaign, July 1812, 263.

Baiæ, kingdom of Naples, 73.

Bakers, bonus given on each sack of flour they purchase (20th October 1811), 253.

Baltic, the, 136, 137.

Bank of France, may lend money to Spain on the security of the crown jewels, 88.

Banishment to the provinces, and enforced residence there, 27, 28, 39, 89, 144, 167-8, 169, 186, 195, 196, 257.

Baptiste-Cadet, actor, gratuity allotted to him, 314.

Barbary Coast, the Regencies, 9, 68.

Barbé-Marbois, Minister of the Public Exchequer, letter addressed to him, 21.

Barberi, Canon of Asti, arrested, 217.

Barbier, actor, gratuity allotted to him, 314.

Barcelona, General Duhesme to remain there and keep order (March 1808), 71, 72 ; General Duhesme's accusation, 179.

Barnevelt, Grand Pensionary of Holland, 203.

Barral, Monsignor de, Bishop of Meaux, Archbishop of Tours, letter addressed to him, 21 ; he is to be given the sum for which he has asked, and 60,000 francs for charitable purposes, 21.

Barthélemy, General, peculation in his command, 201.

Baste, Rear-Admiral, 251.

Batavia, 6.

—— town of, 198.

Batz, Dutch fort, 159, 161, 165.

Bavaria, present from the States-General to Princess Augusta, 28 ; the Emperor demands the arrest of Schneider, 257 ; the Emperor desires General de Wrede may command the Bavarian troops with the Grand Armée (1813), 281.

Bayeux, Calvados, 89.

Baylen, capitulation of, 100, 105, 106.

Bayonne, General Leclerc's advance guard to proceed there (Year IX.), 13 ;

the army massed there (1807), 46; Napoleon's residence and the Spanish Princes' arrival there, 76, 77, 79, 82, 84, 85; the postmaster dismissed, 109; letters dated thence, 76-97.

Bayreuth, Bavaria, 102, 136, 138.

Beauchamp, Mons. de, 45.

Beauharnais, Mons. de, French Minister in Madrid, receives the Order of St. Leopold, 236.

Beaumont, General, 139, 144.

Beaupreau, Maine et Loire, 126, 127.

Beauvau, Léon de, 173.

Beiramar, province of, 13.

Belair, General, 105.

Belgium, bad feeling (Aug. 1809), 144; families and individuals obliged to settle in France, 144, 168; youths forced to enter Lycées, military schools, or regiments, 168; Belgian officers in the Austrian service not to enter Belgium, 199; agitation by the English; despatch of flying columns, gendarmes, and police agents, severe measures (Dec. 1813), 323, 324.

Belliard, General, Governor of Madrid, 81; his weak government—strong measures against the rioters necessary, 114, 115.

Belloy, Monsignor de, Archbishop of Paris: the First Consul requests he may be appointed Cardinal, 20.

Benavente, Spain, letters dated thence, 111, 112.

Berg, Grand Duchy of: troops of the Grand Duchy, 124, 138; disturbances (Jan. 1813), 269, 270.

Bergen-op-Zoom, Holland: the King of Holland's headquarters removed thither (1809), 148; entrance of the French troops (Jan. 1810), 170; supplies for the fortress (Dec. 1813), 325; referred to, 165.

Berlin: Berlin merchants smuggle goods through the blockaded ports, 235; letter dated thence, 35.

Bernadotte, Marshal, Prince of Ponte-Corvo, Prince Royal of Sweden: letter addressed to him, 200; at Libnitz, 126; bad behaviour at Wagram, 140; makes money at Hamburg and Elbing, 157; Fouché desired by the Emperor to remonstrate about his orders of the day to the Saxons and the National Guard, and his intercourse with intriguing persons (12th Sept. 1809),

157; the Emperor authorises him, on being elected Prince Royal of Sweden, to assume Swedish nationality, but he is never to bear arms against France, 200; referred to, 64, 149, 152.

Bernstorf, Mons. de, 76.

Berthier, Alexandre, General, Marshal, Prince de Neufchâtel and de Wagram: letters addressed to him, 9, 29, 30, 35, 75, 91, 99, 110, 114, 131, 144, 185, 200, 201, 222, 284, 285, 291, 316; ordered to remonstrate with the King of Westphalia, 91.

—— General César, blamed for inviting the deported priests in Corsica to dinner, 243.

—— Madame, Princess of Neufchâtel, 332.

Bertin de Vaux, Messrs., editors of the *Journal des Débats*, 43, 210, 211.

Berto, Canon of Florence, 220.

Bertoni, servant to the Pope, 225.

Bertrand, General, Count : letter addressed to him as Governor-General of the Illyrian provinces, 240; his corps d'armée stationed at Coburg (April 1813), 280.

Besnardière, Mons. la, 327.

Besneval, General, 51.

Bessières, Marshal, Duc d'Istrie : letters addressed to him, 81, 165; he commands at Burgos (April 1808), 77, 81; battle of Medina de Rio-Seco, 101; ordered to expel the English from Holland, 165; his affairs arranged after his death, 123; referred to, 149.

—— Madame, Duchesse d'Istrie, the Grand Chancellor ordered to arrange her affairs (1813), 312.

Béthencourt, General, 3.

Beugnot, Comte, Councillor of State, in the King of Westphalia's service, 61, 70, 71.

Bézu, St.-Germains (Aisne), letter dated thence, 331.

Bidassoa, the, 301.

Bignasco, Italy, 37.

Bigot de Préameneu, Minister of Public Worship, letters addressed to him, 112, 119, 143, 156, 198, 218, 266, 274. *See* Public Worship.

Bilbao, Galicia, 104, 105.

Billiot, consul at Stettin : his improper behaviour to a general officer, 200; appointed by mistake to Riga, his affair with General Liébert, 214.

Biscay : the country to be disarmed, 104 ; peculation in that province, 201.

Bishops : the Pope refuses to confer canonical institution on those appointed by the Emperor, 222 ; they are to take the oath to the Regent, 286. *See* Public Worship.

Blacas, Mons. de, 338.

Blangy, Seine Inférieure, 338.

Blockade, the continental, attempts to elude it, and seizure of ships which have broken it, 56, 57 ; not strictly observed in Holland, 160 ; applied to Germany, 238 ; seizure of American ships which have broken it, 248. *See* Licences, and English and Colonial Merchandise.

Blois, Loire et Cher, 332.

Blücher, Prussian General, 126.

Bohemia, referred to, 137, 138.

Bois-le-Duc, Holland, preparation of the fortress (Dec. 1813), 325.

Bois-le-Roi, Seine et Marne, 48.

Bologna, Italy, 135.

Bonneville, printseller, 218.

Books and printed matter, police matters connected with, 123, 178, 205, 213, 228, 239.

Bordeaux, Gironde : troops collecting there, 13 ; hostility of the local nobility to the Government, 49 ; licences granted to the town, 192 ; the national guard to be disarmed and measures taken to put down evil-disposed persons (June 1815), 345, 346 ; referred to, 56, 57 ; letter dated thence, 100.

—— Archbishop of, his Pastoral, 112.

Borghèse, Prince Camillo, Governor-General of the Transalpine Department : letters addressed to him, 147, 164, 217, 218, 222, 233, 235.

—— Pauline Bonaparte, Princess. *See* Pauline Bonaparte.

Borgia, Cæsar, 19.

Borna, Saxony, letter from, 283.

Bouches-de-l'Escaut, Department, flying columns sent there (Dec. 1813), 324.

Bouillerie, Baron de la, letter addressed to him, 331.

Boulogne-sur-Mer, flotilla and camp, 46 ; the police commissary a bumptious chatterbox, 251 ; letters dated thence, 25, 26, 27.

Bourbon, the Duke of, 340.

Bourbon, the Duchess of, 333.

—— the Cardinals, 19.

Bourbonne, Allier, 180.

Bourbons, the, reasons which release the army from its oath to them, 347.

Bourgoin, Mlle, gratuity allotted her, 314.

Bourgoing, Baron, Minister in Saxony : he imperils the dignity of France, 98 ; spy system to be organised in Austria, 118 ; he is to have no intercourse with King Louis (Aug. 1810), 199.

Bourmont, Mons. de : agrees to the pacification, 2 ; has not disarmed his bands, 3 ; reference to a letter from him to General Brune, 4, 5 ; goes to Paris and sees the First Consul, 5.

Bourrienne, Mons.: order to return the portrait given him by the King of Westphalia, 162, 163 ; the Emperor displeased with his conduct at Hamburg, 163 ; his peculations in that town, 292 ; a letter from Hamburg about him, information concerning him to be secretly collected, 247.

Braunau, Austria : the French Ambassador's despatches seized there (March 1809), 121 ; letter dated thence, 124.

Brayer, General, his flying column in the Vendée, 343.

Bread-stuffs, bonus given on every sack of flour bought by the bakers (20th Oct. 1811), 253.

Breda, Holland : entrance of the French troops (Jan. 1810), 170 ; the Emperor desires an attempt may be made to retake the fortress, its armament (Dec. 1813), 324, 325 ; referred to, 165.

Bremen, licences granted to the port, 192, 193.

Brenier, General, is to march troops to a point in the Grand Duchy of Berg, where riots have occurred (Jan. 1813), 269.

Bresson de Valensolles, Mons., 341.

Brest : vagrants are to be sent there and on to St. Domingo, 5.

Brindisi, Italy, 74, 212.

Brixen, Tyrol, 143.

Bruce, Dutch General, 159.

Bruges, Belgium, picked gendarmes sent to keep order (Dec. 1813), 324.

Brugnères, Mons., aide-de-camp to the King of Westphalia, 330.

Bruix, Vice-Admiral, to appear before Cadiz, 11, 12 ; blockaded in Brest by inferior forces, is to leave port and give them chase, 18, 19.

Brune, General Marshal: letter to him when commanding the army of the West, 1; orders to prepare the Western Departments against attempted landing, 1; to send troops towards Vannes, 2; Bourmont's letter to him, 4, 5; orders to be sent him as to the Royalist movement at Marseilles (18th May 1815), 341.

Brünn, Moravia, letter from, 159.

Brunswick, city of, colonial merchandise there, 211; merchants who smuggle goods through the continental blockade, 235; threat of exemplary punishment for bad behaviour, 262.

—— Duke of, his body not to be brought back to Brunswick, 35; passage with reference to him in Mme de Staël's book to be suppressed, 205.

—— Fair, 242.

Bubna, Count, 286.

Bucharest, 36, 166.

Bunzlau, Saxony, letter from, 288.

Buol, Austrian General, 139.

Burghausen, Bavaria, letter from, 124.

Burgos, Spain: the Spanish King and Princes pass through it in 1808, 77, 82, 83; no riot in the town, 87; it is to be occupied in force (Sept. 1808), 104; letters dated thence, 107, 108; referred to, 104.

Busca, Mons., 11.

Bylandt, Mons., to remain in Holland (1810), 198.

Cadiz, 8, 10, 11, 12, 46.

Cadoudal, Georges. See Georges.

Cadzand, island of, 148, 152.

Caen, Calvados, letters from, 235, 236.

Caffarelli, General, 303.

Cagliari, Sardinia, 196.

Cahors, Lot, the Mayor accused of dishonesty about the conscription, 247.

Calvaire, Trappist Monastery of the, 242.

Cambacérès, Prince, Grand Chancellor of the Empire, letters to him, 38, 93, 94, 97, 126, 167, 279, 286, 290, 292, 293, 294, 299, 303, 306, 314, 318, 319, 321, 329, 331, 334, 337; he is ordered to smooth over matters between the Minister and Prefect of Police, 93, 94, 97, 98; to preside over the Council of Ministers, in the Emperor's absence, 151; instructions for misconduct as regards King Louis (Nov. 1813), 321, 322.

Campa, the Pope's florist at Savona, 225.

Campi, Mons., 8.

Campochiaro, Mons., 250.

Campo Formio, treaty of, 17.

Canning, Mr., 78.

Cantal, Department of the, refractory conscripts, 26.

Capraja, isle of, 243.

Caprara, Cardinal, letter to him from the Pope, 158.

Caraffa, Spanish General, 82, 84.

Cardinals, the, kept away from Savona, 154; sent to France, and summoned to Paris (1809), 156, 158; sum allotted for their support, 156; one of them fails to attend the Emperor's marriage, 176; the Emperor allows them to remain at Savona, on condition they interfere in nothing, 252; they are left at Fontainebleau on the same condition (April 1813), 276, 277; they are to be sent to the Genoese Riviera, to Provence, or Languedoc (Jan. 1814), 329.

Caricatures, 112.

Carinthia, 118.

Carlos, Infant Don, 86. See Ferdinand VII.

Carlsbad, 304.

Casimir, King of Poland, 20.

Cassel, Hesse, 97, 137, 138.

Cassini, Mons. and Mme, 168.

Castelfranco, Prince of, 120.

Castiglione, Duke of. See Augereau.

Castile, Old, 82.

Castile, Council of, 88.

Castlereagh, Lord, 328.

Cattaro, Dalmatia, 46; instructions sent to General Bertrand for organising the province (July 1811), 240.

Caulaincourt, General, Duc de Vicence: letters to him, 327, 336; his reception at St. Petersburg, 68, 69; difficulty as to the precedence of the Prince of Oldenburg, 113; exceeds his instructions as to negotiating with Russia, (1810), 178; instructions to be sent him to reassure Russia as to supposed French negotiations with England and Austria (June 1810), 188, 189.

Cavalleri, Canon of Asti, his arrest, 217.

Cavalry, utterly destroyed by cold in the Russian campaign, 264.

Ceccarini, the Pope's surgeon, 225.

Cervara, Trappist Monastery at, 242, 243.

Cesena, Italy, 337.

Cevallos, Mons. de, 83, 84.

Ceylon, 15.

Chaban, Count, Councillor of State, ordered to return to his post at Hamburg, which he had no business to leave, 271.

Chamartin, Castle of, letters from, 109, 110.

Chambarlhac, General : letter to him, 3 ; he directs certain operations of the Army of the West, 1, 2, 3.

Chambéry, Savoy, 17.

Chamber of Commerce, Paris, 141.

Champagny, Count de, Duc de, Cadore : letters to him, 26, 45, 47, 52, 68, 76, 91, 92, 98, 102, 110, 111, 113, 114, 115, 116, 118, 125, 152, 155, 162, 166, 168, 170, 171, 173, 174, 176, 178, 186, 188, 197, 199, 200, 207, 210, 213, 214, 227 ; circular to be sent to the Princes of the Rhenish Confederation to obtain the recall of all princes and great landowners in the Austrian service, 116, 117, 118, 119 ; spy system to be arranged in Austria, 118 ; information to be imparted to Mons. de Metternich, 152, 153 ; intercourse with Persia, Mons. Gardanne's mission, 153 ; instructions from Mons. de St. Marsan, 154 ; instructions to be sent to the Duke of Vicenza (17th Dec. 1809), 166, 167.

Champeaux, General, 2.

Chapelle-Largeau, Deux-Sèvres, 230.

Chaptal, Count, reason he has not been appointed Councillor of State, 18.

Charente Inférieure, Department of the, arrest of refractory priests, 230.

Charles IV., King of Spain, would command the troops if he joined the army in Portugal, 55 ; protests against his abdication and appeals to Napoleon (1808), 77, proceeds to Bayonne, 82-85 ; interview with his son and with Napoleon, 85 ; newspaper article about him, 90 ; his plan of settling at Nice, 95 ; the documents relating to the Queen of Etruria's behaviour to be laid before him, 232, 241 ; his income to be provided for in the treaty with the Prince of the Asturias (Nov. 1813), 323.

—— the Archduke, 136.

Charpentier, General, in command of a flying column in the Vendée(1815),343.

Chastel, General, blamed for having quitted his post through cowardice, 317, 318.

Chasteler, Mons. de, 134, 169.

Chateaubriand, Mons. de, 43.

Chaudron, Loire Inférieure, 127.

Chénier, Marie Joseph, 35.

Chevreuse, the Duc de, orders to find out whether he has a printing-press at Dampierre, and an English governess and four priests to bring up his children, 228.

—— Mme de, Lady of Honour, 90.

Chipault, Chef d'Escadron, 59.

Chouan War, references to the, 1-6. See Vendée.

Cifenti, orders for his execution, 240.

Citerni, eating-house keeper in Paris, 116.

Ciudad Rodrigo, Spain, 53-55, 209.

Civita Vecchia, Italy, 196, 218.

Clarke, General, Count D'Huneburg and Duc de Feltre : letters to him, 38, 53, 85, 105, 119, 126, 145, 148, 151, 163, 164, 165, 179, 187, 190, 197, 206, 243, 244, 245, 248, 256, 268, 269, 271, 272, 275, 277, 278, 283, 295, 297, 300, 309, 310, 313 ; letter dictated by the First Consul, 4 ; repressive measures to be taken against the partisans in Germany, 38, 39 ; blamed for using the telegraph to call on General Delmas to join the army, 279 ; blamed for his letter to King Joseph, after the battle of Vittoria (July 1813), 301, 306.

Clausel, General, left behind in the route after Vittoria (1813), 300 ; retires on Saragossa, 301.

Clauvès-Briant, the brothers, 167.

Clément, aide-de-camp to Desaix, his mission to Egypt, 7, 8.

—— General, 9.

Clergy. See Public Worship.

Coburg, 280.

Colaud, General, 149.

Colditz, Saxony, letter from, 283.

Collin de Sussy, Count, ordered to have ships suspected of coming from England searched, 56.

Colonels-in-Chief, 334.

Colorno, Italy, 95.

Comédie Française, gratuities to the company which travelled to Dresden (1813), 314.

Compiano, Duchy of Parma, 164.

Compiègne, letters from, 177-179, 247-

249 ; assigned as a residence to King Charles IV. of Spain, 95, 122.
Concordate of Fontainebleau, 268.
Condé, House of, 336.
Consalvi, Cardinal, 277.
Conscription a failure in certain Departments, Year XIII., 25 ; levy of 140,000 men (1808), 103 ; levy of 80,000 men (1809), 153; dishonest practices connected with the conscription in the Lot, 247.
Conscripts, refractory, 26, 324 ; orders to give greater liberty to those shut up in the citadel of Ré who are dying for want of space, 244.
Conspiracies and plots : conspiracy of Lahorie, Rivière, etc., 27 ; the anarchist conspiracy, 93.
Contat, Mlle Emily, gratuity allotted her, 314.
Copenhagen, the English expedition, 45, 46.
Coppet, near Geneva, 28, 40, 92.
Corbineau, General, aide-de-camp to the Emperor : in command of a flying column in the Vendée (May 1815), 343.
Corboli, Vicar at Florence, 220.
Corfu, the Russian squadron takes shelter there, 46 ; the Corfu expedition, Cosmao's mistakes, 73, 74, 75 ; communication with the island to be kept open (Oct. 1810), 212.
Corn trade, 140-142, 192, 193.
Corsica, refractory Tuscan and Roman priests deported thither, 218, 258.
Corunna, 12.
Cosmao, Rear-Admiral, the Corfu expedition, his failure, the Emperor's wrath, 73-75.
Cotentin, the, 119.
Côtes du Nord, Department of the, 45.
Cotogni, the Pope's footman at Savona, 225.
Cotton, trade in, 192-194.
Council of the Imperial family, 167.
—— of State, reasons why Chaptal and Ganteaume have not been appointed to it, 18 ; weeding out of the office employés (1815), 337.
Councillors of State, 94.
Courlay, Deux-Sèvres, 230.
Courrier d'Espagne, the, 122.
Cracow, Poland, 118.
Crochaix, Mons. la, 45.
Crossen, 38.

Crown jewels, 21, 334, 335.
—— —— Spanish, 88, 246, 247.
Cuenca, Spain, 101.
Curacoa, island of, 17.
Curione, Canon of Asti, 217.
Customs officers, riot caused by them in Amsterdam (Sept. 1810), 203, 204.
Cüstrin, Germany, 38, 39, 102.
Cuxhaven, port of, 285.
Czernitschef, Mons. de, aide-de-camp to the Emperor of Russia, 228, 230.

DALMATIA. See Ragusa.
—— Duke of. See Soult.
Dambray, Mons., 335.
Dampierre, Chateau de, 228.
—— Charente Inférieure, 230.
Dani, Grand Vicar of Asti, 217.
Dantzig, licences granted to the port, 193 ; the garrison reinforced (1811), 228.
Daru, Count, letter to, 226.
Dauphiné, 29, 119.
David, King, 43.
Davout, Marshal, Prince d'Eckmühl: letters to him, 234, 238, 254, 288, 298, 304, 333, 334, 337, 338, 339, 341, 343 ; strength of his troops in Germany, 102, 103 ; at Vienna, 126 ; movements ordered in Mecklenburg, severe measures to be taken in Hamburg after the capture of that town, line of conduct to be followed as regards Sweden and Mecklenburg (May 1813), 284, 285 ; execution of the severe measures prescribed for Hamburg, 288, 304, 305 ; the Emperor's intentions as to the fine of 48,000,000 to be paid by Hamburg ; he gives Davout authority to conclude an armistice, 298, 299, 305.
Decaen, General, indignation at his evacuation of Willemstadt—he is to be brought before a court of inquiry (Dec. 1813), 324, 325.
Decazes, Mons., 155, 158.
Decorations, foreign, 48.
Decrés, Vice-Admiral, Count and Duke, letters to him, 291, 338, 346.
Defermon, Count, letter to him, 266.
Dejean (Monsignor), Bishop of Asti, 217.
Delaborde, General Count : orders issued to him for putting down disturbances in the Vendée and Anjou (May 1815), 339, 340 ; he is authorised to keep the 26th line regiment, to send flying

columns through the Vendée, to raze La Rochejaquelein's house to the ground, 341, 342 ; his false system; orders for the formation and direction of his flying columns (25th May 1815), 343.

Delmas, General, 279.

Delort, Adjutant-General, peculation in Italy, 29.

Denmark furnishes a contingent for the expedition against Sweden, 76 ; the Emperor demands that the Hamburg refugees shall be removed from Holstein, 289.

Denon, Mons., is to send his letters to the Duc de Cadore, 270.

Desaix, General, 8.

Desaugiers, Mons., 257.

Deserters, 324 ; conscript deserters, 26.

Desmarest, Mons., 51, 185.

Desmasures, Abbé, 164.

Desportes, Felix, 17.

Desprès, Messrs., 169.

Desprez, actor, gratuity allotted him, 314.

Desruisseaux, Mons., 89.

Désure, Abbé and Grand Vicar of Ghent, 143.

Deux-Nèthes, Department of the, refractory conscripts, 26 ; flying columns sent into the Department (Dec. 1813), 324.

Deux-Sèvres, Department of the, 28.

Dillon, Mme, 187.

Disturbances in the Departments, 127, 339, 340, 341, 343, 344, 345. See Chouans.

Dolgorouki, Prince, Russian Minister at Naples, in disfavour with the Emperor, 261.

Dombrowski, General, 288.

Donnadieu, Colonel, 135.

Doria, Cardinals, 156.

—— Monsignor, parted from the Pope and exiled to Naples (Jan. 1811), 226.

Douai, Nord, 7.

Doubrowna, Poland, letter from, 264.

Doucin, refractory priest, 230.

Drainage works, 119.

Drake, Mons., 24, 58.

Dresden, Jerome Buonaparte to mass his troops there (July 1809), 136-139 ; ball to be given by the Imperial Guard on the Emperor's fête-day, 310 ; letters dated thence, 286, 288, 289, 290, 291, 292, 293, 294, 295, 296, 297, 298, 302,

303, 304, 306, 307, 308, 311, 312, 313, 314, 315, 316, 317.

Drouet d'Erlon, General, ordered to put a stop to peculations and abuses in Navarre and Biscay, 201 ; ordered to send General Gardanne back to France, 222.

Drouot, General Count, letter to, 344.

Dubois, Prefect of Police, disagreement with the Minister of Police, 93, 94, 97, 98.

Dufour, General, 119, 126.

—— Mons., 45,

—— Mme, 68.

Dugommier, General, 6.

Duhesme, General, at Barcelona, 71, 72 ; authorised to proceed to Paris to explain the charges brought against him at Barcelona (April 1810), 179.

Dumanoir, Rear-Admiral, 9, 10, 12.

Dunkirk, licensed ships to unload their cargoes there, 192, 193.

Duperré, Vice-Admiral, 291.

Dupont, General Count, at Valladolid, 67 ; his army returns, 72 ; at Toledo, 83 ; capitulation of Baylen, 101, 102, 106.

Dupont-Chaumont, General, Minister in Holland, ordered to take steps with regard to the proposed re-establishment of the nobility in Holland by King Louis, 39, 40.

Dupont de Nemours, Mons., 141.

Durand, Baron, is to make private inquiries at Naples concerning the Spanish crown jewels, 247; disagreement about precedence with Prince Dolgorouki, Russian Minister, 261.

Duroc, General, Duc de Frioul : letters to him, 95, 270 ; instructions as to the journey of Charles IV., King of Spain, to Nice, 95.

EBERSDORF, Austria, letters from, 126, 127.

Eckmühl, battle of, 256.

Edessa, Bishop of, 277, 328.

Egypt referred to, 62. See Army of Egypt.

Eisenach, Saxony, 281.

Elba, refractory priests sent there from Tuscany, 224, 308.

Elberfeld, Grand Duchy of Berg, 269.

Elbing, Prussia, 157.

Elisa Bonaparte, Princess of Lucca and Piombino, Grand Duchess of Tuscany, letters to her, 56, 150, 219, 224, 268, 308; her intercourse with Hainguerlot disapproved, 56; she prevents the carrying out of the Emperor's orders, 128; has no right to interfere with orders given by Ministers, 150; is desired to treat the Florence Chapter, which refuses to acknowledge the Archbishop appointed by the Emperor, with severity, 220.

Elysée, Palace, 333.

Emden, Ems Oriental, riot takes place (May 1811), 233.

Emery, Abbé, 147.

Émigrés, 48, 58; they shirk the conscription for their children, who are sent by force to St. Cyr, 111.

Ems Oriental, Department of the, severe measures to be taken there, 235.

Ernouf, General, 335.

Erfurt, Germany, letters dated thence, 106, 318.

Eschwege, Hesse, 36.

Escoïquiz, Canon, former tutor to the Spanish Princes, 83, 123, 128, 322.

Escurial, palace of the, 82, 83.

Esmenard, censor, dismissed, 230.

Espinay, Mons. de l', the Emperor's orderly officer, 143.

Essling, battle of, 256.

Esterhazy, Prince, 68, 130.

Esteve, Count, ordered to pay over 10,000 francs to Mons. Fabre de l'Aude, 21.

Estramadura, Spain, 15.

Etienne, Mons., Editor of the *Journal des Debats*, 79, 122, 230.

Etruria, kingdom of, the recall of the Nuncio demanded, 31.

Etruria, Queen of. *See* Marie Louise.

Eugène de Beauharnais, Prince: letters to him, 24, 176, 179; report of his marriage with the Queen of Etruria, 25; the Emperor warns him against a dangerous woman, 26.

Eure, Department of the, the conscription there a failure, 26.

Evreux, Eure, 2.

Exchequer, Public, expenditure of the Empress Josephine, 255; sums owed to the Imperial family, 342.

Eylau, battle of, 157, 256.

FABRE DE L'AUDE, President of the Finance section of the Tribunate: letter to him, 21.

Falaise, Calvados, 260.

Farge, printer, 213.

Farnese Palace, Rome, 254.

Fay, Mons., 58.

Fenestrelle, fortress of, 57, 108, 120, 140, 145, 147, 154, 168, 190, 217, 218, 220.

Ferdinand VII., Prince of the Asturias, King of Spain: letter to him, 323; his father abdicates, Napoleon does not recognise him as King, 77, 80, 82, 83; Savary ordered to conduct him to Bayonne, 76-78; at Bayonne, 82; coldly received by his father, 85; sent to Valençay with his uncle and brother, their income, police measures regarding them, 86, 87, 106, 107; their correspondence intercepted, 92; their Spanish servants dismissed, 123; arrest of a supposed English emissary at Valençay, 177; report of his marriage with an Austrian princess, 211; documents relative to the Queen of Etruria's behaviour to be submitted to him, 232; he is forbidden to make expeditions on horseback, 234; Comte Laforest is sent to Valençay to treat for the return of the Princes to Spain (Nov. 1813), 296.

Ferrol, Spain, 10, 11.

Fesch, Cardinal Archbishop of Lyons, Grand Almoner: letter to him, 239; the Emperor's surprise at his having sent to Rimini for priests, 45; the Pères de la Foi, in his diocese, to be suppressed, 58; his Pastoral on the battle of Wagram, 147; his house in Paris, 330.

Fievée, Mons., 43.

Figueiras, Spain, 71, 72.

Finance, prosperous state of the finances of the Empire (Oct. 1810), 208; finances of the Bourbon princely families, (1815), 336.

Finkenstein, castle of, letters from, 40-43.

Finland, Sweden likely to lose the province, 72.

Flahaut, General, aide-de-camp to the Emperor, 281.

Fleury, actor, gratuity allotted him, 314.

Florence, Tuscany: the withdrawal of the Papal Nuncio to be demanded (Sept. 1860), 31; Lucien to retire thither, 73; the Emperor resolved Mme d'Albany shall not remain there, 128; the Pope's letter to the Chapter; the

Canons to be arrested, 219, 220; proposal to reduce the number of Canons, 224; opposition to a parish priest, 308.

Florent, Mons., of Breda, 89.

—— Guyot, senator, 98.

Flushing, English expedition (1809), 151, 152, 153; the English will be driven out by sickness, 159; preparation of the fortress (Dec. 1813), 325.

Fontainebleau, Seine et Marne: proposal to establish the Pope there (August 1809), 145; the Pope's residence there in 1813; police measures, 276, 277; the Pope and the Cardinals removed from Fontainebleau and conveyed to Italy and Southern France (Jan. 1814), 328, 329; letters dated thence, 24, 49, 50-57, 164, 203-215, 267-269, 322.

Fontenay-le-Comte, Vendée, 230.

Foreign Affairs: note on their condition (1806), 31-35; memorandum on continental affairs (Sept. 1807), 45-47; circular to explain the Austrian Alliance and the Emperor's marriage with Marie Louise, 173, 174; circular to be sent to all French Ministers abroad to guide their language as to the battle of Vittoria (July 1813), 302; a report to be printed showing forth the intercourse of the Imperial Government with England, Switzerland, and Naples (27th April 1815), 336. See England, Austria, Spain, Holland, Naples, Prussia, Russia, Sweden, and Caulaincourt, Champagny, Maret, and Talleyrand.

—— —— Ministry of, building of the Ministerial Offices, etc., 237.

Forfait, Minister of the Navy, letter to him, 18.

Fouache, former Sub-Prefect, 338.

Fouché, Comte Duc d'Otrante: letters to him, 23, 25, 26, 27, 29, 30, 31, 35, 39, 40, 41, 43, 44, 48, 49, 50, 57, 68, 72, 78, 87, 89, 90, 92, 93, 100, 108, 109, 111, 112, 116, 120, 121, 122, 123, 127, 128, 131, 132, 133, 134, 135, 139, 140, 143, 144, 145, 146, 147, 150, 154, 155, 157, 158, 159, 162, 164, 167, 168, 169, 172, 175, 177, 178, 183, 189, 335, 337, 338, 339, 340, 343, 345; receipts and expenses of his Ministry, 50-52; he advises Napoleon to divorce, 97; keeps watch on the Princes of Spain and their servants, 86, 87, 106, 107, 123; Napoleon desires he will send him a Chief of Police for Madrid, 110; his disagreement with the Prefect of Police and strange conduct, 93, 94, 97, 98; Napoleon consults him as to where he should cause the Pope to live, 145; desires him to remonstrate with Bernadotte as to his orders of the day to the Saxons and the National Guard and his intercourse with dangerous persons (12th Sept. 1809), 157; the seals put on his property, 187; his intrigues as to the correspondence with England, 188; sent into exile (July 1812), 189, 190; the Emperor aware of his intrigues, 196; no notice to be taken of him, 198; he is allowed to return to his country house, 246; his advice to the Emperor as to the Austrian paper currency, 313.

Foy, Café de, Paris, 116.

Franche-Comté, 27.

François, refractory priest, 230.

Frankfort on the Main, 310.

Frederick VI., King of Denmark, referred to, 76.

—— of Wurtenburg, letters to him, 124, 308.

—— Augustus, King of Saxony, referred to, 99, 280.

—— William III., King of Prussia, 47, 48.

Frémont, priest, 48.

Frenchmen in foreign services forbidden to enter France or the precincts of the Empire, 183, 184.

Fressinet, General, 335.

Friant, General Count, letter to him, 317.

Friedland, battle of, 256.

Frotté, Mons. de, Chouan leader, 1, 3, 5.

Fulda, Hesse, 310.

Fürstenberg, family of, 117, 125.

Fürstenstein, property of, 63, 64. See Lecamus.

GAETA, Italy, 120.

Galbois, Adjutant-General, 316.

Galicia, 71, 85.

—— Austrian, 167.

Galitzin, Prince, 166.

Gallet, dentist, 107.

—— pilot in the English service, steps taken against his wife and children, 249.

Game licences, 50.

Gaming-tables, 45, 50, 51.

Ganteaume, Vice-Admiral: letter to him, 271; prizes captured by him in the Mediterranean, 9; reason he is not appointed Councillor of State, 18; Corfu expedition, his instructions to Cosmao, 73-75; his salary advanced and gratuity given him, 271.

Gardanne, General, summoned to the West by General Brune, 2; his mission to Persia, 153, 154; his mistakes in Portugal, recalled to France, 222.

Gariot, Mons., 93.

Garnier, General, 149.

Gaudin, Count and Duc de Gaëte: letters to him, 56, 132, 254, 271, 336.

Gautier, refractory priest, 230.

Gazette d'Amsterdam to be called *Courier d'Amsterdam* (1810), 195.

Gazette de Bayreuth, 99.

Gazette de France, 25, 135, 139, 146, 172, 212, 252.

Gazette de Madrid, 80, 83, 84.

Gendarmerie employed to watch the Spanish Princes at Valençay, 86, 87; Inspector-General, 52; sent to the Vendée in 1815, 342.

Geneva, Switzerland: the Prefect charged to do all in his power to make it thoroughly French, 227; referred to, 28.

Genoa, Italy: the Archbishop authorised to proceed to Savona, 154; licensed trading ships to unload return cargo there, 194; letters dated thence, 25.

Genoese Riviera, 29.

Gentili, Canon of Florence, 220.

Gentz, author, 92.

Georges Cadoudal. His conspiracy, 27, 45.

—— Mlle, actress, gratuity allotted her, 314.

Geslin, Mons. de, 45.

Ghent: displeasure of the Emperor with the Bishop's management of his diocese, bad spirit amongst the clergy (1809), 143; the director of a seminary arrested, part of the seminarists sent to the army, the rest scattered among the French seminaries, 311; proclamations (Louis XVIII.), 343.

—— Bishop of, Monsignor de Broglie: the Emperor displeased with him, 143; struck off the list of Imperial Almoners,

239; his resignation to be insisted on, and he himself sent sixty leagues from Paris, 257; interned in the diocese of Dijon, 260.

Gibot, Mesdemoiselles, 29.

Gilly, General, 325, 335.

Girard, General, aide-de-camp to the King of Westphalia, 96.

—— refractory priest, 230.

Gironde, Department of the: refractory conscripts, 26.

Givet, Ardennes, 343.

Glogau, Germany, 102.

Gobert, General, 106.

Goes, Dean of the Chapter of Tournay, 315.

Gohier, Mons., 195.

Gonzaga, Ferdinand of, Duke of Mantua, 19.

Gorée, isle of, 149.

Gothenburg, Sweden, 238, 239.

Gottorp. *See* Sweden, Gustavus IV.

Gouvion, St. Cyr, Marshal: letter to him, 316; in Spain, 13; in charge of an expedition in Portugal, 13, 15; ordered to put down disturbances in the 32nd Military Division (Jan. 1813), 268; to take up a defensive position near Bautzen (1st Sept. 1813), 316; removed from the list of Marshals, given a retiring pension, 333.

Gravina, Spanish Admiral, 12, 18.

Grobert, War Commissary, his peculations in Italy, 29.

Grodno, 262, 263.

Gros-Noyer, the, in the Vendée, 230.

Grouchy, Marshal, is desired to make the Duc d'Angoulême sign a promise to give up the crown jewels and not bear arms against France (April 1815), 334, 335; information to be sent him as regards the allied armies (May 1815), 337; the Emperor's hope he will have saved 50,000 men at Waterloo (19th June 1815), 348.

Guard, Imperial, peculation in a Guard regiment, 248, 249; the young Guard sent to the Vendée (May 1815), mode of recruiting it, 343, 344; the navy ordered to furnish men for the artillery of the Guard, 346, 347.

—— Paris, mounted, 159.

—— National, 146, 152, 159, 325.

Guidons for the battalions, 256.

Guillaume, General, 93.

Güntersberg in Prussia, 38.

HAM, castle of, 120.

Hamburg: money made by Bernadotte while there, 157; the King of Westphalia's financial negotiations, 163; the Emperor's plan to unite Hamburg with Holland, 182; licences for the port, 192, 193; Bourrienne's peculations, 292; severe measures to be taken in consequence of the revolt (May 1813), Senators to be arrested, list of absentees made, property confiscated, the most guilty persons shot, a fine of 50,000,000 levied, the town disarmed, sailors and bad characters seized by press-gangs, and possession taken of all warehouses and stores useful to the navy, 284, 285, 288, 289, 290, 304-306; the Emperor refuses to receive a deputation, the fine to be paid in full, but an amnesty may be granted, 304-306; the fortress to be armed and a citadel constructed (May 1813), 285; referred to, 58.

Hanau, Bavaria, 310.

Hanover, decree as to colonial merchandise, 211; taxes levied on property too heavy, 259, 260.

Hauterive, Mons. de, 185.

Havre, old soldiers recalled to service collect there (May 1815), 338.

Haye-St.-Hilaire, Mons. de la, 49, 57.

Hédouville, General, letter to, 4; instructions for the pacification of Western France, 4-6.

—— Mons., brother to the above, 150.

Henri, refractory priest, 230.

Henry, General, sent to command the flying columns in the Sarthe and the Mayenne (Jan. 1813), 267; sent to Bruges to keep the country in order and send back deserters and refractory conscripts to the ranks (Dec. 1813), 324.

—— Prussian Chargé d'Affaires at Madrid, 75.

—— Chouan leader, 5.

Hérault, Department of the, refractory conscripts, 26.

Herbiers, Les, in the Vendée, 230.

Hercules, the ship, 212.

—— the Columns of, 100.

Herman, Secretary of Embassy, 53.

Hersfeld, Hesse, 36.

Hesse, crimes committed there, repressive measures, 36-38.

—— Cassel, the Elector of, 37.

Hogendorp, General, 245.

Hohenlohe, family of, 124, 125.

Holland: Marmont to go there to negotiate a loan (Year VIII.), 6; Dutch troops with the Grande Armée, 124, 135, 139, 159, 162; navy, armament, flotilla, 159-162; re-establishment of the nobility, 39, 40; Dutch troops in Spain, 159; trade kept up with England in spite of the Emperor's orders, 160; Dutch sailors insult the French flag, 160; the English landing (1809), 146, 149, 152, 153, 159, 161; the French troops enter Breda and Bergen-op-Zoom (Jan. 1810), 170; King Louis's unpleasant position, his only way of getting out of it to conform to French policy (20th May 1810), 180-183; the French Ambassador recalled and the Dutch Ambassador in Paris sent away (May 1810), 184; instructions as to the conduct of Serurier at Amsterdam (June 1810), 186; funds due to French privateers kept back by the Dutch, 187; Prince Lebrun sent as the Emperor's Lieutenant-General, preliminary measures prescribed for him (17th July 1810), 194, 195, 197, 198; deputations from the Legislative Body and Councils of State summoned to Paris, 195; the titles and endowments granted by the King suppressed, 198; decree to seize all colonial merchandise in Holland (Sept. 1810), 202; the Emperor's action as regards Holland guided by the general welfare of the Empire, 203; Custom-house riot in Amsterdam, French patriots insulted at Utrecht, riots at Amsterdam and Aurich (1811), 203, 204, 229, 233, 234, 235; communication with England even through the police absolutely forbidden, 238; Frenchmen employed in Holland, and their families, forbidden to cause alarm by leaving the country (March 1813), 273; fortresses to be armed and measures taken to compensate for the evacuation of Willemstadt (Dec. 1813), 324, 325.

Holstein: remonstrance to be made to the Danish Government about the colonial merchandise received in Holstein, 239; the Emperor desires the Hamburg refugees may be sent away, 289.

Hortense de Beauharnais, Queen of Holland: proposed divorce, 167; the property of St. Leu to be made over to her, 226; the management of her household to be reformed, 256; money owed her by the Exchequer (1815), 342.

Hullin, General Count, letter to, 240.

Hulot, Adjutant-General, to be watched and arrested, 315.

—— Mme, 24.

Huscart, Captain, 37.

Hyères, 269.

ILE NAPOLÉON, 131.

Ille et Vilaine, Department of, 45.

Illyria. *See* Ragusa.

Imperial family : family council, 167.

Infantado, Duke del, 85, 107.

Innocent X., Pope, 19.

Intrigante, l', play, the performances to be put a stop to, 274, 275.

Irun, Spain, 84.

Istria, Duke of. *See* Bessières.

Italy, Kingdom of: the Emperor's arrangements about Italian trade (July 1810), 193, 194; refractory Italian priests interned at Bologna and Parma, 198, 199.

JACQUEMONT, Senator, 98.

Jena, battle of, 154, 256.

Jerome Bonaparte, King of Westphalia : letters to him, 61, 62, 63, 67, 69, 70, 96, 97, 117, 120, 124, 133, 135, 206, 259, 262, 265, 288; he borrows from the sinking fund, 56, 96, 120; demands an oath of fidelity from the Frenchmen in his service, 61, 62, 70, 71; his dispute with General Lagrange, 62; the Emperor's displeasure at his bestowing the estate of Fürstenstein on Mons. Lecamus, 63; appointment of a diplomatic agent at Vienna, 67, 68, 69, 70; his circular placing French officers under Westphalian officers, 91 ; the Emperor's complaints of Jerome's Orders of the Day to his army, his way of making war, and military blunders, 133, 134, 135-139; advice as to his pecuniary arrangements and personal occupations, 96, 97; his civil list, 121; his financial negotiations with Hamburg, 163; his bad government, love of display, and foolish expenditure, 61, 62, 70, 71, 117, 118, 120, 121, 124; his debts, 56, 63, 96, 120; objectionable persons about him, 62, 97; he gives his picture to Bourrienne, 162, 163; sits on the Imperial family council,

167 ; foolishly raises a cuirassier regiment, the Emperor gives him advice as to his army and financial arrangements, 214, 215, 259, 260 ; complains that he sends him no news of Bagration (4th July 1812), 263 ; tells him he may go to Westphalia to reorganise his army (Dec. 1812), 265 ; his mistake in not having a French bodyguard, 281, 282 ; he is not to assert, when he modifies the Emperor's orders, that he does so by the Emperor's authority, 288, 289 ; his reception of the former King of Sweden at Cassel described as ridiculous (July 1813), 302 ; his purchase of Stains to be declared void, because he had no right to make it without the Emperor's consent, 319, 320 ; the works there to be stopped, and he to remain quietly at Compiègne (Jan. 1814), 327 ; he is ordered to dismiss his Westphalian household, and have none but Frenchmen about him, sent to take command at Lyons, instructions as to his staff, and the simple manner in which he is to live (Feb. 1814), 329, 330 ; ordered to proceed to Brittany or Berry (April 1814), 332 ; money owed him by the Exchequer (1815), 342.

Jews, 71.

Jollivet, Mons., 61.

Joseph Bonaparte, King of Naples, King of Spain : letters to him, 59, 73, 74, 100, 103, 104, 293, 326, 329, 332, 333, 347 ; the Emperor informs him of his intentions about Lucien, 59-61 ; his orders to Cosmao not sufficiently explicit, 73, 74, 75 ; his position as a King painful, but as a General brilliant, 101 ; recognised King of Spain by Russia, 101 ; unnecessary salaries paid by him to be suppressed, 258, 259 ; to give over the chief command to the Duke of Dalmatia (July 1813), 293 ; to remain at Pampeluna, St. Sebastian, or Bayonne, or retire to Morfontaine and remain there privately, 293, 294, 297, 301, 306-308 ; the Emperor attributes the Spanish catastrophe to him, 299, 300 ; he is to be arrested if he goes to Paris or St. Cloud, 307 ; the officers about his person to be sent to the army, 313 ; the Emperor informs him of his intentions as to the King of Wesphalia, 329, 330 ; the Emperor gives orders for the departure of the various members of the Imperial Family (April 1814), 332; the Master of the Horse to provide Joseph with horses and carriages, he is to choose a residence, but will only receive half his income for 1815 (March 1815), 333; money owed him by the Exchequer, 342; the Emperor tells him of his last hopes and plans for final resistance, 347, 348.

Josephine Beauharnais, Empress of the French: her desire to buy precious stones, 21; at Plombières, 24; her enthusiastic reception at Bayonne, 84; prints of her, with an unsuitable inscription, published after her divorce, 178; Napoleon consents to what she proposes doing as to M. Tascher's marriage, 179, 180; she intends to have building, etc., done at Navarre, 180; proposes to go to the baths of Aix-la-Chapelle (1810), the Emperor's views on the subject, 180; he desires her household may be carefully managed, and will allow no outstanding debts, 255, 266; money owed her by the Exchequer (1815), 342; referred to, 59.

Jouannet, Mme, 247.

Jouberthon, Mme: the Emperor refuses to acknowledge her as Lucien's wife, and desires to force them to separate, 60.

Jourdan, Marshal: the Duke of Dalmatia to send him back to Bayonne (July 1813), 296; he is suspended from duty and sent to his country house, 299, 300; to be allowed to retire, and his aide-de-camps scattered, 313.

Journal des Débats, or *Journal de l'Empire*, 41, 43, 44, 59, 72, 78, 79, 122, 135, 150, 151, 215, 216, 230, 313.

Journal des Défenseurs de la Patrie, 9.

Journal de France, 90.

Journal de Francfort, 311.

Journal de Leipsic, 291.

Journal de Paris, 79, 146.

Joux, fort of, 89.

Judicial proceedings: sentence on Émigrés accused of bearing arms against France, 134; inquiry into dishonest proceedings connected with the conscription in the Department of the Lot (1811), 247.

Julie Clary, Princess Joseph Bonaparte, Queen of Naples, Queen of Spain: let-

ter to her, 258, 259; she is ordered to proceed to Marseilles (April 1814), 332.

Junot, General, Duc d'Abrantès: letters to him, 64, 65, 71; instructions as to his reaching Lisbon without striking a blow, and seizing the Portuguese squadron, 53-55; measures to be taken to put down insurrection in Lisbon, 64; organisation of the French rule in Portugal, financial, military, and police measures, 65-67; he is defeated by Kienmayer (July 1809), 133, 134; his retreat necessitated by Jerome's manœuvres, 136; he commands the Portuguese army (October 1810); the rumours spread about him are false, 209; order to send him away from the army (Jan. 1813), 270; he loses his reason, 297, 298, 312; his daughters sent to Ecouen, 312.

—— Madame, Duchess d'Abrantès, ordered to retire into the country, 312.

Justice, Ministry of, weeding out the officials connected with, 337.

KAAS, Mons. de, Danish Minister, 289.

Kellermann, Marshal, Duc de Valmy: letter to him, 274; ordered to proceed to Mayence, 124.

—— General, son of the above: peculation and abuses in his government in Spain, 200, 201; the Emperor pardons him, and promises him employment for his father's sake, and that of his own conduct at Marengo (March 1813), 274, 278.

Kienmayer, Austrian General, 133, 134.

Knobelsdorf, Mons. de, 34.

Koch, Monsieur, 38.

Königsberg, Prussia, smuggling there, 235.

Koppe, assessor, 103.

Kowno, Poland, 265.

Kroneburg, Denmark, 45.

Kuhn, American consul at Genoa, 48.

LABORDE, General, 135.

Laborie, conspirator, 211.

Lacépède, Comte, Grand Chancellor of the Legion of Honour, referred to, 76.

Lacroix, Pamphile, General, 278.

Lacuée, General, Comte de Cessac: letters to him, 6.

Lafitte, Colonel, 131, 133, 135.

Laforest, Comte: his mission to Spain (1808), 84; should interfere more in the government of that country (18th Feb. 1810), 172; the Spanish crown jewels stolen and taken to Naples, 246; he is sent to Valençay, to negotiate with the Spanish Princes (Nov. 1813), 322, 323.

Lagarde, Monsieur, 341.

Lagorse, Adjutant of the Palace of Fontainebleau, 276, 277; he is ordered to conduct the Pope to Savona (Jan. 1814), 328.

Lagrange, General: letter to him, 36; repressive measures to be carried out by him in Hesse (1807), 36-38; King Jerome reprimanded for his behaviour to him, 62.

Lahaye, ex-deputy, 49.

Lahorie, General, concerned in the Georges Cadoudal conspiracy, 26.

Lalande, the brothers, 45.

Lamalgue, Fort, near Marseilles, 341.

Lamarque, General, sent to command a flying column in the Vendée (1815), 344.

Lamartinière, Senator, 49.

Langeron, Mons. de, a Russian general, 272.

Langlade, Abbé, 112.

Lannes, Marshal, Duc de Montebello, referred to, 64.

Lannes, Mme, Duchess de Montebello, 332.

Laon, Aisne, 348.

Laplace, Comte, letter to him, 204.

Laroche, General, 131.

Latour, doctor to King Louis: Napoleon desires he will join the King, 195.

Lauriston, General, A.D.C. to the First Consul, and to the Emperor: he is to put down the disturbances in the 32nd Military Division (Jan. 1813, 268.

Lavallette, Comte, Councillor of State, Director-General of the Postal Service: letters to him, 43, 55, 57, 75, 92, 109, 216, 261. See Postal Matters.

Lebrun, Prince, Duc de Plaisance, Grand Treasurer of the Empire: letters to him, 194, 197, 202, 203, 229, 231, 233, 234, 235, 237, 238, 273; weakness shown by him in Holland, 229, 234, 235; his useless and harmful proclamations, 231; his daughters and nieces ordered to return to Amsterdam, 273.

Lecamus, Comte de Fürstenstein, 63, 64.

Leclerc, General, 13.

Lecourbe, General, 26, 27.

Ledoulx, consul at Bucharest, 166.

Lefebvre, General, Marshal, Duc de Dantzick: letters to him, 2, 3, 139, 142; instructions for the war in Western France (Year VIII.), 2; he is given command of the 14th Division, 3; is to pacify the Sarthe by means of flying columns, 3, 4; suppression of the Tyrolese rebellion, 139, 140, 142.

Leghorn, Tuscany, 9, 11, 13.

—— Count and Countess of. See Parma and Maria Louise, Queen of Etruria.

Legion of Honour, Order of the, 76; orphanages to be founded, 190, 191.

Lemarois, General: letter to him, 344; referred to, 311.

Lemosy, Mons., 233.

Leroy, Naval Prefect in Egypt, 8.

Lestrange, Mons., 242.

Letort, Major, 38.

Lévis, M. de, aide-de-camp to the Duc de Berry, 337.

Lhermite, Rear-Admiral, 291.

Licences, system of, 192-194; licences granted by the King of Holland, 186, 187; abuses arising out of those issued by the police, 250.

Liébert, General: his matter with the consul of Stettin, 214; referred to, 238.

Liebstadt, Saxony, letter dated thence, 38.

Liechtenstein, family of, 125.

Lieutenant-Generals, 334.

Lille, Nord: the National Guard of that town to be disarmed, 346; letters dated thence, 183, 184, 185.

—— Comte, otherwise Louis XVIII., 48, 90, 339. See Louis XVIII.

Lillo, Holland, 165.

Lintz, Austria, 126.

Lippe, family of, 119.

Lisbon, necessity for the French troops to enter the city under the guise of friendship; instructions to Junot, and to the French Ambassador at Madrid, 53-55; approach of the French troops, 61; revolt of the populace (1808), 64, 65; the town disarmed, a citadel and batteries erected to overawe the town, 69; referred to, 13, 14.

Loan negotiated by Marmont at Amsterdam, 6.

Loire, Department of the : refractory conscripts, 25.

—— Department of the Haute: refractory conscripts, 25.

Loison, General, 36 ; mixed up in Argenton's business, 135 ; leaves his post without permission, 275 ; inquiry to be made as to his reasons, 277, 278 ; the Emperor causes him to be informed of his displeasure, and his hope he will behave better in future, 278.

Lombez, Gers, 43.

Longueil, Mons., 343.

Loo, castle of, 198.

Lorient, Morbihan, referred to, 11.

Lorraine, Charles IV., Duc de, 20.

—— François, Duc de, 20.

—— Leopold, Duc de, 20.

Lot, Department of the : refractory conscripts, 25 ; dishonest behaviour connected with the conscription, 247.

Louis XVI., seizure of the printing blocks of his will, 213.

—— XVIII., reasons which release the army from its oath to him (June 1815), 347. See Lille, Comte de.

—— Bonaparte, King of Holland : letters to him, 180, 184, 325 ; his re-establishment of the orders of nobility in Holland, Napoleon's reproaches, 39, 40 ; death of his eldest son, he writes him from Paris by M. Decazes, 155 ; complaints of his speeches, his army, his bad government, etc., 159-162 ; he removes his headquarters to Bergen-op-Zoom, 148 ; he claims a right, as Constable of the Empire, to command the French troops in Holland, 148, 149 ; proposed divorce from Queen Hortense, 167 ; Holland in an unpleasant predicament ; the only way to get out of it, that the King should change his policy and assimilate it to the Emperor, who reproaches him bitterly (20th May 1810), 180-183 ; rupture of diplomatic intercourse between France and Holland, 184 ; King Louis grants trading licences ; he keeps back money due to French privateers, 186, 187 ; his private papers removed to Paris, 194, 195, 197, 198 ; the Emperor sends him his doctor, 195 ; Mons. Bourgoing not to have any dealings with him, 199 ; his correspondence with the Imperial family

intercepted, 261 ; the Emperor willing to forget and forgive, if he returns to France as a French prince, to serve the Throne ; otherwise he is to be arrested and taken to Compiègne ; the Emperor instructs Madame Mère and Cambacérès on the subject (Nov. 1813), 319-321 ; he arrives in Paris without the Emperor's leave (Jan. 1814) ; to be well received if he comes in a proper frame of mind ; if not, to be sent forty leagues from Paris, 325, 326 ; he is ordered to retire to Montpellier (April 1814), 333 ; money owed him by the Exchequer, 342.

Loverdo de, General, 335.

Lübeck, licences granted to that port, 193 ; fine of fifty millions levied on Hamburg and Lübeck (May 1813), 284.

Lucchesini, Mons. de, 31.

Lucien Bonaparte : letters to him when Ambassador at Madrid, 7, 8, 9, 10, 11, 12, 13, 14, 15, 16 ; object of his mission to Spain, and details concerning it, 7-17 ; complaints of the treaty he has concluded with Portugal, 13-16 ; Napoleon's displeasure at his connection with Madame Jouberthon, 59-61 ; he offers to care for him and his children if he will part from that lady, 59-61 ; his bad behaviour regarding the French in Rome, 73 ; the Emperor writes to the Chancellor of the Senate to have his name struck off the list, and explains his reasons for so doing (Sept. 1810), 204, 205 ; General Miollis ordered to have him watched, and arrested if he attempts to leave Italy, 196 ; he escapes by sea ; the Emperor's displeasure, 211, 212 ; all works of art, etc., belonging to him in Italy, laid under sequestration, 228.

Lugo, Galicia, 114.

Luneburg, Hanover, 285.

Lunéville, treaty of, 17.

Lutzen, battle of : Te Deum to be ordered by the Bishops, 283.

Luynes, estate of, 90.

Lycées, youths sent there by force, 167, 169.

Lyons, Rhône : the Pères de la Foi in the Diocese to be suppressed, 58 ; the Emperor sends King Jérome to command there (Feb. 1814), 330 ; referred to, 122.

MACDONALD, General, Marshal, Duc de Tarente : moves against Tarragona, 209 ; driven back on Görlitz (Aug. 1813), 316.

Mache, Mlle, 338.

Madame Mère : letter to the King of Westphalia's appanage made over to her after 1st January 1808, 56 ; probability that Lucien's daughter will be placed in her care, 59 ; the Emperor begs her to use her influence with King Louis, to induce him to leave France, if he has not come thither in a friendly spirit (Nov. 1813), 320, 321 ; she is advised to go to Nice (April 1814), 332 ; referred to, 319.

Madeira, Island of, 23.

Madrid : energetic steps to be taken by Murat, 79-81 ; disturbances, 87 ; the city furnishes the enemy with horses, 105 ; measures to be taken to keep the populace down, 114, 115 ; letters dated thence, 109, 110, 111.

Magdeburg, Saxony: the taxes laid on the proprietors too heavy, 259 ; the fortress to be prepared for war (Dec. 1812), 265 ; orders to send the Ghent and Tournay Seminarists thither, 311 ; letter dated thence, 301 ; referred to, 309.

Maghella, Minister of Police at Naples, recalled to France on suspicion of treachery, 262 ; referred to, 261.

Maignien, actor, gratuity allotted him, 314.

Malaga, Spain, 10.

Malchus, Mons., answer to be sent him, on Westphalian affairs, 210.

Malet, General, mixed up in a conspiracy ? (1808), 98.

Malmaison, Palace : letter dated thence, 22 ; referred to, 180.

Malouet, Mons., 338.

Malta : the English mean to keep the island, 15 ; Italian ships licensed to trade there, 193, 194 ; referred to, 13, 212.

Mancini, Canon of Florence, 219.

Mans, Le, 4.

Mantua, 59.

Mareschalchi, Comte, ordered to give Signor Melzi details of the Georges conspiracy, 22.

Marescot, General, his arrest ; list of questions he is to answer, 105, 106.

Maret, Mons. Duc de Bassano : letters to him, 232, 236, 237, 241, 242, 244, 246, 257, 261, 262, 263, 264, 286, 287, 289, 301, 302, 322, 323 ; the Minister of Police to send him the reports from Vienna (Jan. 1813), 269 ; referred to, 155.

Maret, Comte, Councillor of State, 254.

Marie Louise of Austria, Empress-Queen: letter to her, 283 ; the Emperor's reason for asking her hand ; the ceremony to be observed in the Courts she passes through, 173, 174 ; her economy, 255 ; she is only to sign documents in the ordinary course of business, while acting as Regent, 279, 280 ; the Emperor summons her to Mayence, her journey and the suite to attend on her (July 1813), 303, 304 ; the Emperor's confidence in her, 331.

—— —— Queen of Spain, 83, 95, 119.

—— —— —— of Etruria : report of her marriage with Prince Eugene, 24 ; she is at Milan, 61 ; her share in the division of Portugal, 71 ; Murat to send her to Bayonne, 84 ; she is to follow the King of Spain to Nice, or proceed to Colorno in Parma, 95 ; she is to be sent to one of the towns on the Genoese coast, 122, 123 ; her behaviour to the Emperor, 232, 241 ; plan to put her in a convent and part her from her son, 235, 236 ; the Emperor orders her to be placed in a convent at Rome, and her son sent to King Charles, 241.

Marmont, General, Marshal, Duc de Raguse : goes to Amsterdam to negotiate a loan (Year VIII.), 6 ; ordered to break down the enemy's bridge at Mühlberg (4th Oct. 1813), 317 ; struck off the list of Marshals (March 1815), 333.

Mars, Mlle, gratuity allotted her, 314.

Marseilles, Bouches-du-Rhone : licensed trading vessels to unload return cargoes there, 194 ; Queen Julie of Spain to retire there, 332 ; the town put in a state of siege ; the National Guard disarmed, and the Royalist leaders imprisoned in Fort Lamalgue (May 1815), 341 ; good effect of these measures, 345.

Masséna, General, Marshal, Prince d'Essling, Duc de Rivoli : in command of the army in Portugal (Oct. 1810), 209 ;

his misconduct, recalled to Paris (April 1815), 335.

Masserano, Prince of, 103.

Materban, refractory priest, 230.

Maury, Cardinal, must be acknowledged as Archbishop of Paris, 215.

Mayence : troops of the Grande Armée recalled thither, to proceed to Spain, 102 ; the Empress to meet the Emperor there (July 1813), 303 ; letters dated thence, 279, 280, 281, 308, 309, 310, 318, 319, 320, 321.

Mayenne : Department of the, disturbances there (Year VIII.), 1, 2 ; flying columns to pursue the robbers infesting the woods (Jan. 1813), 266, 267.

Mazzaredo, Mons., 8.

Mecklenburgh-Schwerin, Grand-Duchy of : complaints of the public press there, 257 ; General Vandamme to take possession of the territory and seize the persons of the Grand-Ducal family (May 1813), 284, 285.

Medina-di-Rio-Seco, battle of, 101.

Meerfeldt, Mons de, Austrian Ambassador at St. Petersburg, 67.

—— Abbé de, 67, 68.

Melzi, Vice-President of the Italian republic, 22.

Ménéval, Mons. de, 109, 332.

Menou, General : letters to him, 108 ; in Egypt, 8, 9 ; to put down disturbances in Tuscany, 109.

Mentone, 95, 123.

Merchandise, British and Colonial, seized, confiscated, sold, or heavily taxed, 53, 56, 57, 105, 202, 213, 238, 239.

Mercy-Argenteau, Mons. de, French Minister to the Bavarian Court, 281.

Merle, General, 335.

Merlin, General, 103.

Mescritz, Hesse, 38.

Mesle, General, 2.

Metternich, Count, Austrian Ambassador in Paris : his couriers stopped, 121 ; news to be communicated to him by Champagny (Aug. 1809), 152 ; present to him on the Emperor's marriage, 176 ; he declares the Austro-French Alliance unbroken (June 1813), 287 ; Caulaincourt's negotiations with him (January 1814), 328.

—— family of, 125.

Metz, mutiny amongst the cadets at the School of Artillery, 85.

Meudon, Seine-et-Oise : the parish priest

sent forty leagues away (May 1815), 340.

Mézeray, Mlle, actress, gratuity allotted her, 314.

Michelot, actor, gratuity allotted him, 314.

Michot, actor, gratuity allotted him, 314.

Milan, Lombardy, letters dated thence, 23, 59.

Minho, province of, 13.

Ministers : their authority is only subject to the Emperor's, 150 ; powers given them in the Emperor's absence, 151.

Minsk, Russia, 264.

Miollis, General : ordered to arrest Cardinal Pacca and the Pope's adherents, 132 ; not to allow vessels to sail from Civita Vecchia without special leave, 196 ; to watch Lucien Bonaparte, and arrest him if he attempts to leave Italy, 196 ; Lucien's escape, 211, 212 ; refractory priests to be sent to Corsica, 218.

Miot, Councillor of State, 51.

Modlin, Poland, 265.

Moiraghi, in the Pope's service, 225.

Moldavia : the Russians march into the country (1806), 36 ; Napoleon has settled that question, 166.

Molitor, General, 229.

Mollerus, Mons., 181.

Mollien, Comte, Minister of the Exchequer : letters to him, 247, 255, 342.

Monaco, Prince of, 95.

Moncabrié, Captain in the imperial navy, 338.

Moncey, General, Marshal, Duc de Conegliano : serves in Spain, 72 ; his retreat on Ocaña, 100 ; his position in Tudela, 104 ; serves in Holland, 149, 152 ; as Senior Marshal, serves on the Imperial family council, 167.

Mondego, river, 15.

Monge, Comte de Peluse, 329.

Moniteur, the : news not to be inserted till it has been approved by the Regency, 286 ; referred to, 9, 71.

Monnet, General, 152, 155.

Monnier, General, 335.

Mons, Belgium, 167.

Montalivet, Comte de : letters to him, 192, 208, 227, 239, 252, 259.

Montauban, Tarn-et-Garonne : measures to be taken to keep ill-disposed persons in order (June 1815), 346.

Montebello, Duc de. See Lannes.

Monteleone, Duke of, 110.

Montenegro, 240.

Montenotte, Prefect of, Mons. de Chabrol: he is to warn the Pope not to interfere in anything, 226; his confidential report on the members of the Pope's household at Savona, 225.

Montesquiou, Comtesse de, governess to the King of Rome: letters to her, 316, 318, 331.

Mont-Genèvre, Trappists of, 242.

Montmarie, General, 339.

Montmorency, Mathieu de, 339.

Montpellier, Hérault, 332.

Morals, 29, 30.

Morand, General, 196.

Morbihan, Department of the, 45.

Moreau, General: his share in the Georges conspiracy, 22; his party, 26; his arrival at Berlin, 315.

Morelli, the Pope's valet-de-chambre, 225.

Morfontaine, 293, 295, 296, 301, 306, 307.

Morin, Gendarmerie officer, 335.

Morio, Colonel, General, in the King of Westphalia's service: the Emperor's poor opinion of him, 91, 117; he is sent to France, 120.

Morlaix, Côtes-du-Nord, the only port whence communication with England is permissible, 227, 244.

Morlot, General, 101.

Mort d' Abel, La, opera, 171.

Mortemart, Mons. de, the Emperor's orderly officer, 178, 245.

Mortier, Marshal, Duc de Treviso: the strength of his corps (Oct. 1809), 163; in command of the army in Andalusia (Oct. 1810), 209.

Moscow, letter dated thence, 263.

Moulin, refractory priest, 230.

Mounier, Mons., the Emperor's private secretary, 185.

Moustier, Mons. de, French Minister to Baden: directions for his behaviour to the ex-Queen of Sweden, 244.

Mozzi or Muzzi, Canon of Florence, 220.

Muhlberg, Saxony, 318.

Munich, Bavaria: letter dated thence, 164.

Muraire, Comte, 155.

Murat, Joachim, Grand-Duke of Berg, King of Naples: letters to him, 71, 76, 79, 81, 83, 84, 88, 100, 107, 128, 212; he concludes an armistice with the Two Sicilies (Year IX.), 10; strong measures to be taken by him in Madrid (1808), 80; he has no right to commute military punishments, 80; complaints of his Order of the Day about the Burgos business, 80; he is to cause the Junta to publish a proclamation, 81, 82; his troops are not to be scattered, 83; blamed for hurrying his horses and property from Berg to Naples, 100; for recalling exiles and returning them their property, 107; ordered to confiscate property held in his kingdom by the Spanish grandees, 107; excommunicated by the Pope, 128; he and his kingdom in debt to the Emperor, 168; his treaty with the Austrians (Jan. 1814), 328; orders to publish a report which will show forth the communications held between him and the Imperial Government (April 1815), 336; he defeats the Austrians at Cesena, 337.

Musset, Comte de, 24.

NAMUR, Monsignor Pisani de la Gaude, Bishop of, 146.

Nantes, Loire-Inférieure: licensed trading ships to unload cargo there, 193; troops not to be left, as the town can defend itself (May 1815), 343.

Naples, Kingdom of: Murat recalls the exiles and reinstates them in their property, 107; confiscation of the property of rebellious Spanish grandees, 107; the English expedition (1809), 146; the country in debt to the Emperor, 168; licensed Neapolitan ships allowed to trade, 194; duty on silk and cloth stuffs, 212; the Spanish crown jewels stolen and conveyed to Naples: inquiries to be made there, 246, 247; arrangement about French ships (Nov. 1811), 257; Maghella suspected of treason and recalled to France, 262; bills to be drawn on the King, in payment for muskets supplied him (March 1813), 272. *See* Murat.

Napoleon I., First Consul, Emperor: he ran no real risk from the Cadoudal conspiracy, 22; his measures as to Jerome Buonaparte and Miss Patterson (*see* Jerome); his quarrels with his brothers (*see* Jerome, Joseph, Louis, and Lucien); apocryphal proclamations, etc., 35; blood-stains on his bust at Bordeaux, 44; he receives the Spanish Princes at Bayonne: his mediation in the Spanish quarrel, 76, 77, 80-85; reports as to his divorce: Fouché's action in that matter, 88, 97; expects to reach the Pillars of Hercules, but not the limits of his power in Spain, 100; his opinion of the Spanish soldiers, 100; presents to be given on the occasion of his second marriage, 176; a Cardinal fails to attend the ceremony, 176; his fête-day to be kept by the army on 10th August 1813 on account of the close of the armistice: his orders as to the festivities, 309; money due to him from the Exchequer (1815), 342.

Nassau regiment, the, 129.

Naval matters: the Spanish fleet to join the French one, 10; purchase of Spanish warships, their crews, 10; Admiral Bruix ordered to leave Brest and chase the English fleet (Year IX.), 18; prizes captured from the English, 23, 24; vessels made over to the kingdom of Naples, 257; appointments of various senior officers, 291, 292; artillery companies to be raised, consisting of naval cadets and midshipmen (June 1815), 346, 347.

Navarre, 104.
—— Castle and estate, 179, 180.

Navy, Spanish: the Spanish squadron to join the French, 10, 12; sale of Spanish ships to France, 10; the First Consul requests Admiral Gravina may be ordered to join Admiral Bruix in his expedition from Brest to give chase to the English fleet, 18.

Necker, the House of, 40.

Negrete, family of, 103.

Neipperg, Count, 328.

Neufchâtel, Prince de. See Berthier.

Neumarkt, Saxony: letter dated thence, 286, 287.

Newspapers: objectionable articles, etc., 24, 43, 44, 87, 122, 135, 139, 140, 150, 151, 172, 173, 212, 215, 216, 230, 257, 313; guidance to be given them, 44, 68, 69, 78, 79, 90, 151, 175; articles to be inserted by Government, or by the police, 23, 24, 36, 41, 44, 72, 77, 78, 89, 112, 114, 207, 236, 308, 310, 311, 334, 335; arrest and imprisonment of editors, 139, 144, 291; the

Emperor requests he may have a recapitulatory statement of his press measures, 209, 210.

Ney, Marshal Duc d'Elchingen, Prince de la Moskowa: in command of the army in Portugal (October 1809), 209; stays behind the Emperor to blow up Smolensk (Nov. 1812), 264; at Weimar with his troops (April 1813), 281; marching on Berlin (May 1813), 284.

Nice, Alpes Maritimes: the Emperor advises his sister Pauline to winter there (Dec. 1807), 59; King Charles IV. of Spain desires to go there, 95; the Queen of Etruria sent there, 122, 123; Pauline Borghèse would have done better to go to Nice than to Hyères, 269; the Emperor wishes Madame to proceed there (April 1814), 332.

Niort, Deux-Sèvres, 119.

Noailles, Comte de, Chamberlain to the Emperor, 173.

Noblejas, Comte de, 110.

Noel, Mons., 195.

Nogent-le-Rotrou, or Nogent-le-Républicain, Eure-et-Loire, 2, 3, 340.

Nogent-sur-Seine, Aube: letters dated thence, 329, 330.

Noyon, Oise: the Vicar of that place preaches an objectionable sermon (March 1809), 120; police agents to be sent there (1815), 343.

Nuremberg, Bavaria, 131.

Ocaña, Spain, 100.

O'Farell, Mons., 77.

Officers: those in King Louis XVIII.'s household are only to be received back into the army with their former rank (May 1815), 338, 339.
—— half-pay, 145, 146.

Oldenburg, Prince and Princess of, 113.

Operas to be performed, subjects to be selected, 171.

Oppizoni, Cardinal, Archbishop of Bologna, absents himself from the Emperor's wedding-ceremony: steps taken against him, 176.

Oracle, L', newspaper, 144.

Orders, religious: heads of orders to be sent to France, 155, 158; expenditure for their support, 156.

Orléans, Louis Philippe, Duc d', 197.
—— Dowager-Duchesse d', 197.
—— family, 336.
—— Loiret, 3.

Orne, Department of the: stripped of troops, 2; General Chambarlhac to remain there, 2; Chouan mobs to be dispersed, 2.

Orphanages to be established in connection with the Legion of Honour, 190, 191.

Osmond, Monsignor d', Bishop of Nancy: appointed Archbishop of Florence; the chapter declines to recognise him, 219, 220.

Osnabrück: Napoleon had thought of uniting it to Holland, 182; referred to, 163.

Ossuna, Duchesse d', 110.

Ostend, Belgium: letter dated thence, 180.

Osterode, Poland: letters dated thence, 39.

Otrante, Duc d'. See Fouché.

Otranto, Italy, 74, 212.

Otto, Comte, French Minister in Bavaria: the manner in which he is to speak of the strength of France and Austria respectively (Jan. 1809), 114; spy system to be organised in Austria, 118; referred to, 124, 199.

Oudinot, Marshal Duc de Reggio: ordered to march into Holland and take command of the Dutch troops, 170; to watch events in Holland and Amsterdam, 185; to break up all mobs and punish them severely, 206; he is struck off the list of Marshals, but allowed a retiring pension (March 1815), 333.

Oultremont, Mons. and Mme d', 169.

Ouvrard, Julien: order to arrest him and put him in solitary confinement at Vincennes (June 1810), 185; his correspondence with England, 188; referred to, 341.

Pacca, Cardinal: to be arrested and taken to Fenestrelle, (1809), 128, 132, 140, 145, 147; referred to, 277.

Palafox, Marquis de: to be placed in solitary confinement at Vincennes, 120; the severity of his imprisonment to be increased, 127, 128.

Palais Royal, the, 333.

Palermo, Sicily, 197.

Palmanova, Venetia, 328.

Palmieri, the Pope's steward at Savona, 225.

Pamphlets and libels, 57, 75, 77.

Panfili, Camillo, Cardinal, 19.

Paris: all the garrison sent to Verneuil (Year VIII.), 1; dangerous rumours and talk to be put a stop to, 116; exaggerated alarm felt there during the campaign of 1809, 126; bad feeling and false reports spread by the English, 132, 133; the Paris Mounted Guard, 159; all Englishmen forbidden to reside there (June 1810), 186; letters dated thence, 1, 2, 3, 4, 5, 6, 7, 8, 9, 10, 11, 12, 13, 16, 17, 18, 19, 22, 28, 61, 62, 63, 64, 65, 67, 68, 69, 70, 71, 72, 73, 74, 115, 116, 117, 118, 119, 121, 122, 123, 165, 168, 169, 170, 171, 172, 173, 174, 175, 176, 202, 216, 217, 218, 219, 220, 221, 222, 224, 225, 226, 227, 228, 229, 230, 231, 245, 258, 259, 260, 261, 262, 265, 266, 269, 270, 271, 273, 274, 275, 276, 323, 324, 325, 326, 327, 328, 333, 334, 335, 336, 337, 338, 339, 340, 341, 342, 343, 344, 345, 346, 347.

—— Governor of: his office expenses, 52.

Parma, Ferdinand, Duke of, 11.

—— Louis, Prince of, Count of Leghorn, King of Etruria, 11, 17.

—— Italy: Madame d'Albany to live there, 128.

Partariew, Mons., 44.

Pas-de-Calais, Department of the: the National Guard sent thence to Flushing (Dec. 1813), 325.

Pasquier, Mons.: the documents from the Dutch Titles Office to be sent to him, 198; Napoleon's regard for him as Prefect of Police, 251.

Paul I., Emperor of Russia, 11.

Pauline Bonaparte, Princess Borghese, Duchesse de Guastalla: letters to her, 59, 90, 269; her journey to Provence (1807), 41; her health: the Emperor's advice concerning it, 59, 90; she sends a mysterious courier to Soissons, 258; her letter to King Louis to be intercepted, 261; bad health again, 269.

Peace, Manuel Godoz, Prince of: Napoleon desires his naval plan of campaign may be made known to him (Year IX.), 9; the First Consul requests he will put a body of Spanish troops under General St. Cyr's orders, 12; he would command the army if he were to join it (1807), 55; idea of making over one half of Portugal to him, 71;

the rebellion at Aranjuez, its consequences, 78; his wealth exaggerated, 78, 79; has an interview with Napoleon at Bayonne, 79, 84; is to live in Paris if he chooses, 95.

Pearl, Peregrina, Spanish jewels, 246, 247.

Pedicini, Cosimo, 225.

Pélet de la Lozère, Councillor of State, 93, 94.

Penitents, Confraternities of, 48, 49.

Penthièvre, Fort, 1.

Pères de la Foi, 58.

Perlet, Mons., 57, 58.

Perrier, priest, 57.

Persia : General Gardanne's mission, 153.

Petroncini, Monsignor Doria's servant, 225.

Peyron, General, 6.

Philippeville, Belgium : letter dated thence, 347.

Piacenza, Duke Charles of : letter to him, 324.

Piedmont, 159.

Pierlot, Comptroller to the Empress Joséphine, 255.

Pietro, Cardinal di : he is removed from Fontainebleau and sent into Burgundy (April 1813), 276.

Pillichadi, Mons., 78.

Pinto, Mons., 14, 16, 17.

Pisa, Tuscany, 73.

Pissolte, Vendée, 230.

Pius VII., Pope : letters to him, 19, 20; he re-establishes the Jesuits, 11; excommunicates Napoleon and his agents (1809), 128; the newspapers forbidden to allude to him, 135; the Emperor sees no objection to his being brought near Paris, and is inclined to settle him at Fontainebleau, 145; he is sent to Savona, arrangements and precautions there, his correspondence intercepted, his confessor sent to Fenestrelle, 147, 148, 154; regret expressed at his having been sent back from Grenoble to Savona, proposal to bring him near Paris, 156; sum paid for his maintenance by the Roman Consulta, 156, 157; his letter to Cardinal Caprara (Sept. 1809), 158; saving to be made on his household expenses to provide for possible journeys, 164; arrest of a priest who goes to see him at Savona, 164; his letters intercepted, 216; his civil list and household expenditure

reduced to punish his misconduct, 221; his servants and attendants removed, 219, 221, 223; his letter to the Florence Chapter concerning Monsignor Osmond's appointment as Archbishop (Jan. 1811), 219, 220; his letter to the Aix Chapter, 221, 222; he refuses to confer canonical institution on Bishops appointed by the Emperor, 222; he is to be forbidden direct communication with the churches of the Empire, 223; his papers seized, and to be sent to Paris, all means of writing to be forbidden him, 223, 224; his household not to be too much reduced, 224; report on the persons in his service, the Emperor's decision as to which are to be kept about him, 225; the Pope will go to Avignon, 268; nobody to be allowed to see him, nor be present at his mass at Fontainebleau, except the Bishops (April 1813), 276, 277; orders for his immediate removal from Fontainebleau to Savona (21st Jan. 1814), 328, 329.

Plauen, Saxony, 137.

Plombières, Vosges, 24, 180.

Police : the police should know no Ambassador, 48; émigrés, political prisoners, 35, 68; arrest and imprisonment of suspected persons, seizure of their papers, 26, 27, 30, 48, 49, 57, 58, 99, 144, 183, 184, 185, 190, 195, 196, 217, 218, 230, 241, 242, 337, 338, 339, 341; release of prisoners, 195, 196; persons sent to provincial towns and detained there, enforced residence in special places, families obliged to leave their own locality, 28, 39, 90, 143, 144, 167, 168, 169, 186, 196; persons expelled from France, 183, 184; police manipulation of public opinion in Paris, 116, 132, 133, 208, 209, 211; police measures as to books, printed matter, caricatures, songs, pamphlets, etc., 23, 57, 58, 123, 178, 205, 206, 213, 239; as to morals, 29, 30, 248; against General Lecourbe, 26, 27; against Mme de Staël, 27, 35, 39, 40, 92, 205, 206, 211, 227; against the Pope (see Pius VII.); as to religious matters (see Public Worship); as to Journalism (see Newspapers); as to Postal Matters (see Postal Matters); as to Plots, etc. (see Conspiracies and

Plots); as to the Spanish Princes (*see* Ferdinand VII. and Marie Louise, Queen of Etruria); complaints of the Paris police after Dubois' departure, 251; police agents sent into the Sarthe and the Mayenne to assist the flying columns (Jan. 1813), 267; surveillance of the Faubourg St. Germain, 272; of suspected persons, 338, 343.

Police Report, 97.
—— Council, 93, 94, 97, 98.
—— Minister of. *See* Fouché and Savary.
—— Ministry of, receipts and expenditure of, 50-52.
—— Prefect of. *See* Dubois.
—— Madrid. *See* Madrid.

Polignac, Mme de, 49.

Pomerania, 102, 235, 239.

Poniatowsky, Prince: the Emperor trusts he is in pursuit of Bagration: desires he will write twice a day to the Major-General (July 1812), 262, 263.

Pont-St.-Esprit, 328.

Ponte-Corvo, Principality of: the son of the King of Naples not to be invested till he can himself swear fidelity to the Emperor, 266.
—— Prince de. *See* Bernadotte.

Porta, the Pope's Doctor, 225.

Portalis, Minister of Public Worship, Councillor of State: he is to communicate with the Bishops as to the persecution of the Irish Catholics, 41; ordered to dissolve the congregation of the Pères de la Foi, 58.

Port-Mahon, Balearic Isles, 11.

Porto-Ferrajo, Elba: Italian priests not to be detained there, 224.

Porto-Lougone, Elba, 224.

Portugal: Spain to be induced to declare war against Portugal (Year IX.), 8; proposed expedition against Portugal, 10, 11, 12, 13; Treaty with France, 11, 13-16; Napoleon desires to force Portugal to close her ports to English ships, 46; line of conduct prescribed to the French Ambassador in Madrid, and to Junot, to enable the Emperor's troops to reach Lisbon unopposed, and there seize the fleet, 53-55; the Prince Regent embarks for Brazil, 61; organisation of the French rule, Military and Police arrangements, 65-67; the public debt, finance, 66; salary of the Administrator-General of the Finances, 65;

Napoleon asserts that Spain desires to divide Portugal between the Queen of Etruria and the Prince of Peace, 71.

Portugal, King Henry of, 20.
—— Sebastian, King of, 20.

Posen, Prussia: letter dated thence, 35.

Postal Matters: Couriers stopped, letters opened and seized, 68, 121, 261; the Pope's letters intercepted, 148, 154, 216, 218, 219; the Spanish Royal Family's letters intercepted, 92; letters from England seized and burnt, 55, 57, 68, 227, 243, 244; the Emperor's express rider seized by the Spaniards, 109.

Potocki, Count, 68.

Prague, Bohemia, 136.

Prefect of Police. *See* Police, Prefect of.

Prefects of Departments: the Emperor complains of several in connection with the conscription, 25; weekly circular to be sent to inform them of current events and guide their opinions, 208.

Préjean conspiracy, 90.

Presents given by the Emperor, 176.

Priests. *See* Public Worship.

Prisoners of war: those expected from Saragossa to be employed on drainage works, 119; none are to be confined in frontier fortresses, 144; Finnish prisoners returned to Russia, 163; their freedom sold to them by French officers in Spain, 201.

Prizes taken at sea, 248.

Promotions: the Emperor reserves himself the right of signing those to superior ranks during the Empress's regency, 279, 280.

Prussia: Prussian armament (1806), must be made to disarm, 30-35; partisans and risings (1807): repressive measures, 38, 39; the French uniform insulted at Königsberg, 47, 48; settlement of the war indemnity (1807), 49, 50; evacuation of the country by the French: Spandau to be blown up first (1808), 102; Napoleon desires Baron von Stein may be given up to him, 111; the King's private expenditure, 121; nothing to be feared from Prussia (1809), 126; the Prussian illusion as to the strength of the Grande Armée, 154; the continental blockade: English goods seized, 213; war fines due to France, 213.
—— Princes of, 38, 40, 43, 254.

Public Worship : police action against ecclesiastics and priests, 28, 48, 57, 58, 164, 190, 198, 199, 218, 219, 220, 224, 230, 231, 242, 311 ; bishops and parish priests dismissed or forced to resign, 143, 257 ; suppression of religious orders and confraternities, 48, 49, 58, 241, 242 ; complaints of pastorals, sermons, etc., 112, 119, 120, 146, 147 ; travelling preachers to be put down, 147 ; refractory Italian priests deported to Corsica, 218 ; no work on ecclesiastical subjects to be printed, 239 ; the Bishops of Ghent, Tournay, and Troyes to resign, 257 ; they are sent to various towns, 258, 260; the bishops and priests in the Sarthe and the Mayenne are expected to do all in their power to assist the military and police (Jan. 1813), 266; the Seminaries at Ghent and Tournay (Aug. 1813), 311, 315 ; removal of parish priests (1815), 340.

Publiciste, Le, newspaper, 78, 140.

Pultusk, Poland : letter dated thence, 35.

Puthod, General, reprimanded for having arrested one of the Emperor's orderly officers, 245.

RAGUSA : orders to General Bertrand about Ragusa and Cattaro (July 1811), 240.

Rambouillet : letters dated thence, 30, 45, 47, 48, 120, 190, 192, 234, 235.

Rampon, General, 149, 152.

Rapallo, Italy, 28.

Rape of the Sabines, ballet, 171.

Rapp, General : blamed for not having given his precedence to the Russian Consul, the Emperor complains of his letter on the subject, 197 ; referred to, 213.

Ré, Ile de, refractory conscripts confined in the Citadel, 244.

Réal, Comte : letter to him, 341 ; the Grand Chancellor ordered to consult him about the quarrel between Fouché and Dubois, 93, 94 ; he is to break the seals in the Duc d'Otrante's house, 187 ; he is sent to the Department of the Ems Oriental in connection with the disturbances there (May 1811), 233.

Reboul, Abbé, to be arrested and his papers seized, 224.

Récamier, Mme, 254.

Regiments : young men forced to join them, 144, 168.

Régnault (Régnaud, Régnauld), de St. Jean d'Angély : receives the order of St. Leopold, 236 ; referred to, 98, 146.

Régnier, Comte, Duc de Massa : letters to him, 134, 247, 248 ; Cambacérès desired to look about for a successor to him as chief judge, 286.

Régnier, General, in command of the army in Portugal (Oct. 1810), 209.

Regulus, the, ship, 9.

Reille, General, the Emperor's displeasure at his having blown up the bridge over the Bidassoa, 301.

Reims, Marne : letters dated thence, 331.

Reinhard, Baron, the Emperor's Minister Plenipotentiary at the Court of Westphalia : letter to him, 281 ; ordered to send a detailed report in cipher on the administration of Westphalia, 115 ; to remonstrate with King Jerome about his objectionable favourites, 163 ; he is to be sure the Emperor never answers the King direct on business matters, 211.

Reinosa, Galicia, 104.

Reiset, General, ordered back to his post (October 1813), 317, 318.

Rémusat, Comte de : letter to him, 171 ; referred to, 95.

Reubell, Mons., 137.

Revolts : in Hesse and Westphalia (1807), 36-38 ; in Germany (1807), 38, 39 ; in Tuscany (1808), 108 ; in Holland (1811), 233, 234, 235 ; in the 32nd Military Division, 267, 268 ; in Hesse (1813), 269, 270.

Rey, General, 311.

Réynier, General, to return at once to his post, which he has left without permission (March 1813), 275.

Rhenish Confederation : circular to the ministers at the various Courts, with reference to Baron von Stein, 111 ; circular to demand the recall of the great German landowners in the Austrian Service, 116, 117, 118 ; the property of such persons to be sequestered, 124, 125. *See* Baden, Bavaria, Saxony, Westphalia, Wurtemberg.

Rhine, the, 6.

Ribaucourt, Mons. de, 169.

Riga, Russia, 214.

Rimini, Italy, 45.

Rippaut, the Emperor's librarian, 40.

Rivaud, Gendarmerie officer, 335.

Roche-Aymon, Mons. de la, 183.

Rochefort, Charente-Inférieure: four thousand men to sail thence for Ferrol (Year IX.), 11.

Rochefoucauld, Mme de la, lady-in-waiting to the Empress Joséphine: letter to her, 173.

Rochejaquelin, Mons. de la: his house to be destroyed (May 1815), 342; a price set on his head, 344.

—— Mlles de la, 28.

Rochelle, La, 119, 192, 230.

Rodier, refractory priest, 230.

Roederer, Comte, Councillor of State: measures he is to take as Secretary of State of the Grand Duchy of Berg, to put down disturbances there, 270; deputed to convey the Emperor's orders to the King of Spain, 294, 307.

Roguet, General, must try to recapture Breda (Dec. 1813), 324.

Rohan, Victor Mériadec de, 134.

Romana, Marquis de la: completely defeated, 112.

Romanzoff, Comte, Russian Foreign Minister: hint about Turkey to be conveyed to him by Mons. de Caulaincourt, 188, 189.

Rome and the Papal States: Lucien Bonaparte to be expelled from Rome, 73; the Legations incorporated with the French Empire, 87; the Roman State divided into two Departments, 132; the Emperor's remarks on Champagny's report on Rome, 168, 169; all property there, belonging to the former King of Naples, to be sequestered, 254; refractory priests deported to Corsica, 258.

Ronsdorf, Grand-Duchy of Berg: disturbances there, 269.

Rotterdam, Holland: rising there (May 1811): repressive measures ordered, 234, 235; letter dated thence, 254.

Rouen, Seine Inférieure: police measures for that town (April 1815), 335; officials to be dismissed, action to be taken by General Lemarois (May 1815), 344, 345.

Rousseau, General, 152.

—— a Belgian in the Austrian service, 199.

Rouyer, General, 139.

Rüchel, Prussian general, 103.

Russia: the line to be taken by the news-
papers as to the Russian Emperor's mediation, 23; the country not in a condition to make another war (1806), 31; no Russian alliance with Turkey exists, 36; the Russian troops enter Moldavia, 36; Russia must force Sweden to declare against England, 47; Russian troops from Cattaro and Corfu, 46; shelter offered the Russian squadron on the French coasts, 46; Russian ships at Toulon, 113; Russia to join France in making representations to Austria, 113; the Emperor makes his Finnish prisoners over to Russia, 163; Mons. de Caulaincourt exceeds his instructions as to his negotiations with Russia (April 1810), 178; he is to reassure Russia as to the supposed negotiations between France, Austria, and England (June 1810), 188, 189; instructions to the Duke of Vicenza with regard to the Russian Ukase, etc. (3rd March 1811), 227, 228; Russian campaign (1812), 262-265. See Caulaincourt.

SAHUGUET, General: letter to him, 3; services with the western army, 3.

Saint-Aignan, Mons. de, 108.

St. Aubin, Mons., 51.

—— Cloud, Seine-et-Oise: the parish priest sent forty leagues from Paris (May 1815), 340.

—— —— Palace of: letters dated thence, 20, 21, 29, 30, 43, 44, 73, 75, 76, 101, 102, 103, 104, 105, 185, 186, 187, 188, 189, 190, 194, 195, 198, 199, 200, 201, 202, 232, 233, 234, 237, 238, 240, 241, 242, 243, 244, 245, 246, 256, 257, 258, 277, 278, 323.

Saint-Cyr Military School: youths sent there by force, 108, 111, 168; referred to, 279.

St. Domingo, island of, 5.

St. Gall, Bishop of, 155.

St. Germain, school of: youths sent there by force, 168; referred to, 279.

Saint-Hilaire. See La-Haye-St.-Hilaire.

St. Leopold, Order of, 236.

St. Leu, Comte de. See Louis Bonaparte, King of Holland.

—— estate of, made over to Queen Hortense, 226.

St. Marsan, Mons. de, French Ambassador at Berlin: information to be sent him as to the strength of the Grande

Armée (Aug. 1809), 154; he is to demand the arrest of the Berlin and Königsberg merchants who practise smuggling, 235.

St. Phal, actor, gratuity allotted him, 314.

St. Prix, actor, gratuity allotted him, 314.

St. Sebastian, Spain : besieged by the English (1813), 311.

Ste.-Foix, Mons. de, 58.

Ste.-Marguérite, isles of, 35.

Sainte-Suzanne, General, 148.

Saintes, Charente-Inférieure, 119.

Salamanca, Spain, referred to, 53.

Salicetti, Police Minister at Naples, 74.

Salmatoris, Comptroller of the Crown property, 156, 164.

Salpêtrière, the, 309.

San-Carlos, Duke of, 123, 322.

San-Clemente, Spain, 100.

San-Remo, Genoese Riviera, 123.

Santa-Fé, Duke of, Spanish Ambassador, 207.

Santander, Spain : threatened riot there (April 1808), 81; the town must be brought to submission (Sept. 1808), 104; peculation by French officials there, 201.

Santarem, Portugal, 66.

Saragossa, Spain : siege and capture of the town, 127; prisoners taken there sent to France, 119.

Sarthe, Department of the : armed gatherings (Year VIII.), 1, 2, 3; flying columns to pursue robbers in that Department (Jan. 1813), 266; the Prefect blamed for not having organised the National Guard there (1815), 345.

Sassi della Tosa to be reprieved, 240.

Saunier, General, to command a flying column in the Deux-Nèthes, and the Bouches-de-l'Escaut (Dec. 1813), 324.

Savary, General, Duc de Rovigo, Minister of Police : letters to him, 185, 186, 187, 189, 190, 195, 196, 198, 199, 205, 209, 211, 212, 213, 215, 216, 217, 219, 221, 224, 225, 227, 228, 229, 230, 232, 233, 234, 235, 237, 241, 242, 243, 245, 246, 249, 250, 252, 257, 258, 260, 266, 267, 269, 272, 273, 274, 276, 289, 292, 296, 297, 307, 308, 311, 312, 313, 315, 323, 327, 328, 330; sent to the Prince of the Asturias at Madrid, 76; his faults and virtues as a general in Spain, 100; he is warned to avoid

diplomatic conversations, and not to send instructions to French Ministers to foreign Courts, 250; the Emperor's displeasure at his apparent endeavour to make him incline to peace, 290, 291; his petty passions, and share in his wife's personal spites, 332; he is ordered to send 500 gendarmes to Antwerp (May 1815), 339.

Savary, Mme Duchesse de Rovigo, 332.

Savoie, Maurice de, 19.

Savona : the Pope's place of residence (1809-1812), 148, 154, 222, 223, 225, 226, 252; the Pope brought back there (Jan. 1814), 328.

—— the Bishop of : summoned to Paris, (Nov. 1810), 216, 225.

Saxe-Coburg, family of, 118.

Saxony : French troops and officials there (1808), 98, 99; Saxon troops with the Grand Armée, 138; Baron de Serra to request the King to send all his remaining cavalry to the Grand Armée (April 1813), 280.

—— Prince Albert of, 113.

Scheldt, the, 161, 165.

Schimmelpenninck, Grand Pensionary of Holland, 160, 183.

Schleitz, Germany, 136, 137.

Schmalkalden, arms factory at, 36, 37.

Schneider, leader of the Vorarlberg rebels, 257.

Schönbrunn, Palace of : letters dated thence, 125, 127, 128, 131, 132, 133, 134, 135, 139, 140, 142, 143, 144, 145, 146, 147, 148, 150, 151, 152, 154, 155, 156, 157, 158, 159, 162, 163.

Schwartzenberg, Prince : present to be made to him on the Emperor's marriage, 176; employed during the Russian campaign, 264.

Schwerin, town of, 284.

Sebastiani, General Comte : his division sent to Spain, 104; commands the army in Andalusia (Oct. 1810), 209.

Séguier, Consul at Trieste, 297.

—— Mme, 224, 225.

Seminaries and Seminarists : seminaries closed, and seminarists sent to the army and to Lycées, 311; professors obliged to take an oath to teach the tenets of 1682, 315.

Sémonville, Comte, receives the order of St. Leopold, 236.

Sénart, Forest of, Trappist monastery, 242.

Senate, the, not involved in the anarchist plot, 1808, Fouché suggests action against it, 93, 94, 97, 98.
—— decree of the, 103.
Sequestration of property belonging to guilty or rebellious persons in France and elsewhere, 49, 108, 111, 237, 258, 342; of the property of the Spanish grandees in rebellion against King Joseph, 107-110; of that of the German princes and nobles in the Austrian service, 117, 125; of that of the former King of Naples, in Rome, 254.
Serra, Baron de, Minister Plenipotentiary to the Saxon Court: letter to him, 280; spy system to be organised in Austria, 118.
Serurier, Mons., Secretary of Embassy in Holland: ordered to take charge of French affairs there (1810), 184; directions as to his line of conduct in Holland (June 1810), 186.
Servan, Senator, 98.
Sheep, seized in Spain, 89.
Sienna, Italy, 109.
Siméon, Comte, Councillor of State, with King Jérome in Westphalia, 61, 62, 70, 71.
Simplon, the, 337.
Sloe, the, 165.
Smugglers, 251.
Smolensk, Russia; blown up by Ney, 265.
Soglia, the Pope's Chaplain at Savona, 225.
Solano, Spanish General, 82, 84, 85.
Souham, General, ordered to destroy the enemy's bridge at Mulberg (4th Oct. 1813), 317, 318.
Soult, General, Marshal, Duc de Dalmatie: letters to him, 22, 101, 103, 347; language to be used by him in dealing with Sweden, 75; strength of his troops in Germany, 102, 103; pursues the English to Lugo, 114; gives warning of Argenton's treason, 131; strength of his troops (Oct. 1809), 163; he commands the army of Andalusia (Oct. 1810), 209; is given chief command of the army in Spain (July 1813), 293, 294, 295, 297, 310; is to have no special pay as the Emperor's Lieutenant-General in Spain, 300.
Spa, gaming tables at, 45.
Spain: ships sent thence to Egypt (Year IX.), 7, 8; Lucien Bonaparte's embassy, negotiations for a treaty against Portugal, 7, 8, 9, 10, 11, 12, 13-17; junction of the Spanish and French fleets, 10; sale of Spanish ships to France, 10; auxiliary Spanish troops serving in Germany, 76; reason given by Napoleon to Portugal for his disagreement with Spain, 71; Charles IV. of Spain protests against his own abdication, 80, 82; the Spanish Princes at Bayonne, 79, 80, 81, 82, 83, 84, 85; regency of the Junta, 81, 82, 83, 84; the Spanish King and Princes in France (see Charles IV. and Ferdinand VII.); disturbances and revolts against the French (April, May 1808), 81, 87; the Spanish crown jewels to be pledged, 88; the Baylen business, 100, 105; French troops withdrawn from Germany for service in Spain, 102; disarmament of the country, hostages to be taken, 104, 105; property owned by rebels, grandees of Spain, or others, to be confiscated, 107, 110; defeat of the English in Galicia, 114, 153; the French strength weakened (October 1809), 163; four Military Governments, plan to incorporate the country, up to the Ebro, with France, orders for the better management of the finances (18th February 1810), 171, 172; desertions from the Irish battalion recruited from English prisoners, 187; abuses and peculation rife in General Kellerman's Military Government, 200; ditto in Biscay and Navarre, 201; complaints of the Spanish authorities as to peculation, etc., by the French Generals, 207; Spanish crown jewels carried off by Frenchmen to Naples, inquiries to be made there (Aug. 1811), 245; excellent military position of the French armies in Spain (October 1810), 208, 209; Napoleon's opinion of the Spanish troops, and of Spaniards in general, 100, 104; he desires his troops may move on the Portuguese frontier, if the English really have retired, 283; French defeat at Vittoria, and its consequences; the chief command conferred on the Duke of Dalmatia (July 1813); the King to retire to Pampeluna, Bayonne, or Morfontaine, and to see nobody, 293, 294, 295, 297, 300, 301; circular to be sent to

French Ministers abroad to guide their language as to the battle of Vittoria (July 1813), 302 ; all wives of generals, officers, and other women, to be sent back across the Garonne, 309 ; Comte Laforest's secret mission to the Prince of the Asturias (Nov. 1813), 322, 323. *See* Army of Spain, Spanish Army, Charles IV., and Ferdinand VII.

Spandau, Prussia, 102.

Spencer Smith, correspondence about, 58.

Spezzia, Gulf of, Italy, 87.

Spies and espionage, 22, 78, 118, 304.

Stadion, Count, 286.

—— family of, 125.

Staël, Madame de : measures to be taken against her, and Napoleon's opinion of her, 27, 35, 39, 40 ; query as to her right to call herself Baroness, 205 ; her book on Germany, passages to be suppressed, 205, 211 ; the Prefect of Geneva not to see her, 227.

Stains, estate of, 321, 327.

Starhemberg, Mons. de, 68.

Stein, Baron von, 111.

—— Fräulein von, 128.

Stephanie-Napoleon, Princess of Baden : letters to her, 29, 265.

Stettin, Prussia, 102, 214, 228.

Stralsund, Pomerania : the French flag insulted there (July 1811), 239.

Strasburg : Tyrolese rebels to be sent to the Citadel, 140, 142.

Strogonoff, Mons. de, 101.

Stuttgart, Germany, 155, 174.

Styria, 118.

Suchet, General, Marshal, Duc d'Albuféra : he lays siege to Tortosa and threatens Valencia (October 1810), 209.

Suwaroff, Russian Marshal, 123.

Sweden : Russia and France to force that country to declare against England, 47 ; newspaper articles to be written against Sweden, 72 ; Napoleon gives Russia a free hand as regards Sweden, 113 ; note on Swedish affairs to be recast by Mons. d'Hauterive, 273 ; directions as to the treatment of the Swedes (May 1813), 284 ; the reception given the former King of Sweden at Cassel likely to embroil France with Sweden, 302.

—— Charles XIII., King of : the Emperor has no intention of dethroning him, 302.

Sweden : Gustavus IV., King of, Count of Gottorp : newspaper articles to be written against him, 44, 207 ; French diplomatic agents in Germany to avoid meeting him, 244.

—— Frederica-Dorothea of Baden, Queen of, 244.

Swiftshire (sic), the, British warship, 18.

Switzerland : raising of four Swiss regiments, 42 ; suggestion that only France and the States connected with France should have the right to draw recruits from Switzerland, 42 ; Swiss in the Portuguese service, 67 ; publication of a report showing forth the communications between the Imperial Government and the Swiss Confederation (April 1815), 36.

TAGUS, the, 15.

Talleyrand, Mons. de, Prince de Benevento : letters to him, 17, 18, 28, 30, 39, 59, 86 ; he is to see the Count of Leghorn is beyond Chambéry on 14th July, 17 ; reasons which should lead the Pope to free him from his priestly vows, 19, 20 ; course he is to take with the Prussian Ambassador to induce Prussia to disarm, 31-34 ; orders he is to transmit to General Dupont Chaumont, French Ambassador in Holland, as to the King's re-establishment of the nobility, 39, 40 ; he receives the Spanish Princes at Valençay, 86 ; inventory of the papers seized in his house (April 1815), 334.

—— Madame de, 86.

Tarento, Italy, 73, 74.

Targhini, the Pope's cook at Savona, 225.

Talma, actor, gratuity allotted him, 314.

Tarragona, Spain, referred to,

Tascher, Messrs., 69 ; they marry in Spain, 170.

Tassoni, Chargé d'Affaires at Naples, dismissed, 201.

Taufers, Tyrol, 142.

Tavera, Mons., 211.

Taylor, correspondence, 58.

Temple, the, Paris, 45, 49.

Testa-Ferrata, Mons., 103.

Teste, General, 289.

Texel, the, 149.

Theatres : expenses connected with, 50 ; scenes in, 47, 48, 144 ; gratuities to

actors and actresses of the Comédie
Française, 314.
Theatrical performances. *See* Operas.
Thénard, actor, gratuity allotted him,
314.
—— Mlle, actress, gratuity allotted her,
314.
Thiébault, General, 36.
Thielman, General, 280.
Thurot, Mons., writes direct to the Em-
peror, 266.
Tiber, Department of the, 132.
Tiflis, town of, 36.
Tippoo-Sultan, 15.
Tissier, refractory priest, 230.
Tobago, Isle of, 17.
Toledo, Spain, 82, 87.
Töplitz, baths of, 304.
Torgau, Saxony, 280.
Tortosa, Spain : besieged by the French
(1810), 209.
Toulon, Var : return of Admiral
Ganteaume, 9 ; sailors might be sent
from Toulon to Malaga, 10 ; Russian
ships there, 113 ; licensed trading-
ships to unload return cargo there, 194;
steps to be taken to keep ill-disposed
people in check (June 1815), 346 ;
siege of Toulon, 149.
Toulouse, Haute-Garonne : letters dated
thence, 98, 99.
Tournay, diocese of : threat to close the
seminary ; arrest of the canons and
professors ; the students sent to the
army, to Lycées, or to various French
seminaries (August 1813), 315.
—— Constant, Canon of, 315.
Tournon, Mons. de, the Emperor's
chamberlain, 86.
Trappists, the, suppression of their
houses, and dispersal of the monks,
241, 242.
Tras-los-Montes, Province of, 13.
Trasimenus, Department of the, Italy,
132.
Trauttmansdorf, Prince : present to be
given him on the occasion of the Emperor's marriage, 176.
Travot, General : commands a flying
column in the Vendée, congratulated
by the Emperor (May 1815), 343, 344.
Treffurt, Saxony, 37.
Treilhard, Councillor of State, 89.
Trianon, Palace : letters dated thence,
166, 167, 196, 197, 271-273, 339,
340.

Trieste, Austria: the port to be closed to
the English, 47.
Trinity Island, 15, 17.
Tromelin, Mons., 45.
Troyes, Aube : letter dated thence, 329.
—— Monsignor de Boulogne, Bishop of :
struck off the list of Imperial Almoners,
239 ; his resignation to be insisted on,
and himself removed sixty leagues
from Paris, 257 ; he is to be released
and interned in a small commune, 258;
sent to Falaise, 260.
Tudela, Spain, 104.
Tuileries, Palace of the, referred to, 167,
333.
Turenne, Comte de, the Emperor's
orderly officer, 67.
Turin, Piedmont, 59.
Turkey: has no alliance with Russia, 36 ;
the Turkish troops enter Wallachia,
36 ; Napoleon forsakes Turkey for
the sake of his Russian alliance, 166.
Tuscany: the Prince of Parma to take
possession without delay, 11 ; the
Ecclesiastical Academy dissolved, 30 ;
revolt (Dec. 1808), 108, 109; opposition to a parish priest in Florence,
308. *See* Elisa Bonaparte.
Tyrol, the, 139, 140, 142, 142.

URQUIJO, Mons. d', Spanish Secretary
of State, under King Joseph: reply to
his communication to Mons. de Champagny, 207.
Utrecht, Holland : French patrols insulted, 229 ; letters dated thence,
252.

VALENÇAY, the residence of the Spanish
Princes, 86, 92, 106, 123, 177, 322.
Valencia, Spain, 209.
Valenciennes, Nord, 199.
Valentini, Florentine lawyer, 220, 224.
Valladolid, Spain : General Dupont's
army massed there (Jan. 1808), 67 ;
disturbances there suppressed (1809),
115 ; letters dated thence, 114, 115.
Valmy, Comte de, 278.
Vandamme, General : accused of brigandage during the Russian campaign, 263 ;
is to be sent towards Mecklenburgh,
284 ; the Emperor expresses his satisfaction with his behaviour, and desires
he may be spared, 285 ; he would ap-

pear to have committed suicide after his defeat, he did not take sufficient precautions (August 1813), 316, 317.

Van der Leyen, Mons., 169.

Vandewerke, Mons., 169.

Vannes, Morbihan, 1, 2.

Van Praet, Mons., 169.

Varin, Father, Superior of the Pères de la Foi, 58.

Vedel, General, 106.

Vence, Colonel de, 338.

Vendée, the: disturbances in that province (Year VIII.), 1-6; arrest of refractory priests, 230, 231; Matthieu de Montmorency, the Comte de Lille's agent there (May 1815), 339; flying columns to be sent through the country to put down disturbance (May 1815), 339, 340; a Military Court to sentence the rebels, 341; La Rochejaquelin's house to be destroyed, 342.

Venice, Italy: the Russian garrison from Cattaro lands there, 46; licences granted to the port, 193, 194; referred to, 328.

Verdier, General, to command at Marseilles (May 1815), 341.

Verdun, Mons., 330.

Vermoesand, Mons., 169.

Verneuil, Eure, 1, 2, 3.

Verrerie, La, in Vendée, 230.

Versailles, referred to, 6.

Vertumnus and Pomona, ballet, 171.

Viaud, parish priest of Livière, 230.

Vichy, Allier, 180.

Victor, General, Marshal, Duc de Bellune: in command of the army of Andalusia (Oct. 1810), 209; his conduct in 1814, 328; struck off the list of Marshals and granted a retiring pension (March 1815), 333, 334.

Vienna, Austria: disturbances, the French insulted, steps to be taken to insure order, supplies to be insured, 128-131.

Vienne, Dauphiné, 28.

Vieusseux, Mons., Etienne, 89.

Vignolle, General, 271.

Vigny, actor, gratuity allotted him, 314.

Villaret-Joyeuse, Admiral, 12.

Villeneuve, Admiral, 23.

Vilvorde, Belgium, 190.

Vincennes, Castle of: State prisoners confined there, 120, 127, 128, 140, 162, 184, 185, 231, 335.

Vittoria, Spain: the Spanish King and

Princes pass through the town, 77, 83, 85; rout of the French troops (June-July 1813), 293, 294, 295, 297, 299, 300-302.

Vorarlberg, the: revolt against the French (1809), the country disarmed and the rebellion suppressed, 139, 144, 155.

WACHT, Hesse, 36.

Wagram, battle of, 140, 146, 256.

Walcheren, island of, 152, 159, 161.

Waldheim, Saxony: letter dated thence, 284.

Wallachia, 36, 166, 167.

Walther, General, 87.

Warsaw, Poland: letters dated thence, 36, 38.

Watteville, orderly officer to the Emperor, 188.

Weimar, Saxony: Marshal Ney arrives there (20th April 1813), 281; referred to, 92.

Wellesley, Lord, 188.

Wesel, Rhenish Province: the Emperor proposes to change the population, 144; the Ghent seminarists to be sent there, 311; letter dated thence, 255.

Weser, the, 57.

Westphalia, Kingdom of: the Emperor desires his Ambassador will send detailed reports of the Government and internal administration of the Kingdom, 115; King Jerome's bad government, 117, 124; revolt (April 1809), 124; the French troops there uncomfortable (October 1810), 206; the King blamed for raising a cuirassier regiment, 214, 215; the French troops in Westphalia only to be inspected by French officers, 215; too heavy taxes imposed in Hanover and Magdeburg, 259; faults in the composition of the army, and its bad feeling (Dec. 1811), 260; it should be reorganised for the spring of 1813 (Dec. 1812), 265; the King's mistake in not having a French Guard, 281, 282.

Willaumez, Rear-Admiral, does not possess the Emperor's confidence, 297.

Willemstadt, Holland: the Emperor's displeasure at its having been evacuated, 324, 325.

Wilna, Lithuania: letter dated thence, 262.

Wimereux, 251.

Wintzingerode, Count, Westphalian Ambassador in Paris, 215.

Wittenberg, Saxony: letters dated thence, 299, 300.

Wrede, General: the Emperor wishes him to command the Bavarian troops, in 1813, 281.

Würtschen, battle of, 286.

Würtzburg, Bavaria, 309.

ZAMORA, regiment, 28.

Zealand, 160.

Zezere, Portuguese river, 222.

Zinzendorf, family of, 125.

Znaïm, armistice of, 136.

Printed by T. and A. CONSTABLE, Printers to Her Majesty
at the Edinburgh University Press

Mr. William Heinemann's

Autumn Announcements

mdcccxcvii

ibistorp anð Biograpbp

NEW LETTERS OF NAPOLEON I.

Omitted from the Collection published under the
Auspices of Napoleon III.

TRANSLATED FROM THE FRENCH BY

LADY MARY LOYD

In One Volume, demy 8vo, with Frontispiece, price **15s.** net

The monumental twenty-eight volumes of Napoleon I.'s letters, published under the direction of the Commission appointed by Napoleon III. to edit and arrange his uncle's correspondence, were by no means exhaustive. The *Correspondence*, as originally issued, contained, indeed, some 22,000 pieces. Many of these, however, were decrees, orders of the day, bulletins, &c., and the original minutes in the French archives show a total of over 30,000 letters. It is notorious that the Commission, of which Prince Napoleon was President, exercised its prerogative of suppression with great freedom. The reasons for its action in the matter are obvious. In some cases, letters were set aside as wanting in interest, or as going over ground already covered by other documents. But in the majority of instances, a pardonable zeal for the family glory came into play, urging the with-holding of anything that might dim the lustre of Napoleon's fame, or reflect unpleasantly on his near relatives. Governed by considerations of this nature, the Commission set aside a series of letters of extra-ordinary historical interest—some dealing with the quarrels of Napoleon and his brothers, and the long struggle with the Pope, others containing trenchant criticisms of the capacity and conduct of eminent generals and officials, or bearing witness to the iron hand with which the greatest organiser the world has ever seen, carried out his " system," and ordered the affairs of the press, the police, and all the minutiæ of his vast economy.

The object of the two supplementary volumes recently published in France is to repair these deliberate omissions, and to make the former collection practically complete. A considerable part of these two volumes is naturally wanting in novelty and interest. But they contain so much that is fresh and new, so much of exceptional value historically, and they throw so many new lights on the actors of that wonderful drama of the First Empire, especially on the masterful character of its creator, that the English publisher is confident that a selection, with a view to the general interest felt for Napoleon I., is bound to be welcome.

WILLIAM SHAKESPEARE

A Critical Study

By GEORG BRANDES, Ph.D.

Translated from the Danish by WILLIAM ARCHER and
DIANA WHITE

In Two Volumes, demy 8vo, price **24s.**

Dr. Georg Brandes's "William Shake speare" may best be called, perhaps, an exhaustive critical biography. Keeping fully abreast of the latest English and German researches and criticism, Dr. Brandes preserves that breadth and sanity of view which are apt to be sacrificed by the mere Shakespearologist. He places the poet in his political and literary environment, and studies each play not as an isolated phenomenon, but as the record of a stage in Shakespeare's spiritual history. Dr. Brandes has achieved German thoroughness without German heaviness, and has produced what must be regarded as a standard work.

CATHERINE SFORZA

A Study. By COUNT PASOLINI

Adapted from the Italian by PAUL SYLVESTER

Demy 8vo, with many Illustrations

Count Pasolini is a lineal descendant of the hereditary enemies of the Sforza family. His work is enriched by numerous illustrations, facsimiles of handwriting, seals, and quotations from some five hundred letters of the Madonna of Forli. It combines the charm of romance with the dignity of history, and brings within the reader's ken, not only the militant princess who held the Fort of St. Angelo against the Conclave (thus arresting the affairs of Europe until her own were settled), who circumvented Machiavelli and defied Cesar Borgia, but the private woman in her court and home, her domestic and social relations.

A HISTORY OF THE LIVERPOOL PRIVATEERS

And Letters of Marque, Including the Slave Trade.

By GOMER WILLIAMS

In one Volume, demy 8vo, price **12s.** net

ROBERT, EARL NUGENT

A Memoir

By CLAUD NUGENT

In One Volume, demy 8vo, with a number of Portraits and
other Illustrations

𝕰ducational

𝕲reat 𝕰ducators

Each subject forms a complete volume, crown 8vo, 5s.

THOMAS AND MATTHEW ARNOLD
And Their Influence on English Education

By Sir JOSHUA FITCH, M.A., LL.D., formerly Her Majesty's Inspector of Training Colleges

Volumes Previously Published

Aristotle. By T. DAVIDSON	**Abelard.** By J. G. COMPAYRÉ.
Loyola. By Rev.T. HUGHES, S.J.	**Herbart.** By Prof. DE GARMO.
Alcuin. By A. F. WEST	*In Preparation volumes on*
Froebel. By H. COURTHOPE	**Rosseau; Horace Mann;**
BOWEN.	**Pestalozzi**

THE WOMEN OF HOMER
By WALTER COPLAND PERRY

With numerous Illustrations, large crown 8vo, **6s.**

This work is intended to give to those who are interested in Greek antiquity, but have not mastered the Greek language, some insight into the Fairy World of Homer's Epics.

The Gods and Heroes of Homer have been much more frequently portrayed than their female counterparts. The author has therefore chosen " The Women of Homer " as his main subject, which may be thought, in some respects, to be the more attractive of the two.

THE STORY OF THE GREEKS
By H. A. GRUEBER

Small crown 8vo, 288 pp., with Illustrations

This Elementary History of Greece is intended for supplementary reading or as a first text-book for young pupils ; for, while history proper is largely beyond the comprehension of children, they are able at an early age to understand and enjoy anecdotes of people, especially of those in the childhood of civilisation. It has been the author's intention to write a book which will give pleasure to read, and will thus counteract the impression that history is uninteresting.

To be Published on Trafalgar Day, October 21

A SCHOOL PRIZE EDITION OF

THE LIFE OF NELSON

By ROBERT SOUTHEY, Poet Laureate

A New Edition. Edited by DAVID HANNAY

Crown 8vo, with Portrait of Lord Nelson, after Hoppner

price **3s. 6d.**

A HISTORY OF DANCING

From the Earliest Ages to Our Own Times

FROM THE FRENCH OF

GASTON VUILLIER

With 25 Plates in Photogravure and about 400 Illustrations in the Text
In One Volume, 4to. Price 36s. net

Also 35 copies printed on Japanese Vellum (containing 3 additional
Plates), with a duplicate set of the plates on India paper for framing.
Each copy numbered and signed, price **twelve guineas** net.

Copious as are the incidental studies of the various phases of the
Art of Dancing, no comprehensive attempt has yet been made in our
own times to evolve from the rich material available a synthesis that
shall be not only a serious contribution to social history, but a treasury
of quaint information and artistic pleasure for those who wish to be
amused as well as instructed. M. Vuillier has undertaken this interesting task. The History of Dancing is traced from its dawn in Egypt,
throughout all its developments in the sacred dances of the Hebrews,
the Greeks, the Romans, and the early Christians. The author
sketches the decline of religious feeling in this form of art, and the
gradual debasement of the poetry of motion to the level of licentious
pantomime. He deals with its renaissance in the age of chivalry,
notes the more animated and voluptuous character impressed on it by
Italian influences, and shows how the ballet, the masquerade, and the
masked ball were the outcome of this further development. From this
he passes on to the age *par excellence* of social pageants, the eighteenth
century, when dancing reached its apogee of elegance in the minuet and
the gavotte, and glancing at such sinister offshoots of the art as the
Carmagnole of the Revolution, depicts the rise of modern dancing,
signalised on the stage by the appearance of Taglioni and Fanny Elssler,
and in social life by the introduction of the waltz, the galop, and the
polka—forerunners of the fashionable skirt-dance of the moment.

An Illustrated Prospectus on Application

JUDGE JEFFREYS

A Study

By H. B. IRVING

In One Volume

Literatures of the World

A SERIES OF SHORT HISTORIES

Edited by EDMUND GOSSE

Each Volume Large Crown 8vo, Cloth 6s.

A HISTORY OF FRENCH LITERATURE

By EDWARD DOWDEN, D.C.L.,.LL.D., Professor
of Oratory and English Literature in the
University of Dublin

In October

A HISTORY OF MODERN ENGLISH LITERATURE

By EDMUND GOSSE, Hon. M.A. of Trinity
College, Cambridge

In January

A HISTORY OF ITALIAN LITERATURE

By RICHARD GARNETT, C.B., LL.D., Keeper of
Printed Books in the British Museum

Previously published

A HISTORY OF ANCIENT GREEK LITERATURE.

By GILBERT MURRAY, M.A., Professor of Greek in the University
of Glasgow.

The Times.—"A sketch to which the much-abused word 'brilliant'
may be justly applied. Dealing in 400 pages with a subject which is
both immense and well worn, Mr. Murray presents us with a treatment
at once comprehensive, penetrating and fresh. By dint of a clear,
freely moving intelligence, and by dint also of a style at once compact
and lucid, he has produced a book which fairly represents the best
conclusions of modern scholarship."

The Athenæum.—"The book is brilliant and stimulating, while its
freshness of treatment and recognition of the latest German research
amply justify its existence. Professor Murray has made these old
Greek bones live."

In preparation the following volumes

A HISTORY OF SPANISH LITERATURE. By J. FITZ-MAURICE-KELLY.

A HISTORY OF JAPANESE LITERATURE. By WILLIAM GEORGE ASTON, C.M.G., M.A.

A HISTORY OF MODERN SCANDINAVIAN LITERATURE. By Dr. GEORG BRANDES.

A HISTORY OF SANSCRIT LITERATURE. By A. A. MACDONNELL, M.A.

A HISTORY OF HUNGARIAN LITERATURE. By Dr. ZOLTAN BEÖTHY.

A HISTORY OF AMERICAN LITERATURE. By Professor MOSES COIT TYLER.

A HISTORY OF GERMAN LITERATURE. By Dr. C. H. HERFORD.

A HISTORY OF LATIN LITERATURE. By Dr. A. W. VERRALL.

Also volumes dealing with RUSSIAN, ARABIC, DUTCH, MODERN GREEK.

Philosophy

THE NON-RELIGION OF THE FUTURE

From the French of MARIE JEAN GUYAU

In One Volume, demy 8vo, **17s.** net

This work traces the connection between religion, æsthetics and morals, and the inevitable decomposition of all systems of dogmatic religion. It also deals with the state of "non-religion" toward which the human mind seems to tend. It explains the exact sense in which one must understand the non-religion as distinguished from the "religion of the future," and sets forth the value and utility, for the time being, of religion.

Uniform with the above, price **17s.** *net each*

By MAX NORDAU	By MAX NORDAU
Paradoxes	**Degeneration**
Conventional Lies of Our Civilization	By Dr. WILLIAM HIRSCH
	Genius and Degeneration

Travel

CUBA IN WARTIME
By RICHARD HARDING DAVIS
Author of " Soldiers of Fortune "

With Numerous Illustrations by FREDERIC REMINGTON

Crown 8vo, price **3s. 6d.**

WITH THE FIGHTING JAPS
Naval Experiences during the late Chino-Japanese War
By J. CHALMERS

Crown 8vo.

MY FOURTH TOUR IN WESTERN AUSTRALIA
By ALBERT F. CALVERT, F.R.G.S.

4to, with many Illustrations and Photographs, price **21s.** net.

Verse

POEMS FROM THE DIVAN OF HAFIZ
Translated from the Persian by
GERTRUDE LOWTHIAN BELL
Small crown 8vo, price **6s.**

A SELECTION FROM THE POEMS OF WILFRED SCAWEN BLUNT
With an Introduction by W. E. HENLEY

Crown 8vo, price **6s.**

IN CAP AND GOWN
Three Centuries of Cambridge Wit.
Selected and arranged by CHARLES WHIBLEY

A New Edition, with Frontispiece, price **3s. 6d.**

Great Lives and Events

Uniformly bound in cloth, price 6s. each

THE NEW VOLUME

SIXTY YEARS OF EMPIRE

A Symposium

With over 70 Portraits and Diagrams

This volume gathers together the remarkable series of articles which attracted such general attention when they first appeared in the *Daily Chronicle*, on the occasion of the Queen's Jubilee. Embracing as they do the whole field of national and Imperial interests, written each by an expert in the subject of which he treats (Sir Charles Dilke, Mr. John Burns, Mr. A. B. Walkeley and Mr. Joseph Pennell are among the contributors), illustrated with portraits and diagrams, the papers thus collected supply what this Jubilee year has hitherto failed to produce—a brief, comprehensive and authoritative review of the period covered by Her Majesty's reign.

The following volumes have been published in this Series

By K. WALISZEWSKI.

The Romance of an Empress. Catherine II. of Russia.

The Story of a Throne. Catherine II. of Russia.

By F. MASSON.

Napoleon and the Fair Sex.

By PAUL GAULOT.

A Friend of the Queen. Marie Antoinette and Count Fersen.

The Memoirs of the Prince de Joinville.

By ARTHUR WAUGH

Alfred Lord Tennyson.

By EDMUND GOSSE.

The Naturalist of the Seashore. The Life of Philip Henry Gosse.

LUMEN

Fcap. 8vo, cloth, price 3s. 6d.

By CAMILLE FLAMMARION

M. Flammarion, the distinguished French astronomer, has in his volume entitled *Lumen* added to his exact scientific knowledge a new and interesting attempt to bring before his readers a speculative theory of life in another planet.

In France the volume has been widely read, for more than 50,000 copies have been sold in the original.

THE WORKS OF LORD BYRON

Edited by WILLIAM ERNEST HENLEY

To be completed in Twelve Volumes

The Letters, Diaries, Controversies, Speeches, &c., in Four,
and the Verse in Eight

Small Crown 8vo, price 5s. net each

VERSE VOLUME I.   Containing "Hours of Idleness" and
"English Bards and Scotch Reviewers." With a Portrait after
SANDERS.   [*In October.*

I. LETTERS, 1804–1813.   With a Portrait after PHILLIPS.
                                                [*Is now ready.*

"Mr. W. E. Henley is not only steeped to the lips in Byronic poetry,
but he has also a very familiar acquaintance with the remarkable
characters who formed 'the Byronic set' and he knows the manners
and customs of the Regency epoch to an extent that gives him full
mastery of his subject.   There is originality in the very form of this
edition.

"He manages to give in a few vigorous sentences vivid sketches of
the wide circle of Byron's friends and enemies."—*Pall Mall Gazette.*

"The first volume is delightfully handy and the type excellent."
                                        ANDREW LANG.

"These Byron Letters (Vol. I.) Mr. Henley has annotated as never
surely were letters annotated before. His notes provide simply a complete series of little biographies—miniature biographies with such
vital selection, such concise completion without dry-as-dustness—such
interest as no other writer but Mr. Henley could compass.   It may
fairly be said that he has discovered a new art, the art of biographic
cameos. . . . It is safe to say that henceforth the typical edition of
Byron can never be separated from these notes.   In conclusion, if Byron
has waited long for a heaven-sent editor, he has him at last."
                                        Academy.

"Mr. Henley, so far as elucidation and illustration are concerned,
is fully equipped."—*Athenæum.*

There will also be an Edition, limited to 150 sets for sale
in Great Britain, printed on Van Gelder's hand-made paper,
price Six Guineas net, subscriptions for which are now being
received.

STUDIES IN FRANKNESS

By CHARLES WHIBLEY

Crown 8vo, with Frontispiece, price 7s. 6d.

By the same Author, uniform with the above

A BOOK OF SCOUNDRELS

Crown 8vo, buckram, price 7s. 6d.

A New and Enlarged Edition

THE GENTLE ART OF MAKING ENEMIES

As pleasingly exemplified in many instances, wherein the serious ones of this earth, carefully exasperated, have been prettily spurred on to indiscretions and unseemliness, while overcome by an undue sense of right.

By JAMES McNEILL WHISTLER

The continued demand for this unique work has enabled the publisher to induce Mr. Whistler to consent to the issue of another edition, which will be further enriched by the addition of much new material.

A few copies of the Large Paper issue of the first edition are on sale, price **£2 2s.** net.

The Drama

18mo, cloth, **2s. 6d.** each, or paper, **1s. 6d.**

ADMIRAL GUINEA   MACAIRE

By W. E. HENLEY and R. L. STEVENSON

Previously Published.

Deacon Brodie | **Beau Austin**

16mo, paper covers, **1s. 6d.** ; or cloth, **2s. 6d.**

THE PRINCESS AND THE BUTTERFLY

By ARTHUR W. PINERO

Previously Published

The Times	The Benefit of the Doubt
The Profligate	Dandy Dick
The Cabinet Minister	Sweet Lavender
The Hobby Horse	The School-mistress
Lady Bountiful	The Weaker Sex
The Magistrate	The Amazons
The Notorious Mrs. Ebbsmith	The Second Mrs. Tanqueray

The above 14 Volumes are now uniformly bound in *Leather*, in case, price on application.

THE WEAVERS   LONELY LIVES

By GERHART HAUPTMANN

Previously Published price **5s.**

Hannele: A Dream Poem. Translated by WILLIAM ARCHER.

New Fiction

In One Volume at **6s.**

ST. IVES

Being the Adventures of a French Prisoner in England

By ROBERT LOUIS STEVENSON

By the same Author, price 6s.
The Ebb-Tide

THE BETH BOOK

By SARAH GRAND

By the same Author, price 6s. each
The Heavenly Twins | Ideala | Our Manifold Nature

MARIETTA'S MARRIAGE

By W. E. NORRIS

By the same Author, price 6s. each
The Dancer in Yellow | A Victim of Good Luck
The Countess Radna

WHAT MAISIE KNEW

By HENRY JAMES

By the same Author, price 6s. each

The Spoils of Poynton | The Other House
Embarrassments | Terminations

THE WAR OF THE WORLDS

By H. G. WELLS

By the same Author

The Island of Dr. Moreau. 6s.
The Time Machine. Paper, 1s. 6d.; cloth, 2s. 6d.

GOD'S FOUNDLING

By A. J. DAWSON

THE LONDONERS

By ROBERT HICHENS

By the same Author, 6s. each

An Imaginative Man   The Folly of Eustace   Flames
Also in The Pioneer Series, paper **2s. 6d.** *net; cloth* **3s** *net.*
The Green Carnation

New Fiction

In One Volume, at **6s.**

A NEW VOLUME

By STEPHEN CRANE

By the same Author

The Red Badge of Courage (*Pioneer Series, paper* **2s. 6d.** *net;* cloth **3s.** *net.*)	**The Little Regiment** (*Pioneer Series, paper* **2s. 6d.** *net;* cloth **3s.** *net.*)
Maggie. Price **2s.**	**The Black Riders.** Price **3s.** net

The Third Violet. Price **6s.**

A NEW NOVEL

By HAROLD FREDERIC

By the same Author

Illumination. Price **6s.**	**The Return of the O'Mahony** Price **3s. 6d.**
In the Valley. Price **3s. 6d.**	
The Copperhead. Price **3s. 6d.**	**The New Exodus.** Price **16s.**

TONY DRUM

A Cockney Boy

By EDWIN PUGH

By the same Author

The Man of Straw Price **6s.**	**A Street in Suburbia** (*Pioneer Series, paper* **2s. 6d.** *net;* cloth **3s.** *net.*)

THE GADFLY

By E. L. VOYNICH

THE GODS ARRIVE

By ANNIE E. HOLDSWORTH

By the same Author

The Years that the Locust hath Eaten. **6s.**

And in the Pioneer Series

Joanna Traill, Spinster. Cloth, **3s.** net, paper, **2s. 6d.** net.

THE FREEDOM OF HENRY MEREDYTH

By M. HAMILTON

By the same Author **6s.** *each*

Mcleod of the Camerons | **A Self-Denying Ordinance**

And, in the Pioneer Series

Across an Ulster Bog. Cloth **3s.** net, paper, **2s. 6d.** net.

New Fiction

In One Volume at **6s.**

THE NIGGER OF "THE NARCISSUS"
By JOSEPH CONRAD

THE DRONES MUST DIE
By MAX NORDAU

By the same Author **6s.** *each*
The Malady of the Century | A Comedy of Sentiment

THE FOURTH NAPOLEON
By CHARLES BENHAM

A ROMANCE OF THE FIRST CONSUL
From the Swedish of M. MALLING, by ANNA MOLBOE

THE MASTER-KNOT
By J. A. STEUART

THE LAKE OF WINE
By B. E. J. CAPES

EZEKIEL'S SIN
By J. H. PEARCE

By the same Author **3s. 6d.** *each*
Eli's Daughter | Inconsequent Lives

A CHAMPION OF THE SEVENTIES
By EDITH A. BARNETT

In One Volume at **3s. 6d.**

MRS. JOHN FORSTER
By CHARLES GRANVILLE

New Fiction

In One Volume at 6s.

NEW VOLUMES OF SHORT STORIES

DREAMERS OF THE GHETTO

By I. ZANGWILL

By the same Author

Children of the Ghetto. 6s.	The King of Schnorrers. 6s.
The Premier and the Painter. 6s.	The Old Maid's Club. Boards. 2s., cloth, 3s. 6d.

IN THE PERMANENT WAY

By FLORA ANNIE STEEL

By the same Author, price 6s. each

On the Face of the Waters | From the Five Rivers
The Potter's Thumb

· LAST STUDIES

By HUBERT CRACKANTHORPE

With an Introduction by HENRY JAMES, and a Portrait

By the same Author

Sentimental Studies. 6s. | Wreckage. 3s. 6d

A New Volume of the Pioneer Series

Price 2s. 6d. net in paper, and 3s. net in cloth

A MAN WITH A MAID. By Mrs. HENRY DUDENEY.

Two New Volumes of the International Library

In paper cover, 2s. 6d. ; cloth, 3s. 6d.

THE OLD ADAM AND THE NEW EVE
Translated from the German of RUDOLF GOLM.

NIOBE. Translated from the Norwegian of JONAS LIE.

The New Volume of Ivan Turgenev's Novels

Fcap. 8vo, cloth, 3s. net

THE TORRENTS OF SPRING
Translated by CONSTANCE GARNETT.

Two New Volumes of Björnstjerne Björnson's Novels

Fcap. 8vo, cloth, 3s. net each Volume

CAPTAIN MANSANA AND MOTHER'S HANDS
ABSALOM'S HAIR AND A PAINFUL MEMORY

AN ALPHABET

By WILLIAM NICHOLSON

Will be Published in September 1897

In three Editions

1. *The Popular Edition.* Lithographed in Colours, on stout Cartridge Paper. Price **5s.**
2. *The Library Edition* (Limited). Lithographed in Colours, on Dutch Hand-made Paper, mounted on brown paper and bound in Cloth, Gilt edges. Price **12s. 6d.**
3. *The Edition de Luxe* (Limited). Printed from the Original Wood-blocks. Hand-coloured, and signed by the Artist. In Vellum Portfolio. Price **£12 12s.**

AN ILLUSTRATED PROSPECTUS ON APPLICATION

The art of the coloured woodcut, which was brought to its highest perfection in Japan, has been comparatively neglected of recent years in Europe, and its revival is due, probably, to the discovery of the inadequacy of all mechanical processes for certain artistic effects. Mr. Pennell has recently given enthusiastic testimony to the extraordinary merit of the few examples of Mr. Nicholson's art which have hitherto been published. If, as he said, "the colour prints of Utamoro are Japanese, the colour prints of Nicholson are English," the publisher is confident that Mr. Nicholson establishes himself, with this illuminated alphabet, as *facile princeps* in this country as was the great Japanese in Japan.

An ALMANAC of TWELVE SPORTS for 1898

By WILLIAM NICHOLSON

Will be Published in November 1897

In three Editions

1. *The Popular Edition.* Lithographed in Colours, on stout Cartridge Paper. Price **2s.**
2. *The Library Edition* (Limited). Lithographed in Colours, on Japanese Vellum, and bound in Cloth. Price **7s. 6d.**
3. *The Edition de Luxe* (Limited). Printed from the Original Wood-blocks. Hand-coloured, and signed by the Artist. In Vellum Portfolio. Price **£5 5s.**

AN ILLUSTRATED PROSPECTUS ON APPLICATION

These pictures, done by one of the most distinguished younger artists England can boast of, are English to the core, and will be delighted in, not only for a momentary perusal but more so even if framed and daily seen, as indeed their subject, and assuredly also their artistic merit, warrants.

www.ingramcontent.com/pod-product-compliance
Lightning Source LLC
Chambersburg PA
CBHW032312280326
41932CB00009B/786